# [Ab]Using Power

## The Canadian Experience

*edited by Susan C. Boyd, Dorothy E. Chunn and Robert Menzies*

Fernwood Publishing • Halifax, Nova Scotia

for Margaret A. Jackson,
consummate scholar, mentor, colleague and friend

Editing: Douglas Beall
Cover art: Richard Slye
Design and production: Beverley Rach
Printed and bound in Canada by: Hignell Printing Limited

A publication of:
Fernwood Publishing
Box 9409, Station A
Halifax, Nova Scotia
B3K 5S3

Fernwood Publishing Company Limited gratefully acknowledges the financial
support of the Department of Canadian Heritage and the Canada Council for the Arts
for our publishing program.


Canadian Cataloguing in Publication Data

[Ab]Using power: the Canadian experience

Includes bibliographical references.
ISBN 1-55266-047-8

1. Power (Social sciences)--Canada. 2. Social justice--Canada. I. Boyd, Susan C.,
1953- II. Chunn, Dorothy E. (Dorothy Ellen), 1943- III. Menzies, Robert, 1951-

HN49.P6A28 2001     303.3'0971     C00-901778-X

# Contents

### Part Four
### Professions / 161

# About the Editors and Authors

**Susan C. Boyd** is an associate professor in the Department of Sociology and Criminology, Saint Mary's University.

**Dorothy E. Chunn** teaches in the School of Criminology, Simon Fraser University.

**J.F. Conway** is a professor of Sociology at the University of Regina.

**Tana Dineen** is a psychologist, lecturer and author living in Victoria.

**John Dixon** is a philosopher, civil libertarian and author who teaches at Capilano College.

**Stuart Farson** teaches political science at Simon Fraser University.

**Edgar Z. Friedenberg** passed away on June 1, 2000; he was professor emeritus in the School of Education at Dalhousie University.

**Judy Fudge** is an associate professor at Osgoode Hall Law School, York University.

**Gayle K. Horii** is co-founder of the Strength in Sisterhood (SIS) Society and serves on the board of the West Coast Prison Justice Society (WCPJS).

**Dianne L. Martin** is an associate professor at Osgoode Hall Law School, York University.

**John McMullan** is a professor in the Department of Sociology and Criminology at Saint Mary's University.

**Robert Menzies** teaches in the School of Criminology at Simon Fraser University.

**P. Susan Penfold** is a professor of Psychiatry at the University of British Columbia and a clinical director of an inpatient unit for disturbed children at B.C.'s Children's Hospital.

**Judy Rebick** is an activist, journalist, broadcaster, teacher and author living in Toronto.

**Ted Schrecker** is a political theorist, consultant and author living in Montréal.

**Laureen Snider** is a professor of Sociology at Queen's University.

**Sunera Thobani** is an assistant professor in the Women's Studies program and at the Centre for Research in Women's Studies and Gender Relations at the University of British Columbia.

**Toni Williams** is an associate professor at Osgoode Hall Law School, York University.

# Acknowledgements

This book was spawned by a symposium of the same name held at the Harbour Centre downtown Vancouver campus of Simon Fraser University on May 7–9, 1998. An SFU Molson Prize and Social Sciences and Humanities Research Council of Canada Small Grant awarded to Robert Menzies helped lay much of the groundwork for both the conference and book, as did the remarkable research assistance of Ian Forrester and Yuefang Wang. The symposium funders were SSHRC; the Ministry of Attorney General of British Columbia (our special thanks to Maureen Maloney and Ann Ratel); and SFU through its university conference grants committee, and the offices of (as they were then) President Jack Blaney, Vice-Presidents/Academic Jock Munro and David Gagan, Dean of Arts John Pierce and School of Criminology Director Margaret Jackson. Throughout the life of this project we have benefited from the wonderful administrative and technical input of Sandi Cole-Pay, Christine Eastlick, Deborah Palliser, Donna Robertson, Jane Roth, Sharon Rynders and Liz Straker. Carol Knight and Marie Krbavac, respectively, designed the conference documents and website. Contributors to the symposium included Nick Blomley, John-Paul Boyd, Neil Boyd, Christine Boyle, Kate Braid, Joan Brockman, Stevie Cameron, Harold Cardinal, Mark Carter, Murray Dobbin, Richard Ericson, Corky Evans, Jim Fulton, Herschel Hardin, Melody Hessing, Dean Jobb, Karin Mickelson, Kim Pate, the Raging Grannies, Svend Robinson, Julie Rupert, Stuart Rush, Renee Taylor and Jerald Zaslove. And, of course, we owe the greatest debt to our fifteen authors, whose collective erudition, insight, conscience and commitment permeate the pages that follow.

Elizabeth Comack originally suggested that we approach Fernwood Publishing with the proposal for this collection. Publisher Errol Sharpe embraced the idea from the outset and was a bedrock of support throughout. Douglas Beall edited the manuscript with a master's eye for clarity and form and Beverley Rach artfully shepherded the production process through to completion. Richard Slye crafted an absolutely inspired cover design.

A version of Chapter 3, by Sunera Thobani, originally appeared in the journal *Race and Class* in June 2000 under the title "Closing Ranks: Racism and Sexism in Canada's Immigration Policy."

Chapter 15, by Gayle K. Horii, is adapted from her article first published in Kelly Hannah-Moffat and Margaret Shaw's *An Ideal Prison? Critical Essays on Women's Imprisonment in Canada* (2000). Our thanks go out to Fernwood Publishing for sharing this work.

On behalf of the contributors and Fernwood, royalties from sales of this book are being donated to End Legislated Poverty of Vancouver.

# Introduction

*Robert Menzies, Dorothy E. Chunn and Susan C. Boyd*

## Of Crime Waves and Crime Tsunamis

By most accounts, Canada is in the throes of a rampant crime wave. From coast to coast to coast, the lives and property of law-abiding citizens, and the safety and security of our communities, are in grave jeopardy. The "bad apples" among us wreak havoc on the public peace, drain billions of dollars from the economy and subject ever-increasing numbers of ordinary Canadians to their wicked ways. The law-abiding seem virtually powerless to stem this tide of violence, disorder and deceit. Lenient and liberal lawmakers, incompetent or complicit judicial officials, disempowered police forces, and an uninformed public have precious little impact on, and may even intensify, the untold risks that surround us. In our society the criminal element wields the real power and, more often than not, vested authorities are either in their employ or under their control. With impunity these "others" systematically inflict incalculable damage in the pursuit of profit, comfort, status and self-interest. The rest of us are at their mercy, with little recourse other than to defend ourselves as best we can. Ultimately, it is only through all-out combat against these dangerous forces—through more and tougher laws, redoubled political resolve, heightened security and surveillance, fortified police, courts and prisons and, if necessary, direct vigilante action—that the abuses can be stemmed. Our way of life and our basic rights as Canadian citizens hang in the balance.

This inflammatory rhetoric no doubt rings all too familiar to the ears of most Canadians. Such "lawandorder" talk (Ericson and Baranek 1982) has become a dominant and daily feature of public culture as we embark on this new millennium. In our latter-day "risk society" (Brown and Pratt 2000; Ericson and Haggerty 1997; O'Malley 1998), security is purportedly in short supply and menacing outsiders imperil us from all sides. News and entertainment media are replete with images of rising crime rates, predatory strangers, street violence and crime warfare that have come to signify our worst anxieties about a society facing danger and decay (Ericson, Baranek and Chan 1989, 1991). And by all appearances, our pan-Canadian obsession with "the crime problem" has been surging to ever more elevated levels since 1990.

Perhaps this most recent bout of fear and loathing should come as no great surprise. Since the alleged victory of capitalism over communism, and amid the ensuing *Pax Americana* era of relative national security and domestic prosperity for the affluent states and social classes of the "developed" world, external enemies have become an endangered species (Chomsky and Herman 1988). At the same time, internal crises brought on by the economic recessions of the early 1980s and 1990s—along with the erosion of the social welfare net, deepening class divisions, and other conflicts based on race, gender, sexuality, ability and age—have fostered a climate of insecurity and resentment in liberal democracies for which causes must be found and blame attributed.

Street crime becomes the ideal representation of all that is wrong. As Taylor (1983), Kaminer (1995), McCormick (1995), and Ferrell and Websdale (1999) have observed, commonplace images of predatory criminals, and foreboding crime statistics unleashed by police bureaus and government offices, are potent symbols of a social world in chaos. They crystallize public anxieties; they offer compelling explanations for our assorted domestic troubles; they seem far more immediate and intense than other recognized social problems such as suicide, disease, poverty and environmental desecration; they justify repressive laws and nurture policies that make everyone less free; and they divert our collective attention away from the wider structures of inequality, injustice and oppression that engulf us. For those who rely on these images and numbers to amass money and power—from right-wing politicians to crime-control practitioners to the mainstream media—the idea of an ever-burgeoning crime problem is an indispensable token of political and cultural capital.

But this generally accepted portrait of "normal" crime is fatally flawed. Every piece of criminological evidence available to us shows that the rhetoric is, quite simply, wrong. Latter-day assertions about accelerating crime waves are variously founded in stereotype, moral panic and myth (Fishman 1998; Kappeler, Blumberg and Potter 2000; Pepinsky and Jesilow 1984). As it happens, rates of officially recorded criminality in Canada have been plummeting for nearly a decade (Canadian Centre for Justice Statistics 1999; Hackler 2000; Silverman, Teevan and Sacco 2000). In 1999 they dropped for the eighth straight year (Skelton 2000). By every account, the "average" Canadian today is less likely to be victimized criminally by another individual than at any time since the 1970s.

Of course, the compelling substance of this fact in no way diminishes the devastating impact of violent and property crime on those who have encountered it. Nor should it downplay the disproportionate experience of criminality among disadvantaged peoples, including the poor, inner-city dwellers, and/or First Nations communities across Canada. At the same time this evidence of falling crime rates offers a forceful rebuttal of many of the most fiercely held conventional wisdoms about crime in Canada. It also challenges the claims of those who manufacture the exaggerated images of criminal anarchy; who demand that ever more resources be funnelled into the business of suppressing, detecting and locking up wrongdoers; and who capitalize on the resulting hysteria for personal and institutional gain.

Still, there are further complexities and contradictions to consider. The problem, we would argue, is not so much that the dire visions and accusations referenced above are blatantly untruthful—it is more the case that they are tragically misdirected. The sheer scope and quantity of the harms being perpetrated on the Canadian public are indeed colossal, and the resulting economic, social and personal costs are beyond measure. In allocating blame for this sorry state of affairs, however, our efforts have been stupefyingly off course. If we have so badly misjudged and mismanaged the crime problem over the years, it is because we—professional criminologists, policy-makers, criminal justice authorities, the media and the public alike—have been looking for crime in all the wrong places. To flush out those perpetrators who systematically inflict the greatest share of suffering, abuse, penury and misery on their co-citizens requires a depth of comprehension and a level of creativity that have repeatedly eluded the majority of otherwise sensible and compassionate Canadians. Again and again, the powerful ideologies of crime control have seemingly retarded our capacity to envision, name and remedy the numerous problems that surround us.

The process of achieving an informed understanding of "crime" and effecting genuine change for the better must begin by recognizing that the sum total of violence, transgression, damage and disorder inflicted by the entire population of "mainstream" criminals—as serious as this issue is for countless Canadians (Lowman and MacLean 1992)—is utterly eclipsed by the infinitely more grievous depredations of the powerful. By fixating on street crime waves, we have virtually ignored the tsunamis generated by "suite crime." By every possible measure—money wasted, property destroyed, lives ruined, people killed—the affluent are more dangerous than the poor. Authorities wreak more havoc than their subjects. The "average" Canadian is more likely to suffer at the hands of government, elected and appointed officials, business organizations, professionals or white-, blue- and khaki-collared criminals than from all the street thugs, youth gangs, home invaders, illegal (im)migrants, pot growers and squeegie kids that our society can produce. In Canada, criminologists have estimated that corporate wrongdoing alone—through illicit mergers and monopolies, unsafe goods and products, fraud, false advertising, kickbacks, profiteering, price-fixing, pollution, hazardous workplaces, exploitation of labour, and so forth—accounts for twenty-five times more injuries, six times more deaths and ten times more economic loss than do offences under the *Criminal Code* (Ellis 1987: 94–95; McMullan 1992: 24, 34–35; Snider 1993: 1–8). When other kinds of "elite deviance" (Coleman 1994; Simon 1999) are added to the equation—misconduct by doctors, lawyers, clerics and teachers; government corruption; crimes by criminal justice officials; state-sanctioned assault on the environment; violations of human rights—the aggregate impact is staggering and beyond measure.

Despite its international reputation as a "peaceable kingdom" of order and good government, and a bastion of democracy and civil liberty, Canada is an ideal exemplar for the study of "upperworld" wrongdoing. From the very first appearance of European colonialists on the easternmost points of the continent some five centuries ago, successive generations of state authorities, corporate organizations and elites have been carving out an impressive legacy of desecration, atrocity, exploitation, perfidy and greed. Historians, social scientists and journalists in this country have charted in detail a galaxy of harms visited by the rich and powerful upon the people and land around them.

Through the years Canadians and their forebears have witnessed, *inter alia*,

the systematic economic and cultural assault on First Nations and other Aboriginal peoples across the country (Cardinal 1969, Culhane 1997); the government's
active or clandestine involvement in immoral wars and "police actions" around
the world (Brown and Brown 1973; Culhane 1972); the sellout of Canadian
resources and industry through so-called "free trade" agreements (Barlow 1990;
McQuaig 1998); endless incidents of political corruption from the Pacific Scandal
of John A. Macdonald's era (McDonald 1996) to the Mulroney boondoggles of
the 1980s (Cameron 1994); the state's harassment, surveillance and assault of its
own citizens (Dion 1982; Mann and Lee 1979; Vallières 1971); the legally
sanctioned execution of 701 people between Confederation and 1961 (Anderson
1973) and the wrongful or needless imprisonment of untold others (Anderson
and Anderson 1998); the racially motivated exclusion of Asian and Jewish
migrants (Abella and Troper 1982; Johnson 1989; Roberts 1988); the internment
of Japanese Canadians in the British Columbia interior during World War II
(Adachi 1991); the political disenfranchisement of women (Backhouse 1991;
Boyd 1997; Kealey and Sangster 1989); the legal subordination of lesbian, gay,
bisexual and transgendered peoples (Herman 1994; Kinsman 1996; Ross 1995);
tens of thousands of worker fatalities at the hands of negligent and abusive
company owners (Leyton 1997; Reasons, Ross and Paterson 1981; Tucker 1990);
consumer deaths by the millions from the ingestion of tobacco, alcohol, assorted
other drugs and unsafe food (Breggin and Cohen 1999; Cunningham 1996;
Lexchin 1984; Nottingham 1998); the defilement of oceans, rivers and forests in
the pursuit of profit (Howard 1991; Marchak 1995; Mowat 1984); countless
chronicles of physical, sexual, mental and economic abuse by organizations and
people in authority such as religious institutions, the psychiatric profession,
financial "trusts," legal firms and educators (Collins 1988; Hyde 1991; Miller
1996; Penfold 1998; Ross 1987); and the "private" terrorization and coercion of
women and their children by men wielding patriarchal power in the homeplace
(Bonnycastle and Rigakos 1998; Comack 1993).

More recent illustrations of such upperworld malfeasance in Canada have
been legion. Canadian citizens have been subjected to an extraordinary number
and range of crimes and harms committed by powerful people. However ironic
our opening "crime wave" imagery was meant to be, when it comes to
"ordinary" felonies, it does seem a very apt metaphor for describing the tsunami
of transgressions that has been bearing down on us from high places since the
1970s and 1980s.

Examples of these wrongs and harms abound, many of which our authors
chronicle in the chapters that follow. In the political arena we have witnessed the
self-immolation of the federal Tory government, and a sorry succession of scandals among British Columbia Socreds, Nova Scotia Liberals and Saskatchewan
Conservatives (Jones 2000; Leslie 1991; McCormick 1999; Sawatsky 1991).
Individual politicians like Colin Thatcher, Gerald Regan and Jack Ramsey have
achieved notoriety for dubious reasons of their own (Boomer 1999; Greenaway
1999; Wilson and Wilson 1985). The involvement of Canada's military in Soma-

lia, Rwanda, the Balkans and the Persian Gulf has tarnished our standing as an international peacekeeper around the globe (Kashmeri 1991; Loomis 1997; Miller 1994). Closer to home, Hydro-Québec laid waste to thousands of hectares of pristine wilderness and threatened to obliterate an entire way of life before the northern Cree mobilized to bring the Great Whale Project to its knees (Niezen 1998). The disasters of the Ocean Ranger and Westray once again revealed the vulnerability of working Canadians to raw corporate power (House 1987; Jobb 1994; McCormick 1999). In Nova Scotia, the Sydney Steel Corporation has dumped tons of toxic waste into city tar ponds; likewise, the Alcan aluminum smelter in Kitimat, British Columbia, disgorged massive quantities of sulphur dioxide and hydrocarbons into the surrounding environment during the 1980s (McMullan 1992: 33); and the Grassy Narrows Aboriginal reserve in northern Ontario was decimated by more than a decade of mercury poisoning from the Reed Paper processing plant in Dryden (Shkilnyk 1985). The Bre-X and Vancouver Stock Exchange fiascos and the Royal Trust case have exposed the rot of corruption undergirding many sectors of the finance industry (Goold and Willis 1997). The Anglican Church hovers on the brink of bankruptcy as revelations continue to surface about Aboriginal lives destroyed under its alleged care (Miller 1996). The criminal justice system has been far from exempt, with police shootings of African Canadian and Indigenous people in Montréal, Toronto and Winnipeg; high-profile wrongful conviction cases such as Donald Marshall, Guy Paul Morin and David Milgaard; the pepper spraying of peaceful anti-APEC protesters in Vancouver and anti-poverty demonstrators in Toronto; epidemic corruption in the Winnipeg judicial system; unexplained deaths behind bars at municipal, provincial and federal levels; and assorted rights violations against women prisoners at the former Prison for Women in Kingston (Cayley 1997; Hannah-Moffat and Shaw 2000; Harris 1986; Karp and Rosner 1991; Makin 1992; Pue 2000). These are just samples from an inventory of abuse that stretches on and on and to which the fifteen chapters of this book bear witness.

## Terms of Engagement

How could all this happen? How can our society routinely ignore, condone or even applaud the destructive policies and practices of privileged institutions and people, yet at the same time demonize individual street criminals and devote the majority of attention, social control machinery and resources (some $10 billion annually) to regulating crime in the streets? Why does crime in the suites seem so innocuous to so many despite its chilling, meticulously documented and utterly devastating impact on us all? Conversely, why does street crime seem so threatening to so many, especially during a period of falling crime rates? And how can those with status, wealth and power repeatedly transgress against society, ethics and the law with such impunity? Why is there no "lawandorder" campaign against elite criminality, demanding tougher laws against abusive and malevolent businesses, government authorities and professionals? Why are these issues not daily on the front pages of national newspapers and at the forefront of our elected officials' legislative agendae? Most importantly, what steps can be taken to change this dismal state of affairs? How can we raise the profile of upperworld wrongdoing, educate the public and convince those in positions of influence that our priorities have been all wrong? In conventional crime control parlance, what are the prospects for a successful "war" against crimes of power?

With these questions (and many others) in mind, we convened a symposium on May 7–9, 1998, to explore the many aspects and experiences of upperworld wrongdoing in Canada. In establishing a theme for the meetings, we opted not to look exclusively at "crimes of authority," "state and corporate criminality," "white collar crime" or "human rights violations." Instead we enlisted the more encompassing concept of power, coining the slightly postmodern term "power [ab]use" to emphasize that the use and abuse of power cannot be studied separately. One flows from the other; they are reflexively involved and mutually implicated; the systematic exercise of power inherently implies the possibility of abuse. Our aim in taking on this project, then, was to canvass alternative ways of defining, observing, understanding, resisting and overcoming power [ab]use in various sectors of Canadian society. We worked from the assumption that only through a multidimensional approach, in which a range of topics would be addressed and diverse perspectives heard, could we capture the full depth and breadth of the critical social problems that we were addressing.

During the three-day symposium, thirty speakers told their stories of power [ab]use. The presenters, who encompassed many different backgrounds, interests and regions of the country, included researchers, writers, academics, politicians, legal practitioners, activists and community members. They covered a spectrum of topics relating to the illegitimate, unethical, dangerous and harmful conduct of the state, political elites, private corporations, professionals and other authorities that offend against people, the law, the environment and the economy. In total, 125 participants attended the keynote and panel sessions. The discussions ranged widely, but in differing ways all focused on the need to integrate the varied experiences, observations and prescriptions of participants into a coordinated approach to understand, confront and transcend power [ab]use in Canada.

This book is the product of that symposium. In what follows, thirteen of the symposium presenters, and two authors added for their expertise on mass media representations of corporate crime and women's imprisonment respectively, offer their understandings and analyses of power [ab]use—and its many causes, conditions, guises and consequences—in the Canadian context. We view this collection above all else as an exercise in the writing of critical and feminist criminology. Each of the chapters can be seen as a case study in the general investigation of upperworld transgression.

Our Introduction offers a framework for reading these essays. In what follows we look at power [ab]use as an organizing concept for this project; we review some of the remarkable transformations in the discipline of criminology that have made such an inquiry possible; and we outline the main themes and subjects that are featured in the five parts and fifteen chapters of this reader.

## Power [Ab]Use and Canadian Criminology

Power has long been a subject of concern for social scientists of all persuasions. It is an inescapable, yet deeply enigmatic, feature of modern life. Across the centuries, power has proven to be a "will-o'-the-wisp" (Morriss 1987: 1) which has assumed an array of shapes and forms, and has meant many things to many people. While treatises on power date back to the very beginnings of philosophy and social thought—with writers as diverse as Aristotle, Plato, Hobbes, Hume and Machiavelli reflecting on its nature—it is the autocracies and democracies of the nineteenth, twentieth and twenty-first centuries that have spawned the most concerted efforts to gain understanding and mastery over the workings of social power. In his groundbreaking analysis of political economy and culture, Karl Marx (1967 [1867]) equated power with the historical dialectic of material existence and, in capitalist society, with class struggle and consciousness. For Max Weber (1954 [1925]), power represented the capacity to achieve one's aims over the opposition of others. The U.S. social critic C. Wright Mills (1956) saw power as a commodity that was monopolized by a small cabal of influential political, industrial and cultural elites.

More recently, feminists and post-colonialists have located power within a matrix of structural hierarchies and social relations based on class, gender, race, ethnicity, sexuality, (dis)ability and generation. Postmodernists and post-Marxists have adopted a more diffuse, destructured, polycentric and mobile representation of power relations and social movements that are in a continuous state of fluidity and flux. The influential social theorist Pierre Bourdieu situates power in relation to "fields," or systems, that constitute social positions of dominance, subordination or equivalency; whereas Michel Foucault conceives of power as a relational, reflexive, dynamic, capillary phenomenon that is intimately tied to the flow of knowledge relations and inherently embodies resistance as much as it does authority (see generally Barrett 1991; Dean 1999; Foucault 1980, 1990; Fraser 1989; Isaac 1987; Jenkins 1992; Lash 1990; Lukes 1974; Morris 1987).

In this book, no single theory of power predominates. We have eschewed a one-sided or doctrinaire analysis of power and its origins, character, whereabouts and implications in favour of an open-ended attitude that selectively enlists the insights of various writers and researchers. This approach, we think, far better reflects the extraordinary complexity of the issues involved and more accurately represents the diverse disciplinary backgrounds and perspectives of our fifteen contributors. At the same time, the influences on us in the development of this project have been very clear from the outset. From Marxism we draw an awareness of the structural and ideological conditions of capitalism that frame the [ab]use of power in modern society and in liberal (democratic) states in particular. From Mills and other critical sociologists we derive our concentration on the wrongs and harms committed by upper echelons of the social order. Feminism has sensitized us to the correspondences between the private and public realms, and the intersecting relations of gender, class, race and other dimensions of hierarchy. Finally, from Foucault we extract the idea that power is not a static instrument of oppression, but rather a set of relations and sites of contention where every display of power ignites its own oppositions, and where even the most seemingly "marginal" people and groups are far from impotent. All of these ideas are to be found in the fifteen studies of power [ab]use that comprise this collection, just as they have all been instrumental in fuelling the critical movement in criminology with which the book identifies.

When it comes to the study of power, the criminological enterprise has lagged far behind related disciplines such as philosophy, sociology and political science for most of its history. Prior to the late 1960s, criminologists seldom even considered the role of power in causing crime, defining criminals, generating law or shaping the policies, institutions and practices that comprise criminal justice and correctional systems.

Moreover, from the biological positivism of the late 1800s through to the twentieth-century psycho-sociological schools of individual and social pathology, ecological criminology, learning theory, differential association, subculture and labelling, criminology was uniformly, and heedlessly, about the trespasses of powerless people. The discipline both followed and fuelled public and media images about the primacy of street crime, stranger danger and random violence as the supposed monopoly of the most marginal sectors of society. The criminality of the poor and of racial and ethnic minorities comprised the raw material of criminological inquiry. At the same time, the notion that institutions and elites might merit the attention of professional criminologists, or that crimes of the powerful could be equal to or even more pernicious than the actions of marginal groups, was almost inconceivable. These biases were embedded in the very fabric of the discipline and were evident in every facet of its practice, from the production of crime statistics to the chosen interests of academic, private and state researchers to the composition of university curricula and the topics deemed eligible for research funding. Moreover, they dovetailed with wider political and community beliefs about the nature, distribution and suppression of crime.

But as the 1960s and 1970s unfolded, the topography of the discipline began to shift. With the rise of the "new criminology" in Britain (Cohen 1988; Taylor, Walton and Young 1973; Walton and Young 1998) and "radical criminology" in the United States (Inciardi 1980; Pepinsky and Quinney 1993; Quinney 1974), some members of the discipline began to challenge conventional wisdoms about the phenomenon of crime, its causes and distribution, and the conditions of its social and legal control. Books with titles such as *Law, Order and Power* (Chambliss and Seidman 1982), *Crimes of the Powerful* (Pearce 1976) and *Power, Crime and Mystification* (Box 1983) began to appear. A paradigm shift was underway, and the concept of power was at its core. Over the subsequent quarter century, an impressive array of approaches imported from other disciplines—including Marxism, feminism, left realism, abolitionism, peacemaking and postmodernism—forever reshaped the theory and practice of criminology.

Out of this unprecedented wave of alternative criminologies have emerged new and different ways of thinking about crime. Increasingly, many criminologists have been concerned less with charting and preventing criminality in its conventional forms, and more with rethinking the crime concept itself and relocating it within structures of authority and privilege. In turn, these trends have spawned an influential body of research and writing that is concentrated on the relationships between crime, social class, gender, race/ethnicity, sexuality, generational structures and other aspects of social hierarchy; and on the political, moral and legal dimensions of harms committed by persons and organizations that have not traditionally been the focus of criminological inquiry.

With these objectives in mind, since the 1970s, researchers, theorists and activists have attempted to map and explain patterns of wrongdoing among privileged members of society and to assess their impact. During a period of intense public concern with the repression of street crime, critical criminologists studying corporate, political, organizational, professional and elite criminality have succeeded in documenting the economic, ecological, social and human carnage inflicted by those who rule and control. A succession of studies on numerous subjects in a wealth of different settings has proven that the risks and costs associated with upperworld power [ab]use—including rights violations, repression, collusion, corruption, transgression and outright lawbreaking—eclipse in every way the "ordinary crimes" perpetrated by the powerless and poor. This work has again and again revealed the exceptional frequency, range and impact of upperworld criminality. It has also exposed the alarming tendency of elite deviance to remain underdetected and underpunished as criminal justice systems doggedly persist in training their attention, revenues and powers on the disadvantaged and the weak (e.g., Barak 1991; Braithwaite 1989; Clinard and Yeager 1980; Ermann and Lundman 1987; Pearce and Snider 1995; Pearce and Woodiwiss 1993; Pearce and Tombs 1998; Reiman 1990; Rosoff, Pontell and Tillman 1998; Simon and Hagan 1999).

In Canada, too, critical and feminist criminologies have flourished. In academic, activist and applied circles, Canadian criminologists over recent years have shown far less deference to authority (Friedenberg 1980) than did prior generations. While traditional conservative genera of the discipline have endured, and new administrative and biological strains have emerged, by the same token increasing numbers of criminologists have turned to broader and more ambitious projects focusing on the vitally important correspondences between crime, law, power and social (in)justice. Along with these shifting emphases has come awareness that criminality in all its guises is inextricably tied to regimes of dominance and subordination. The resulting body of research and theory extends beyond mere "exposé criminology" (Taylor, Walton and Young 1973)—it is far more than just a cataloguing of power and its negative effects on Canadians. There is growing recognition that any lasting solution to the "crime problem" hinges on our collective willingness to challenge traditional power structures and become involved in struggles for social change (see Chunn and Lacombe 2000; Chunn and Menzies 1995; Comack 1999; Comack and Brickey 1991; Fleming

1985; Hinch 1994; MacLean 1986; MacLean and Milovanovic 1991; Schissel and Mahood 1996).

Towards this end, the criminological study of power [ab]use has come alive in Canada. As noted above, this burgeoning field of research encompasses crimes of warfare and genocide; political terrorism; crimes against the "Third World"; breaches of human rights; environmental desecration; crimes against the economy; political corruption; corporate wrongdoing; violations of trust by professionals; violence against women; crimes against ethnic, racial, linguistic and sexual minorities; the endangerment and exploitation of workers; the abuse and victimization of children; and crimes of authority in the criminal justice system and other public institutions (see, e.g., Cameron 1994; Dobbin 1998; Goff and Reasons 1978; Hannah-Moffat and Shaw 2000; Hessing and Howlett 1998; Jobb 1994; Leyton, 1997; McCormick 1999; McMullan 1992; McQuaig 1991; Penfold 1998; Reasons, Ross and Paterson 1991; Rebick and Roach 1996; Sawatsky 1991; Shearing1981; Schrecker 1997; Snider 1993; Tucker 1990). Unifying this diverse body of work is the understanding that crime is a far more complex and political phenomenon than has been acknowledged by criminologists of the past. This recognition has irreversibly altered the content and character of academic criminology in this country. It has changed the very way that we think about crime and power in Canadian society.

Finally, power [ab]use research in Canada also breaches the customary boundaries of academic criminology. Some of the most influential writing in this field has come from the keyboards and pens of activists, journalists, practising lawyers, consultants and private researchers—and especially from those who have witnessed the [ab]use of power first-hand (ibid.). This diversity of background, experience and perspective is represented throughout this book. It is an essential ingredient, we believe, for any project aimed at mapping the full breadth and impact of power [ab]use in Canada. It also demonstrates that criminology—critical and otherwise—is daily being practised far beyond the cloistered halls of university and government. Academic criminologists have much to learn from this work. Furthermore, it is within these numerous contexts, both public and private, that most of the important struggles for social justice are being waged and praxis in its many forms is most likely to be found.

## Organization, Themes and Contents

At its core, this is a book about crime, law, power and social (in)justice in Canada. The fifteen contributors comprise academics, legal practitioners, journalists and social activists who have been studying and struggling for years against the [ab]use of power in myriad realms of Canadian life. Many are leading researchers and writers in their respective fields. *[Ab]Using Power: The Canadian Experience* is conceived as the first systematic effort in this country to integrate a variety of interrelated topics, all connected to power [ab]use, into a single collection aimed at identifying and exploring common themes, issues, problems and remedies. Each chapter has been selected because it furthers an understanding of power relations and illuminates the problem of upperworld wrongdoing in Canada.

The selected topics represent some of the most controversial issues and notorious examples of power [ab]use in recent Canadian history. In developing and drafting their respective chapters, the authors have extrapolated from their personal and professional experiences to address the circumstances in which abuses of power are most likely to occur, the strategies needed to combat such abuses, and the legal and social policies that might help to promote regulation and prevention.

The book is organized in five interconnected parts: The State; The Political Elite; Corporations; Professions; and Criminal (In)justice. These somewhat arbitrary divisions belie the many subjects and themes common to every chapter but reflect the fact that each topic has developed as a relatively independent area of study both within and beyond the field of criminology. Preserving these sections within a comparatively open-ended book structure, therefore, has both organizational and instructional value.

The struggle against power [ab]use and for social justice is the central theme of every essay in this book. Our authors chart the human experience of power and resistance in a multiplicity of places and times, and explore the wider contexts within which such struggles are waged. Several contributors demonstrate that, against the background of transworld capitalism and the internationalization of political culture, virtually every exercise of power resonates globally, nationally and locally. On a worldwide plane this polydynamic aspect of power [ab]use is seen in the explosion of global corporate capitalism, in the assaults of neo-colonialism against impoverished nations and in the ominous threat of unrestrained "free trade." At the level of nation-states such as Canada, the struggles pivot around the restructuring of the welfare state at both federal and provincial levels; around divisions of class, race, ethnicity, gender, sexuality, (dis)ability and generation; and around critical changes in the relationship between government and citizen under conditions of advanced capitalism. And at the local level, as some authors point out, a range of questions related to praxis, political mobilization, the quest for social change and the power of collective action needs to be addressed.

Visions of hope, emancipatory possibilities, and the capacity of individuals and collectives to resist and overcome power [ab]use are also at the core of this book. Each chapter should be read as a blueprint for future social justice as much as a litany of past and present injustice. The sometimes overt, occasionally tacit message of our authors is that as an initial step towards effecting genuine and lasting change we need first and foremost, and with deceptive simplicity, to "imagine democracy" (Rebick 2000a).

Part One establishes a political context for the book by considering how the Canadian state has fostered the structural and cultural conditions for power [ab]use in this country. Judy Rebick reviews some of the main economic and social dilemmas currently facing the Canadian Left. She argues that global restructuring, deregulation, privatization, corporatism and the ascendancy of neo-conservative ideologies in government and media have eroded the gains made by previous generations of human justice and collective rights activists. But, as she also maintains, there is much opportunity for a new cohort of politically conscious citizens to regain the initiative, develop progressive strategies of participatory democracy and "take back the agenda" for social justice and against the abuse of power. In his essay, Ted Schrecker chronicles the dismantling of the welfare state, the rise of marketplace economics, and the recommodification of labour that have characterized political economies in Canada and elsewhere over the past twenty years. He charts the devastating effects for powerless Canadians who are cast adrift as allegedly unable or unwilling to contribute to this "new economic reality." Next, Sunera Thobani enlists the federal Immigration Policy Review of 1994 to demonstrate how the Canadian state has mobilized gendered, racialized and class-based constructions of citizenship to erect barriers against the immigration of women of colour. Like Rebick and Schrecker, she situates her analysis within the context of structural and ideological shifts in the relationship between the Canadian state and its citizenry. She shows how authorities wield their power to exclude marginal outsiders, and manufacture legitimacy for prohibitionist policies by purporting to represent the "nation's interests."

Part Two addresses [ab]uses of power by Canadian political elites. John Dixon recounts the extraordinary chain of events leading up to and following the torture and killing of Shidane Arone by members of the Canadian Forces Airborne Division in Somalia on March 16, 1992. For Dixon, this sorry incident harbours critical lessons about the nature of power and its [ab]use in Canada. He argues that the de-democratization of politics and the disempowerment of the citizenry are responsible for breeding a political and civic culture within which authorities are unaccountable and atrocities such as this can be committed with impunity. For his part, Stuart Farson chronicles the history of the federal government's signals intelligence operations leading to the establishment of the Canadian Security Establishment (CSE) in the 1970s. He charts initiatives undertaken by the executive branch to conceal the existence and operations of such surveillance organizations from Parliament and the public. J.F. Conway then details the legacy of scandal, fraud and betrayal of trust bequeathed by the Conservative government of Grant Devine in Saskatchewan. This was perhaps the most corrupt political administration in Canadian history. Yet as Conway argues, the individual pecca-dilloes of mercenary politicians did not even begin to measure up to the systemic [ab]uses of power committed by this same government as it downsized and privatized its services, forged unholy alliances with corporate interests and tried to gerrymander its way back to power in the 1991 provincial election.

The contributors to Part Three focus their attention on the corporate [ab]use of power. First, Laureen Snider looks at the corporate counter-revolution that has succeeded in virtually erasing the idea that economic institutions are even capable of malfeasance. Free market competition, deregulation and the triumph of the profit motive are all implicated in the near disappearance of corporate crime as a subject of public policy and legal control. Snider reviews the decriminalization and normalization of various forms of corporate power [ab]use, and links these trends with the increasing economic polarization of Canada and other "developed" nations, the escalating scale and profitability of corporate institutions, and the alienation of citizens from government policy and practice. Pursuing similar themes, John McMullan examines media representations of the May 9, 1992 explosion at Westray, Canada's worst mining disaster of the past generation, in which twenty-six men perished. McMullan demonstrates how the press participated in the manufacture of "regimes of truth" (Foucault 1980, 1990) which nullified the experience of dead miners and their grieving families, and reinforced the corporate and state version of Westray as nothing more than a regrettable accident. Judy Fudge extends the discussion beyond Canada's borders in her analysis of labour abuse by transnational corporations. Fudge looks at the recent rise of activism against Nike, the world's largest manufacturer of sports apparel, which, she observes, "epitomizes the global sweatshop" in its exploitation of women workers in impoverished nations. With a restrained optimism, she notes that consumer activism has caused some progressive change in Nike's labour practices and codes of conduct. She argues that campaigns against corporate transgressors can potentially facilitate international solidarity and raise living and working standards both at home and abroad.

In Part Four, the authors focus on power [ab]use among Canadian professional elites. First, Tana Dineen looks at the psychology industry. A vast and profitable institution, psychology has infiltrated increasingly wide expanses of the social terrain. Its practitioners have benefited hugely from their recognized status as experts in human living. Dineen enumerates three forms of professional power [ab]use perpetrated by psychology—namely, the maintenance of power through pseudo-science, the control over publicly available knowledge about its activities, and the dissemination of fear for the purpose of selling its services. Susan Penfold shifts attention to the profession of psychiatry, mapping the gender-based power structures on which psychiatry is built. Penfold catalogues the many varieties of abuse inflicted upon women by mental health practitioners. A remedy to systemic abuses of patients by professionals, she argues, can be found only by acknowledging, understanding and working to overcome the gendered relations of power that prevail between male psychiatrists and their women patients. Edgar Z. Friedenberg offers an analysis of homophobia inside this country's school systems. While the Canadian educational industry (with the exception of so-called Christian private schools) does not officially promote homophobia, nonetheless it encourages a cultural and institutional regime within which lesbian and gay students are marked as rebellious outsiders and their worlds go unrepresented in curricula and classrooms. In this sense, education systems are inseparable from the wider structures of discrimination and prejudice that surround them, and which they in turn nourish.

The concluding part looks at the state of criminal (in)justice in Canada. Toni Williams examines the Commission on Systemic Racism in the Ontario criminal justice system, which was established in partial response to the police shootings of at least eleven black Ontarians between 1979 and 1992. Williams documents the role of black communities and activists in framing the problem of police power [ab]use upon which the commission focused. In order to promote real change, she argues, energies must be directed toward uncovering and transforming the entrenched, normalized and everyday repression that pervades this country's criminal justice system. Dianne L. Martin's contribution recounts the compelling story of Leonard Peltier, the American Indian Movement (AIM) leader who is serving consecutive life sentences for allegedly having shot to death two FBI special agents on the Pine Ridge Reservation in South Dakota on June 26, 1975. Martin argues that Peltier was both wrongfully convicted and unjustly extradited from Canada to the United States. She sees the Peltier case as a paradigmatic example of power [ab]use by judicial authorities which also illuminates the limitations of legal redress for First Nations and other disenfranchised groups, and the need to seek justice beyond law, within the realm of politics. Finally, Gayle K. Horii considers the habitual abuse of power against incarcerated women in Canada, well documented in Madam Justice Arbour's inquiry into the guard riot at the Kingston Prison for Women, in the life stories of prisoners, and by other investigations. Horii locates the subjugation and mistreatment of women prisoners within the wider arena of systemic gender bias, and she reviews various strategies available for empowering women and effecting progressive change both inside and beyond the prison walls.

## Summary

This book explores the human experience and social impact of power [ab]use in Canada at the outset of a new millennium. Our contributors document the many domains of Canadian life where the powerful and powerless are in conflict. It also addresses the origins, nature and implications of power, authority, regulation and resistance. In light of the growing national and international literature on the subject, the authors consider the many implications of the cultural, politico-economic and legal problems to which they bear witness. In this sense, the collection represents one small step towards establishing an interdisciplinary program of "power studies" that would be devoted to understanding power and its use as well as the struggle against its abuse in diverse spheres of Canadian society.

Along with its relevance for students, researchers, activists, members of the public and practitioners working outside university contexts, we intend this book as a resource for critical and feminist criminologists, legal scholars and individuals involved in a wide range of related disciplines. We hope that it will be useful not only as a primary text in criminology and law courses but also as a secondary reader for others who want to establish links among their teaching and research in environmental studies, feminist studies, communications, economics, political science, corporate law, criminal justice and the sociology of professions.

Part One
# The State

Chapter 1

# Active Citizenship Is the Best Defence against Abuse of Power

*Judy Rebick*

Corporate globalization is not fundamentally new. Adam Smith said the vile maxim of capitalists is "everything for ourselves and nothing for anyone else." In a capitalist society, the corporations always want to maximize their profits. For a variety of reasons, we are now at a stage of capitalism where corporations pursue this goal at almost any cost.

Many argue that we have never seen this level of corporate power in the world. They maintain that the corporations have usurped the power of governments and that today our focus should be on corporate power rather than state power.

Much youth activism is focused on corporate power and the international trade organizations which enforce that power, particularly in developing countries. Internationally, more and more young people see the overthrow or significant reform of corporate rule as the only possible direction for social change. In 1998, when I gave the speech at Simon Fraser University (SFU) on which this chapter is based, I pointed to the defeat of the Multilateral Agreement on Investment (MAI) and the student demonstrations against the Asia-Pacific Economic Co-operation Conference (APEC) as a sign of this growing movement. Later, of course, the Battle of Seattle against the World Trade Organization (WTO) has made the developing movement visible even to those on the Right who have been declaring for years that the Left is dead.

Unchecked corporate power of necessity leads to abuse. In fact the unchecked power of any group in society leads to abuse. In my speech in 1998, I argued that instead of just analyzing abuses of power, it was important to counter them. (At that time I was in the early stages of developing an argument that appears in my book *Imagine Democracy* (Rebick 2000a), that the deepening of democracy is the best way to counter the abuses of power inherent in corporate globalization.)

The voracious appetites of capital are nothing new. At the time of the symposium at SFU, I was preparing a speech for a conference on the 150th Anniversary of the *Communist Manifesto*. First published in 1848, the *Manifesto* defines the nature of unrestrained capitalism:

> The bourgeoisie, wherever it has got the upper hand, has put an end to

all feudal, patriarchal [we wish], idyllic relations. It has pitilessly torn asunder the motley feudal ties that bound man to his "natural superiors," and has left remaining no other nexus between man and man than naked self-interest, than callous "cash payment." It has drowned the most heavenly ecstasies of religious fervour, of chivalrous enthusiasm, of philistine sentimentalism, in the icy water of egotistical calculation. It has resolved personal worth into exchange value, and in place of the numberless indefeasible chartered freedoms, has set up that single, unconscionable freedom—free trade. In one word, for exploitation, veiled by religious and political illusions, it has substituted naked, shameless, direct, brutal exploitation.... The need of a constantly expanding market for its products chases the bourgeoisie over the whole surface of the globe. It must nestle everywhere, settle everywhere, establish connections everywhere. (Marx and Engels 1998 [1848]: 37)

This analysis could have been written yesterday, if we substitute "cultural and economic illusions" for "religious illusions." The newest stage of capitalism, what we call "globalization," is, however, different in several respects from previous stages. The most important difference is that economic force has replaced military force as the primary way that the capitalist countries impose their agenda on developing countries. As famed civil rights activist and U.S. presidential candidate Jesse Jackson said in 1993, "They no longer use bullets and ropes. They use the World Bank and the IMF [International Monetary Fund] (PIRM, 1999).

Colonialism and imperialism used primarily armed force to impose their will on the developing world. Colonialism used the armies of the imperial nation-state to open new markets and new territories for the ruling elites of the imperial state. When revolutionary nationalist movements successfully resisted colonial rule, the stage of imperialism developed to enable the same economic exploitation, but this time in a nominally independent state often ruled over by a dictator—or what we used to call the "comprador bourgeoisie."

The other central feature of imperialism was the battle to prevent the spread of Communism. Whatever the highfaluting rhetoric of the U.S. administrations, the Cold War was primarily about protecting and expanding markets, not about democracy. If you doubt that, have a look at the record of the regimes supported by the U.S. during that period.

While armed might is still used against what the U.S. calls "rogue states," it is the economic might of the transnational corporations, and the trade deals and international organizations that represent their interests, that keep markets open and profitable for capital.

From slavery to imperialism, exploitation has always been part of human society. Corporate globalization reaches even further into the lives of people around the globe than colonialism or imperialism ever did. Resistance seems futile. Deliberate economic policies designed to enrich a minority at the expense of the majority are made to appear to be the only alternative.

When tanks and torturers crush democratic expression, organizing resistance may be dangerous, but as history has shown, it is inevitable that those struggling for freedom cannot be stopped forever by repression. But when the instrument of repression is the slow erosion of the levers of democratic control through the imposition of a single economic system on every country, regardless of the needs of the people, it is much harder to dream of the day when this repression might be overturned. And it is dreams—whether of freedom, democracy or equality—which motivate large-scaled organized resistance. Persuading people that no collective solutions are possible, and that a better world lies in informed self-interest, is the slyest and most insidious way to erode democratic participation yet invented.

Corporate globalization puts real pressures on governments to carry out policies that benefit corporate profit. You know the list: cutbacks, privatization, deregulation, balanced budgets, smaller public sectors; the market knows best; the private sector is more efficient than the public sector; services can be delivered more effectively by private interests. Some neo-liberal ideologues go so far as to say that individuals have more power as consumers than as citizens. After all, government bureaucracy is not responsive to citizens, but the marketplace does respond to consumers, so consumer power is more potent than people's power, the story goes.

The impact of international capital, trade agreements and the Breton Woods institutions (the IMF and the World Bank) on national governments has turned the attention of many activists to the global level. On one sense this is a correct response to corporate globalization. The defeat, or at least derailment, of the Multilateral Agreement on Investment was due to an international lobby campaign led in part by our own Council of Canadians. MAI was, as activist Tony Clarke put it, "NAFTA [the North American Free Trade Agreement] on steroids." Its imposition would have even more severely restricted our government in making policy that meets the needs of our citizens. The most disturbing provision of the MAI was the right given to corporations to sue a national government if they felt that a law or regulation interfered with their ability to make a profit. This provision already exists in NAFTA but was strengthened in the MAI. The case where the federal government dropped its ban of the chemical MMT in gasoline and paid the Ethyl corporation $13 million to settle a lawsuit gives a glimpse of the problem. Where is democracy if government initiatives can be overturned, not in the public interest but for the profit of a single multinational corporation?

As Marx pointed out, capitalism creates the seeds of its own destruction. Globalization has also created the possibility of a *people's globalization*. Naomi Klein is a young progressive journalist who researched the anti-corporate youth movement for her book, *No Logo*. "There is this free flowing rage against multinational corporations among young people," says Klein. "It's a backlash that was waiting to happen" (interview 1999).

Klein argues that the anti-corporate movement sweeping campuses in the United States and the streets of England was caused by the collision of three major factors—"No Space, No Choice, No Jobs." The loss of public space is epitomized by ads in schools and bathrooms. This aggressive infiltration of public space has instigated "Reclaim the Streets," an international grassroots movement centred in England. Klein attributes this backlash to corporations increasing their profit without creating more jobs: "Nike is the symbol of this corporate disconnect because they have totally severed marketing from any sense that you might get a job from them. Nowhere is this more pronounced than in the inner city. They are feeding off the culture of black youth in the inner city without providing jobs. They've made themselves into tribal icons but they've also lost their protection." These multinationals are therefore both more in your face and less protected. When asked where this resistance to corporate rule is going, Klein responds: "The most lasting legacy of the sixties is this unwillingness to actually commit to where this movement is going. At this point it is enough to have a critique and resist and that's about as far as it goes. Which isn't to say that it's not radical" (interview 1999).

In a way, this generation of anti-corporate activists mirrors the birth of the New Left in the 1960s. We too found the historical Left of communism and social democracy undemocratic and unappealing. We believed that we could transform the world through the power of our ideas and our movement. In many ways we succeeded through the civil rights movement, the women's movement, the environmental movement and the anti–Vietnam War movement. But in many ways we failed.

Resistance is the first and most important step of any movement for social change. Today, resistance seems to be focusing on reforming global institutions and opposing or modifying trade deals. However, it is hard to imagine democratizing global institutions without democratizing national, provincial and local institutions. Grassroots movements can become international through electronic organizing, but when they try to influence the international institutions of power, the nation-state—especially the United States—reacts. International institutions, no matter how undemocratic, all draw their power from nation states.

The repression of student demonstrations at APEC and the WTO demonstrates this link. Demonstrators were exercising democracy protesting its restriction by undemocratic economic organizations such as APEC. They also protested attempts by the RCMP—and, it appears, the Chrétien government—to curb their right to demonstrate. Globalization was the context, but the real issue was democracy.

The need to democratize international institutions such as the World Bank and the IMF was a major preoccupation at the U.N.'s NGO Women's Conference I attended in Beijing in 1995. Gita Sen, representing Development Alternatives for Women in a New Era (DAWN), talked about the rapidity of globalization and how it undermines the economic role of the state and its ability to provide services. She said the Breton Woods institutions have acted like storm troopers to break the state's ability to resist. But, she noted, the state's repressive power remains intact: "Governments that can no longer provide even minimal health and education are maintaining huge arsenals." In most countries, the transfer of wealth through investment in the Third World benefits a tiny minority who use armed force to protect their privileges.

We see a similar development in the countries of the North, with the revival of Victorian distinctions between the "deserving" and "undeserving" poor. For the majority to accept a society where dire poverty exists amidst so much wealth, the poor must be considered responsible for their own misfortune. We talk about child poverty as if their parents didn't exist. We are willing to provide benefits to the working poor at the expense of people on welfare. Social assistance is disappearing as a public issue. Politicians of every ideological stripe style themselves the saviours of medicare and education—the concerns of the middle class. So the people who are hurt most by the zeal for deficit reduction are helped least in the post-deficit era. In Ontario, Mike Harris is well on his way to criminalizing the poor through his so-called "squeegee law."

The dangers of these attacks on the poor are best seen in the United States where they started almost thirty years ago. In her article "Reforming the Welfare State," sociologist Francis Fox Piven points out that high poverty levels in the United States also explain

> other unique features of the American labour market in the 1980's, including the collapse of unionism, falling wage levels, lengthening work hours, explosive growth in low-wage and irregular jobs, and widening income polarization. In short, history was providing a virtual laboratory for the examination of the significance of welfare-state related programs for class inequalities and class power relations. (Piven 1992: 68)

Criminalization of the poor went hand in hand with cuts to social assistance in the U.S. No one is in prison simply for being poor, but without income or access to decent jobs, more and more young people will turn to escape through drugs or profit through crime. The United States has imprisoned a significant percentage of its poor male population. Between 1985 and 1998, the *per capita* prison population in the U.S. more than doubled from 313 to 668 prisoners for every 100,000 residents. At end of 1997 the incarceration rate for black males in their late twenties was 8,630 per 100,000 people, compared to 868 for white males. Blacks were at least six times more likely than whites to be in local, state and federal prisons, and 7.5 times more apt to be locked up in a local jail (U.S. Department of Justice 1999a: 1, 9; 1999b: 1, 2; 1999c: 12). In total, two million Americans were in prison in 2000 (Davis 2000). About 60 percent of federal inmates and 23 percent of state prisoners are there for possessing or dealing drugs (U.S. Department of Justice 1999d: 3). Some analysts have estimated that U.S.

unemployment rates would be two percentage points higher if they included men in prison.

American writer Barbara Ehrenreich, speaking at a 1998 conference held in Vancouver and broadcast by CBC Radio's *Ideas* program, points to the danger to democracy:

> When government spends little or nothing on social assistance and more and more on the repressive forces of the state—police, prisons and military—poor people begin to see government as the problem rather than a solution. All a ghetto-dwelling black male sees of the government is police and prison guards. The idea that electing a politician could promote community interests becomes more and more remote.

That is one explanation for the alienation of the majority of Americans from their electoral system.

Poor people become marginalized and alienated from government, and middle-class people with good intentions feel there is not much that can be done beyond charity. What Linda McQuaig (1998) has called the "cult of impotence" is a critically important ideological weapon in the arsenal of neo-liberalism. Even governments of the centre and the left echo the right-wing threat that if we try to control the behaviour of corporations, they will flee our jurisdiction.

The unbridled power of international capital right now is the result of conscious policy changes by governments. Governments could re-regulate capital if there were enough social unrest and political pressure to force them to do so. Direct action against corporations can certainly help in this effort, but in the end it is governments that must act. Many European states, such as France and Sweden, have much more successfully resisted the pressure of international capital to implement a right-wing agenda than Canada has.

If it is true that multinational corporations have inordinate power and influence in our society today, it is equally true that national governments have allowed them to grow like "the Blob," becoming bigger and more powerful by ingesting everything in their path. Environmentalist David Suzuki tells us that cancer is the only organism in nature that grows without limit. The cancer of multinational corporations has been allowed to spread across the globe with barely any attempt to contain it. We do need some international solutions, such as the Tobin Tax, which would slow speculation and encourage a more democratic system of world government. The Tobin Tax proposal is for a modest, perhaps one percent, tax on all financial transactions, levied on an international level and used to fund the fight against urgent world problems, such as hunger and AIDS. But even the movement for the Tobin Tax must begin in a single nation-state. "Globaphobia"—the fear that national governments can do nothing to stop the worldwide spread of savage capitalism—works in the interests of the economic elites. Yet many on the left have fallen victim to the same beliefs.

Despite the upsurge in Seattle, right-wing politics still dominates much of the public agenda, particularly in North America. During the 1990s, the right in Canada succeeded in convincing people that the deficit was the central problem and that social program cutbacks were the only solution. Now, in the post-deficit era, they are trying to repeat that success by arguing for tax cuts. While there is still tremendous public support for publicly funded universal medicare and education, this too can be eroded by deteriorating public services and domination of the debate by those who support tax cuts. The erosion of public health care and education, particularly in Ontario and Alberta, has been frighteningly rapid. Everywhere social assistance has become more punitive than ever before, and the homeless population has skyrocketed in major cities. When you've been persuaded that collective solutions no longer work and that governments are powerless to help their citizens, it's easy to accept that self-reliance is more important than solidarity.

In the face of what appears to be the overwhelming power of the right these days, a lot of people are retrenching. Many activists and academics of my generation are withdrawing from public action.

The younger generation is much more focused on financial security. Twentysomethings are convinced that they should be putting away for their retirement because government pensions won't be around. The other day, my niece, an articling law student, told me that she and her friends always discuss the contradiction between wanting to do good and needing to take care of themselves financially, usually deciding that doing well financially is the most important thing. At her age, I never worried about money because jobs were plentiful.

Among activists there is an increasing aversion to electoral politics as the parties look more and more alike. The cynicism about the mass media is even greater. If progressive people withdraw from mass institutions of public discourse, two things happen: the progressive people who are there get silenced because they don't seem to represent anyone; then the mass of people don't see their ideas reflected in the media or in Parliament. This has happened in the U.S., where much of the population is excluded from public discourse. We can't let it happen in Canada.

Since the free trade debate of 1988, the left in Canada has been on the defensive. In my youth there were competing visions of an alternative society, and many ideas about what such a society would look like and how it would be constructed. Today the left and centre seem reduced to responding to the ideas of the right. What is needed, in my view, is to revive and develop the ideas of the left in a contemporary context. To develop that new vision we have to have all the voices—women and men, people of colour and white people, people of all sexual orientations. The struggles we had in the eighties and nineties, which are sometimes labelled "identity politics," are critical to developing that vision. The kind of democracy that will counter corporate globalization has to include the most marginalized people or it will produce new abuses of power.

The social movements of the 1960s that dreamed of creating a new society achieved change but left society's basic unequal structure in place. A range of social groups, enticed into temporary residence in the corridors of power, focused too much on lobbying and not enough on organizing and mobilizing. It is a difficult process to resist.

Any group fighting for social change knows the drill. First, others discount you and deny there is a problem. You are ignored or ridiculed in the media. If you make enough noise, provide enough studies and mobilize enough people, the media starts to notice, and if you persist, the politicians invite you in for discussions—the first step to co-optation. Once you are actually talking to people in power, the legitimacy of protest is questioned. If I had a dollar for every time a journalist attacked NAC (National Action Committee on the Status of Women) for participating in sixties-style protest politics, I'd be rich today.

My generation has gotten kind of spoiled. We started our activism in the midst of a widespread youth radicalization. The social revolution of the 1960s was strong enough to set the agenda for an entire historic period: women's rights, environmentalism, expansion of the welfare state, human rights etc. I was always surprised when right-wing viewers of the debate show *Face Off* on CBC Newsworld, which I co-hosted from 1994 to 1998, would write, "people like Judy Rebick have run the country long enough." People like me, whether socialists or feminists, have never even gotten near to running the country, but it is true that for a long time we were able to set the agenda and force politicians to respond to our demands.

Then the right regrouped and, beginning with Ronald Reagan in 1985 and Margaret Thatcher a couple of years later, they took back the agenda big time. The fall of Communism and the rise of the computer revolution enabled a massive global expansion of capitalism that rivals the expansion that Marx and Engels talked about in the *Communist Manifesto*.

Up until now our generation had never seen unbridled savage capitalism. Our parents and grandparents saw it in the 1930s, and before that at the turn of the century when industrialization took hold. Each time capitalism ran rampant over their rights, people fought back. The modern workers' political movement, both communist and socialist, emerged from the working-class struggles of the late nineteenth century and early twentieth century. The modern labour movement emerged from the struggles of the 1930s. In the post-war period, a social contract which provided workers in the North with a larger share of the economic pie laid the basis for a long period of prosperity and social peace that culminated in the social justice movements of our youth. That historical period came to an end with the rise of neo-liberalism in the form of Reagan and Thatcher. Many of the rights fought for and won over the entire twentieth century are being lost.

Because of the time we live in, it is necessary to internationalize the struggle, and to integrate into our strategies the lessons of the last thirty years and the insights of a new generation which has grown up in this period of globalization.

Despite the domination of right-wing ideas in the media and in Parliament in the last ten years, Canada maintains a very strong attachment to the ideas of social justice and equality. Poll after poll shows that while many people have accepted fiscal conservatism, they continue to prioritize health care, education, and child poverty above tax cuts.

Progressive forces are having more success in presenting some alternatives in the post-deficit era. In the run-up to the 2000 federal budget, many groups laid out an important new social agenda in support of families that includes a national child care program and expanded income supports. Most social groups are accepting the framework of a balanced budget and the need for tax cuts and debt reduction. Other groups are mobilizing support for health care and education. Still others have raised public awareness about poverty and homelessness.

Surprising people are sometimes involved in such movements. A silver lining in the terrible turn to the right over the last few years is that many people who work in the public sector are becoming radicalized. The Council of Canadians found a lot of support, for example, in municipal councils in their campaign against the MAI. Similarly, on the issue of homelessness, municipal politicians, not only from the left, have been some of the strongest advocates for more spending on social housing.

The Alternate Federal Budget and a handful of left-wing think-tanks are beginning to make inroads in presenting alternative economic arguments, although it is hard to tell from reading Conrad Black's newspapers.

The movements against the MAI and WTO are making the point that we don't have to adapt to these trade deals, which are fundamentally anti-democratic. We oppose these deals because we are opposed to a system of international trade where only a small elite benefits and everyone else loses. This is the wrong framework for international economic relations because it imposes one economic and cultural solution on everyone. It's wrong. It's anti-democratic and it won't work. The right contends that those of us who oppose free trade deals are afraid of progress. It's not that we are against international trade. On the contrary, we want to see new economic relationships of equality.

Last year I heard Noam Chomsky speak at Massey Hall in Toronto. The event was sold out and almost everyone there was young. Chomsky spoke in a scholarly manner and I had to listen carefully to understand what he was saying. He said that democracy and capitalism don't mix very well. Capitalists who have fought for democracy have consistently been defeated. If we want to fight for democracy, we have to take on the economic inequalities of capitalism.

It's not very popular these days to talk critically about capitalism. Socialism, we are told, has been discredited and it is certainly nowhere on the public agenda. Democracy, however, is very much on the agenda. As I have mentioned, much of the battle against globalization is a battle to defend the democracy we already have.

In Latin America, progressive groups have moved to significantly expand democracy to include forms of citizen participation. In Porto Alegre, Brazil, the Workers Party government has developed an extraordinary process called the

Participatory Budget which brings thousands of ordinary citizens into policy-making. After eleven years of successful democratic experience at the municipal level, they have just been elected to the state government of Rio Grande do Sul, where they will further develop their ideas of participatory democracy in a state with twelve million people.

In Canada, the Reform Party has argued for broader and deeper forms of democracy. Now, the United Alternative (the party formerly known as CRAPP), seems to be morphing from a populist party into a professional electoral machine. No doubt, issues of direct democracy will also fall to the periphery of their vision.

In my book *Imagine Democracy,* I argue that progressives should pursue the expansion of democracy as the best way to resist the repressive forces of globalization. What I maintain is that the abuse of power is inherent in a capitalist society because of the voracious nature of such an economic system. Those abuses are curbed only when people resist them and, when successful, turn that resistance into laws and policies such as labour standards or the equality provisions of the Charter. The less resistance, the more abuses. We recognize that tendency in authoritarian states where armed force prevents open resistance. It is a more subtle process in Western democracies but works in similar ways. When people are convinced that resistance is futile, when movements are marginalized and demoralized, when groups of people such as immigrants, gays or poor people are successfully demonized, abuses of power are more frequent than in periods when progressive social movements are on the rise.

In other words, when democracy is working, abuse of power is less likely. We need to deepen our ideas of democracy to go beyond the nineteenth-century notion of representative democracy to what I call active citizenship (Rebick 2000a). Restructuring the state to include citizen participation at every level is a way to ensure that the kinds of abuses of power discussed in this volume decrease rather than increase.

Chapter 2

# From the Welfare State to the No-Second-Chances State

*Ted Schrecker*

## The Rise of Insecurity

The thin young man in dust-covered denim sat in the parking lot under my hotel window, holding his head in bony hands in the dull pre-dawn light. I couldn't see his face and didn't need to—his posture radiated despair.

Street people of all ages are very visible in downtown Vancouver these days, as in most North American cities. For me, at least, their vulnerability was always a subtle whisper in the background during the conference that inspired this chapter. The homeless, and those who are just one crisis away from homelessness, are the most serious casualties of the economic insecurity that has affected all but the most privileged in our society. Canadians as a whole have experienced two lost decades in income growth: in constant dollars, average family income before taxes in 1997 was about the same as in 1980 and still substantially below its 1989 peak (Statistics Canada 1999a: 13). Many households were able to avoid downward mobility only because they included two full-time income earners; the economic trajectory of households for which this was not a possibility was correspondingly bleak (Yalnizyan 1998: 35–42). Indeed, the economic security of Canada's population as a whole, measured with reference to the risks of unemployment, ill health, single-parent poverty and poverty in old age, has deteriorated almost continuously since 1973 (Osberg and Sharpe 1999: 40–52). Although the calculations that generated this conclusion did not incorporate household debt levels, "keeping up" by way of rising levels of consumer debt may be another important source of longer-term insecurity (MacKinnon 1998; for comparable U.S. data, see Mishel, Bernstein and Schmitt 1999: 274–75).

To explain trends in the distribution of income and economic opportunity, we need to look both at the structure of the economy and at government policies. The role of structural economic change is best assessed in the first instance by looking at changes over time in market incomes of households or families—that is, at incomes before taxes and transfers from government. In constant dollars, the average market income of the poorest 20 percent of Canadian families with children under eighteen fell by an astounding 48 percent between 1980 and 1996, while the average market income of the richest 10 percent grew by 14 percent (Yalnizyan 1998: 123–25). In the United States, again in constant dollars, the average income before taxes of the poorest 20 percent of families with children fell by 21 percent between 1978–80 and 1994–96, while the average income of the richest 20 percent of families rose by 30 percent (Larin and McNichol 1997). The U.S. figures, unlike the Canadian ones, include income from government transfers, which is received disproportionately by the poorest families; however, they also exclude the much larger value of income from capital gains, received almost exclusively by the richest. Consequently, they substantially understate the structurally generated increase in economic inequality over the period in question.

Official Canadian unemployment rates have been declining, but these rates fail to capture the relations between employment status and economic insecurity. Between 1989 and 1997, the percentage of Canada's unemployed who had been out of work for at least one year more than doubled, to 38.4 percent (Human Resources Development Canada 1998: 44). The incidence of involuntary part-time work (the number of people who are working part-time only because they are unable to find suitable full-time jobs) has increased steadily in Canada since 1976, albeit with some cyclical variations (Schellenberg 1997: 39). Recalculations that included involuntary part-time work and discouraged people who had stopped looking for work raised the official unemployment rate in 1998 from 8.3 percent to 11.5 percent, with especially dramatic increases in Atlantic Canada (Statistics Canada 1999b: 32–39). Self-employment accounted for roughly 75 percent of net new job creation in Canada between 1990 and 1996 (Gauthier and Roy 1997: 9). A different data set, for the period between 1992 and 1997, indicates a bimodal distribution of incomes: the self-employed were concentrated at the lower end of the income scale, with another, smaller peak at the high end presumably representing self-employed professionals such as physicians (Yalnizyan 1998: 29). Unfortunately, no data analogous to those on involuntary part-time employment appear to exist on involuntary self-employment; such data would contribute substantially to our understanding of economic insecurity, because the self-employed are ineligible for Employment Insurance (EI), employer-provided pension contributions or medical benefits.

Any discussion of inequality and structural economic change must further emphasize that work, even though it may be considered a sacrament by the ideologues of the right, provides no insulation from extreme economic hardship. One of several disturbing trends in North American labour markets is the proliferation of demanding, low-wage jobs in fast food, retail and other areas of the service sector. Even when they are full-time, such jobs don't provide a minimally adequate income (Economic Council of Canada 1990: 10–17; Ehrenreich 1999; Kilborn 1995; Mishel, Bernstein and Schmitt 1999: 171–74, 189–95; Passell 1998; Uchitelle 1993). "A full-time, full-year job at the minimum wage ($6.85 and frozen since 1995) would generate $14,250 before taxes. That's not quite two-thirds of the poverty line for a single parent and one child in Toronto in 1997" (Yalnizyan 1998: 93; for comparable U.S. data, see Blank 1997: 79–82). For a family of three in large Canadian cities, that minimum-wage income would correspond to just half the 1997 Statistics Canada Low-Income

Cutoff (LICO) of $28,119, which is the threshold referred to by Yalnizyan. Canadians who think the LICO too generous as a measure of poverty, such as Andrew Coyne (1997), probably have never had to live anywhere near it.

## Technology, "Globalization" and Labour Markets

Several factors have contributed to the combination of more polarization and less economic security. Two major Canadian recessions were at least partly policy-induced: by the interest rate policies of the Bank of Canada in the early 1980s, and by implementation of the Canada-U.S. Free Trade Agreement at the end of the decade. The remarkable growth of microelectronics applications, some of them (such as the automation of routine financial transactions) with major job-displacing effects, draws our attention to a new "techno-economic paradigm" characterized by innovations with "such widespread consequences for all sectors of the economy that their diffusion is accompanied by a major structural crisis of adjustment"(Freeman and Perez 1988: 38). The sanguine view of this process of adjustment (e.g., Lynch 1996) is that the industries that arise as part of the paradigm shift will provide increased living standards for everyone. A blunter and more realistic view provided by a senior executive of the investment banking firm Lazard Frères is that the new high-productivity economy means "the promise of higher incomes for more efficient workers and fewer jobs for everyone else" (Rattner 1993: 54).

The new paradigm involves not only technological change, but also the interaction of new technological capabilities with "transnational economic integration"—a term more accurate than globalization (see Boyer and Drache 1996; Dieken 1998). In the words of a 1994 *Business Week* feature article on the changing nature of employment, "A global economy ... demands such change; rapidly evolving technology allows it" (Hammonds 1994: 77). Perhaps the most familiar manifestation of the "global economy" is the reduction of impediments to trade through such multilateral accords as NAFTA and the WTO Agreement. These accords are about direct investment—that is, about facilitating the profit-able reorganization of production for a continental or global market—as much as they are about trade in the textbook sense of the exchange of commodities between two economies. This point is dramatically illustrated by the fact that, according to one estimate, "around 60% of international trade involves transac-tions between two related parts of multinationals" (Bishop 2000: 18). Cross-border reorganization of production has, in turn, made it meaningful to speak of the emergence of a truly global labour market (World Bank 1995). Although this process is only in its early stages, its importance is captured in the 1980s comment of a Canadian executive with Goodyear Tire and Rubber that, "Until we get real [North American] wage levels down much closer to those of the Brazils and Koreas, we cannot pass along productivity gains to wages and still be competitive" (quoted in Palmer 1994: 103).

Perhaps even more importantly in the effect on labour markets, the elimination of many restrictions on cross-border financial flows (Helleiner 1994;

Peterson 1995) has intensified competition among firms and political jurisdictions for hypermobile capital. The World Bank (1999: 35–36) notes that "well-run developing countries offering solid returns can expect to supplement their [domestic] savings with resources from all over the globe." The resulting shift in political power, enabling investors to define whether a country is well-run or not, and exposing rich and poor countries alike to the prospect that their residents will shift investments abroad, is best described in terms of the emergence of a "global, cross-border economic electorate" (Sassen 1996: 40) defined by its ownership of financial assets.

The author of a front-page article in *The Wall Street Journal* observed in 1995: "Just as Japan perfected the just-in-time inventory system, America is well on its way to perfecting the just-in-time work force, notwithstanding the grim toll it takes on labour. The harsh truth is that it is a major productivity plus" (Wysocki 1995). Among the more immediately visible manifestations of this new flexibility in labour markets are: the replacement of full-time, waged work by stereotypically Third World forms of work organization, such as piecework done at home for low wages and no benefits (Gringeri 1994; Ross 1999); and the remarkable growth of short-term, temporary or project-based employment relationships (Bradsher 1996; DiTomaso in press; Mishel, Bernstein and Schmitt 1999: 242–50; Uchitelle 1995; Washington 1995).

Insecurity now affects a very large proportion of the work force, as managers and professionals as well as production workers have experienced downsizing (Mishel, Bernstein and Schmitt 1999: 235–41; Newman 1988; Uchitelle et al. 1996). One executive interviewed for the 1994 *Business Week* feature admitted that "we have fewer people doing much more work, much of which is knowledge-based, and we're paying people less" (in Hammonds 1994: 86). Another elaborated:

> This year, I had to downsize my area by 25%. Nothing has changed in terms of the workload. It's very emotionally draining. I find myself not wanting to go in to work, because I'm going to have to push people to do more, and I look at their eyes and they're sinking into the back of their heads.... But they're not going to complain, because they don't want to be the next 25%. (in Hammonds 1994: 84)

Examples such as these from south of the border are directly relevant to Canadians because transnational (and most particularly continental) economic integration may present the choice between accepting this model of work organization and living with the consequences of rapid disinvestment.

Not everyone loses from the economic transitions that are now underway. In a rather simplistic effort to identify winners and losers in the labour markets of the future, former U.S. Secretary of Labour Robert Reich (1992: 171–224) distinguished among routine producers (exemplified by assembly-line workers), providers of in-person services and "symbolic analysts." According to Reich, the first two groups can, in general, look forward to job losses and stagnant or declining earnings as the globalization of labour markets progresses. Conversely, the prospects for those "who solve, identify and broker new problems" are generally bright because of the increasingly knowledge-intensive nature of most forms of economic activity and the fact that, as an employee, "your real competitive position in the *world* economy is coming to depend on the function you perform in it" (Reich 1992: 208, emphasis added). Winners in that economy have competencies or capabilities that make them individually valuable and internationally marketable to entrepreneurs, large corporate employers or the owners of financial assets. Recent rhetoric about the brain drain from Canada to the United States is undoubtedly exaggerated for strategic effect, but nevertheless underscores a genuine structural characteristic of contemporary labour markets.

Owners of financial assets, analytically distinct from Reich's symbolic analysts but in practice often the same people, comprise an equally significant category of winners. High-income households can take advantage of new opportunities for cross-border investment by shifting their assets into firms or jurisdictions that control labour costs most effectively, becoming partisans in a global class struggle waged via the world's stock markets (cf. Fishman 1997). Even within national borders, the new economy has meant dramatic divergence between the returns to capital and the returns to most forms of labour—a divergence that has almost certainly contributed to the growing polarization of household incomes. As an illustration of the amounts involved, in June 1995 the *New York Times* reported that the value of American stocks had increased by approximately $673 billion that year, according to an index that tracks "roughly 90 percent of the market value of all American stocks"—enough "to give every American worker a $5,100 bonus" (Nasar 1995).

Needless to say, few such bonuses were forthcoming; most employees were losing, not gaining, from the economic boom that was generating such increases in stock prices (Mishel, Bernstein and Schmitt 1999: 119–218). U.S. data show that stock ownership, and therefore the distribution of direct benefits from the post-1987 financial boom, is heavily concentrated among the 6.4 percent of households at the top of the income distribution. They account for 54.2 percent of all shares owned by U.S. households either directly or through mutual funds, retirement accounts and defined contribution pension plans (Mishel, Bernstein and Schmitt 1999: 271–73). Direct Canada-U.S. comparisons are impossible because the last Statistics Canada survey of household wealth was undertaken in 1984, when the Toronto Stock Exchange (TSE) 300 composite index stood at approximately 2,500 and the Dow Jones Industrial Average (DJIA) at approximately 1,200 (in March 2000 the TSE 300 broke 10,000 and the DJIA stood at around 11,000). Useful inferences can nevertheless be drawn from the fact that, in 1996, 38 percent of all dividend income and 57 percent of all capital gains on shares were reported by only *0.7 percent* of individual Canadian tax filers, those with before-tax incomes over $150,000 (calculated from Revenue Canada 1998, Tables 2 and 9).[1]

## Social Provision: The Fraying Safety Net

On a national level, Canada's social programs have so far kept income inequality after taxes and transfers from increasing in parallel with market incomes (Statistics Canada 1999a: 19–21; Yalnizyan 1998: 53–56). This macro-level outcome must not divert our attention from a number of distressing phenomena. "In 1980, Canada had no food banks, but 20 years later there were more than 2,000" (Prince 1999: 189). In 1997, 17.2 percent of all Canadians and 19.6 percent of children under eighteen were living on incomes below the LICO; both figures are considerably higher than the comparable percentages in 1980 (National Council of Welfare 1999: 10–11). In the City of Toronto, 37.3 percent of children lived in households with incomes below the LICO in 1996—more than twice as many, in percentage terms, as in the adjoining suburbs and edge cities of Durham, Halton and York Regions (Toronto Children's Services 1999: 10). The 1991 census suggested that U.S.-style concentrations of poverty in distressed neighbourhoods were coming to Canada, at least in Québec City, Montréal and Winnipeg (Hatfield 1997). Child poverty data from the 1996 census suggest the emergence of similar concentrations in Toronto (Toronto Children's Services 1999: 33; also see Hill 1997).

The incomes provided by provincial social assistance ("welfare") continue to be remarkably inadequate. For a single parent with one child, welfare income in 1998 ranged from 50 percent of the LICO (in Alberta) to 69 percent of the LICO (in Newfoundland) (National Council of Welfare 2000a: 40–41). For single persons deemed employable, and for disabled people, the gap between the LICO and social assistance income was even more dramatic in some provinces. To emphasize a point made earlier in this chapter, those who think LICO-level incomes are generous should try living on them for a while. Interestingly, welfare support for a single parent with one child was the same (61 percent of the LICO) in Ontario and British Columbia. British Columbia had a New Democratic government, while Ontario had been governed since 1995 by Mike Harris's Conservatives, who had campaigned aggressively against the supposed generosity of the province's welfare levels, cut them by 21 percent immediately upon assuming office, made eligibility rules more restrictive and instituted a U.S.-style workfare program (Morrison 1998). This comparison suggests a remarkable cross-party consensus on the part of political elites and electoral pluralities about what the most economically vulnerable Canadians (don't) deserve.

The percentage of unemployed Canadians, as officially defined, receiving EI or its predecessor declined from 83 percent to 42 percent between 1991 and 1997 (Human Resources Development Canada 1998: 13), representing "an area of remarkable convergence in social policy" between Canada and the United States (Hoberg, Banting and Simeon 1999: 17). Only part of this decline is directly attributable to changes in eligibility criteria. Other factors include the increase in part-time employment, which voids eligibility for EI, and the fact that, as noted earlier, the percentage of unemployed Canadians out of work for more than twelve months, which also voids eligibility for EI, roughly doubled between 1976 and 1997 (Human Resources Development Canada 1998: 44). The federal government did not alter EI to respond to such labour market changes, even though the program had accumulated a surplus of more than $20 billion by late 1999—leading to the conclusion that convergence with the United States' relentlessly market-driven labour market policy represents an intentional outcome whose implications were, and are, fully understood.

The impact of changes in government commitments that do not involve direct income support is likely to be even more significant in the long term. Long delays in obtaining essential care threaten to undermine public support for universal, publicly financed health insurance at least among people who could afford, or whose employers could afford, to buy insurance in the private market (Evans 1997b: 449–55; Schrecker 1998). Portions of the medical profession are becoming increasingly vocal in their support for privatization (Orovan 1998). Recent, well publicized crises in hospital emergency rooms across the country (Foss 1999a, 1999b; Gray 1999; Peritz and Picard 2000; Sher 2000; Stackhouse 2000; Zacharias 1999) have the air of a problem deliberately allowed to worsen in order to generate support for a powerful elite consensus on the need for more private, for-profit provision and financing of health care. University tuition increases, especially in Ontario where fees for some professional programs have been completely deregulated, are rolling the clock back to the 1950s for students with limited resources (Galt 1999). Post-secondary education as a whole is an area of social provision in which Canada significantly underperforms the United States, both in public financing for universities (British Columbia 1999) and in making university programs accessible on a part-time, affordable and flexible basis consistent with the needs of working people. Among other consequences, Canada's failure in this respect makes the "lifelong learning" advocated as a way of adapting to fast-changing contemporary labour markets (Esping-Andersen 1997; Moses, 1999b) a bitter joke except for the minority whose choices early in their working lives have either enabled them to accumulate substantial savings or led them to employers willing to invest in their continued training.

Several of these developments are related to the changing nature of fiscal federalism, specifically, the 1995 replacement of conditional federal transfers to the provinces for health, income support and post-secondary education with a block grant—the Canada Health and Social Transfer, or CHST (Battle 1998; Moscovitch 1997; Prince 1999). The value of federal transfers to the provinces was substantially reduced in the first years of the CHST, as part of cuts in federal program spending meant to reduce the deficit. More significantly, the CHST is for all practical purposes an unconditional grant, unlike the programs that preceded it. Since money is fungible, provincial governments have a strong financial incentive to cut back social policy expenditures, especially those whose beneficiaries are relatively powerless, in favour of programs with more obvious political returns.

In theory, incremental reductions in the CHST can be used to enforce provisions of the *Canada Health Act* limiting the role of private health care.

However, the importance of federal transfers in the revenue budgets of the richest provinces is declining: federal transfers accounted for 15.9 percent of Ontario government revenues in 1995–96, but just 8.2 percent in 1998–99. Ontario and Alberta may soon decide to accept reduced federal transfers in exchange for greater autonomy in financing health services, which would enable them to deliver further tax cuts (Evans and Barer 1998: 31). Those cuts would almost certainly provide disproportionate benefits to the richest households, as have the tax cuts instituted by the Harris Conservatives since 1995 (see Ontario 1999). As with changes to EI, such outcomes must have been anticipated and understood at the time the CHST was put in place. When such a change occurs, responsible social science recognizes that it did not "just happen," and insists that it be regarded as demanding an explanation, rather than as providing one.

## The Politics of Secession

Recent changes in Canada's social programs are magnifying rather than reducing the economic insecurity associated with changing labour markets. How can we best account for this ironic outcome? Program spending cuts that Canadian governments have undertaken in order to balance their budgets have been driven by the fact that deficits undermine the confidence of investors and credit-rating institutions (Bloomberg 1995; Sinclair 1994). However, under the most optimistic assumptions imaginable, the persistent deficits of the 1980s and early 1990s would eventually have succumbed to their own inexorable arithmetic. Thus, the verdict of international financial markets merely hastened the time when deficits could no longer be used to defer domestic class conflicts about the appropriate level of social provision and the appropriate magnitude of the costs.

Even when budgets are balanced, investors and corporate managers may shy away from countries with relatively expansive welfare states because they inhibit the development of U.S.-style labour market flexibility (see, e.g., Sachs 1996). Canada's Business Council on National Issues, comprising the chief executive officers of 150 of Canada's largest corporations, has warned that "governments ... must make it easier for jobs to disappear" (BCNI 2000: 11) if the country is to avoid economic stagnation, or worse. However, the primary barrier to the pursuit of welfare-state policies that effectively counteract the polarizing effects of structural economic change is the difficulty of sustaining the necessary domestic electoral coalitions. Why might the political coalitions that historically have provided qualified support, or at least assent, to the Canadian welfare state be fragmenting now?

Sustained elite pressure is one answer, but not a complete or sufficient one. When incomes are stagnant, as for many Canadians over the past two decades, most people understandably pay closer attention to the value received for their tax dollars—and, perhaps more importantly, to who is receiving that value. The first casualties in terms of public support are expenditures on people who can credibly be branded as undeserving, such as the welfare recipients used as scapegoats in Mike Harris's 1995 Ontario election campaign. The equation of reliance on social provision with moral weakness has a particularly long history in U.S. social policy (Backer 1993, 1995; Withorn 1996) and explains the political attractiveness of the vicious welfare "reforms" signed into law by President Clinton in 1996. The inference of individual weakness is reflected in the title of the legislation: the *Personal Responsibility and Work Opportunity Reconciliation Act.* Similar inferences help us to understand the persistent inadequacy of Canadian welfare incomes. In addition, a majority of the population expects never to need welfare.

The political dynamics of tax-financed programs that serve a majority of the population, such as public schools and health insurance, are different. These programs must be supported, or at least not energetically opposed, by a substantial proportion of the "middle class"—a colloquialism that eludes precise definition but is understandable in this context. They must (a) perceive themselves as receiving significant benefits from the programs in question, and/or (b) perceive that they might receive benefits in the future that are commensurate with the programs' present costs in tax dollars and/or (c) be willing to live with the lack of benefit from any particular program as part of a broader social bargain without "too strict an accounting of what the bargain is worth" (Ignatieff 1987: 979).

The radical individualism of the new techno-managerial labour market, with its vocabulary of human capital and networking (see any issue of the magazine *Fast Company* for abundant examples), is antithetical to this third basis of support. We are exhorted to plan our working futures around the concept of "Me, Incorporated" (Moses 1999a; Onstad 1996; Surowiecki 1998)—a revealing phrase, since corporations are legal devices that facilitate the effective pursuit of profit and the avoidance of liability. Career consultant Jack Groppel (in Brackey 2000) describes the contemporary working environment this way: "You are a performer. You are expected to perform at the highest level, over long hours, while someone younger is waiting to take your job." Some cognitive baggage goes along with economic success in the context of insecurity: "To the extent that skill has become more important as an explanatory factor of quite visible wage inequalities, such inequalities come to have a more 'biographical' character: they seem to be more related to personal history and qualifications than to class as traditionally understood" (Vandenbroucke 1998: 47). Against this background, which may explain why so few academics concern themselves with the issues discussed in this chapter, fewer and fewer members of the middle class view the costs of solidarity as worth bearing.

Reich (1991) argues that changes in the nature of economic activity and economic opportunity are leading to "the secession of the successful." As their incomes rise, a small but expanding cohort of affluent households finds private purchase of various services attractive, especially if they can avoid financing a similar quality of services for others. The geography of secession can be observed in the spread of gated communities, sometimes run by homeowners' associations that function as private governments (Blakely and Snyder 1997; McKenzie

1994); it is also evident in the flight of the affluent to suburbs with good schools—the combination of ample tax bases and the U.S. regime of highly localized education funding means that home buyers are buying educational quality for their own children and their neighbours', but not for a broader cross-section of the population. "If generosity and solidarity end at the border of similarly valued properties, then the most fortunate can be virtuous citizens at little cost" (Reich 1991: 42). Economist Robert Evans (1997a: 47; 1997b) identifies the same calculation behind pressures to increase privately purchased health care, or health insurance, in Canada: "Private markets can offer a (real or perceived) higher standard of care for those willing or able to pay for it, without their having to pay taxes to support a similar standard for others."

This may always have been the case, but both Reich's analysis and the income distribution figures cited earlier in this chapter suggest that the proportion of the population for whom private purchase of services appears attractive may be growing—especially if they can anticipate offsetting tax reductions. In February 2000, *The Globe and Mail* profiled a professional couple who were "going broke on $300k a year" (MacDonald 2000). The single largest item in their annual household budget was personal income tax ($105,000). Next was private-school tuition for their three children ($39,000): presumably they had concluded, with much justification, that their province's public schools were broken beyond immediate repair. For such people, what form of collective social provision is likely to offset the attraction of substantial income tax reductions?

Not many Canadian households are in this poster couple's income bracket. However, once people like them are able to set the dynamic of secession in motion, the process quickly becomes self-reinforcing. Deterioration in public services such as health care and education quickly generates a spiral of declining quality and an intensified search for privately financed alternatives, whose results are evident in the current state of public schools in most U.S. cities (see, e.g., Kozol 1991). "Ultimately any of us will take our children out of a crumbling inner-city school rather than persevere with civic mindedness simply for the sake of principle" (Ignatieff 1987: 980). Ignatieff might have added that not all of us can afford this option and—more importantly—that those who can barely do so often become the most highly motivated partisans of tax reductions, financed by program cuts that hurt those left behind. The clientele for publicly provided and financed services soon consists primarily of those who have no other choices, and little political impact. Zygmunt Bauman (1993: 244; passim 223–50) eloquently describes the end point as "a nation divided between the premium payers and the benefit recipients," with the former nursing a growing resentment against the latter and, "sooner or later, buying themselves out of collective responsibility."

Welfare state programs are only viable if voters assent to the requisite levels of taxation. Wealthy taxpayers can effectively veto programs by giving parties with a record of cutting taxes for the rich, such as Harris's Conservatives in Ontario, enough money to keep competitors from mounting an effective electoral challenge (see Mackie 1999). Governments may also alter their policies from fear that capital flight from emigration by internationally mobile high-income households will cause fiscal crisis. Both prospects are being invoked by elites seeking support for income tax cuts at the national level (BCNI 2000; Simpson 2000; Taber 1999). Economist Dani Rodrik, who is on balance an enthusiast of globalization, nevertheless concedes that programs to compensate its losers may be thwarted if, once transnational economic integration is sufficiently advanced, "the government can no longer finance the requisite income transfers because the tax base becomes too footloose" (Rodrik 1997: 55; Bishop 2000: 15–21).

Claims that tax cuts are necessary, or that the welfare state in its present form is unaffordable, are often made in the language of the public interest: jobs must be created, the tax base maintained, the brain drain plugged. Warnings of unaffordability or inevitability (for numerous examples, see BCNI 2000) cloaks an underlying exercise of power: the threat of disinvestment or emigration, which pre-empts objections to the concessions that the owners of capital in market economies always seek and promote with reference to some greater good (Lindblom 1977: 170–221). Transnational economic integration has increased the credibility of such demands, in effect reintroducing property ownership as a condition for political participation (Harris 1998). Perhaps as a corollary of these circumstances, pure self-interest is enjoying renewed respectability as the basis for domestic political allegiances. The head of the Conservatives' advertising agency for the 1995 Ontario campaign describes their research as showing

> that the suburbanite became much more the mean kind of person, you know, like, "Look, I'm in the car for an hour and a half, two hours a day, I pay high taxes, I live a stressful life, I want what gets done to benefit me and my family." That kind of attitude. So some of the traditional value systems of universality and "Let's take care of the poor first" seemed to move down the hierarchy of priorities, and that group wanted to seize control of their own lives, that was their objective. So issues like tax relief became big. (quoted in Dale 1999: 108)

This may, in the end, be the most enduring accomplishment of the new right in restructuring the language and values of Canadian politics.

## Conclusion: The No-Second-Chances State

As noted earlier, structural economic change has already driven even many people with "good" jobs to organize their working lives around enhancing the "personal, self-managed career portfolio containing the unique combination of assets that defines us individually. This combination will ultimately determine what we have to sell" (Moses 1999b: 30). Those who lose their jobs are exhorted to "network broadly" and "think multiple income streams.... Increasingly today people cobble together a living through a variety of work options. This may mean, for example, owning vending machines, taking on consulting assignments, and teaching a course at a local college" (Moses 1999c). Labour market participants less favoured by skill, opportunity and chance can expect limited assistance from governments that define the only legitimate goals of social policy in terms of enhancing individual economic competitiveness. As this trend plays out, social programs that remain are likely to highlight the rhetoric of equality of opportunity (cf. Esping-Andersen 1997), but the dark subtext will be a retreat from any responsibility for those who fail to make the most of the chances they have supposedly been offered.

Charles Murray (1984: 233–34), an intellectual progenitor of the 1996 U.S. welfare "reforms" whose work is essential reading for anyone wanting to understand the logic of attacks on the North American welfare state, explains the organizing principle succinctly: "Some people are better than others. They deserve more of society's rewards, of which money is only one small part. A principal function of social policy is to make sure they have the opportunity to reap those rewards." Conversely, Murray conceded well before the latest waves of economic dislocation that the best the U.S. economy could offer many of its citizens was "probably no more than getting by"; that "to promise much more is a fraud"; and that people were best induced to accept this bleak prospect by what he called "negative incentives"—in other words, the prospect either of jail or of a level of economic hardship "so uncomfortable that any job will be preferable to" an existence on income support (Murray 1984: 176–77).

Obsessive concern with individual economic competitiveness has spread far and wide outside government. Thus, public expenditures to ensure that children "get off to a good start in life" are justified with the claim that "investing in high quality social and physical environments makes good economic sense" and with explanations of how such investments, especially if and as they are directed toward the first few years of life, will enable today's children to compete more effectively in tomorrow's labour market (Guy 1997[2]; BCNI 2000: 10).

The matters at stake go far beyond semantics. As market criteria infuse the areas of social life they have not already penetrated, the equation of the unmarketable with the worthless will be reinforced in very concrete ways. The homeless young man in the parking lot should beware, lest his presence discomfit local high-rollers or California tourists coming and going from the boutique a few blocks away. Canadian municipalities have not yet followed the lead of their U.S. counterparts in actively criminalizing homelessness (see, e.g., Bumiller 1999; Herszenhorn 1999; Simon 1995; Smith 1996), but anti-panhandling bylaws recently enacted in some Canadian cities provide early warning signs (Cernetig 1998; Schafer 1998). So does the Harris government's 1999 *Safe Streets Act,* aimed at Toronto's squeegee kids to ensure suburbanites' untroubled passage between the automated teller machine and the supermarket—an extension of the urban enclosure movement that can be observed throughout North America's downtowns (Boddy 1992). Recent social history tells us quite a lot about what happens when the worthless, defined by economic vulnerability and social exclusion, have the temerity to become inconvenient to the propertied (Chevigny 1995: 145–201; Scheper-Hughes and Hoffman 1998). The death squads may be coming, sooner than we think.

## Notes

1.  This figure overstates the concentration of wealth at the top end of the income scale because it does not include the many Canadians whose pension funds have grown impressively thanks to the post-1987 increase in share values. On the other hand, the concentration of wealth may be understated because Canadian income tax data are reported on an individual rather than household basis. This is why the lack of post-1984 data on the nature and distribution of household assets is so important.

2.  Among the sponsors of the book from which these observations are drawn were the Imperial Oil Charitable Foundation and the revealingly named Invest in Kids Foundation. Although the government of Canada's financial involvement is unspecified, the book's copyright is held by Health Canada.

# Chapter 3

# Closing the Nation's Ranks:
## Racism, Sexism and the Abuse of Power in Canadian Immigration Policy

*Sunera Thobani*[1]

## Canadian Nation-Building and the 1994 Review of Immigration Policy

Immigration policies have been central to the production and reproduction of the Canadian nation, whose founding was predicated upon the colonization of Aboriginal peoples and the appropriation of their lands (Culhane 1997; Dyck 1991; Frideres 1990; Green 1995; Maracle 1993). The development of capitalism during this early phase took the form of integrating the global economy through European colonialization. Canada's "national" territory was acquired as part of this process.

In tandem with appropriating Aboriginal lands, racialized immigration policies enabled land settlement by Europeans who were subsequently integrated into the "national" population. Canadian immigration policies overtly distinguished between immigrants of "preferred races" and "non-preferred races" until the 1960s and 1970s. Policies such as the Head Tax, the *Exclusion Act* and the Continuous Passage requirement strictly controlled immigration by Third World peoples, while European immigrants were actively recruited for settlement (Bolaria and Li 1985; Buchignani, Indra and Srivastava 1985; Hawkins 1989; Jakubowski 1997; Stasiulis and Jhappan 1995).

In the post–World War II period, national liberation movements in colonized countries undermined the British Empire. Concomitantly, growing antiracist movements in advanced capitalist countries discredited the "scientific" racist theories of the previous era. With European immigration declining in this changed global climate, the Canadian state pragmatically removed overt references to race in immigration policy and entrenched the point system in the *Immigration Act, 1976–1977*. Selection criteria were based on the skills and qualifications of applicants (under the independent category) and their family relationships (under the family category). As a consequence, immigration source countries changed significantly throughout the 1980s and 1990s. By 1993, 51 percent of all immigrants came from Asia and the Pacific, 14 percent from Africa and the Middle East, and 13 percent from South and Central America. Only 3 percent came from the United States and 18 percent from Europe (CIC 1994a: 5). Predominantly European immigration had definitely ended by the 1990s.

With more immigration under the family category than under the independent category, Third World women gained relatively increased opportunities to come to Canada and claim citizenship. However, in 1994 the Canadian state organized a review of immigration policy, which sought to reduce access to citizenship, as part of the process of restructuring the economy.

The following examination of the 1994 review (CIC 1994a–h) focuses on how the state has defined "problems" with immigration. I seek to reveal, and challenge, the Canadian state's racialization of the "relations of ruling" (Smith 1990), and its ideological practices in contemporary nation-building.

## Restructuring the Immigration Program

The immigration policy review of 1994 was mandated to develop, through extensive public consultations, an immigration strategy for the twenty-first century. The state argued that policy changes were necessitated by changing global conditions which posed "challenges" to the "effective management" of the immigration program (CIC 1994d: 1).

While Immigration Minister Sergio Marchi repeatedly stated his commitment to "include" Canadians in "making choices" for the future, the review began with a private meeting of thirty individuals. This meeting was organized by the Public Policy Forum, drawing participants from the three levels of government, from "international and social organizations, business, labour, academic institutions, and media representatives," and "public safety and service agencies" (CIC 1994d: 2). Organizations representing immigrants and immigrant men and women are not recorded as having participated in this meeting. Ten key issues for discussion in the public consultations were identified at this meeting, as were the "elements of an approach" for "the most productive discussion of these issues" (CIC 1994f: 2). Extensive public consultations were then organized across the country.

Although the public consultations looked like a democratic process allowing Canadians to raise their "concerns," the issues up for public discussion had been pre-selected, which, of course, limited the responses. Thus, the "problems" identified by the state became the major focus during the public consultations. The whole exercise, therefore, drew Canadians into a pre-set agenda and served to popularize it by giving participants a stake in "solving" the problems through a restructuring of the national immigration program. Immigration was presented as a "problem-in-common" shared by the state and Canadian citizens, and was defined from the state's perspective. Through the consultations, the state invited citizens to "own" subsequent policy changes as being in the nation's, and therefore their own, best interest.

## Framing the Consultations

The first issue for public discussion—the development of a "Vision of Canada"—raised questions about the impact of immigration on the population, "cultural" diversity and the economy. The background information provided to the participants stated: "In 1991, the Economic Council of Canada found that immigration has a small but positive impact on our economy" (CIC 1994b: 3). This is an extraordinary starting point for a discussion on immigration policy in a country colonized and populated by immigrants. The statement makes sense only if the reader disassociates the immigration of predominantly Third World peoples in the 1990s from the pre-1970s immigration of predominantly European immigrants. This reading of Canadian history is racialized, as it defines "Canadians" as not having themselves been immigrants. As a starting point it naturalizes the nation, making it an entity predating immigration, and separates "Canadians-as-members-of-the-nation" from immigrants.

"Immigrants" make a contribution to "our" economy, the text informs "Canadians." "Our" economy is defined as belonging to "us," and although "immigrants" contribute by working and living in Canada, it is not "their" economy. The questions which frame this part of the discussion draw attention specifically to "cultural diversity": "What role should immigration play in fostering the development of Canada's economy? How does immigration affect the social and cultural life of Canada? What are the benefits of cultural diversity?" (CIC 1994b: 3). The text separates economic development from "social and cultural" life, setting the stage for the weighing of "economic" benefits in opposition to "social" and "cultural" benefits.

By linking questions of social and cultural diversity to immigration, the text implicitly constructs "Canadians" as socially and culturally homogeneous. As a number of theorists have demonstrated, "cultural diversity" has come to stand in for "racial diversity" in the "new racism" of the post–World War II period (Balibar 1991; Barker 1981; Gilroy 1991). By questioning the benefits of cultural diversity, the text makes it clear that the "immigrants" whose "benefits" are to be evaluated are those who are culturally and socially "diverse." The texts invite "Canadians," as a culturally and socially homogeneous group, to work with the state in assessing the impact of "diverse immigrants" on the nation. With this very first issue, the text places Canadians who are culturally and socially "diverse" outside the partnership of the nation and state, giving people of colour who are Canadian citizens no authority to speak. In defining "immigrants" as different culturally and socially, all people of colour are pushed aside in the subsequent defining of the national interest. This racialized use of the category "immigrant" identifies all people of colour as being part of the same "problem" which the "immigrants" under present discussion represent.

The background information framing the second issue directs attention to two categories of immigration: the independent category—also referred to here as the "economic category"—and the family category. The text informs the reader that the criteria for admission under the independent category are based upon the education, skills and occupation of the applicants, and says that this category is easily managed through adjustment of the allocation of points. The independent category is thus constructed as easily managed and as making an "economic" contribution to the nation. This category is constructed as one of *future* members of the nation. It is not linked with social or cultural diversity, nor associated with costs to the nation.

The presentation of the family category, however, stands in stark contrast. The text makes no reference to the economic contributions to the nation from those who may fall in this category. Rather, this category is constructed as making no contributions to the nation. The text presents this category as allowing entry so long as applicants have family members in Canada and meet "standards for good health and character" (CIC 1994b: 3). The text does not specify that applicants need sponsors who have to meet specific requirements under the sponsorship regulations, nor does it point out that this category is also controlled by strict criteria such as family relationships and financial obligations. For example, in June 1989, immigration policy allowed sponsorship of single, adult children of sponsors. Adult children were previously not defined as eligible for family sponsorship. With this change attracting more applicants than the department had anticipated, changes were introduced in April 1992 to reduce the eligibility of adult offspring (CIC 1994g: 8).

Annual plans tabled by the immigration minister set numerical targets for the family category, as they do for the independent category. The text therefore hides the reality that the family category is also subject to control and management, presenting it instead as allowing potentially limitless and uncontrollable immigration into the country.

Having thus constructed the family and independent categories, the discussion question, "Should immigration be managed according to business cycles or long-term social goals?" (CIC 1994b: 3), presents a choice between opposing "economic" and "social" goals. When the text asks "How much importance should the principle of family reunification be given?" (CIC 1994b: 3), it specifically calls into question the principle underlying this category. Considered in light of the first issue, which defines "immigrants" as responsible for cultural and social diversity, the family category becomes constructed as the source of this diversity, as not making economic contributions and as allowing potentially limitless entry into the country. In this way, the text specifically targets the family category as problematic.

Six of the ten issues set out for discussion in the consultations raise specific questions about the costs of immigration, linking "increased" demands on social programs with "immigrants": "Have recent immigration and economic trends created needs which current programming and resources cannot meet?" "Should newcomers receive materials explaining the rights and responsibilities of consuming public services?" "How far are Canadians prepared to go to ensure their generosity and openness are not abused?" "What are the groups, institutions and programs which need to be protected?" "What factors should we consider in shaping our immigration programs to increase economic benefits at low cost?" and "How do we build partnerships among all levels of government" to "improve the detection of abuse?" (CIC 1994b: 3–6). These questions direct attention to the range of fiscal, social and political "problems" with immigration, and the need to "protect" "Canadians" from "immigrants." In the background to the first issue, reference is made to the fact that "immigrants" are less likely to claim welfare and other benefits than "Canadians," and that "immigrants" contribute more in taxes than they consume in social services. But this information is not used to inform the framing of the questions for discussion, and the rest of the document reiterates the view that "immigrants" represent a burden on social services, especially in the areas of housing, health, education, social assistance and policing. Three of the ten issues directly present "immigrants" as threatening national institutions by "abusing" social services (CIC 1994b). The text's linking of "immigrants" with criminality and abuse of social services sets up every "Canadian" as being vulnerable.

The text's linking of "immigrants" with increased demands on social services provides the motive for the direct involvement of all "Canadians" in the subsequent restructuring of the immigration program and gives every "Canadian" a direct investment in protecting herself or himself individually, as well as their fellow "citizens," from being taken advantage of by "immigrants." Further, the text erases the reality that sponsorship regulations expressly forbid individuals in the family category from accessing social security programs such as social housing and social assistance (EIC 1983).

Even as the text links "immigrants" in general, and the family category in particular, with economic costs and "abusing" the "generosity of Canadians," it constructs all "Canadians" as citizen-taxpayers who are equally in danger of being manipulated by the potentially "abusive" "immigrant" women who enter under this category and, legitimately or otherwise, overburden social programs. The text constructs for "Canadians," as taxpayers, an interest-in-common in restricting the access of immigrant women to social programs by reducing their further entry into Canada. The textual practices give "Canadians" a direct stake in controlling immigration in the family category, inviting them into a partnership with the state on this issue.

None of the issues for discussion address the inequalities confronted by "immigrant" women in Canada, nor do they address the deeply entrenched racism in Canadian society. The only exception is one question which raises the problem of the non-recognition of "foreign" educational and professional credentials of "immigrants" (CIC 1994b: 5). The text does not mention the reality that sponsored "immigrants" are made into second-class citizens by regulations which give them unequal access to social entitlements. Nor does it mention that sponsors, who are citizens and landed immigrants—and taxpayers—have to forfeit their claims to social assistance in order to sponsor family members. Throughout the document, it is "immigrants" who are presented as a "problem," not the various agencies of the state which reproduce racialized inequalities. Nor are "Canadians" and the racism they help to reproduce raised as problems.

None of the ten issues refer to the unequal treatment of workers who enter the country under the Live-in Care Giver Program, which allows domestic workers to apply for landed status only after doing domestic work for two years (Arat-Koc 1992; Bakan 1987), nor to the Non–Immigrant Employment Authorization Program which has allowed increasing numbers of workers to enter the country on temporary work permits (Sharma 1997; Bolaria 1992). The existence of these programs is made invisible in the textual reality being constructed.

In producing the conceptual framework for the review, the state imposed an ideological "knowledge" of the "problems" upon the lived experiences of consultation participants, mediating the relationship of participants with reality through this lens. As Smith (1990) points out, entering textual realities is entering into a circularity where the words that initially stood in for actuality subsequently become imposed upon actuality through the practices of individuals and their institutions.

Where the textual reality produced by the state conflicted with the lived experiences of individuals, individuals were compelled to articulate their lived experiences in relation to the textual reality. Participants would articulate their lived reality as a subjective and individual reality, whereas the texts were said to represent an objective, collective reality experienced by the nation. If the individual experiences of participants contradicted the texts' knowledge of the "problems," their individualized experiences were juxtaposed with the collective problems of the "nation." Once the conceptual framework of the textual reality was entered, participants could only challenge it within its own terms of reference. Their own lived "knowledge" of "problems" would be overshadowed by the state's "knowledge" of "problems" confronting the nation. In short, the consultation documents constructed a textual reality through which participants were to view reality, and this conceptual framework became the lens through which participants, as "Canadians," were asked to relate to "immigrants."

## What the State Heard

The contributions to the review made through the public consultations included the following four themes: (1) defining a "national" vision for the twenty-first century, (2) the "quality" of "immigrants," (3) the appropriate balance between the independent and family categories and (4) "protecting" the security of "Canadians" and national institutions.

### A National Vision

The first theme defines a "national" vision and character, calling for its preservation as a key goal of future immigration. The majority are summarized as being in cautious agreement with continuing immigration, although some participants called for an end to immigration altogether and others for a reduction in the numbers. The texts record support for continued immigration and then immediately counter this support by repeatedly raising the "problems" with immigration. The benefits of immigration are defined as "economic," and the "problems" as based on a social and cultural diversity that "inflames" racial "intolerance." In the texts, "immigrants" are constructed as being responsible for these problems, not the racism of "Canadian" society.

The cautious support presented for continuing immigration is therefore made conditional upon recognizing the potential "dangers" of racial diversity: "the importance of the whole must be emphasized ... we must be a choir, not a cacophony"; and "ethnic diversity has no benefits, it only creates tension" (CIC 1994f: 19).

The text's construction of "diversity" as a characteristic of "immigrants"— not of "Canadians"—and a divisive and fractious one at that, is achieved through its repeated warnings about the dangers that "diversity" presents to the national "vision" and values shared by "Canadians." These values are defined as including "freedom," "democracy," the "rule of law," "the principles of justice, fairness, tolerance, and respect for our fellow citizens," and "equality" (CIC 1994f: 21). One submission is singled out for special mention as "capturing" the "Canadian" character:

> Canadians value honesty and fairness. They respect hard work and people with integrity. And they are willing to give people a second or even third chance. But Canadians also expect their fellow Canadians to respect the system that is in place, and to not take advantage of their generosity. (CIC 1994f: 20)

The text's repeated definitions of the "Canadian" identity and core "Canadian values" construct a national self-image, a character, which "Canadians" are said to have defined. However, the textual practices shape this national character and simultaneously invite "Canadians" to claim it as their own. The ideological construction of this national character as committed to "tolerance," "accepting of differences" and "humane" stands in sharp contrast to the actual recommendations of many of these "Canadians" to end immigration altogether, to allow immigration only from European countries and to contain, or even eliminate, "cultural" diversity. Frequent recommendations to "close the doors" to "immigrants" are not allowed to interfere with the text's construction of the "Canadian" character as "fair" and "just." The textual reality constructs "immigrants" as threatening national values by "their" cultural and social diversity. "Immigrants" are defined not only as failing to share "Canadian" values, but also as threatening to erode these values and the cohesiveness of the nation. On the basis of cultural and social "diversity," the textual reality reconstructs racialized definitions of "immigrants" and "Canadians," defining all people of colour as outsiders to the nation, regardless of their actual legal status.

The national character is given substance in direct opposition to "immigrants," who are constructed as not sharing it: "Throughout the consultation process, Canadians have expressed concern that their Canada is disappearing, that "its values and lifestyle are being eroded and degraded" (CIC 1994f: 22). A number of submissions were made with respect to Canada's character. According to the texts, a list of the elements of the country's basic belief system should look something like this: non-violence, justice, democracy, equality, honesty, acceptance, and fairness. As one submission quoted in the final report states, "There is no doubt that Departmental personnel want these core values to be retained and strengthened by immigration, not threatened" (CIC 1994h: 1).

The problem constructed by the texts is not so much that "immigrants" do not share national values, but they "erode" and "degrade" these values. The values of "immigrants" are constructed as the opposite of "Canadian values" as the texts delineate the ideological borders of the nation. Whereas "Canadians" are defined as respecting "the rule of law" and being "honest," "hardworking" and "fair," "immigrants" are defined as "abusers." Participants in the consultations are said to want "a government which takes effective action against abuse of our systems instead of allowing chronic abusers of our immigration and welfare systems to go unchecked" (CIC, 1994d: 42).

State officials are reported to be frustrated with a system which stops them from dealing quickly and efficiently with fraud and abuse. They are disturbed by the fact that "some" people arrive at "our" borders with "instructions on how to use the system to their advantage" (CIC 1994h: 6). "Immigrants'" effective use of the system becomes equated with "fraud" and "abuse." The texts present "immigrants" who know how to use the system as a "problem," and those who don't know "our" system as also a problem because they don't "know" democracy and the "rule of law"!

Challenges of the racialized construction of "immigrants" can be found in a number of study group reports, but these were left out of the final reports. Contributions which challenged the racist stereotype that immigrants "live off the fat of the taxpayer" (CIC 1994e: 6) were ignored, as were contributions which challenged the view that "Canadians" and "immigrants" have opposing values. The textual practices of the state did not allow these oppositional views to enter the textual reality under construction, because they would have challenged its fundamental assumptions about the nation and "immigrants." These contributions were silenced by being denied entry into the final report, which ends by reiterating the numerous "threats" "immigrants" present to the health and safety of "Canadians" and national institutions. "Immigrants" are defined again and again as representing criminality, disease, laziness, and ignorance of democratic values and the rule of law, when not openly flaunting them. The state is presented as committed only to protecting the nation and national values in partnership with "Canadians."

These textual practices hide the actuality that people in Canada are divided by the social relations of race, class and gender. The text's production of a "unified" national character counters, at the ideological level, the increasing material polarization which has resulted from the economic restructuring of the 1990s. Growing race, class and gender inequalities have been demonstrated by a number of studies (Brodie 1995; Khosla 1993; Ralph 1996). This polarization, which creates differing interests among Canadians, is not allowed to enter the textual reality. The texts construct the national character as united with a shared national interest which would work to transcend internal polarization.

### The "Quality" of Immigrants

While the first theme racializes the "quality" of immigrants, the second theme specifically genders this "problem" of quality by constructing "immigrant" women as threatening to erode the nation culturally and socially with their allegedly boundless fecundity. "Immigrants" are constructed as "threatening" the national "way of life" by overwhelming the nation's resources through over-population. The following statement is offered as one which "reflects the views of many":

> Growth as an ever increasing and self-sustaining way of life, leading to increased consumption, has been our North American way of life. All of these treasured ideas and much of what we call "our way of life" is now ending. (CIC 1994f: 17)

Immigration is associated with the "ending" of "our way of life." The texts define "our" "treasured" "North American way of life" as leading to "increased consumption." They thereby negate the reality of Aboriginal peoples, whose experience of "our" way of life has been an experience of colonization. The actuality that "our" "North American way of life" increased "consumption" only for some sectors of the population at the expense of others, and through the exploitation of the resources of Aboriginal peoples, is not mentioned.

The texts go on to present the "dangers" of overpopulation as a widespread "concern" of "Canadians." Canada has a "fragile ecology" (CIC 1994f: 18) and "climatic conditions" and "geography" that are unable to sustain more than the "ideal population," which has already been "surpassed" (CIC 1994f: 18). The use of geographical and climatic conditions to justify curtailing immigration from Third World countries is a familiar theme in Canadian history: arguments that Asian and African immigrants were incapable of adapting to the climate were used to restrict their immigration in the nineteenth and twentieth centuries (Bolaria and Li 1985; Buchiganani, Indra and Srivastava 1985; Hawkins 1989). The review gives new currency to these older rationales. The "dangers" of population growth through immigration are summed up as follows:

> The effect that population growth will have on our environment and quality of life seems to be of primary concern. Environmental deterio-ration, air and water pollution, traffic congestion, increased crime rates, over burdened social services, garbage disposal problems and shortages in housing, food and energy, are some of the problems that people identify with over-population. They are concerned as Canada's popu-lation grows, these problems will increase in severity. (CIC 1994f: 18)

In this passage, the text begins by associating immigration with "population growth," which it then immediately equates with overpopulation. "Immigrants" become responsible here for "environmental deterioration," "pollution," "increased crime," "over burdened social services," food and housing "shortages" etc., etc. The causes of these complex problems are reduced simply to the presence of "immigrants." Making "immigrants" the cause of these problems, the text directs attention away from the effects of state policies and corporate practices. The textual reality under construction reverses actually existing social relations: "immigrants" are attributed with the power to devastate the nation and the environment. Although population levels in Canada actually face decline in the year 2010 without continued immigration (CIC 1994b; Hawkins 1989), the texts incorporate an unfounded "concern" about "over-population" without challenge.

The texts signal that the "problem" is not solely population growth, but the nature of this growth, because they simultaneously forward a proposal for increasing population levels by giving "Canadians" incentives to reproduce (CIC 1994f: 18). The population growth of "Canadians" is not the "problem," it is specifically the population growth of "immigrants" which is the problem. By blaming "immigrants" for overpopulating, and listing the myriad problems associated with overpopulation, the texts link "immigrants" to "problems" which Third World peoples have historically been associated with in the Western imagination, problems such as increased crime, disease, pollution, "excessive" breeding and "excessive" demands on resources (Ahmed 1992; Mies 1986; Said 1978). Indeed, one would be hard pressed to find a more racially charged representation of "immigrants" than the one constructed in the texts' discussion of overpopulation. In contrast, the texts construct "Canadian" society as "dedicated to the preservation of a healthy environment" (CIC 1994f: 21).

The gendered consequences of the textual practices linking "immigrants" with overpopulation are also unmistakable. It is women, after all, who "populate," and it is Third World women in particular who have been associated in the Western imagination with "over-population" (Amos and Parmar 1984; Barroso and Bruschini 1991; Barbee and Little 2000; Correa 1994; Mintzes, Hardon and Hanhart 1993).

Contemporary population debates draw upon Malthusian theories which define population growth in Third World countries as an explosion endangering the very survival of the human species. High population levels are blamed for causing economic stagnation, environmental devastation and poverty. Overpopulation has created excessive demands on scarce resources, the popular argument goes, and population control is the only solution (Barroso and Bruschini 1991; Correa 1994; Hartmann 1995). Indeed, the "excessive" fertility of Third World women has, in the "Canadian" imagination, long presented a "danger" of "polluting" the whiteness of the nation. The discussion of overpopulation in the immigration policy review carries the racialized and gendered historical undertones of previous immigration policies that specifically sought to prevent the entry of "non-preferred race" women into the country. The text uses these "concerns" to rally "Canadians" against the menace of the abundant fecundity of "immigrant" women. "Immigrant" women and their potential offspring thus come to be equated with the "garbage" and "pollution" mentioned by the writers of the texts.

That the "problem" of overpopulation does not concern all types of immigration becomes clearer in subsequent sections of the text, which make repeated recommendations to aggressively increase the recruitment of applicants under the independent category, and to recruit more immigrants who speak English and French (CIC 1994f: 26, 65). Very explicitly, the text states that the problem is one of the "quality" of "immigrants," not their quantity (CIC 1994d: 61), and records recommendations to return to the original European source countries to attract immigrants who are compatible with the nation (CIC 1994f: 26). Fluency in English and French is repeatedly recommended as a criterion by which the "quality" of potential immigrants should be evaluated. This criterion would of course privilege Europeans, who would be the group most likely to meet it, and who would embody the "quality" most socially and culturally compatible with the nation.

The "problem" of overpopulation thus operates at two levels: the presence of "immigrant" women and their fertility becomes the "problem." The "problems" of the "quantity" and "quality" of "immigrants" are specifically related to the bodies of "immigrant" women.

## Balancing Immigration Categories

The third theme relates to the appropriate balance between the independent and family categories. The texts define the independent category as making "economic" contributions: and by defining the family category as one of "dependents," they make it responsible for the "costs" of immigration and for overburdening social programs. The independent category is not associated with social, cultural and linguistic diversity, nor is it associated with any costs to the nation. As I have argued elsewhere, the ideological practices of the state construct this category by masculinizing it, associating it with the "male" characteristics of independent, "economic" actors, underscoring its compatibility with the national interest, while feminizing the family category as "non-economic" and "dependent" (Thobani 1998). The textual reality here constructs the family category, and the "immigrant" women who enter under it, as responsible for "lowering" the "quality" of immigrants. It is the family category and "immigrant" women who are constructed as the biggest "problem" for "management" by the state.

The framing of the family and independent categories shaped the responses from participants in the consultations, so that, with very few exceptions, most replies reproduced the state's ideological constructions. The question, "What criteria should we set for selecting immigrants in order to achieve our social and economic objectives?" (CIC, 1994b: 3), provoked calls for increasing restrictions to reduce the family category because it is unaffordable. The texts propose that economic considerations mean that:

> weight must be given to official language ability, education levels and
> potential to contribute to Canada.... Potential to contribute to Canada
> must be viewed in terms of (a) ability to demonstrate willingness to
> integrate socially and culturally; and (b) proven ability and demon-
> strated willingness to be productive economically. (CIC 1994f: 26)

Given that the starting point for the public consultation was the construction of
the family category as not "economically" productive, recommendations for
increasing the "economic" benefits of immigration inevitably translate into
recommendations for reducing the family category, as well as increasing internal
controls to limit the access of sponsored immigrants to social programs. Recommendations call for requiring "immigrants" to pay the costs of settlement services
themselves (CIC 1994h: 7), and for obligating "immigrant communities" to fund
settlement services for new "immigrants."

> Immigrant communities can play an important role in the integration
> of new arrivals. They should be encouraged in this respect, to provide
> language and settlement services to other immigrants, particularly
> where existing delivery mechanisms are underfunded or overburdened
> and if possible to provide Canadian job experience as a transition into
> the broader labour market (perhaps through a form of sponsorship).
> These measures will help raise the economic contribution of immi-
> grants while reducing the costs of traditional settlement delivery
> mechanisms. (CIC 1994c: 11)

This extraordinary recommendation constructs all people of colour as "immigrant communities," regardless of their citizenship status, and makes them
responsible for their own kind. The reality that "immigrant communities"—as
taxpayers—fund "our" national social programs is unacknowledged by this
recommendation. Other measures recommended by the text to reduce the costs
of immigration include the introduction of a $20,000 "sponsorship bond"
(DeVoretz 1995: 8). Another recommendation calls for raising the income levels
sponsors need to have in order to qualify for sponsorship (CIC, 1994c: 11), and
yet another prescribes the outright ending of family sponsorship for low-income
immigrants, arguing that "being separated from one's family is a choice that every
immigrant must make" (CIC 1994f: 28).

While the text recommends restrictions on the numbers in the family
category and their access to social programs, it simultaneously calls for increasing
and supporting the immigration of the independent category. The texts recommend "aggressive" recruitment and "promotion" of this category, specifically
calling for increasing the numbers of "economic" immigrants and correspondingly decreasing the family category to keep overall immigration levels low.

## Protecting National Institutions

The fourth theme identifies "threats" to national institutions from "immigrants" who are constructed as engaged in widespread criminal activities and abuse of social services. Every "Canadian" as a taxpayer is said to be in danger as a consequence of defaulting sponsorships: "There is increasing concern that immigrants are not respecting these responsibilities, thus placing demands on already over-burdened social support programs, funded by Canadian taxpayers" (CIC 1994c: 10–11).

The textual reality being produced brings right-wing anti-immigrant views and more liberal views to the same conclusion. If it is accepted that "immigrants" are engaged in massive abuse of social services, as the right claims, then the "solution" to cutting costs becomes one of restricting immigration. A more liberal view might reject this wholesale stereotyping and instead define "immigrants" who claim assistance as victims of economic conditions beyond their control, and as such, unwittingly precipitating a crisis in social services. The "solution" to reducing costs in this liberal view would also be to reduce immigration levels, even if only as a temporary measure. The "problem" constructed in the text is such that there is only one "solution." The state's ideological construction of "immigrants" as outsiders to the nation makes their unequal rights, and unequal treatment by the Canadian state, politically acceptable, while erasing the actuality that immigrants, including sponsored family members, also pay taxes.

The important point here is not whether "immigrants" do or don't use social services. After all, the very basis for the creation of social programs, especially social assistance, is the recognition that individuals are not responsible for the labour market conditions which create unemployment and poverty, and that they need protection from economic cycles by having access to social programs. The point here is that defining "immigrants" as outsiders to the nation legitimizes their unequal rights and entitlements. The point is not whether "immigrants" make claims to social programs; rather, it is the state's legitimization and normalization of unequal rights and entitlements for "immigrants" through its ideological practices—"they" should not have the same rights as "us."

## What the Consultations Accomplished

Throughout the review texts, the construction of "immigrant" women as presenting various forms of threats to the nation remains constant, and so does the construction of the state as the defender of the interests of "Canadians" against "immigrants" in general, and "immigrant" women in particular. The textual reality presents the state as committed only to protecting the nation, and the public consultations are defined as demonstrating the commitment of the state to a partnership with an active citizenry to resolve their problems.

In the textual reality produced, reducing the access of Third World women to formal citizenship in Canada and policing the access of all "immigrant" women to social security programs was made not only feasible but absolutely necessary to protect "Canadians" and "our" national institutions.

The review ended with the tabling of the report for the years 1995–2000, *A Broader Vision: Immigration and Citizenship*, and a long-term strategy plan, *Into the 21st Century: A Strategy for Immigration and Citizenship*. This strategy plan outlines the direction for immigration policy into the twenty-first century and, as such, is an extremely significant document. A number of its recommendations have been implemented since 1995.

The plan for the years 1995–2000 made an outright reduction in overall immigration levels and significantly reduced the family category. Increased restrictions on eligibility criteria for sponsorship include a sponsorship contract and allowing provincial governments to prosecute defaulting sponsors. Greater surveillance of sponsored immigrants' access to social assistance programs will be facilitated by increased cooperation between the federal immigration department and provincial social service agencies. The introduction of a $975 head tax in the 1995 federal budget will disproportionately limit Third World women's immigration due to their unequal access to financial resources. Additionally, a state-commissioned legislative report, *Not Just Numbers*, contains many of the recommendations made in the review, including making fluency in one of the "national" languages, English or French, a selection criterion for immigrants. This report calls for a new *Immigration Act* and for privatizing the costs of all settlement and language-training programs.

Peoples of colour, and immigrant and refugee rights groups, have responded to the above changes by organizing campaigns such as those against the head tax and against making fluency in English and French a selection criterion. While these are certainly important initiatives, what is required in fighting the state-organized racism against women of colour is a much more fundamental challenge to the status quo. Rather than focusing only on the discriminatory treatment of Third World immigrants—and these policy changes are specifically aimed at them—what is urgently required is a transformation of the Canadian nation.

A fundamental principle underpinning the Canadian nation is the ongoing colonization of Aboriginal peoples. Ending this colonial and racial domination through resolution of the struggles of Aboriginal peoples for self-determination and title to land are key to any progressive social change in Canada. As long as Canada is officially defined as being bicultural and bilingual, i.e., English and French, the nation continues to be identified in colonial terms and to be racialized as white. A second principle underlying the Canadian nation is the racialization of all immigrants: white immigrants have historically been, and continue to be, integrated into the white nation as members, while people of colour are marginalized as "immigrants," as outsiders to the nation.

Challenging and transforming the fundamental racialization of the nation as bilingual and bicultural is urgent if Canadian society is to become more just. So long as this racialized definition of the nation is accepted, its membership will remain exclusionary, and the racialized marginalization of "immigrants" as outsiders will remain inevitable. An examination of how nation-building is currently being organized demonstrates that although the specific content of the "national" interest has changed over time, what has not changed is the state's construction of the whiteness of the nation and the definition of women of colour as not belonging to it. As long as the nation is defined by racialized cultural, linguistic and social characteristics, women of colour will continue to be defined as outsiders who undermine the "unity" and cohesiveness of the nation.

There is a pressing need for coalitions among Aboriginal women and women of colour to challenge the Canadian state's nation-building practices. A dialogue between Aboriginal communities and people of colour on immigration is urgently needed if we are to stop the state from pitting these communities against one another. Aboriginal voices were given no space in the 1994 review, and the struggles of Aboriginal peoples now receive little support from people of colour. Coalitions of Aboriginal women and women of colour committed to working across historical divisions have to be a priority for the anti-racist organizing of women of colour.

The state has made "immigrant" women one of the most significant "problems" confronting the nation. While women of colour are organizing against racist immigration policies, it is up to "Canadians" to challenge their own racialization, which is the basis of their membership in the nation, and to rupture their "partnership" with "their" state. The question women of colour *must* ask "Canadians" is this: If the state is not acting in your interest by closing the nation's doors to "immigrant" women, where are your voices?

## Conclusion

Immigration policy regulates access to citizenship in Canada, and membership in the nation. As long as this policy continues to distinguish between those who "contribute" to the nation and those whom it constructs as "dependents" and hence a "burden" on the nation, the unequal treatment of "Canadians" and "immigrants" is inevitable.

The current phase of globalization has encouraged increased international migration as a result of both the growing global polarization between North and South and the environmental devastation that is the fruit of neo-conservative "free trade" policies. And it is the very people who are forced to migrate as a result of these policies that the Canadian state seeks to keep from entering Canada as permanent residents who can later claim citizenship.

As long as immigration policy controls borders to organize the unequal treatment of "citizens," "immigrants" and "non-citizens," it cannot but organize and regulate inequalities between them. Once we accept that there should be unequal treatment of citizens, immigrants and non-citizens, the only remaining question is how unequal that treatment should be.

Appealing to "Canadians" in overtly racialized ways, the immigration policy review sought to spur them to defend the state's practices for the twenty-first century. The 1994 review enabled the state to claim to be the defender of the "national" interest against "immigrant" women. It enabled the state to claim a partnership between nation and state on the basis of "shared goals" and "shared responsibilities" between "government and its citizens" (CIC 1994f: 1).

In the textual reality produced by the state, whether "economic," "social," "cultural" or linguistic criteria are used for immigrant selection, the family category is placed in a no-win situation. It comes up short on "economic" criteria by having been ideologically constructed as making no "economic" contribution to the nation. The family category also comes up short on "social" and "cultural" criteria by having been ideologically constructed as "culturally" and "socially" diverse and, as such, undermining the national character by increasing racial "tensions." Once the textual reality produced by this review is entered, the only way to maximize the "economic" contributions of the immigration program and to lessen "racial tensions" lies in reducing the family category. The text's construction of this particular "problem" rules out any other possibility, except, of course, to reject its entire conceptual framework and underlying assumptions.

## Note

1.    The author wishes to thank Yasmin Jiwani and Fatima Jaffer for their comments on this chapter.

Part Two
# The Political Elite

Chapter 4

# The Somalia Affair:
## A Personal Account of Speaking Truth to Power

*John Dixon*

The Somalia Affair began as a scandal within the military but eventually involved all of the "estates" of the Canadian establishment—the executive and legislative branches of the federal government, the federal civil service, the media and, finally, the legal culture. Originally billed as a kind of fierce interrogation of our political elites, it ended quietly five years later with the tabling of Justice Dickson's report on the military justice system. That report accomplished little beyond confirming the old saying of the Department of Justice that "military justice is to justice what military music is to music." No national institution, inside or outside the military, either suffered or enjoyed significant reform as a consequence of the Somalia Affair.

This is, in large part, a tribute to deft management by the Chrétien government. Ultimately, however, this triumph of damage control depended upon a characteristically Canadian disinterest in pursuing the matter to a bitter end. "Scandal fatigue" was a popular description of the condition, though I will argue that Canadians couldn't wait to be bored.

I was a minor actor in the drama and so bring, I am sure, a full measure of myopic animus to my account. On the other hand, I was, I believe, an unusual observer, interestingly placed.

I came to that place in a roundabout way. In January of 1990, I was seconded from teaching philosophy at Capilano College in B.C. to serve as senior policy adviser to the then deputy minister of justice and attorney general for Canada, John Tait. At that time, I was president of the B.C. Civil Liberties Association, and although I severed my connection with the BCCLA while in Ottawa, I could not imagine giving up civil rights activism for a long period. Indeed, I had turned down the original offer of a seven-year appointment in Ottawa. I was never on a "career track," which freed me from many of that city's standard forms of discipline.

I served Mr. Tait for two years as a kind of interlocutor between his office and that of his minister, Kim Campbell. Though I answered to Mr. Tait, I addressed—with his permission—all of my notes "To Minister, Deputy Minister," and these were simultaneously routed to both recipients.

When Minister Campbell was shuffled from Justice to National Defence in January 1992, she borrowed me from Mr. Tait to serve as her special policy adviser on national defence. She also took Richard Clair and Marianne Campbell with her, both of whom had been key members of her policy staff at Justice. I had long experience of collegiality with her staff, and Minister Campbell wanted a seasoned team to support her in meeting the challenges of a new ministry. All of us had the highest Canadian security clearance of Top Secret/Cosmic Access.

This is relevant, because it meant that during the emergence of the Somalia Affair, the minister of national defence and her staff were fresh from years of working together on the most consequential and delicate legal files in the nation. We were not a pick-up team for a novice or second-tier minister; nor were we strangers to the restraints and prerogatives of judicial institutions. Further, when trouble came, we reflexively turned to our colleagues in Justice. More on this below.

But first the "facts" of the case, the events that set the Somalia Affair in motion. On March 16, 1992, a sixteen-year-old Somali youth, Shidane Arone, was tortured to death by several members of the Canadian Forces Airborne Division, which was engaged in a humanitarian mission in Somalia. Arone had been detained as he attempted to infiltrate the Canadian compound, presumably on a mission of theft. Exasperated and embarrassed by the success of such thieving expeditions directed at the Airborne, the responsible Canadian officer had ordered his troops to make an example of anyone they caught. Arone's body was broken with pipes and boots; he was suffocated, burned with cigars on the soles of his feet, and probably sodomized with a riot baton before he died of his injuries. Arone's screams and cries of "Canada! Canada!" were heard by practically the entire regiment through his long night of agony. No one intervened. Over thirty "trophy pictures" of his torment were taken by Canadian soldiers. The following day, one of the torturers was taken into custody, and later cut down when he was found hanging in his cell.

This story was covered up by the national defence establishment for more than two weeks. That is, the military did not tell the civil authority established by the *National Defence Act*, which is the minister of national defence. Instead, the minister and her staff, including me, were fed a thin stream of half-truths and misinformation.

The first trickle was a couple of significant incident reports (SIRs). The report of March 17 informed the minister that a Somali national had died the previous day in Canadian custody. The death was characterized there and in an accompanying secret briefing note of the same date from the vice-chief of defence staff as "mysterious" and "perplexing," because "a medical officer's preliminary investigation indicates that the Somali had only one bruise in the area of his mouth and another on the right side of his chest.... The Headquarters of the Canadian Joint Force in Somalia is attempting to obtain the services of a pathologist so that the cause of death can be determined." It is important to recall that these documents describe a person who had been beaten to death. Photographs of Arone taken by his torturers and published a year later in *Maclean's* magazine show that his injuries were so severe that he was scarcely recognizable as a human being. There was no need for refined study to determine the cause of Shidane Arone's death.

A second, seemingly unrelated, SIR informed us that a Canadian soldier, Master Corporal Clayton Matchee, had apparently attempted suicide by hanging while under detention in Somalia.

Both of these Significant Incident Reports were noticed by the relevant minister's staffers—Richard Clair on the peacekeeping desk and Marianne Campbell on personnel—and mentioned to me in passing. Neither, however, seemed particularly worrisome to us. A minister's staff hears of many very serious issues, so these matters, while significant, did not require ministerial attention.

The second trickle came a day or so later, suggesting a connection between the death of the Somali and Matchee's attempted suicide. By utter chance, a Pembroke reporter had seen Matchee being carried from his cell. We were cautioned by the military to keep it a secret until the investigative team had completed its work.

This revelation gave the original reports more weight and raised the question of why someone would attempt suicide over an incident in which medical examination found Canadians responsible for only two small bruises?

I recall Marianne Campbell speculating that perhaps Corporal Matchee had used excessive force capturing Arone, and since Matchee was an Aboriginal person, he had been guilt-stricken when his captive had died. Or perhaps poor health had contributed to the prisoner's death. Malnutrition was endemic among the Somali population: indeed, the principal purpose of the military intervention was to facilitate food distribution. When we asked the military for clarification, the response was always the same. The matter was still under investigation and, until that investigation was concluded, the connection between the dead Somali and Matchee had to remain a secret.

This raised a second question for us. Why was the army so anxious about the "connection" between Matchee's attempted suicide and Arone's death? What could Matchee have done that was so horrible, if, as reported, the Somali's body showed no significant trauma? The minister's staff continued to pull on this thread more urgently as days became weeks with still no credible explanation. What had seemed fairly straightforward appeared ever more suspect.

On March 30, in response to an urgent March 29 request from our office for information, we were informed that "an autopsy was not conducted" because the body of Shidane Arone had been quickly retrieved by the family, that the "investigation is ongoing" and that "there is the possibility that up to a total of seven persons may have been involved." How, we asked, could seven persons be involved in inflicting two minor bruises? At this point, Marianne Campbell informed the minister that "we are having trouble getting information out of the department."

Finally, the military abandoned its attempt at cover-up. On the morning of March 31, 1992, over two weeks after the murder, and following renewed demands from us on March 30 for frankness, Richard Clair and I were briefed by the acting Judge Advocate General (JAG). We were informed that Arone had been tortured to death by Matchee and others, that videotaped confessions had been obtained, that torture implements and trophy pictures had been seized as evidence, and that charges would soon be laid by the commanding officer in the field. Mr. Clair and I were flabbergasted.

At the same time, the JAG issued a legal caution. Because the *National Defence Act* prescribed several roles for the minister in the administration of military justice, she must say or do nothing that could be construed as prejudicial of anything that could become an issue at the trials. An investigation had begun, and it was important that its work not be compromised by public discussion of the facts.

When we adjourned, I wrote an explanatory note to the minister and offered some opinions on how she should view and react to this stunning turn of events. She was also independently advised by the deputy minister and the chief of defence staff. I advised her that:

> The Forces wanted to keep separate, in their communications, the death of the Somali and the attempted suicide of Matchee. We insisted that this simply invited a later implication, by the media, that a "cover-up" was attempted. We did not imagine, until this morning, what actually had occurred. If anything, it makes more urgent a course of openness which is conditioned only by the rights of the accused.

From this point on, the minister and her staff were engaged in a kind of covert war with the National Defence establishment over the issue of "openness." It was obvious to the military that we knew there had been an attempt at a cover-up.

What was not at all obvious was the level of command at which the cover-up had been contrived, and the extent to which we were now confronted with an effort to "cover up a cover-up." Where, precisely, had the crucial information about the torture/murder been from March 16 to March 31? Had it come forward to Defence headquarters in bits and pieces, or all at once? Who had created and maintained the principal cover story of a "medical examination" that had revealed only two small bruises? Was this an "in-country" initiative that became untenable, or a spin put on the story as it proceeded up the chain of command? And what else was going on that we did not know about?

It was the last question that caused us the greatest immediate concern. The *National Defence Act* unequivocally identifies the minister of national defence as the official ultimately responsible for the conduct of Canadian Forces. "The Minister," the *Act* provides, "has the management and direction of the Canadian Forces and of all matters relating to national defense." The chief of staff, in contrast, is "charged with the control and administration of the Canadian Forces … subject to the regulations and under the direction of the Minister." The minister bore final responsibility for whatever Canadian Forces were doing in Somalia. What was to be done?

When we think of "abuse of power," we usually have in mind the arrogant overstepping of legitimate authority. But sometimes the very possession of legitimate authority requires its dutiful and diligent exercise, and the failure to use power in such circumstances can become a form of abuse. There are both positive and negative abuses of power.

We certainly did not miss this fundamental point, and neither did Parliament. In the wake of a cryptic announcement by General Reay on April 1 that blandly described Arone's death as a homicide occurring "after contact with several members of the Airborne Regiment," members of the Opposition began demanding explanation in the House of Commons. Where had this information been languishing? Was the minister awake and alive to her duties to Canadians and Parliament? The media already smelled blood, even though the word "torture" had not yet been publicly uttered. That shockwave would not hit until the actual charges were laid, almost two months later.

The media treatment of the Somalia Affair is a subject deserving extensive treatment on its own, but one or two brief observations should be made. In general, the only media organization that "got" the story and followed it with professional tenacity from beginning to end was the *Toronto Star*. The *Globe and Mail*, which was then a much more consequential national force (and as distinctly Tory as the *Star* was Grit), decided at the outset that Somalia was a *Star* story. The *Globe* tended to treat the story as an "Ottawa" piece about bureaucratic warfare, and the Southam papers echoed this perspective. Only at the very end, when the Somalia commission was shut down, did all Canadian media acknowledge that something very serious had happened.

The period from March 31 until early May, when it was finally revealed that Canadian soldiers were being charged with torture, was excruciating. At one point, soon after General Reay's April 1 press conference, I was briefing the deputy prime minister for Question Period in a small conference room in the office of the privy council. Minister Campbell was not in Ottawa, and Harvey André was taking questions for her. Several other ministers were present, and the deputy prime minister made it clear that he intended to aggressively "stick up for our boys," who were doubtlessly carrying out their duties in Somalia in the best tradition of the Canadian armed forces.

As noted above, JAG had advised us that we had a duty to maintain strict secrecy with respect to the facts of the affair as they had been revealed to us, and that on no account were we to communicate those facts to other ministers. However, if I failed to give Mr. André some sense of what was actually happening, I would be setting him up for future embarrassment and—at least arguably—to mislead Parliament. I took Mr. André firmly by the arm and led him out of the conference room to his office and gave him the bare outline of what we knew. Mr. André was just as astonished as we had been previously. I told him that we had been advised by JAG that none of what I had said could be communicated to Parliament.

This was an intolerable state of affairs. I strongly felt that JAG's advice to

Defence Minister Campbell would effectively draw her—and other ministers—into collaboration in a cover-up.

I did two things. First, I went to David Merner, the special counsel to the deputy attorney general of Canada, and told him everything we knew. Secrecy might be the drug of choice at National Defence headquarters, but I was convinced that it was causing brain damage. From April 1 forward, I regularly briefed Mr. Merner, who briefed Mr. Tait, and I spoke directly to Mr. Tait himself about the Somalia Affair on several occasions.

Second, I made an urgent request to the acting JAG to prepare a comprehensive note for the defence minister, documenting his precise legal sense of the minister's dilemma along with her options and telling her how the defence establishment had previously dealt with such situations. We remarked at this time that at the Department of Justice such a note would have appeared before the minister and her staff had recognized the need for it. This point was vigorously seconded by Mr. Merner, who emphasized the importance of getting the full advice of JAG on paper.

JAG responded on April 4, not with the requested note to the minister, but with a fateful memo to me which began, "I understand that in spite of the explanations that have been provided to you, you still have difficulty with the idea that the Minister should not attempt to exercise political influence over the unfolding of these processes." The note goes on to threaten that "one may imagine the effect on the Minister's present situation [contesting the leadership of her party] should it be revealed that she had interfered, or attempted to do so, with the course of military justice in this highly sensitive case." As an example of such reckless interference, JAG darkly referred to an instance of the minister actually talking to the chief of defence staff (CDS) about Somalia: "I believe that the preceding (sic) paragraphs should explain the concern in the Canadian Forces about the Minister's telephone call to the Chief of the Defence Staff on Thursday last"—this in reference to a woman who had served for three years with distinction as minister of justice and attorney general for Canada.

Since the note was addressed to me, and copied to the chief of defence staff and the deputy minister, it was not advice to the minister and hence was accessible under the provisions of the *Freedom of Information Act*. The "should it be revealed" clauses would seem to strongly suggest, to anyone ignorant of the innocent and appropriate request that had brought forth the note, that the minister had, in order to advance her political fortunes, actually "interfered, or attempted to do so, with the course of military justice." In the heated atmosphere of a race for prime minister, the damage flowing from such a misperception would be very difficult to deflect or undo. JAG had made a bomb and was holding a lighted match to its fuse.

Upon receipt of this note, we dispatched Mr. Clair to meet with the CDS and the deputy minister to demand that JAG retract his insinuations and apologize for the note. Their counter-suggestion was that the three copies of the note should be shredded, and the hard drive from JAG's home computer, upon which the note had been composed, destroyed. If no note exists, the problem disappears. When Mr. Clair returned to us with this proposal, we quickly determined that acting on it would involve us in the wrongful destruction of a public document. However dangerous the existence of JAG's note was to the minister, complicity in its destruction would fatally compromise the integrity of our office. It would also, we noted, put the minister in the compromising position of sharing a guilty secret with the military establishment.

We locked up JAG's note in Mr. Clair's safe and refused, in the face of the most pressing demands, to destroy it. On April 23, JAG sent a note to the deputy minister unreservedly retracting the inferences of his note of April 4. We then gave the office of the CDS and the deputy minister copies of the original note for their files. These photocopies, Marianne Campbell pointed out, bore the stamp of the office of the minister of national defence, making it clear that they were not the documents originally sent to the CDS and the deputy minister by JAG.

When Mr. Clair and I showed the original JAG note to the minister, her response was immediate and unequivocal. She asked me to get the deputy attorney general, Mr. Tait, on the phone so she could read the note to him. In the presence of Mr. Clair and myself, she reported to Mr. Tait our information concerning the destruction of copies of the note at the Department of National Defence, and added that she would be formally seeking his advice. The minister then directed me to prepare a concise version of my original question, as I had posed it to JAG, for the attorney general. I did so, and on April 22 the Minister Campbell wrote to the deputy minister, effectively discharging JAG as her legal counsel and directing the deputy minister to communicate the crucial question to Mr. Tait.

The text of the question for the attorney general outlined the Minister's responsibilities according to the *National Defence Act* and noted the quasi-judicial functions she performed in the system of military justice—principally certain powers of mercy. "The question raised by these considerations," the note concluded, "is as follows: how ought the Minister of National Defence conduct herself when it appears that she may be fettered by her limited role within the system of military justice from the timely discharge of her duty and responsibility to govern the Canadian Forces?"

This note of April 23 brought the deputy attorney general and several of his officials to the Department of National Defence offices on April 24. It was immediately decided and advised by Mr. Tait that the defence minister's duty to manage and direct the Canadian Forces could not and should not be nullified by her very limited role within the system of military justice. It was determined that she could immediately convene a special inquiry to go to Somalia and determine, on an emergency basis, whether Canadian Forces could honourably continue their service there. As long as the inquiry did not press into those areas under active investigation in connection with Arone's murder, it should be possible to determine if there was a crisis of morale or leadership. At the very least, the minister could discharge her responsibility to ensure that, if it were necessary, she would have the information needed to withdraw our forces to prevent further criminal activity and national disgrace.

There was no attempt at this time, either by us or the attorney general, to address the underlying cover-up issue. There were two reasons for this. First, it was very difficult to see how such an initiative could avoid interference with the investigation of the torture and murder, not to mention the subsequent trials of those who would be charged with that crime. Canada's system of military justice provides that only officers in the field can lay criminal charges, and by late April 1992 that crucial step had still not been taken. Any suggestion on the part of the minister's office that the delay seemed excessive was rebuffed by dark implications of "political interference." Second, it was clear that nothing less than a full public inquiry could marshal the resources and authority needed to get to the bottom of the affair. In this connection, it seemed obvious to us that once the trials were concluded and their findings made public, the government of Canada would be under tremendous political pressure to convene such an inquiry.

In early 1995 the government commissioned an inquiry into the deployment of Canadian Forces to Somalia. The commission's mandate was to cover all aspects of the affair—pre-deployment, in-theatre and, finally, the issue of a possible attempt at a cover-up.

From the outset, the commission experienced tenacious and determined opposition to its work from the military. Relevant documents were lost, not produced in a timely fashion or "hidden" in—literally—thousands of pages of extraneous and irrelevant material. At one point, after almost a year of examining of document alteration in the Communications Directorate, the chief of defence staff was implicated and forced to resign.

This delay in coming to grips with the central issue of an attempted cover-up, however expensive, provided the government with a bolt-hole. Citing the need for thrift and the pressing need to move forward with reforms to the Canadian Forces, cabinet effectively ended the Somalia commission by refusing to extend its reporting deadline. Never mind that the promised reforms would necessarily exclude consideration of the possible participation of the highest officials of the defence establishment in an attempted cover-up.

I felt very strongly that this result was a travesty of justice and a national disgrace. What First World nation would tolerate the intervention of government in a public commission of inquiry charged with the investigation of a cover-up of a torture/murder on the part of its highest officials? If I did not literally find it impossible to believe, I certainly found it impossible to accept. That the cabinet possessed the raw power to shut down the commission was obvious—it accomplished that purpose by simply refusing to extend its mandate. The commission was, in strict legal terms, the creature of the government; and what the government had given, the government could take away. Such a step, however, had never been taken before in the history of our country. Commissions struck under the *Public Inquiries Act* had come to take on what the Supreme Court of Canada has identified as "a vital role in our democratic institutions" and, as is often the case in a parliamentary democracy, an inviolate robe of traditional practice had come to protect them from the prospect of government interference.

I retained counsel and brought forward an application for standing to testify before the commission. It had several weeks left to run, and I reasoned that if Marianne Campbell and I had an opportunity to testify concerning our experiences it would be impossible for the government to persevere in its plan.

In this connection I wish to make it very clear that I nor any other members of the minister's staff, nor the minister herself, possessed knowledge concerning the participation of any specific individual in the cover-up of the torture/murder. Knowing that there has been a cover-up is very different from knowing who is responsible for it. Only the commission of inquiry, with its power to command documents and testimony, could have thrown light on these matters. The most telling information we had to offer concerned what we did *not* know, and should have known, very soon after March 16, 1993. I could not and did not prejudge, because I had not been informed of the torture by official $A$ or $B$ that $X$ and $Y$ were involved in a cover-up. For all I knew then (and know now) $X$ and $Y$ could have been as much a victim of a cover-up as the minister and Parliament.

Only the commission could do justice, and it could only do justice if it were permitted to discharge its mandate. In the event, the commissioners decided to reject my application for standing, arguing that my testimony, which I outlined to them in a supporting affidavit, would necessitate their hearing the chief of defence staff, the deputy minister and the minister herself. This could not be accomplished in a manner consistent with the demands of due process in the time remaining to them. They praised Marianne Campbell and me for our diligence, and roundly condemned the abusive arrogance of the government, but declared that, in the final analysis, they were bound by the will of cabinet.

Although I respected the difficulties faced by the commission, I could not accept this decision. As quickly as possible, I filed an application in federal court for a writ of *mandamus* against the commission, and brought an action against the cabinet for exceeding its lawful authority in shutting it down. *Mandamus* is a prerogative writ ordering an official or governmental institution to discharge its full and lawful duty. The mandate of the commission, established by orders-in-council, included inquiry into a possible cover-up of the Somalia atrocity. I had made it clear in my affidavit that there had, indeed, been a cover-up, and that I was anxious to give sworn testimony which would establish that fact. As long as the commission was still in force and knew of the significance of my testimony, it had a duty to hear me.

I expected the Somalia commission to defend against my application for *mandamus* by testifying that, although they regarded my testimony as highly significant, they could not responsibly hear it without committing to hear testimony from persons implicated by it. This was not possible in the several weeks remaining to them. So their defence against *mandamus* would be that the government had effectively prohibited them from discharging the very mandate the government had imposed upon them. That defence I then expected to use in support of my principal legal thrust, which was to argue that it was not lawful for the government to establish a legal duty for a public inquiry and then withhold from that inquiry the bare resources needed to discharge that duty. This was the core of my argument that, in shutting down the commission, the government had acted *ultra vires*, literally "beyond its lawful authority."

My counsel, Joseph Arvay, and I both understood that this was a hard case in which we were advancing novel legal concepts. On the other hand, we had good authority for the democratic importance of commissions of inquiry in recent decisions of the Supreme Court of Canada, and a strong general sense throughout the country that the government's action was an arrogant abuse of power.

In the event, I won. Judge Sandra Simpson of the federal trial division decided that a writ of *mandamus* could not hold against the commission because it was clear that the government had effectively deprived them of the means to discharge their mandate. Further, and most importantly, she ruled that the federal cabinet had acted *ultra vires* in shutting down the commission without issuing new or amending orders-in-council relieving it of those elements of its mandate that it could no longer discharge. The commission might be the creature of the government, but it was a special sort of Canadian creature that had come to occupy a special role in the preservation of confidence in the integrity of government. If the Somalia commission was to be shut down by government, then government was going to have to do it in a manner that made its action politically transparent.

Of all of the disappointments that I felt in connection with the Somalia Affair, none was more keen than my disappointment that the commission did not take the opportunity afforded them by the decision in federal court to immediately summon me to Ottawa to testify. In subsequent conversations with the president of the commission, Giles Letourneau, and commissioner Desbarats, they pointed out that by the time the Simpson decision was rendered, they were so demoralized that they could not conceive of carrying on. While I appreciate the honesty of this excuse, I do not think, given the gravity of their mandate and duty to Canadians, that it is acceptable. As it was, the commissioners cooperated with the privy council in crafting a new order-in-council to shut themselves down in accordance with the Simpson decision; and they got on with packing up their desks.

In the following months, Mr. Desbarats published a book about his experience as a commissioner, based upon notes he made during the tenure of the inquiry (Desbarats 1997). Just before its publication, he approached me with a request for an extensive set of interviews from which he hoped to glean the material he needed to give his book—which was to be titled *Somalia Coverup*—some real punch. I suggested that, along with my sworn affidavit, he must have had access, as a commissioner, to far more information than I could ever provide him. He responded that, in order to protect himself from charges of conflict of interest when he published his book, he had made it a point of honour not to read any document that touched on the issue of the actual torture/murder or subsequent cover-up. This was, I believe, an inappropriate balancing of his duties as a commissioner and his professional journalistic principles.

Clearly, the central "abuse of power" in the Somalia Affair was perpetrated by the federal cabinet. However, as I suggested earlier, the failure to use legitimate power can be a form of abuse as well. Such "negative" abuse coloured, to some extent, the final days of the Somalia commission, but it was most egregiously present in the passivity of the Canadian people.

The ultimate political elite in a democratic polity is its citizenry. They stand at the apex of their system of government as its genuine, as opposed to figurative, sovereign. But there is a big problem with the Canadian sovereign these days, because, as I noted at the outset, when the citizens of Canada were inundated with the machinations surrounding the Somalia Affair, they essentially responded that they were tired of trying to pay attention and were ready to go along with the government's inclination to bury it.

How could this have happened? Why were Canadians so easily tired—a condition almost obsessively tracked by government polling—of the work of the Somalia commission? Why did they feel no sense of connection with or responsibility for the commissioners? How has so much political power managed to cut itself off from its authorizing source and escape genuine accountability? It is as though, to borrow an idea of John Ralston Saul, Canada is increasingly becoming an "unconscious civilization"—a polity in which the ultimate political agents are unconscious of their own great office and its related powers and responsibilities.

I will conclude with a suggestion of what I think are the most important elements contributing to this political malaise. The worst problem is that our educational system neglects to awaken the citizenry to the fact of their great office or to lift their incumbency beyond the range of mere formality. That would take generations to change, but the second component of the problem—which is nothing less than the gradual disappearance of the legislative branch of government—might be changed more quickly.

The fundamental political act of a citizen is to vote for her or his most immediate governing instruments—legislative representatives. Members of Parliament, however, have gradually become nonentities in the Canadian system. Not only the executive, but even the legislative business of government, is now transacted by a handful of cabinet ministers who are advised and directed by a proportionally tiny number of unelected, anonymous and unaccountable deputy ministers. To an extent unparalleled in any of the other Western parliamentary democracies, Canadian political parties maintain a tyrannical discipline over the voting of their members, and this has transformed Parliament from a genuine political assembly into a highly stylized theatre.

The simplest step needed to restore our legislative assemblies to some semblance of political vigour and authenticity is reform of this distinctly Canadian practice of iron caucus discipline. Without such reform, Canadians will become more and more alienated from their politics, which they will come to understand as a lottery of political will which, at regularly scheduled intervals, endorses a kind of regency. This is the condition of democratic decay that Rousseau warned against in 1762 in his slightly overstated criticism of English parliamentary government in *The Social Contract*:

> The people of England regards itself as free; but it is grossly mistaken; it is free only during the election of members of parliament. As soon as they are elected, slavery overtakes it, and it is nothing. The use it makes of the short moments of liberty it enjoys shows indeed that it deserves to lose them. (Rousseau 1762)

The citizenry of Canada hold the great sovereign office that can never be delegated or authored away, and when its incumbents nod off—as they did at the close of the Somalia Affair—all hope of political accountability disappears.

Chapter 5

# "So you don't like our cover story. Well, we have others":
The Development of Canada's Signals Intelligence Capacity through Administrative Sleight of Hand, 1941–2000

*Stuart Farson*

Power may be the quintessential element of politics, but monitoring its use is an ideal tool for discerning how states adhere to democratic principles. Yet power is frequently conceptualized in far too clear-cut terms. Often it is perceived as unproblematic, as where its use accords with a country's constitution and legal systems. Conversely, where it benefits specific individuals or groups, or covers up intended or actual wrongdoing, power is said to be corrupted. But conceiving power in such a binary fashion has serious consequences, both by removing important topics from view and by obscuring the many ethical dilemmas political elites face.

This chapter focuses on the development of Canada's signals intelligence (SIGINT) capacity over more than fifty years. This historical analysis shows how power is frequently used in ways not readily categorized in absolute terms. When the government first established a SIGINT unit, it used means now falling outside governmental norms. There were then, however, good reasons for doing so. Canada was at war, its intelligence resources needed protection and there were established precedents for employing the legal instruments used. Later, as the Cold War developed, administrative sleight of hand was again used to keep Canada's SIGINT capacity from view. Once more the objective was to pursue what intelligence officials believed was a higher noble cause, the defeat of Soviet communism. But in this instance, those seeking the high ground were not entirely pure of heart. While atomic weapons made the Soviet threat tangible, these officials' actions were swayed by the benefits of membership in an intelligence club recently forged between the United States, Britain and the principal dominions. The Soviet Union's demise has since dramatically changed the national security threat. Rationales used to support a special status for SIGINT agencies are no longer sustainable.

This chapter begins with a discussion of delegated legislation, the mechanism chosen to establish and amend Canada's SIGINT capacity. The next section illustrates how it was used administratively and shows how power was employed to effect secrecy and prevent elected officials from scrutinizing Canada's SIGINT capacity. The chapter then focuses on pressures to improve oversight, explaining why current review mechanisms are inadequate and arguing that Canada's SIGINT organizations require a statutory basis.

## A Change in Attitudes toward Delegated Legislation

Cabinet's authority to make regulations—delegated legislation—stems from two sources. One is the Crown's prerogative, which, while diminished, still includes the appointment of the prime minister and other ministers, the conduct of foreign policy (including the right to make treaties) and the capacity to declare war (Hogg 1992: 14–15). Statutory provisions enacted by Parliament constitute the other source.

Prior to the Second World War, delegated legislation could be enacted and enforced without public knowledge or parliamentary review. Wartime demands required publicizing regulations, and by war's end it was standard practice to make the public aware of most delegated legislation and to table orders-in-council in the legislature. While fewer than five percent of the ten thousand orders-in-council passed each year during the war and immediate post-war period were of a legislative character, the import of some of these executive actions was considerable (Heeney 1946: 287). Some executive agencies had wide discretionary powers to make policy (Mallory 1982: 133). In fact, governments have accepted that democratic principles can be diluted during times of crisis, and such attitudes find much public support (see Sallot 1985).

Though some curtailment of liberty may be warranted, wartime expediencies have overstayed their welcome. The *War Measures Act* and the *Official Secrets Act* are good examples. The former was adopted in 1914 and remained in effect until the mid-1980s. Similar to Britain's *Defence of the Realm Act*, it transferred during wartime virtually the whole legislative authority of Parliament to cabinet (Hogg 1992: 342). According to the *War Measures Act,* in times of "real or apprehended war, invasion or insurrection" the government could pass orders and regulations having the force of law to ensure the "security, defence, peace, order and welfare of Canada."[1] During the Second World War, the Canadian Government used the legislation to enact some 6,414 orders without parliamentary debate (Bothwell et al. 1981). Such regulations often abridged civil liberties. Canadians of Japanese extraction were among the most seriously victimized— most were detained in camps, and many had their possessions confiscated and sold at fire-sale prices.

Adopted in 1939, ostensibly to prevent spying, the *Official Secrets Act* also served to enhance investigatory powers, curtail legal protections and reverse the burden of proof in prosecuting espionage cases. At war's end, Parliament was specifically told that there were no secret wartime orders still in effect. Nevertheless, the *Official Secrets Act* underpinned a secret order-in-council issued in 1946[2] after Russian cipher clerk Igor Gouzenko defected from the Soviet embassy in Ottawa (see Whitaker and Marcuse 1994). This allowed individuals suspected of communicating secrets to be detained and interrogated, and permitted the RCMP to enter and search their premises (Kersell 1960: 11). The royal commission established by order-in-council to investigate Soviet espionage also had extraordinarily broad powers.[3] Besides having the right to set its own procedures and detain witnesses, it often prevented such people from having access to counsel and abridged their right not to have their testimony used against them in subsequent proceedings (Rosen 1981: 11). When the existence of the order-in-council became public knowledge with the commission's establishment, it caused a stir in Parliament that led to the provision of legal safeguards under the *Statutory Orders and Regulations Order, 1947* (Kersell 1960: 11).

## Deep Cover: 1941–1969

Delegated legislation was also used to create organizations. Although the military rejected an independent code-breaking unit in late 1940, the Department of External Affairs saw its potential. Through an agreement with the National Research Council (NRC), it located a civilian cryptographic bureau under the NRC's auspices disguised as a code-*developing* office. External Affairs not only bankrolled the unit but also retained operational and policy control. Not for a further nine months was cabinet officially informed (Wark 1987: 644).

In hindsight, establishing the unit in the NRC appears odd. Yet it met the needs of the day. Using an executive order instead of an enabling statute ensured fast action, avoided the more public legislative process and limited knowledge of the intelligence resource to those involved. Locating it inside the NRC also had other major benefits. But consolidating it within an armed service, arguably the most logical location, might have both increased service rivalries and made it a focus for Axis infiltration. Similarly, the NRC's hiring process did not have to follow the Civil Service Commission's open procedures. Thus, housing it within an organization not expected to perform intelligence activities allowed the NRC not only to become the covert conduit by which SIGINT was secretly administered and funded but also deceived the enemy. To bolster its cover story, the new unit was innocuously named the "Examination Unit." Its location adjacent to the prime minister's Ottawa residence ensured adequate security without drawing attention (St. John 1984: 9).

By war's end, SIGINT's value to the Allied effort was established. So too was its significance as an entrée into the exclusive intelligence-sharing club run by the British and Americans. The Canadian government therefore took steps not only to maintain the cryptographic bureau, but also to extend the intelligence collection and sharing arrangement it had developed with its principal allies. New life was effected through delegated legislation. A Treasury Board minute set pay scales,[4] and an order-in-council authorized the reappointment of 179 wartime appointees in the NRC under section 10(f) of the *Research Council Act* of 1924.[5] The nature of the work was extremely well hidden. Instead of mentioning a particular organization, the order merely referred to "a project which, throughout the war, did work of great value not only to Canada but also to the United

Kingdom and the United States." Nor was any explanation provided about why it was "essential" to continue this "project" on a post-war basis.[6] Only later would the functions be generalized as "Signals Intelligence" and "Communications-Electronic Security (COMSEC)."[7] While it is not known to what extent the original establishment owed its authority to the *War Measures Act*, after Gouzenko's defection the Canadian government extended orders established under that *Act* through the *National Emergency Transitional Powers Act* of 1945 and every year thereafter until 1951 (Friedland 1979: 111).

Though wartime demanded that regulations be better publicized, there was no statutory obligation to make them public or for Parliament to scrutinize them. However, in 1950, Parliament adopted the *Regulation Act*. Besides requiring the publication and tabling of orders and regulations, this *Act* obliged cabinet to scrutinize them for clarity and uniformity. But, not surprisingly, the legislation had little impact on the Communications Branch of the National Research Council (CBNRC). Mallory has observed that such scrutiny was generally perfunctory, and that provisions in the 1960 *Bill of Rights* requiring the minister of justice to check such delegated legislation for consistency with the *Bill* were even less successful (Mallory 1982: 135).

There is still no statutory obligation to make public international agreements that the government has signed. Thus, when Canada became a formal party to the Allied SIGINT sharing agreement after the war, Parliament was not informed even in the broadest of terms. In fact, few in cabinet knew of its existence. And since then only a handful of ministers have been fully briefed on its content. This crucial intelligence-sharing agreement remains one of the most closely guarded secrets of the Canadian state. Few acknowledgements of its existence have ever been made.

## Demystification and Remistification: 1970–1981

The 1970s marked a point of departure and were characterized by paradoxical processes that both demystified and remistified the work of SIGINT agencies. The invocation of the *War Measures Act* during the October Crisis of 1970 again focused attention on the use of emergency powers emanating from orders-in-council. On this occasion the powers were mobilized to thwart an "apprehended insurrection." In all some 467 people were arrested. Of these, only sixty-seven were ever charged and only eighteen were found guilty (Peppin 1993: 183). In 1972 the old *Regulations Act* was replaced by the *Statutory Instruments Act*. The new legislation reiterated the obligation placed by the earlier statute on the clerk of the privy council and the deputy minister of justice to scrutinize all statutory instruments before enactment. The purpose was to ensure that such instruments did not go beyond the powers authorized in the originating enabling legislation. A joint standing committee on regulations and other statutory instruments was created. Copies of all statutory instruments had to be published in the *Canada Gazette* and *permanently* referred to a parliamentary committee. Exempted, however, were instruments which might be injurious to "the conduct of international affairs, the defence of Canada or any state allied or associated with Canada ... or the detection, prevention or suppression of subversive or hostile activities."[8]

It was in this context that the CBNRC began to emerge from the shadows and to be demystified. The process started in 1972 with a feature interview with a former SIGINT officer in the magazine *Ramparts*. This article publicly identified how the National Security Agency (NSA) operated, and it confirmed SIGINT's immense value to U.S. intelligence efforts. At the time, some fifteen thousand people were said to work for the NSA, either at its Fort Meade headquarters or in one of its over 2,000 field stations worldwide. In addition to monitoring and ensuring the security of U.S. communications, the principal job of the NSA was to break the military, diplomatic and commercial codes of *every* nation around the globe. In all, some 80 percent of the data produced by U.S Intelligence came from the NSA. The *Ramparts* article also provided details of the UKUSA treaty and identified the CBNRC as a secondary partner alongside British, Australian and New Zealand agencies. Finally, it indicated impropriety. Not only did the U.S. contravene the International Telecommunications Convention when it listened in on its principal target, the Soviet Union, but it also breached its own UKUSA treaty by routinely listening in on its partners (Anonymous 1972).

The *Ramparts* story caught the attention of the Canadian Broadcasting Corporation (CBC), which in early 1974 aired an hour-long documentary entitled, "The Fifth Estate: The Espionage Establishment." This broadcast revealed aspects of Canada's SIGINT activities. It identified the CBNRC; showed how its SIGINT product was passed to the RCMP, External Affairs and Canada's allies; and disclosed the CBNRC's close working relationship with the NSA. According to the *Globe and Mail*, even Prime Minister Trudeau may not have really known about the agency prior to the CBC program. When probed about the organization, Kevin O'Neill, then head of the CBNRC, replied he could not release any information without it being cleared by senior authorities. When asked to whom he reported, O'Neill indicated that "he had spent most of the morning trying to determine just that" (Carruthers 1974: 8). While the response sounds like a line from *Yes, Minister*, the chief was firmly on the horns of a dilemma. Had he answered, the NRC president, the prime minister, or a cabinet committee, O'Neill would have opened these parties to questions about their involvement in directing the Communications Security Establishment (CSE) and their knowledge of the UKUSA Agreement.

Although relocating CBNRC had been considered when the intelligence committee was restructured in 1972, rising media interest in SIGINT led the government to reconsider how best to hide CBNRC's programs from closer scrutiny. Work on an improved cover story began in early 1973. By year's end the Interdepartmental Committee on Security and Intelligence (ICSI) had agreed to replace the old cover story ("The [CBNRC] carries out research, development and production of aids in the field of communications for the defence and other departments") with a revamped version ("The [CBNRC] carries out research, development and production in the field of communications security for federal government departments. It also provides advice to departments in the field as required. Communications security measures are highly sensitive and no further information on the subject can be divulged.")[9]

The CBC program quickly made this cover story redundant and caused ICSI to consider moving the CBNRC functions to another location where better cover could be provided. The Department of National Defence (DND) was deemed the best option for several reasons, not least of which was its ability to hide the SIGINT budgets and personnel within a large, highly secure environment that was the largest user of COMSEC programs. To ensure that the growing interests of non-military SIGINT users were accommodated, ICSI continued to provide policy guidance and annual program forecast reviews.[10]

Delegated legislation was again used to enshroud Canada's SIGINT capacity in yet another layer of mist by transferring what was a fully fledged SIGINT processing agency with six hundred staff to DND. This process was achieved through five orders-in-council issued on three separate dates in early 1975.[11] While some of these orders appeared in the *Canada Gazette*, others did not. The most important, the one actually transferring the Communications Branch, was issued under the *Public Service Rearrangement and Transfer of Duties Act*. It made no mention of a change in name; nor did it identify the powers and duties transferred, or for what the minister of national defence and chief of defence staff would be responsible. It also glossed over the transfer's legality, as the chairman of the NRC may never have had the authority to control and supervise such a unit either under his *Act* or in actual practice. Orders appointing personnel to the CSE similarly failed to mention their previous employer; they were also broad in compass and provided exclusions from the *Public Service Employment Act*. They made no reference to Canada's principal SIGINT agency, nor to ICSI's budgetary and policy role. Ironically, though the Soviets would have known of CSE's dual role, its name conveyed—to Canadians at least—only its COMSEC mandate.

## The Decision to "Avow" the Existence of the CSE

It was not until 1983, when a special committee of the Senate evaluated Bill C-157—the Liberal government's first attempt at passing the *Canadian Security Intelligence Service* (CSIS) *Act*—that a Canadian minister formally acknowledged the agency's SIGINT role.[12] Although Alan Lawrence (the former Progressive Conservative solicitor general) had broached CSE's SIGINT role in his evidence (Canada, Senate 1983a: 26–27), the decision to avow the CSE's dual mandate had been under discussion for some time.[13] CSIS becoming the first intelligence agency to receive a legislative mandate approved by Parliament demanded broader acknowledgement. Moreover, CSE management saw benefits accruing to the agency—including easier recruiting, better external liaison relationships, simplified purchasing and acquisitions, higher profile within the intelligence community and removal of stress—if the SIGINT role were divulged. Still the subsequent acknowledgement of CSE's broader role was strictly limited. The testimony of Secretary of State for Foreign Relations Jean-Luc Pepin provided only the briefest description of CSE's SIGINT role and the assistance it received from the Canadian Forces Supplementary Radio System (CFSRS) (Canada, Senate 1983b: 19). No mention was made of the bifurcated accountability system recently approved by ICSI for the chief of the CSE.

Further information about the limited control and accountability mechanisms came from Alan Lawrence. In his testimony, Lawrence posited that he and Allan McKinnon, the defence minister in the short-lived Clark government, had been the first ministers to visit the CSE's Ottawa headquarters. He believed there was no real supervision governing the agency (Anonymous 1983: 11) and that a committee of senior officials, reporting not to the defence minister but to a cabinet committee, were in charge. In Lawrence's view, the lack of a legal mandate posed "a very grave potential threat to a citizen's privacy and the potential for abuse [was] very great."[14] McKinnon was equally concerned about ministerial control. Apparently, some of their predecessors had not wanted to know about the agency (Macdonald 1985). Robert Kaplan, the minister responsible for the CSIS Act, had turned down requests for independent review, saying it would be inappropriate to include a defence ministry agency under the same body as one responsible to the solicitor general (Sallot 1984b: 5). Demands some three years later by the Liberals when in Opposition were therefore not without irony (Moon 1987b: A13).

It is evident from the Commons debates on the CSIS Act that Opposition parties were concerned about the legality of CSE operations and their threat to civil liberties. They believed the CSE should be brought under controls similar to those of CSIS, and they demanded that the justice committee be provided with the mandate under which the agency operated (Sallot 1984b: 5). The government refused all such demands. Kaplan tried to assuage critics by claiming that the CSE operated under a "very conservative" interpretation of the criminal law and did not need warrants to cover its operations. He declined to provide the justice committee with a copy of the agency's nine-year-old secret mandate,[15] arguing that the CSE did not intercept private telephone calls and limited its activities to monitoring radio signals that provide intelligence about foreign countries.

Kaplan refused to reveal, however, whether the CSE was in the practice of intercepting such other forms of communications as telex, electronic mail and computer data, which were frequently transmitted by satellite or microwave. Apparently, the minister and his advisers believed that warrants were not required to cover such forms of communication. Their reasoning was that satellite and microwave transmissions were in the public domain and could be lawfully gathered. At issue was whether the public had a reasonable expectation of privacy in making long-distance communications, as all transmissions travelling more than 600 kilometres left land lines and went by microwave link (Sallot 1984a: 3). A legal opinion obtained by the justice committee contradicted the solicitor general's views. It argued that such long-distance calls were private communications under the *Criminal Code* and could be intercepted only by judicial warrant or under the *Official Secrets Act* in national security investigations (Sallot 1984b: 5).

## Movement towards the Light

The auditor general's annual report (Canada, Auditor General 1996: s.27.47, 6) suggested that parliamentary interest in Canada's foreign intelligence sector had been limited. This statement was both true and misleading.

If one compares the time spent by Parliament on security intelligence versus foreign intelligence, or on CSIS versus the CSE, the report makes a valid point. Following a lengthy public inquiry into RCMP security service wrongdoing in the 1970s, Parliament spent much time debating legislation that established a new civilian security intelligence agency operating under a fixed mandate with review bodies and strict accountability mechanisms. The *CSIS Act* requires a public report of the Security Intelligence Review Committee (SIRC) to be tabled annually to Parliament. The law also obliged Parliament to conduct a five-year review of the law, which occurred in 1989–90. Following that review, Parliament established a sub-committee on national security, reporting to the justice committee.

In contrast to this focus on security intelligence, Parliament missed many opportunities for examining the foreign intelligence sector. Foreign intelligence is used primarily to aid policy, and its principal beneficiaries are the Department of Foreign Affairs and DND. Yet, when joint committees of the House of Commons and the Senate separately examined foreign and defence policies, they failed to consider foreign intelligence as a component of the study. Why this was so is the subject of conjecture. Certainly it was not because they were not alerted to its importance.

But the auditor general's picture of an indifferent Parliament is also deficient in not taking into consideration the occasions when Parliament has interested itself in the CSE. Several backbench MPs have tried to develop a private member's bill providing the agency with a statutory mandate.[16] That none ever reached a form in which it could be tabled says much about the difficulty of researching this area. Nonetheless it was parliamentary pressure, mainly from members of the sub-committee on national security, that was to lead to the establishment of a CSE commissioner in 1996. Interestingly, this step was achieved through all-party support for a motion on the order paper. However, the main reason why Parliament has not developed a sustained interest in the CSE is that consecutive governments have not wanted it to probe too deeply. Despite Parliament's legitimate concerns about propriety, officials have responded negatively to parliamentary soundings of CSE activities. Some have not been forthcoming, others have obfuscated the facts, and on occasions Parliament has simply been misled.

Questions about the CSE's mandate and accountability were again raised in 1987 following media accounts claiming that the CSE had propped up an ailing high technology firm (Moon 1987a: 1, 11). On that occasion it was the

Progressive Conservative government that ignored demands that the CSE be placed under a review process similar to that for CSIS. According to the junior defence minister, the CSE was operating within the laws of Canada and was subject to normal lines of ministerial authority. As a division of DND its business could ostensibly be raised with the national defence committee "at any time" (Anonymous 1987; Moon 1987b: A13).

For the last decade, responsibility for answering questions about the CSE has been left to senior privy council office (PCO) officials. A consistent position has been that CSE operates within the law, does not target Canadians and has adequate accountability mechanisms in place. During the five-year review of the CSIS Act, Parliament sought testimony from senior officials regarding these issues. Their information did not, however, go much beyond Pepin's earlier statement. For example, Senator Michael Pitfield, Trudeau's secretary to the cabinet, felt constrained by his privy council oath from answering questions about whether the cabinet had ever directly tasked CSE. However, he was categorical in stating that "clearly some degree of accountability is going to be necessary for that institution, because [it] has very great powers of an exceptional nature and it is a simple law of public administration and democracy that this sort of power should be under some sort of constraint" (Canada, House of Commons 1990a: 8). Gordon Osbaldeston, a subsequent secretary, was similarly unforthcoming about ICSI's role, as he did not know how it currently operated (Canada, House of Commons 1990e: 5).

In contrast to Pitfield, Blair Seaborn, the first person to hold the office of intelligence and security coordinator (and thus to take direct line responsibility for CSE policy and operations), did not even think external monitoring of CSE was justified (Canada, House of Commons 1990b: 14). As to questions of operational propriety and technological capacity, he felt similarly hampered by his oath of office from going beyond Pepin's avowal statement. When asked whether the CSE ever intercepted the communications of Canadians within Canada, he stated that that was an operational matter he could not discuss. The generalities in the evidence of Seaborn's successor, Ward Elcock, only infuriated the special committee, causing its chair to cut short the meeting and apologize to those present (Moon 1991a: A1).[17] When asked specifically to describe what checks and balances existed, Elcock merely stated that he was personally satisfied with the current system. The chief of CSE was accountable to him for policy and operations. The minister was briefed and advised regularly. And justice department lawyers reviewed CSE activities (Canada, House of Commons 1990d: 13).

The special committee did, however, receive solid evidence about the legality of CSE's operations, and some criticisms of the law governing communications interception. Ironically, these came from Robert Kaplan, who was by then no longer an MP. Kaplan stated it was only a "legal technicality" that permitted the CSE to intercept telephone calls. When one spoke by telephone and the call went through a wire, it was protected by law; however, if it went through the air, it was in the public domain. Consequently, Kaplan believed that arguments for oversight were just as compelling as for CSIS, and he confirmed that the Liberal government had intended to provide the CSE with a statutory basis if re-elected (Canada, House of Commons 1990c: 26).

Since the end of the Cold War the government has become less reticent about the CSE's functions. Senior bureaucrats have appeared before standing committees to discuss its work. During the last months of the Conservative government, Elcock appeared before the sub-committee on national security. This included an historic first *in camera* meeting with the Chief of the CSE, Stewart Woolner. Later, in public session, Elcock provided some details about how the CSE reported through two deputy ministers to the minister of national defence and indicated that the government was giving active consideration to additional accountability mechanisms. He also acknowledged it had a staff of 875, some of whom operated outside Canada. However, Elcock maintained that CSE did not target Canadians by intercepting their cellular, microwave-link land-line telephone calls (Canada, House of Commons 1993).

Two years later when the Liberals were again in office, Margaret Bloodworth, Elcock's replacement as deputy clerk of security and intelligence, appeared before the defence committee along with CSE chief Woolner (Canada, House of Commons 1995). On this occasion, Woolner responded to committee questions in open session. Together they provided the most detailed briefing on the CSE to date. For the first time, specific budget and resource figures were revealed, though not those of the CFSRS or the split between its intelligence gathering and security functions.[18] Bloodworth also acknowledged the role of the CFSRS and its operation of several stations in Canada.

As well, Bloodworth commented on the UKUSA agreement and the unusual accountability system governing CSE.[19] The chief of the CSE reports to two deputy heads: (1) the deputy minister of national defence on administrative matters and (2) the deputy clerk of security and intelligence regarding policy and operations. Both the deputy clerk and the deputy minister are accountable to the defence minister, who in turn is responsible to the prime minister and to Parliament for the CSE. The deputy clerk also advises the prime minister and cabinet on security and intelligence matters, and oversees and coordinates the security and intelligence activities of government departments and agencies. The CSE now has in-house legal counsel with access to all operational information, and Bloodworth reported that the government was looking for ways to strengthen external oversight.

## Steps into the Sunlight

During the 1990s, former insiders brought the propriety of CSE operations to public attention. In a series of articles based on interviews with former CSE employees, Peter Moon asserted that the agency's partners routinely cooperated in intercepting communications, such that each could gather personal information about its own citizens without breaking its laws (Moon 1991a: A1). In another story he commented on working arrangements between CSE and CSIS.

Apparently, a judicial warrant was reissued annually to provide the legal basis for round-the-clock surveillance of the Soviet embassy. CSIS then subcontracted most of the surveillance work to the CSE (Moon 1991b: A6). Moon also obtained on-the-record comments from Jean-Jacques Blais about his term as defence minister in the early 1980s. Blais stated that his knowledge when minister for the CSE was very superficial, opining that only the prime minister could provide information about the CSE's operational responsibility and accountability as it reported to the PCO for operational direction (Moon 1991c: A4).

In 1994, Michael Frost, a former senior communications officer with the CSE, published an unauthorized memoir that made several claims which question the propriety of CSE's actions and contradicted official positions. Apparently, in the late 1970s Canada's intelligence partners threatened to stem the flow of foreign intelligence to Canada. This caused a renaissance at CSE (Robinson 1991), which included the acquisition in 1985 of a Cray supercomputer to make Canada a serious contender in cryptanalysis. The CSE also received key-word computer technology from the Americans. Another development was the "Pilgrim" project, under which Canada began to collect intelligence abroad by intercepting foreign communications from its embassies. The memoir also contended that the agency repeatedly spied on Canadians. For example, the CSE intercepted communications between the French government and leaders of the Québec sovereignty movement. Frost also listed several domestic operations of dubious nature. One in which he claimed personal involvement concerned intercepting the possible drug dealings of Prime Minister Trudeau's wife. He also mentioned an occasion when his boss went to the United Kingdom to intercept the communications of two British ministers at the behest of the British SIGINT agency after that agency had turned down Prime Minister Thatcher's direct request (Frost and Gratton 1994).

The following year, Jane Shorten, a former senior CSE analyst, also risked prosecution under the *Official Secrets Act*. In interviews with CTV News, Shorten contradicted the view that Canada did not spy on its friends and neighbours (CTV 1995). She had been personally involved in analyzing intercepted communications between the South Korean embassy in Ottawa and its foreign ministry in Seoul. She also claimed Canada had intercepted Japanese embassy traffic and had monitored the communications of Mexican trade representatives during the North American Free Trade Agreement (NAFTA) negotiations. Shorten's main point, however, was that Canadians frequently got caught in such gathering, particularly when working at foreign embassies in Canada. In one case, which involved a woman talking to her doctor about gynecological problems, Shorten had been so appalled about the invasion of privacy that she questioned her boss on its legality (Benzie 1995).

Besides establishing institutions, enabling legislation often provides special review and monitoring mechanisms. The *CSIS Act*, for example, established SIRC and the inspector general of CSIS. In addition to such specialized review bodies, Canada has several institutions that have specific but broad review functions. For example, the office of the auditor general (OAG) acts as the government's auditor for all departments. In addition, there are several mini-ombuds offices that scrutinize government departments to ensure compliance with such legislation as the *Access to Information Act* and the *Privacy Act.*

Until the mid-1990s, such independent bodies had not reviewed CSE. Matters, however, changed dramatically in 1996 when the government acted on the Commons' motion to establish an independent review mechanism for CSE. Once again it relied on an order-in-council, thereby avoiding parliamentary debate and the fact that its mechanism fell short of what MPs had intended. Under the order, Claude Bisson, a recently retired judge, was appointed on a part-time basis as commissioner of the CSE for a period of three years.[20] The office's initial mandate focused on whether CSE activities complied with law. The annual review leads to a report being submitted to the minister of national defence. When the commissioner believes activities are not in compliance, he or she must report the fact to the responsible minister and the attorney general (Canada, OAG 1996: 8). Unlike SIRC, the commissioner is restricted in what he or she may put into the annual report—it must not include classified information. To ensure this, the senior security and intelligence official in the PCO first vets the report. However, the commissioner may submit confidential reports containing classified information to the minister at any time. When reappointed in 1999, Bisson's mandate was extended to permit him to notify complainants of his findings. The order-in-council also obliges the defence minister to table the commissioner's report in Parliament.

Commissioner Bisson has not proven to be particularly helpful to parliamentarians. His reports have been limited in focus and content, and he has given few media interviews and appeared only once before a parliamentary committee—and that was *in camera*. Nonetheless, the commissioner insists that the CSE has not breached the law or targeted Canadians. In the latter regard, he has stressed that this is true of all Canadians, "including the people of Quebec. CSE does not target Quebec communications, or the Quebec sovereignty movement, and it does not have a 'French Section'" (Canada, Commissioner of the Communications Security Establishment 1998: 4). Although Bisson has made important recommendations concerning the complaint process, only an extension of his mandate to cover complaints has been adopted; and while he quickly supported enabling legislation, his reports have been short on supporting arguments or discussion of broader accountability and control issues.

A month after the commissioner's initial appointment, the office of the privacy commissioner reported on the CSE's activities (Canada, Privacy Commissioner 1996: 52). This audit was one of the most complex ever undertaken. Privacy audits normally rely on an organization's enabling legislation to assess compliance with the *Privacy Act*. In this case, there was no legislated mandate—only a stated one—to act as a benchmark against which information management could be assessed. The investigators found no evidence of the CSE targeting Canadians or monitoring their communications. Nevertheless, they noted it was inevitable that the monitoring of foreign electronic communications would inadvertently trap information about some Canadians, and they went on to make a strong case for enabling legislation which would explicitly establish a legal framework and review mechanisms to monitor the CSE's activities. In the privacy commissioner's view, these steps would permit personnel information management practices to be measured objectively, provide legal protections for Canadian's liberties and give CSE operations a clear underpinning.

For years, ministers and bureaucrats have told Parliament that effective accountability systems and control mechanisms govern the foreign intelligence sector generally and the CSE in particular. However, the OAG's 1996 report challenged such assertions. Despite its moderated language, the report suggested that serious flaws existed.

First, the OAG found no internal or external review processes that could provide ministers with systematic assurances that control and accountability mechanisms were working effectively (Canada, OAG 1996: 99). Furthermore, it noted that until Commissioner Bisson's appointment, there were no mechanisms dedicated to reviewing the foreign intelligence side. The OAG did, however, acknowledge the improvements in the CSE's public accountability with the new external review body (ibid: 65).

Second, the OAG was even less positive regarding the accountability mechanisms needed to ensure the CSE's performance and capacity. Of critical importance here is the process by which national intelligence priorities are developed. For most of the Cold War, Canadian intelligence was essentially self-tasking: intelligence agencies identified priorities and the government approved their proposals. In many ways, this was appropriate for the times. Both within Canada and among its principal allies with whom it shared the workload and intelligence product there was general agreement about the nature of the threat and what had to be done to thwart it. With the demise of the Soviet Union, the intelligence priority-setting process has become more problematic because the international environment has become more complex. This broadening of the target frame has occurred as certainty in international relations has declined. Whereas state and sub-state actors were previously controlled like pawns in a giant chess game initiated by the major powers, they now operate more independently. Moreover, priority-setting is increasingly affected by the globalization of markets, dramatic changes in technology and diminishing intelligence community resources.

Not surprisingly, the OAG found the articulation of intelligence priorities to be a recent phenomenon (see Canada OAG 1996: 79–87). On the security intelligence side, an articulation process only began in 1989. Following recommendations made by an independent advisory team on CSIS (Canada, Independent Advisory Team 1987: 36–37), the government required the service to develop an annual overview of the security threats facing Canada. This is accomplished through an annual memorandum to cabinet. On the basis of this submission and subsequent decisions made by cabinet, the solicitor general provides CSIS with a set of national security intelligence priorities. Foreign intelligence priorities, however, are of more recent vintage (the first having been developed in 1991 in response to the Soviet Union's disintegration), and they are not formalized to the same degree as those on the security side. And although foreign intelligence requirements should serve government policy-making, it appears that a broader consultation process involving major consumers within government did not begin until 1995 (Canada, OAG 1996: 83).

The OAG was critical about the political executive's involvement in the priority-setting process. It questioned the relevance of ministerial direction where the approval of security or foreign intelligence priorities occurred late in the year to which they applied (Canada, OAG 1996: 85). It levies further criticism against the executive for its failure to rank priorities. The government had not taken steps to assess whether intelligence collection adhered to established priorities and whether gaps in coverage existed. Without refining the ranking of priorities and doing follow-up analyses, it is difficult to see how the annual strategic planning process which the various intelligence agencies appear to undergo can be useful (Canada, OAG 1996: 79–87). Another problematic area concerns how operational policies are determined and approved. It appears that the CSE has developed its own policies and procedures without the request or guidance of responsible ministers. Furthermore, the political executive has not approved these; also worrying is the failure to implement reviews and audits establishing whether the CSE has complied with them (Canada, OAG 1996: 104, 106). Under such circumstances, it is difficult to see how the defence minister could possibly be accountable to Parliament for the CSE in a meaningful way.

As is usual practice, the OAG revisited its audit for a two-year period. While it observed some progress in strengthening the accountability and control mechanisms, it noted that certain initiatives were still incomplete (Canada, OAG 1996: 321). Of particular importance was the need for a legislative mandate. The coordinator's 1997 response to the public accounts committee suggested that proposals to provide the CSE with enabling legislation were then under consideration.[21] However, the 1998 response indicated that such proposals had been deferred to the next year.[22] The response also acknowledged that the CSE's internal policy needed higher level direction from government and that the agency's accountability structure should be clarified and strengthened. To this end, in 1997 the coordinator had instituted a mandate and authorities project, which was approved the following year (CSE Commissioner 1998–99: 11). However, this action could at best offer only the possibility that legislation might result.

## Conclusions

Delegated legislation has been used to restructure Canada's SIGINT capacity for nearly sixty years, and government has claimed that the principal reason for using this strategy has been to protect the agency from prying eyes. Yet it seems that only Canadian taxpayers and their representatives have actually been thwarted from looking at the mandate and the laws under which the CSE operates. Committees of both houses of Parliament, the CSE commissioner, the privacy commissioner and the OAG have all argued that enabling legislation is long overdue and that the CSE needs a permanent review mechanism.

There is a strong argument for providing the CSE and the CFSRS (now consolidated in the Canadian Forces Information Operations Group) with governing legislation. The principle of ministerial responsibility is of paramount importance in Canada's system of government. This idea holds that ministers are accountable *in* and *to* Parliament for the activities of agencies under their charge. However, for accountability to work, Parliament needs to know what questions to ask responsible ministers. Without a statutory framework and access to independent review bodies, it is impossible for Parliament to know for what to hold ministers accountable.

The management system at CSE leaves much to be desired. It is overly complex and too layered. The agency is sufficiently important to Canada's intelligence effort, and in terms of the total resources employed and funds expended, to warrant a separate existence with its own deputy head. Given the change in operational tasks since the end of the Cold War and the fact that budgets are now revealed publicly, serious questions should be asked about whether DND is still the most logical location.

While contemporary intelligence officials may be honourable individuals deserving of public trust, Canadians should not have to rely on their personal integrity to protect their rights and freedoms. Today's commitments are an insufficient guarantee of tomorrow's liberties. Not only can delegated legislation be readily changed to meet future needs, but tomorrow's officials may also be of a different stripe. Governments have a duty to ensure that contemporary organizations with the capacity to damage the democratic fabric have known and explicit mandates as well as permanent independent review mechanisms. Without knowing the details of their mandates, and how CSE/CFSRS go about fulfilling them, Canadians have no way of knowing whether existing law really protects their privacy.

Britain has been one of the most secretive nations when it comes to intelligence, and has routinely relied on delegated legislation for governance of the intelligence sector. Yet Britain has recently brought its services out of the shadows. With the exception of its military intelligence services, all of its agencies now have statutory mandates. The *Intelligence Services Act* of 1994 specifically provides Britain's SIGINT agency with the authority to exercise its functions beyond traditional national security areas; it permits involvement in economic espionage outside the British Isles, and in the prevention and detection of serious crime. CSE is also involved in these areas. The RCMP has long been acknowledged as a substantial user of SIGINT. Although the powers of section 4 of the *National Defence Act* are broad indeed, it is difficult to envisage how they cover these areas.

The current review process is inadequate and needs rethinking. Neither the post of commissioner nor the office has permanency. Because they have been derived from delegated legislation, they can be as easily discarded as renewed. Moreover, the commissioner's mandate focuses entirely on compliance with Canadian law and complaints against the CSE. There is no obligation to assess the sufficiency of the current legal regime governing communications interception and the expectations of Canadians to privacy. Nor is consideration anticipated on matters of international law, memoranda of understandings between intelligence agencies, Canadian treaty obligations or the laws of other states. Similarly, there is no mandate to determine whether agencies with which the CSE works, such as CFSRS, also comply with such obligations, whether a warrants system is appropriate or whether extant law is adequate. Likewise, the commissioner's office has no legal burden to comment on whether CSE activities comply with internal policies, whether regulations are appropriate and lawful, or whether the agency is meeting performance standards or has the capacity to meet current and future intelligence needs. In conducting his audits, the commissioner ostensibly has access to the CSE's staff and its relevant documentation (Government of Canada 1996). However, the CSE and its employees are not required by the current order-in-council to comply. Significantly, CFSRS, the body doing most of the intercepting, is not included within the current review rubric.

Enabling legislation is a two-edged sword. While review and oversight bodies can use it to establish benchmarks for assessing compliance, performance and capacity, such legislation can also protect employees. While the CSE may not overtly target Canadians, their communications can inadvertently be trapped in the process of collecting foreign intelligence. Having a specific public mandate not only reduces naiveté about what the CSE can and cannot do, but also protects employees against exploitation and unlawful orders.

## Notes

1.  *War Measures Act*, RS 1952, c.288 (as amended).
2.  Order-in-Council PC 411, February 5, 1946.
3.  For the order's preventive rather than punitive intent, see Canada, Royal Commission (1946: 649ff).
4.  Treasury Board Minute T307012B, April 13, 1944.
5.  In addition, almost five hundred servicemen were allocated to high-speed monitoring work (see Granatstein 1981: 500).
6.  Order-in Council PC 54/35235, April 13, 1946.
7.  See the declassified version of the *History of the CBNRC*, Vol. 1 (August 1986): 1. COMSEC is now called "Information Security (INFOSEC)."
8.  See Canada, *Statutory Instruments Act*, c.S-32, s.20.
9.  Memorandum from W.R. Luyendyk to ICSI, "Proposed CBNRC Cover Story," November 27, 1973, as released under the *Access to Information Act*.
10. See "Policy Guidance and Ministerial Responsibility for the CBNRC and the SIGINT and COMSEC Programs," considered by ICSI on September 4, 1974, as released under the *Access to Information Act*.
11. Orders-in-Council 1975–95, 685, 686, 708 and 709.

12. That is not to say ministers had not commented on the CBNRC/CSE's role. Bud Drury had talked of the CBNRC monitoring "Hertzian radio waves" on March 24, 1975. Prime Minister Trudeau suggested two days later that DND was the "main user of the kind of intelligence which might be gathered by this unit." Material released under the *Access to Information Act*.

13. Material released under the *Access to Information Act*.

14. In 1984, Lawrence noted that neither he nor the defence minister, who was responsible to Parliament for the CSE, had been informed of the agency when sworn in (Sallot 1984a: 3).

15. CSE's mandate has not been released. Two documents in the *History of the CBNRC* offer glimpses of its authority: "Responsibilities and Functions of the Communications Security Establishment" (February 1975) and "Control of Signals Intelligence in Canada" (August 24, 1977) (http://watserv1.uwaterloo.ca/~brobinso/csememo.html).

16. Confidential interview with research branch of the Library of Parliament, March 1997.

17. For the chair's remarks, see Special Committee on the Review of the *CSIS Act* and *Security Offences Act, Minutes of Proceedings and Evidence*, No. 27 (April 24, 1990), 21–22. Though the chair intended for the witness to appear at an *in camera* hearing, the committee was unable to secure his attendance.

18. Such a figure could have been determined from the testimony of CSE's director-general of INFOSEC. In 1991, Alan Pickering informed members of the public accounts committee that INFOSEC received about 20–22 percent of CSE's total budget. This left 78–80 percent for SIGINT and administration (Canada, Standing Committee on Public Accounts 1991).

19. Bud Drury was likely the first minister to comment on UKUSA when he responded as minister of science and technology to a question put in committee by Perrin Beatty (Canada, House of Commons 1975: 17–21).

20. Canada, Privy Council Office, Order-in-Council 1996-899 (June 19, 1996).

21. Letter of John Tait to the clerk of the committee, October 6, 1997.

22. Classified response of the coordinator entitled, "Follow-up Action Plan Status" (October 27, 1998), as released under the *Access to Information Act*.

Chapter 6

# The Devine Regime in Saskatchewan, 1982–1991:
## The Tory Caucus Fraud Scandal and Other Abuses of Power[1]

*J.F. Conway*

> Political corruption is endemic to Latin American countries, Asia and perhaps Eastern European jurisdictions. But it has never seriously been suggested that corruption permeates Canadian politics, at least until a fraud of this scale was revealed.—Judge W.R. Matheson, Court of Queen's Bench, as he jailed former cabinet minister John Gerich to two years less a day on February 21, 1997

> I don't know of a more distasteful duty than to impose sentence on a former justice minister.—Provincial Court Judge Diane Morris as she fined Bob Andrew $5,500 and ordered $4,224.57 in restitution after a guilty plea to fraud, May 24, 1997

> The theft … was motivated by greed and committed while in high office.—Judge Frank Gerein, Court of Queen's Bench, as he sentenced former deputy premier and now senator Eric Berntson to twelve months in jail for fraud and ordered $41,735 in restitution, March 16, 1999

The people of Saskatchewan have endured two episodes of Tory rule during the province's brief history, and both have been thoroughly unpleasant experiences, deeply dividing the province and poisoning its political culture for years afterward.

Having been shut out of office since the province's founding in 1905, when Prime Minister Laurier created Saskatchewan and Alberta and appointed Liberal premiers in both provinces, the Tories, desperate and hungry for office, cultivated two strategic alliances during the 1920s: one with the farmers' movement that echoed an agrarian critique of the Saskatchewan Liberal patronage machine; the other, more ominously and significantly, with the Ku Klux Klan (KKK), which enjoyed a meteoric life in Saskatchewan politics during the late 1920s and early

1930s. The KKK emerged as a frontal attack on Catholics, continental European immigrants (especially Eastern Europeans), Jews, Asians, the French language—indeed, upon any forces they perceived as eroding "true" morality, patriotism, British institutions and the Anglo-Saxon "race." These groups were attacked in language that can only be described as violent, abusive and potentially dangerous, yet the KKK received enormous support. The Grand Wizard was a prominent Tory. J.T.M. Anderson, the Tory leader and 1929 premier, helped the KKK organize Saskatoon by providing membership lists of his party and many Protestant clergymen joined. Members of all political parties joined the Klan, but the Tories led the field. At its apotheosis the KKK had between twenty thousand and thirty thousand members. The Klan was decisive in electing aldermen to city councils, had a big effect on who became mayor in the larger centres and, in the 1929 election, aided in unseating the Liberal government.

The Tory-led coalition government of 1929–34 was a defeated government when it took office in September 1929. Less than two months later the Depression began. The government's response was typical of the day—retrenchment, higher taxes, wage rollbacks, staff cuts and reduced services. For this they were bitterly attacked. Early in the Depression, Tory premier Anderson, speaking at Yorkton, made a promise that came back to haunt him—"no one will starve," he promised. Many did, however, and Anderson and the Tories were never forgiven. In the 1934 election the Tories were wiped out, failing to win a single seat and ceasing to exist as a significant force in provincial politics for forty years before finally replacing the Liberals as the alternative to the Cooperative Commonwealth Federation (CCF)/New Democratic Party (NDP) in the election of 1978.

The second episode of Tory rule occurred in the context of the global realignment of the political right around the neo-conservative counter-revolution, which saw the election of Margaret Thatcher in the U.K. and Ronald Reagan in the U.S. Saskatchewan's Tory leader, Grant Devine, caught the right-wing wave that brought Brian Mulroney to office in Ottawa in 1984 and neo-conservatives to power in every other western province that same decade. This movement triumphed as the dominant political ideology in Canadian political culture when the NDP, under Bob Rae in Ontario and Audrey McLaughlin federally, embraced neo-conservative doctrines. The Devine sweep in Saskatchewan in 1982—fifty-five seats and 54 percent of the vote—reduced the NDP under Allan Blakeney to nine seats and 38 percent, the party's worst showing since 1938. Seats held by the party since 1934 were lost, the party's citadels of working-class urban support largely voted Tory, and the party was virtually annihilated in rural areas. As a result, Saskatchewan became a beacon of hope for neo-conservatism in Canada. Many saw the humiliation of the NDP in the cradle of Canadian social democracy as a watershed in Canadian politics.

And it was. Canada entered one of its most turbulent political decades during which neo-conservative governments strove to implement what became the dominant agenda: (1) cutbacks in social spending, including a significant erosion of Canada's social security net, (2) an assault on the incomes and living standards of wage and salary earners, while the total share of wealth flowing to capital and its privileged servants was increased, (3) a weakening of federal power *vis-à-vis* the provinces, (4) a program of deregulation and privatization and a move to free market forces as the engine of social and economic development, (5) a free trade deal with the U.S. as a prelude to the establishment of a continental and ultimately a global free market, and (6) a deliberate process of discrediting and disabling government as a popular democratic tool available to the people to shape the economy and society, achieved largely by burdening governments with huge annual deficits and a crippling debt. The Devine government participated eagerly in this rewriting of the post-Depression, post–WW II welfare-state political consensus.

After just over nine years in power the Devine Tories were badly defeated in October 1991. Two years after that defeat, the Tory caucus fraud scandal become public and completed the destruction of the Tory party.

## Abuses of Power: A Recapitulation of the Devine Regime

Aware that a deep recession in Saskatchewan's resource and agricultural sectors had more to do with his victory than neo-conservative ideological leanings, Devine hesitated after his 1982 landslide. Compared to what was to come later, the Devine government only played cat-and-mouse with the neo-conservative agenda during its first term. The civil service was purged of socialists and NDPers, but there were no cuts in its size. The province was declared "open for business," and the government catered to the business lobby with deregulation, a legislative attack on trade union rights, and a host of tax breaks for corporations, resource companies and the affluent. Government support for free enterprise came through an endless stream of public cash grants and loan guarantees to help big and small entrepreneurs develop projects, from barbecue briquettes and shopping carts to pork plants and oil upgraders. Many of these schemes were foolish, self-evident failures from the outset. Others were fiscally irresponsible, and some were suspected to be outright frauds. But all had the effect of mortgaging the future of the province through deepening debt and creating appalling future financial liabilities through loan guarantees.

The Devine government attacked Saskatchewan's large crown corporations. They were curtailed, bled of revenues, hamstrung with hostile boards and CEOs and deprived of their public policy role. Yet there were only a few privatizations, and a sell-off of blocks of government shares in a variety of key enterprises. The government denied that it intended to privatize the crowns, while simultaneously preparing the way: "participation" bonds were sold in SaskOil, and eventually one-third of the oil crown's shares were sold off at low prices; bonds were sold in the utility crown, and small pieces of SaskPower's assets were sold off. The Crown-owned Prince Albert Pulp Co. (Papco) was sold back to Weyerhaeuser, and this created considerable controversy, if only because the original pulp deal had been instrumental in the fall of the Thatcher government in 1971. Meanwhile the government's accumulated deficit grew—as a result of a combination of the continuing depression, uncontrolled spending and irresponsible cuts on the revenue side—from nothing to over $1.7 billion in four years.

Despite these efforts to steer a "moderate" right-wing course, while carefully preparing the ground for the future, public support for the Devine government collapsed. The extent of the erosion in Tory support was tested in two by-elections in 1985—both seats that had been won by the Tories in 1982. In a March by-election in Thunder Creek, the rural seat vacated by Colin Thatcher after his conviction for murdering his ex-wife, Tory support fell by 20 percent, from 62 to 42 percent. Although the Tories held the seat, it appeared that even their hard-rock rural base was abandoning them. In a November by-election in Regina North East, a seat vacated by an incumbent's resignation and formerly an NDP stronghold, Tory support fell a full 34 percent, from 57 to 23 percent, while the NDP's shot up from 39 to 71 percent. Clearly the urban NDP vote was coming home in an unprecedented way, just as Tory rural support was slipping out the back door, going largely to the Liberals.

Devine was haunted by "Blakeney's nightmare." During the constitutional battle with Ottawa over control of resources in the 1970s, then-premier Allan Blakeney had frequently argued that Saskatchewan's world-market-dependent and vulnerable resource-based economy made it imperative that the province have control of its resources to maximize revenue for the province and plan the pace of development. Then, with an economy based on a diversified range of resources such as oil, potash, uranium and grains, the province could weather a downturn in one resource sector by relying on the others and avoid the kind of calamity that hit wheat-dependent Saskatchewan in the 1930s. Asked at a press conference what would happen if all resource sectors experienced a downturn at the same time, Blakeney answered, "That would be an economic nightmare."

By the mid-1980s, Devine lived that nightmare. Oil prices had collapsed, triggering a deep recession in the oil patch. Potash prices were low and markets sluggish. Uranium was just beginning to limp out of the doldrums of the early 1980s, when the nuclear disaster at Chernobyl in the Ukraine had made many countries abandon nuclear-generated electrical power. And agriculture faced a long-term crunch, as world prices collapsed because of the wheat wars and a third of Saskatchewan's farmers teetered on the brink of bankruptcy. No incumbent government had ever survived such an economic collapse. The recession that helped elect Devine had become a full-scale depression four years later and defeat seemed inevitable.

It was in this context that Devine opted for his rural election strategy. The strategy was simple and brutal—write off the urban centres as NDP strongholds where Tory support was soft in the first place, and concentrate on rural and small-town Saskatchewan. In pursuit of this strategy the Devine government encouraged an unprecedented political polarization between rural and urban Saskatchewan. Welfare recipients were attacked as abusers of the system, social support programs for urban residents were slashed and trade unions were bashed. The premier railed against outside labour big shots and red-baited the NDP as Marxist monsters. Grant Schmidt, a small-town lawyer and Tory labour minister, went so far as to attack trade unionists and city professionals as unduly affluent people whose outlandish wage and salary demands were made at the expense of poor farmers and rural residents.

Meanwhile, the Devine government poured largesse and sympathetic attention on Saskatchewan's crisis-ridden farmers. The premier personally took over the agriculture portfolio to deal with the farm crisis. Whirlwind trips to Ottawa by the premier squeezed concessions from the "feds." He also dashed off to meetings in the U.S. and Europe to plead for a stop to the wheat wars. More concretely, Devine promised to put the provincial treasury at risk to save rural Saskatchewan; and he did so, mounting a series of programs from cheap money to production cost relief; from hog incentives to farm purchase support; from loan guarantees to tax relief. These programs, estimated by the premier's own officials to amount to $36,000 per farmer for a total of $2.4 billion, added a new dimension to the old idea of buying an election.

During what turned out to be a pivotal election in reshaping Canada's national political culture, the Tories waged the most deceptive campaign in the province's history. Devine invoked the ghost of Tommy Douglas and claimed that the traditional CCF populist turf now belonged to him. The government lied about its post-election intentions regarding privatization and social spending. The public accounts were kept under wraps, while Finance Minister Gary Lane predicted a deficit of under $400 million. (After the election it became clear he had "underestimated" the deficit by more than $800 million.) Further, there was an orgy of spending promises to buy the rural vote. And, for good measure, hundreds of millions in subsidized mortgages, low-interest home improvement loans and matching grants were given out to woo urban voters. Still unsure of victory, Devine begged Brian Mulroney for help. Mulroney intervened at the last moment with a billion-dollar deficiency payment to western farmers, half of which was earmarked for Saskatchewan farmers.

Devine's rural strategy paid handsome dividends on October 20, 1986, when the Tories won thirty-three of thirty-six predominantly rural seats. With a half-billion-dollar nudge from Mulroney, Devine had bought the farm vote. The last minute Tory effort to buy some of the urban vote with its $300 million housing program netted five of twenty-six urban seats, four of which were middle-class seats in Regina and Saskatoon. The Tories won the rural seats with about 53 percent of the vote and their few urban seats with 37 percent. The NDP, on the other hand, swept the major urban centres, twenty-one seats with 52 percent, while being decimated in the countryside, two seats with 38 percent of the vote. The NDP also easily took the two northern seats.

Tensions in the province were increased by the fact that the NDP had won more of the popular vote but not enough seats to form the government. For the first time in the province's history there was a government in power with a large majority of seats despite having won less of the popular vote than the major opposition party. This unprecedented situation occurred because the NDP won "big" in most urban seats, while the Tories won the countryside. An urban vote carried less weight than a rural vote, and Tories had used that disparity to good advantage. Its failure to win a plurality of votes immediately called into question the legitimacy of the Tory government and raised serious questions about just how democratic the system really was.

The next five years were politically ugly. Having won a second mandate in a tough, "no holds barred" contest, Devine began to implement the neo-conservative agenda with all the zeal of a crusader. Saskatchewan, after long years of social democratic rule, had a comparatively well-developed and expansive social and health security system, as well as a very large public sector. To retain their rural hegemony, the Tories gave urban problems—those of the unem-ployed, the welfare recipient and the poor—short shrift. Thus, as the government cut back spending and raised taxes, it imposed the lion's share of the pain on urban Saskatchewan, especially the working and lower middle classes.

The Devine counter-revolution was paced in two overlapping phases: the first was a process of ransacking the social and health security system, and the second was a program of privatization of public assets. In preparation, the government established a Draconian dictatorship through the *Government Or-ganization Act*, granting the cabinet the power to make sweeping changes without debate in the legislature. Then, in the spring of 1987—what came to be known as "the year of the cutting knives"—the assault began on Saskatchewan's elaborate social and health security system, a system described in the legislature by Social Services Minister Grant Schmidt as "a hammock" in which "a lot of people [are] laying [sic] ... having a good time at the expense of a majority of taxpayers." Schmidt later summed up the government's credo: "If you work hard, you eat. If you won't work, you don't eat. And if you can't work, then we'll take care of you. That's what social programs are for" (*Regina Leader Post*, October 9, 1990).

There followed a blizzard of budget cuts issued by order-in-council. Each day brought new announcements, coming so quickly that the media found it impossible to keep up: two thousand civil servant job cuts, school board funding cuts, layoffs of Potash Corporation workers, cuts for municipalities, nursing-home fee increases, cancellation of promised construction projects, the closure of the Regina branch of the provincial medical school, a funding freeze on universities, cuts to the large human service and support sector, cuts in legal aid; cuts in the prescription drug program, the cancellation of the children's dental plan and the sacking of four hundred dental technicians. The list went on and on as the public watched, first in stunned disbelief, then in anger. Then came tax hikes on incomes and gasoline, and an end to controls on utility rates—all of which hit the ordinary taxpayer hardest. The Coalition for Social Justice, a united front of labour and social activists, organized the largest protest demonstration in the province's history in June 1987.

The Devine government's ambitious privatization plans were implemented by a new Orwellian department, the Department of Public Participation.

Throughout 1988 and 1989, a host of public assets were privatized at firesale prices: a sodium sulfate mine, a peat moss operation, most of what was left of SaskOil, the government printing company, a forest product company, the crown computer utility, pieces of SaskTel (from the phone book to the computer division), SaskPower's natural gas reserves (worth $1 billion) sold for $325 million, the government's vast uranium holdings in existing mines, and its huge potash company, which was put up for half its value. And the already well-developed policy of contracting out continued to accelerate. Public support for privatization plummeted, especially after the potash decision, but public opposition became rage after the move to privatize the crown natural gas utility and the general insurance arm of the crown insurance company. The NDP opposition, under new leader Roy Romanow, provided only desultory resistance until public pressure grew. Finally, as the anti-privatization extra-parliamentary movement grew in size and anger, Romanow acted when the privatization of the gas utility was proposed, bringing the legislature to a procedural standstill. Devine backed off, shuffled his cabinet and decided to "re-examine" his privatization strategy. In the end, the big utility crowns were saved, but not before many other things were lost.

The Devine government also began to be tainted by a series of scandals that wounded it deeply and undermined public trust. During the first term there had been the usual stories of excessive patronage flowing freely to Tories and friends of the government: a consultant's job for the premier's brother-in-law, government work and contracts granted without tender, the collapse of Pioneer Trust, and the proposed Rafferty-Alameda dam in the premier's riding. But during Devine's second term a number of more serious scandals developed, starting with revelations about the true size of the deficit and the reversal of Devine's personal assurances regarding privatization and program cuts. The juiciest scandal in 1989 involved GigaText Translation Services, which received $5.25 million in government investment and loans to produce perfect English-to-French translation by computer. No translations ever took place, but the GigaText "hustlers" took the money and disappeared.

The public money squandered on GigaText paled next to the $140 million for the Rafferty-Alameda dam, which proceeded in 1988 after the release of a much-criticized provincial environmental assessment. Since the project affected both interprovincial and international water flows, a federal licence and environmental assessment were required. Devine violated federal law by ignoring these requirements. By the time the legal issues had been resolved, the project was a *fait accompli*. The scandal involving the purchase of buses for the publicly owned Saskatchewan Transportation Company (STC), received still larger headlines. STC's president and vice president of operations were charged with fraud for taking a $50,000 kickback to arrange the purchase of $3 million worth of buses from Eagle International of Texas. Then there were constant stories of business failures, involving nearly $60 million in questionable public loans and grants to a variety of entrepreneurs, involving equal measures of bad judgement and economic desperation, and amid widespread public suspicion that larceny was involved.

Although Devine emerged personally relatively unscathed by the more seedy stories of patronage and scandal, during his second term he was criticized for abusing power, showing contempt for democracy and violating parliamentary norms and conventions. The premier's contempt for the system was already well-known among MLAs and close political watchers, but by his second term he habitually used his power to punish those who defied him, including the legislature's law clerk, the provincial ombudsman and the provincial auditor.

As its second term unfolded, the Devine government tried to solidify its rural strategy. Deep cuts in social spending, an aggressive program of privatizing much of Saskatchewan's large public sector, and a rhetorical defence of the farm sector characterized the premier's continuing efforts to polarize the province along rural/urban and ideological lines. An attempt was made to ensure a replication of the 1986 result in a future election by enshrining that voting pattern in a legislated gerrymander through the *Electoral Boundaries Commission Act, 1986, 1987, 1988* and *The Representation Act, 1989.*

Having put the province deeply in debt (by the end of the Devine government the public debt reached $15,000 for every man, woman and child, the worst provincial debt load in Canada), and with his Ottawa ally in no position to provide expensive political bailouts again, the premier's credibility was wearing thin. His folksy rhetoric and his urban bashing made less and less sense to embattled farmers, who needed friends and not enemies in urban areas. Cuts in social and health spending and unpopular privatization moves were not received in rural areas with the automatic enthusiasm the premier had expected. Threats of legal action by a coalition of lawyers, academics and trade unionists forced the government to refer the constitutionality of its gerrymander to the Saskatchewan Court of Appeal. As a result, Devine's rural strategy increasingly was in tatters. Public and private polls put the NDP fifteen to twenty points ahead of the Tories at mid-term. And Liberal support was holding, a politically fatal fact for the Tories in many rural seats.

With a provincial election constitutionally required by November 1991, the government made a last-ditch effort to bolster its faltering rural strategy. A government "budget review" shocked many by presenting the "harmonization" of the provincial sales tax (PST) with the federal goods and services tax (GST) as a necessary measure to "pay for the protection of Saskatchewan farmers, through programs such as the Gross Revenue Insurance Program (GRIP) and the Net Income Stabilization Account (NISA)." The harmonization—which simply meant adding the 7 percent PST onto the 7 percent GST, thereby extending the PST into many new areas—constituted an extra tax grab of $105 million in the first year and $150 million in each subsequent year. This was the first time in Saskatchewan history that a specific tax levied on everyone had been openly targeted by a government to benefit only one specific group of citizens.

The message was not lost. Urban dwellers and non-farmers were told this extra tax burden would go to help farmers. Farmers knew they should be grateful to the government for bringing them this small measure of additional relief. By this crude pre-election move, the Devine government had again clearly written off urban voters, except the most affluent who benefited from the regime's generally pro-business policies, while openly begging for continuing electoral support in rural areas.

A last desperate measure to woo rural voters was the Fair Share program, which promised a huge decentralization of government services and departments, and up to two thousand jobs in both urban and rural areas. This strategy backfired; public opposition to this program was particularly sustained and bitter throughout the province. The depth of opposition shocked the premier, especially when an independent poll revealed that the gap separating his party from the NDP had grown to 44 percent after the announcement of the Fair Share program.

Thereafter the Devine government began to unravel. Already suffering from the loss through retirement of every cabinet minister but one since his 1982 victory, the premier now faced mutiny in his own ranks. Grant Hodgins, a young rising star in the cabinet and often mentioned as a natural successor to Devine, abruptly announced his resignation on June 17, 1991. He did this dramatically in the House, without having informed the premier. The next day, amid rumours that many Tory backbenchers might fail to show up to support the government in a non-confidence vote, Devine suddenly prorogued the legislature, despite the fact that the budget and a raft of proposed bills, many with important fiscal implications, remained unpassed. The premier himself admitted that he might not have been able to get the budget approved by the legislature. Rather than calling an immediate election, as many expected and convention required, Devine made clear his intention to continue in power. His government began routinely to spend money not approved by the legislature and continued to act as if many of its bills were already law.

By doing so, Devine violated the principle of responsible government. A premier and his cabinet, though appointed by the lieutenant-governor, can only govern as long as they enjoy the confidence of the legislative assembly. Events suggested that the premier no longer commanded the support of a majority in the assembly. Devine was also violating two fundamental principles found in British constitutional practice: governments cannot be arbitrary and subject to the whim of the ruler, but are themselves subject to the law; and new taxes cannot be lawfully imposed without the consent of a parliament.

However, Devine's constitutional sins went much further. He was also violating the spirit of the 1689 *Bill of Rights* which, following the English civil war between king and parliament, had established the principle of the supremacy of parliament over the monarch and his or her ministers, begun the political process that finally led to responsible government, and made it clearly illegal for a government to spend public money without the approval of its parliament. In Saskatchewan, during the last days of the Devine government, the people suffered

under what can only be described as a dictatorship. It was a dictatorship with a
time limit, because the premier was constitutionally required to hold an election
before November 12, 1991, and one that had had its origins in the parliamentary
system, but it was a dictatorship nevertheless.

Devine had intended to call an election during the spring of 1991, in the
midst of the implementation of the PST/GST harmonization and the Fair Share
program. Unfortunately for the premier, on March 6, 1991, the Saskatchewan
Court of Appeal unanimously ruled that the boundaries drawn under his regime's
legislation were unconstitutional. Though the Supreme Court of Canada agreed
to fast-track the Saskatchewan government's appeal of that decision, an election
had to be delayed pending the final outcome. On June 6, 1991, the Supreme
Court voted six to three to overturn the Court of Appeal and upheld the
constitutionality of the boundaries. From that time to the October 21, 1991,
election, Devine "ran scared" up and down the province's rural areas begging for
support. The besieged premier made unabashedly desperate and shockingly
cynical appeals to rural voters: even if the NDP wins more votes, if you stay with
me, we can win again. Devine's behaviour was reminiscent of that of Macbeth
running half-mad through the corridors of Dunsinane castle, unaware until the
very end that Birnam Wood had arrived and Macduff was on the threshold, sword
in hand. Mixing literary metaphors, the final incarnation of Devine was very
much a Frankenstein of the Supreme Court's fateful decision.

It had not needed to be so. Devine's final days need not have been such as
to leave a bad aftertaste and taint the province's history books. Devine's end could
have been one of some dignity rather than the deeply disturbing spectacle that
unfolded in front of the Saskatchewan people. After the unanimous March
decision by the Court of Appeal short-circuited his rural strategy, suddenly the
premier had become a chastened and more thoughtful man. The expected April
election had been postponed. New and fairer boundaries legislation had been
introduced in the legislature. Devine had begun to behave a little more like a
proper premier, respectful of the law, constitution and parliamentary system.

However, the Supreme Court decision changed all that. Devine again had
his electoral trump card, though now soiled. When the legislature began to slip
from his control and his own front benches began to disintegrate, the premier
took the unconstitutional course that led to the 1991 election. The legislature was
shut down, the budget and a whole series of laws were left unpassed, and the
premier began his one-man government, contemptuous of the constitution and
the parliamentary system, unrestrained by law or convention.

On October 21, 1991, the Saskatchewan electorate badly defeated the
Devine government, granting fifty-five seats to the NDP, ten to the Tories and one
to the Liberals. Devine's popular vote was cut to 25.54 percent, just a nose ahead
of the Liberals' 23.29 percent, while Romanow and the NDP received 51.05
percent. The gerrymander had had its effect. After the final enumeration had been
done, the average voter population of the thirty-five rural seats had stood at
9,101, while that of the twenty-nine urban seats was 11,029. Thus, on average,

it took 121 urban votes to equal 100 rural votes. The NDP took twenty-eight of twenty-nine urban seats, with 58 percent of the vote, and twenty-five of the thirty-five rural seats. The rural/urban polarization of the Devine years remained, however, though cloaked by the size of the NDP victory, the strong showing by the Liberals and Devine's unpopularity. The chasm between rural and urban Saskatchewan created by Devine was in fact long-lived, as subsequent elections confirmed. In 1995 the NDP took twenty-six of twenty-eight urban seats and only fourteen of twenty-eight largely rural seats. In 1999, faced by the new Reform/ Tory coalition, the Saskatchewan Party, the NDP was wiped out in rural Saskatchewan, winning only one rural seat (along with twenty-six urban seats and the two northern seats), only clinging to power by entering into a coalition government with the four Liberals elected.

## The Tory Caucus Fraud Scandal: "Operation Fiddle"

The fraud scandal had nothing to do with the defeat of the Devine government nor with any clearly proven criminal wrongdoing, but everything to do with the government's political sins. Certainly many, perhaps most, people in Saskatchewan believed something was terribly wrong with the provincial ship of state. The hints of scandal had been legion, from the Eagle bus kickback scheme to the selling of public assets at low prices, to loan guarantees and outright grants for businesses that never came to fruition. Some of this was seen as old-fashioned patronage—gifts and benefits to political friends, probably legal but unethical. Some was seen in political terms—the Tories were rewarding their class friends, the business lobby and investors in general by pillaging public assets—again, though a moral breach of the public trust, probably technically legal.

Many viewed the Devine regime as just another example of a pro-business government blindly devoted to right-wing ideology, serving the interests of business during the life of the government and receiving their perfectly legal rewards after departure from public office (jobs, seats on boards, consulting fees, insider trading information etc.). After all, in Canada this is one route to upward mobility—win public office, betray the trust of those who elected you, serve the rich, leave office, get rich and live out your life in comfort, if not luxury. The legal line, of course, is usually never crossed. One never takes bribes, kickbacks or benefits from the business lobby while in office. One has to be patient. Brian Mulroney is the most recent beneficiary of this informal reward system. Having served as corporate capital's loyal lieutenant during his years at 24 Sussex Drive, the rewards fell into Mulroney's lap after he resigned from office, like manna from corporate heaven: a seat on the boards of directors or advisory committees of Barrick Gold, Horsham Corporation, Clark USA, Archer-Daniels-Midland, Petrofina SA, Pro-Agro, China International Trust and Investment, Chemical Bank, Power Corporation and Bombardier. Many in Saskatchewan expected to see the same scenario unfold after the defeat of the Devine government—the premier and at least his key ministers would be in payback heaven. As a result of the fraud scandal, this has not happened. Devine and his political cronies have not reaped the legal rewards they might have expected. The business lobby apparently does not want to be linked with what has been the biggest and most sordid fraud scandal in Canadian political history.

The fraud scandal did not become public until February 1993, when the RCMP and the NDP justice minister admitted that there was an investigation underway involving the misuse of caucus expense money. The headlines and general public knowledge did not really start until the first charges were laid on July 28, 1994, against Lorne McLaren, former Tory labour minister and caucus chair, and John Scraba, the former Tory communications director. McLaren was charged with two counts of fraud over $1,000, conspiracy to commit fraud, theft over $1,000, and two counts of breach of trust. Scraba was charged with fraud over $1,000, conspiracy to commit fraud, and the possession of $240,000 cash and a car obtained by means of the commission of an offence.

But for two events that could just as easily not have occurred, the entire scam might never have been exposed. The first event occurred in a Regina hotel bar in spring 1991 when an employee of a crown corporation learned of the suspicions of some employees in the financial offices of the legislature that irregularities appeared to be epidemic in the ways expense money was disbursed to Tory members of the legislative assembly. In July 1991 that employee finally went to the RCMP with information and the investigation began. The police began to interview all those involved in MLA expense funds and their control and distribution, and to obtain the relevant records.

The second event occurred in June 1992 when, as a result of bank branch closures and consolidations, CIBC officials endeavoured to contact all safety deposit box clients, including a certain "Fred Peters" with the address "201 Legislative Building" (in 1990 one of the offices of the Tory caucus). Unable to find Peters, the bank drilled open the box and found $150,000 in one-thousand-dollar bills. The police were called. Records revealed that Mr. Peters had rented the safety deposit box in 1990 and visited it five times that year. Mr. Peters's final visit occurred on January 31, 1991, at which time he paid for two year's rent and informed bank officials he would be out of the country for some time. After a search of records, CIBC officials discovered Mr. Peters had another safety deposit box at the main branch, rented on September 11, 1991, and not visited thereafter. The box was opened after police obtained a search warrant, and $90,000 in one-thousand-dollar bills was discovered. Subsequent police investigation revealed that "Fred Peters" was an alias used by John Scraba to rent the boxes, and the $240,000 was part of the more than half a million dollars that their investigation had already revealed had been siphoned from the Tory MLAs' communications allowances.

These two events—the conversation in a bar and the accidental discovery of the cash in the first safety deposit box—were the keys that unlocked the scam. Investigations after the initial report to the police on the bar conversation had borne some fruit, but only with difficulty and after painstaking reconstruction of many transactions through official records of invoices, cancelled cheques and individual bank records. All financial records of the Tory caucus office had been destroyed. Investigations revealed many, many cash transactions, which are always difficult to reconstruct. Four numbered companies (582806, 582807, 582808 and 593297) had been incorporated in Saskatchewan to issue false invoices (under the imaginative names of Airwaves Advertising, Images Consulting, Communications Group Advertising and System Management Services) and to launder money. All included Scraba and/or Joan Woulds, the Tory caucus office administrator, as officers of the companies. After the defeat of the Tories, the companies had been dissolved and the records destroyed.

Confronted with the evidence, Scraba appears to have struck a deal with investigators and prosecutors, though he continues to deny this. In what is widely believed to have been an exchange for a guilty plea, the provision of ongoing assistance in the investigation and an agreement to act as the key prosecution witness, Scraba got a very light sentence (two years in jail and an order of restitution in the amount of $12,000). Formal deal or not, with Scraba as guide, prosecutors were able to reconstruct many details of the scheme, to assemble enough of a paper trail to embark on a series of successful convictions, and to extract a number of guilty pleas. Lorne McLaren, former labour minister and Tory caucus chair, pleaded guilty and was sentenced to three and a half years in prison; Grant Hodgins, former government house leader, was convicted, granted a conditional discharge and ordered to pay $3,645 restitution; Harold Martens, former associate minister of agriculture, was convicted, granted a conditional discharge and ordered to pay $5,840 restitution; Ray Meiklejohn, former education minister, was convicted, granted a conditional discharge and ordered to pay $4,500 restitution; Michael Hopfner, former Tory caucus chair, was convicted, sentenced to eighteen months in prison and ordered to pay $56,000 restitution; John Gerich, former associate minister of economic development and tourism, was convicted, sentenced to two years in prison and ordered to pay $12,264 restitution; Sherwin Petersen, former highways minister, was convicted, granted a conditional discharge and ordered to pay $9,285 restitution; Harry Baker, former MLA, was convicted, given a one year conditional sentence under curfew in the community and ordered to pay $22,545 restitution; Joan Duncan, former minister of economic development and tourism, pleaded guilty, was fined $5,000 and ordered to pay $12,405 restitution; Bob Andrew, former justice minister, pleaded guilty, was fined $5,500 and ordered to pay $4,500 restitution; Gerald Muirhead, former MLA, was convicted and fined $5,000; Michael McCafferty, former caucus employee, pleaded guilty and was sentenced to one year community service; Beattie Martin, former provincial minister of the family, pleaded guilty and was granted a conditional discharge; and Eric Bernston, former deputy premier and now senator, was convicted, sentenced to one year in jail and ordered to pay $41,735 restitution. The last trial, that of Ralph Katzman, a former MLA and a key figure in handling what were termed "surplus caucus funds," was still pending at the time of writing. Jack Wolfe, a former minister of community services, committed suicide in 1995 while under investigation.

The scheme, dubbed by the RCMP as "Operation Fiddle," was simple. Tory MLAs were encouraged to pool one-quarter of their $13,000 annual personal communication allowance for the general use of the caucus. Participating MLAs (thirty-three of thirty-eight MLAs in 1987 and 1988, for example) signed blank requisitions and these were then attached to fake invoices from one of the numbered companies under the general name of "Communications Group." Cheques were issued by the legislature's accounting office and deposited in the bank accounts of the numbered companies. Cheques would then be written on one of the numbered company accounts payable to the PC caucus. These cheques would be deposited to the caucus account by Scraba who would then withdraw large amounts of cash. The cash would then be distributed variously to individual MLAs, caucus employees, the Tory party and safety deposit boxes. In addition to substantial amounts paid to prominent members of caucus such as McLaren and Bernston, and allegedly to the Tory party, smaller additional amounts from caucus funds—usually as cash in envelopes—were distributed as bonuses to individual MLAs, various minor caucus employees, the party whip and deputy whip, the director of caucus research and the director of communications (Scraba).

Few believe that the whole story has come out, and clearly the police and prosecutors have refrained from charging everyone involved, keeping their attention focused on the key figures. Given the almost total destruction of files and records, except for those documents submitted to and retained by the financial office of the legislature, the full extent of the fraud will probably never be revealed. There are a variety of pressing, unanswered questions. The Regina Metro Progressive Conservative Council trust fund still holds about $2.5 million and paid out about $700,000 to the Tory party between 1993 and 1996. Trust officials claim the fund came from anonymous donors, a violation of *The Election Act*, and refuse to reveal the names, though they insist that no funds from the fraud scam were received. Did some share of these funds come from the fraud scheme, as many still believe? Was a system of kickbacks from entrepreneurs receiving government grants and loan guarantees in place under the Tories? Was influence peddling going on?

Then there is the $455,000 in "surplus" caucus funds that went into the personal bank account of Tory MLA Ralph Katzman. All but $69,000 of these funds disappeared. (In one trial where he testified as a witness, Katzman claimed $250,000 in cash was given by him to someone at a cocktail party, though he had forgotten just who that person was.) Another MLA, testifying at another trial, claimed that Premier Devine himself approved a plan to put Katzman in charge of the management of "surplus caucus funds," a claim the former premier continues to deny.

The Tories had been able to avoid fallout from the fraud scandal during the 1991 election; the investigation had just begun and, though there were many rumours, the lid was kept on until 1993. The 1995 election was a different story, as the electorate learned of the scandal. The Tories won only five seats and just under 18 percent of the vote. All five seats were rural, and four were in loyal, right-wing Tory areas in the southeast and southwest corners of the province.

In the summer of 1997 the Reform Party decided to fill the vacuum on the right created by the collapse of support for the provincial Tories. In response, the five Tory MLAs pushed through the dissolution of the provincial Tories and joined right-wing Liberals and many Reformers in creating the Saskatchewan Party as the new party of the right to challenge the NDP and the remaining Liberals. The Tories, as such, no longer exist as a provincial party in Saskatchewan, the final consequence of "Operation Fiddle" and Devine's lasting legacy to Saskatchewan political history.

## Conclusion

By late March of 1999, fifteen former Tory party officials and MLAs, including ten of cabinet rank, had either pleaded guilty or been convicted of charges including fraud, theft and breach of trust. One other still awaited trial. Four others had been charged, tried and acquitted. In one case the judge dismissed the charge, and in another the former cabinet minister committed suicide while under investigation. The "Tory caucus scam," as many on "coffee row" call it, had captured a great deal of media attention and public comment. No other government or political party in Canadian history has ever been so thoroughly and publicly discredited as a result of criminal trials and convictions.

However, this fraud scam involving the misappropriation of an estimated $1 million to $2 million in communications and research allowances annually provided to sitting MLAs was really a minor abuse of power compared to other actions of the Devine government. The Tories sold off public assets at outrageously low prices, trampled on parliamentary traditions and procedures, governed without apology on behalf of business interests and contrary to the public good, and attempted a blatant gerrymander in an effort to steal the 1991 election. Canada's existing criminal law can catch and punish an MLA or cabinet minister who fraudulently "rips off" a saddle, a computer or some cash, but apparently is unable to bring to justice those guilty of systematically governing contrary to the public interest.

Perhaps the deepest wound, as yet unhealed, that was inflicted by the Devine government on Saskatchewan's civil society was the deliberate creation of a deep rural/urban split that has poisoned Saskatchewan politics.

## Note

1.   The research for this chapter was based in part on Biggs and Stobbe (1991), Conway (1993, 1994), Courtney, MacKinnon and Smith (1992), Pitsula and Rasmussen (1990) and selections from the *Regina Leader Post*, 1982–2000. For additional detail and insight on the Saskatchewan Tory fraud scandal, see Jones (2000).

Part Three
# Corporations

Chapter 7

# Abusing Corporate Power:
## The Death of a Concept

*Laureen Snider*

This chapter is about corporate abuse of power and its disappearance as both a concept and in law. I argue that a corporate counter-revolution has transformed business, politics and society since 1980, and that its greatest success has been the virtual eclipse of the idea that corporations abuse power. Today, *potentially profitable acts cannot be wrong*. As corporate power in all spheres of social life has increased, virtually all of the anti-social, acquisitive, profit-generating acts of business have been redefined, normalized and "de-juridified." In law, this means that many former crimes such as price fixing, creating monopolies, false advertising, poisoning the air and soil or failing to maintain a safe workplace have been transformed into minor regulatory transgressions. Other formerly criminal activities have been completely deregulated, had their legal sanctions removed and are neither *mala in se* (inherently wrong) nor *mala prohibita* (wrong according to social convention). Ideologically, corporate executives whose negligence or greed leads to fraud, injury or death are not presented in the media or seen in popular culture as "criminals." The public relations machines of corporate capital present chief executive officers as blameless.

If offences must be acknowledged, they are called accidental misdeeds caused by the complexity and pace of technology, the intricacies of hierarchy or mindless, whimsical "market forces." Corporate frauds that cannot be denied are portrayed as an unfortunate result of the need to remain competitive in the global marketplace. Market forces themselves are viewed as sacrosanct because they produce, it is argued, Canada's high standard of living. Such forces must not be tampered with for fear of killing the golden goose of prosperity. They are, and must remain, beyond the control of any nation-state or human decision-maker. Zero tolerance for the anti-social but profitable acts of corporate capital is literally unthinkable in economic and political circles today.

Business is not restrained by government or censured by media or religious elites when it removes the economic base of entire towns to generate higher profits for owners and shareholders. It is not illegal for corporations to accept millions of dollars in start-up grants and tax-free allowances and then relocate or shut down when the tax holiday ends; it is perfectly acceptable to pay CEOs millions of dollars in salary and stock options when the company is losing money and firing long-term employees. Such activities are seen not as criminality or greed, but as the unavoidable price to be paid (by employees, not employers or corporate capital) to create "flexible" economic systems. Paying employees wages insufficient to meet their daily needs is not regarded as inhumane. Forcing employees to work sixty-hour weeks or evening and weekend shifts—practices that can destroy family life and impair the ability to parent in a responsible manner—are not censured as criminogenic corporate behaviour. However, should employees take too long for lunch or surf the Internet on company time, they are guilty of "theft of time." In the many U.S. states with "right to work" laws, if workers attempt to fight back by forming unions they may be guilty of felonies. Should employees get injured on the job in the relentless quest to increase productivity, their employers will argue that the worker caused the accident by being careless, hungover or negligent. The message is that employees, rather then employers, lower productivity, take advantage of their bosses, commit crimes and abuse power.

A massive abuse of corporate power has taken place since 1980 as power has increasingly been transferred from citizen and nation-state to corporate capital. As legal fact and ideological category, corporate crime has virtually disappeared. The effects of this corporate counter-revolution, for the average Canadian, have been overwhelmingly negative. To enrich a small percentage of people and organizations at the top of the elite structure has meant that the lives of citizens overall have been impoverished; the sense of Canada as a set of communities where values other than profit maximization are in force has been weakened; and the ability of Canadians to address national problems or forge distinct Canadian solutions has virtually disappeared.

## The Disappearance of Corporate Crime

At the structural and institutional level, corporate crime has been eliminated through downsizing, deregulation and decriminalization. Of course, there is considerable variation in the ways and degrees to which this has been accomplished in different areas of the economy, in different nation-states and for different types of corporate crime. But there is a basic consistency here: In all cases and countries the tendency has been to decrease the recording, monitoring, investigation and punishment of corporate crime. Proposals to strengthen state regulation have been removed from the vocabularies and agendas of government. Pro-regulatory groups must work flat out merely to retain the regulatory structure already in place. Despite business claims, deregulation is not about minimizing the coercive or punitive powers of the state; massive increases in state control over traditional blue-collar criminality have gone hand in hand with massive decreases in state control over crimes of capital. Oblivious to falling rates of (traditional) crime, rates of incarceration in the United States doubled and tripled throughout the 1980s and 1990s, with three strikes laws, boot camps, the abolishment of parole and relentless criminalization of the homeless and unemployed (Cayley 1997; Christie 1993; Snider 1998). Other Western liberal democracies besides Canada have exhibited similar, if somewhat less dramatic, trends. Everywhere we have witnessed zero tolerance of the transgressions of the least privileged people and maximum tolerance of crimes of the powerful.

To document this disappearance of corporate crime, let us examine its two main types, usually characterized as financial and social offences (Cranston 1982; Edelhertz 1970). Financial corporate crimes include competition/combines offences, insider trading and similar frauds against the market; social crimes consist of occupational health and safety offences and environmental crimes. My geographic focus will be on North America.

## Financial Crimes
### Competition, Combines and Deceptive Trade Practices
Competition/combines offences are (or were) anti-competitive practices designed to inflate profits by restraining trade through conspiracies, mergers and monopolies, predatory pricing, price discrimination, resale price maintenance or refusal to supply retailers deemed to be selling too cheaply. The *Combines Investigation Act* passed in Canada in 1889 and the 1890 U.S. *Sherman Act* represent early attempts to proscribe profitable economic practices in the name of citizen protection. The ninety-six-year history of Canada's *Combines Investigation Act* is typical: the enabling legislation was weak (no successful prosecutions under the monopoly provisions were ever registered); it never had adequate funding or enforcement; and each attempt to strengthen it was vigorously opposed by business (Snider 1978). In the post-war period, governments with liberal credentials often sought to reform the *Act*, most notably in 1969 when an *Interim Report on Competition Policy* (Economic Council of Canada 1969) recommended modest reforms, including tighter controls on conspiracies, bid-rigging and other monopolistic practices, and expanded rights for consumers. Predictably, business denounced these "radical" proposals through its national lobbying organizations and the business press. The report was withdrawn and the cabinet minister responsible for its introduction was deposed. For the next ten years new versions of the Bill were introduced, each weaker than the last, each dying an unnatural death. In January of 1976, attempts to reform sections of the *Act* governing restraint of trade were abandoned, and a very modest *Act* was finally passed that provided higher maximum fines for false advertising, extended existing regulations to cover services (such as real estate) as well as products, and prohibited practices such as bait and switch, bid-rigging and pyramid selling (Stanbury 1977).

In 1984 a Conservative government was elected and the new prime minister, Brian Mulroney, denounced the "anti-American," "anti-business" stance of the preceding Liberal government. A blue-ribbon committee to revise the *Combines Investigation Act* was appointed, with representatives from the Canadian Manufacturers Association, Chambers of Commerce, the Grocery Products Manufacturers of Canada—the very groups that had lobbied so successfully against stringent legislation in the past. Notably absent were labour and consumer representatives (although the deputy minister insisted, when pressed, that the

Consumers Association of Canada and "interested academics" were "also consulted"). The committee recommended abolishing the *Combines Investigation Act*, and the requisite legislation was swiftly introduced and enacted, experiencing none of the delays or resistance that stymied attempts to strengthen the *Act*. Its replacement, the *Competition Act* of 1986, had very different goals: to provide a stable and predictable climate for business, to promote competitiveness and to enhance business prosperity. To achieve these goals, it removed criminal sanctions from the merger/monopoly sector, offered businesses advance approval for mergers or monopolies they were contemplating and embraced a "compliance-centred" approach. This major policy reverse passed largely unnoticed in mainstream media and public discourse (Canada, Bureau of Competition Policy 1989; Snider 1993; Stanbury 1986–87).

With corporate capital driving government policy, scrutiny of mergers and monopolies went from weak to virtually nonexistent. From 1986 to 1989, a total of 402 merger files were opened, most of which were unilaterally approved by the new regulatory body. Of the total, it was decided to "monitor" twenty-six proposed mergers, seven were abandoned, nine restructured, five sent to the Competition Tribunal for judgment and two appealed. The number of mergers questioned by government declined until, in 1995–96, only 228 files were opened. In 1996–97 this went up to 319, with 23 deemed problematic enough to require follow-up. Three hundred and sixty-nine were slated for review in 1997–98 (Canada, Industry Canada 1998). This modest increase—in reviews, not charges—was described by the business press as "a crack down by the competition cops" (*Globe and Mail*, March 30, 1998: B4). More significantly, these numbers indicate that most mergers are quickly approved; in fact, so few cases go to the Competition Tribunal that even front-line staff worry that "too many negotiated compromises occur" (Doern 1995a: 77).

In the Marketing Practices Branch, responsible for false and misleading advertising and price misrepresentation, decriminalization was initially resisted. The official goal remained the achievement of "fair treatment of consumers" (Doern 1995a: 89). However, this was the same branch hardest hit by downsizing and the 1986 *Act*. In the following decade it lost most of its staff and budget, its regional structure was eliminated and almost all of the regional offices—part of a protective network that once stretched from sea to sea—were closed. The rationale was in part technological; the whole operation was to be rendered more accessible by going online. Staff who survived downsizing were subjected to compulsory "re-education," presumably to disabuse them of the quaint notion that charging and sanctioning corporate offenders (now renamed "clients") is a socially useful practice. Under the new regime, deceptive advertising—a fraud that produces massive profit windfalls—is presented as primarily an accidental act requiring noncriminal remedies and, perhaps, gentle counselling.

Given this dramatic shift, it is not surprising that levels of prosecution plunged. Charges for conspiracy, discriminatory and predatory pricing, misleading or deceptive practices and price maintenance declined by 33 percent, from thirty-seven in 1982–84 and thirty-six in 1984–86 to twenty-three in 1986–88. This was not the result of higher business standards or declining complaint levels. Only in 1995–96, when the closure of regional offices of the Competition Bureau reduced visibility and made it difficult for the average citizen to register a complaint, did complaint numbers fall. Thus the number of false advertising complaints logged fell from 15,130 in 1991–92 to 6,751 in 1995–96. Similarly, eighty-two follow-up inquiries began in 1991–92, but only eight in 1995–96. The number of cases referred by regulators to the attorney general for charges also declined (the branch cannot lay criminal charges; it can only recommend that they be laid). From 1991–92 to 1995–96, cases recommended for charges dropped from fifty-five to seven, prosecutions declined from forty-four to seven, and convictions from forty-three to fourteen. As these statistics reveal, most complaints were abandoned at the earliest stage of investigation. In the spring of 1998, the final nail was hammered into this coffin when a Bill to officially decriminalize deceptive and fraudulent marketing was introduced in the House of Commons (Canada, Industry Canada 1998: 3; *Globe and Mail*, May 5, 1998: B3). The initiative was spearheaded, ironically, by the same Liberal party that had struggled, only a scant decade earlier, to strengthen criminalization.

The 1986 *Competition Act*, then, represented the end of an era. It valorized competition, not citizen protection. This "reform" was supposed to remedy the defects in the *Combines Investigation Act*, particularly the legally unenforceable stipulation requiring the Crown to prove that each proposed monopoly represented "a detriment to the public." Instead the *Act* eliminated "public interest" as the measuring rod for regulators to evaluate a proposed merger or monopoly and substituted the goal of seeking "efficiency" through a "competitive economy." This new holy grail will, it is presumed, maximize economic welfare. Social welfare is ignored. Corporatist thinking assumes that we are what we consume, so this becomes the identity and goal of citizens and government. But the basic concept of "efficiency" is far from problem-free; it comes replete with ideological and cultural baggage. Is the objective of efficiency to be "the means that will accomplish the desired end at the least net cost" (Wuthnow 1994: 631) or "the optimal use of scarce resources" (Marshall 1998: 184–85)? Can we assume, as the *Act* appears to do, that individual and collective welfare are compatible rather than competitive objectives? Why is maximizing individual "freedom of choice"—the ability of individuals to buy goods—automatically privileged over other goals such as achieving a civil society, equality or full employment? Why do unelected business and intellectual elites, the CEOs and economic gurus whose thinking permeates policy, have the power to decree that "rational" individuals want to maximize income above all else, or that state intervention in the affairs of business is "coercive," but the ubiquitous and undefined "market forces" are "beneficial"? For that matter, when did Canadians vote to make "the spread of market principles to all walks of life" a major goal of Canadian government policy (Doern 1995b: 9–10)? All of these highly political and contentious notions are hidden in corporate law reform, disguised as "technical details" on competition policy that only experts can understand and debate. In this way, then, changing laws that govern offences of the powerless (such as legalizing marijuana or increasing penalties for welfare fraud) become the stuff of public debate; everyone has the right to voice an opinion on these. But removing criminal penalties for corporate fraud or theft is an issue only economists and trade experts can debate.

In true Canadian fashion[1] the 1986 *Competition Act* was modelled upon practices originating in the United States, driven by knowledge claims originating in right-wing economic think-tanks. As we shall see again and again, the corporate counter-revolution was officially inaugurated by the return of the Republican party to power and the 1980 election of Ronald Reagan in the United States. (The election of Margaret Thatcher's Conservatives in the United Kingdom was of secondary importance to Canadian policy-makers, though it too fed the ideological counter-revolution.) Large cuts in corporate tax rates and the onset of the takeover craze of the 1980s began transforming corporate America. Between 1980 and 1988, 26,671 mergers and acquisitions involving assets of $1,083.4 billion took place in the U.S. (Adams and Brock 1986). The Federal Trade Commission (FTC), the body responsible for overseeing mergers and monopolies, had never been effective in restraining capital's monopolistic urges (Green et al. 1972; Nader and Green 1973), largely because the unrivalled social capital of business in America made every government restriction on capital morally suspect and politically perilous (Calavita et al. 1997). In addition, pro-enforcement social movements such as consumers' groups never had much lobbying power or clout compared to business. Thus, outraged defrauded consumers have never been the major players forcing the FTC to take regulatory action; the primary activists have been other corporations seeking to use the FTC to weaken competing firms.[2] Thus, in 1996–97 the FTC and the Justice Department investigated just 150 of 3,700 planned mergers in the United States, intervened in 60 and filed court actions against 14 (Milner 1998: B1, 3).[3] However, the American position on monopolization is an interesting one because, while there is something approaching consensus among economists on the supremacy of competition as a policy goal (Doern 1995b: 11–12), there is also an ongoing, virulent hatred of government regulation as a means of achieving this or any policy objective. Thus U.S. competition policy reflects shifts in the balance of power between government-hating politicians and business elites versus combine-hating economists and policy gurus.

### Frauds against the Market

Deregulation, downsizing and decriminalization have also occurred in the regulation of stock exchanges. Here again the American example, given U.S. domination of the world economy, and the Canadian economy in particular, is pivotal. The Securities and Exchange Commission (SEC), a national, federal regulatory agency, was established in 1933–34 as a key component of Roosevelt's New Deal reforms (Condon 1992; Seligman 1982). Although the SEC was essential in rescuing capitalism at the height of the Depression, and although fair, competitive markets of exchange are basic to the survival of capitalist economies (Snider 1991), capital in general and American capital in particular have never fully accepted state regulation. This is particularly true of the fractions of capital dominating the Republican party. Reagan's presidency resulted in three hundred SEC staff losses between 1981 and 1986 and extensive deregulation, even though the aforementioned takeover frenzy of the 1980s doubled the number of securities the SEC was charged with monitoring. The resurgence of the Republicans in the House of Representatives in the congressional elections of 1994 had a similar effect.

Struggles to regulate this area of economic crime also run up against the quintessentially libertarian resistance to government that dominates American political and economic discourse. Rationally, it is very much in the interests of capital as a class[4] to control the cowboys of capitalism. Fraud artists who sell shares in non-existent gold mines or Florida swampland, or owners who systematically "loot" company assets to drive them into bankruptcy, undermine public confidence in the economic system, thereby jeopardizing the supply of investment capital.

Thus it is instructive to consider the non-rational response by economic elites and the U.S. Congress to the savings and loan (S&L) crisis, a massive fraud that was a direct result of 1980s deregulation in the banking sector. Before 1980, federal laws had restricted investments by owners and managers of savings and loan institutions (known as "thrifts") to solid and safe areas of the economy. S&Ls had to maintain a certain percentage of their assets as capital reserve, and U.S. states were not allowed to override or circumvent these rules. But in the early 1980s these regulations were systematically repealed, with the sole (and criminogenic) exception of the provision guaranteeing S&L losses through federal insurance.

By the latter half of the decade, large numbers of S&Ls were going bankrupt, stealing the savings of thousands of ordinary Americans. Because of the federal guarantee, secured creditors, typically large corporations and banks, suffered far less. In the end, 284 institutions failed, the majority in states with minimal state regulation, such as Texas and California. Mean losses were put at $500 billion ($12 million per institution). This amounted to about $5,000 for every American household—at the time, the most expensive fraud ever perpetrated. Investigation showed that S&L executives had perfected several types of theft. "Hot deals" were frauds where the owners of S&Ls engaged in land flips, nominee loans and reciprocal lending, with huge sums "lent" in return for deposits. "Looting" occurred when owners siphoned off monies they were supposed to invest, paid themselves enormous salaries and bonuses, and charged expensive holidays, yachts and limousines to company accounts. "Falsifying records" took place when misleading or inaccurate financial accounts were produced. Audits, required by U.S. law, mysteriously certified blatantly mismanaged companies with unwieldy debt loads and scores of bad investments as financially sound and healthy, sometimes merely days before they collapsed. As a result, every major accounting firm in the United States (except one) was implicated in the S&L frauds for producing false, dishonest and misleading audit/account statements (Calavita et al. 1997; New York Times, June 10, 1990; Observer, April 8, 1990; Zey 1993).[5]

Most perpetrators of S&L frauds were never charged or sanctioned.[6] Nonetheless, the cost of investigating and prosecuting the tiny minority who were indicted challenged the resources of the world's richest country. However, enforcement costs, estimated from 1989 to July 1996 alone to be $500 billion (Calavita et al. 1997), were only one of several key factors that allowed most perpetrators to escape unscathed (the political and economic power of the offenders was even more crucial). Because deregulation was an obvious cause of this disaster, which was for a very short time a *cause célèbre* in the U.S. media, Congress was forced to take action to put back the regulations it had earlier repealed. But this re-regulation was short-lived: the minute the Republicans took control of the House of Representatives in 1994, deregulation was back on the agenda. Federal controls on banks were once again relaxed or repealed (producing a 276 percent increase in the number of independent commercial banks) (American Bankers Association, *Harper's Index*, July 1998: 13). And, in 1995, legislation to downsize the SEC was once again introduced (Calavita et al. 1997; Fishman 1998; New York Times, June 10, 1990; Observer, April 8, 1990; Zey 1993).

The last major type of financial crime, insider trading, appears at first glance to be an exception to the deregulatory craze. The United States is recognized worldwide as the leader in promulgating laws and prosecuting corporate insiders for profiting on inside knowledge that is not available to the wider investment community. In this area the SEC is depicted as a tough no-nonsense regulator with zero tolerance for miscreants, as illustrated by the prosecution of high-profile, high-flying entrepreneurs such as Michael Milken, Ivan Boesky, Dennis Levine and Martin Siegel in the late 1980s. Government investigators, it is said, effectively put an end to "a system of mutual back scratching" by "takeover specialists seeking to buy or sell companies, the investment bankers who arranged the deals and the speculators who purchased the stocks of the companies in play" (*Globe and Mail*, July 13, 1991: B5). Between 1985 and late 1999 the SEC had pursued "nearly 500 cases of illegal insider trading and raked in penalties totalling $4.5 billion U.S." (*Globe and Mail*, October 18, 1999: B10). Thus average small investors, at least in the United States, can be assured of a level playing field when they invest their money in the stock market. Capital is disciplining its most blatant antisocial actors, behaving rationally to safeguard its own long-term interest in creating investor confidence.

Why is it, then, that "Americans lose about $1 million *an hour* to securities fraud," according to the North American Securities Administrators Association (Fishman 1998: 41, emphasis mine)? It is well known that companies routinely issue false statements about their expected or actual earnings, misleading and defrauding the average investor. For example, Cendant Corporation, a giant software/financial services firm created in 1997 through the merger of CUC International and HFS Inc., inflated its 1997 earnings by $100 million. The stock fell 47 percent on April 16, 1998, when Cendant "restated" (that is, corrected) its earlier announcement, and "an internal audit revealed that accounting 'irregularities' had inflated CUC's 1995–97 income by $500 million" (Fishman 1998: 38–9). Stock swindlers hyping worthless stocks steal an average of $6 billion a year, and million-dollar thefts are a "near daily occurrence" (Fishman 1998: 40–41). Of the $5.2 billion in fines levied by the SEC on companies since 1985, only $2.7 billion has been collected (Fishman 1998: 41).[7] This is tight regulation? Indeed, the few and feeble efforts made by regulators to tighten control have been met by impassioned resistance from financial interests on Wall Street and its lobbyists, backed with massive campaign donations to candidates opposing increased regulation. In 1995, laws making it harder for investors to sue securities firms for fraud were passed, while in the 1996 elections, twelve of the top forty corporate donors were securities firms (Fishman 1998: 38).

Thus even where stock market fraud seems poised to destroy the system of exchange that is the very foundation of capitalism, deregulatory ideology retains its hold on financial elites (and thus on U.S. law). This does not mean total deregulation is the rule. As noted, the security of exchange markets is pivotal to world capitalism. Thus, particularly in the U.S., massive frauds regularly occur and are regularly assessed sanctions which are a small proportion of the amounts extorted, as in the Drexel Burnham scandal where $650 million in fines and a ten-year prison sentence (Milken served four years) were assessed for insider trading and failure to disclose information (Zey 1993).

Other capitalist countries have done even less than the U.S. to control corporate fraud. A recent investigation of insider trading in Canada by journalists, not government regulators, revealed that "of the 28 friendly mergers or acquisitions announced between July 31, 1998 and July 31, 1999, valued at more than $150 million, the share price of almost half rose by more than 25% between the times the companies began talking and the night before the deal was disclosed" (*Globe and Mail*, October 18, 1999: B1). In many of the deals, shares rose 50 percent or more, while stock prices overall, as measured by the Toronto Stock Exchange Index (and other relevant indicators), rose two to three percent during the same period. Clearly inside parties were benefitting from their knowledge. None of these deals has led to charges by the Ontario Securities Commission or any other regulatory body. The Bre-X scandal in Canada (where it was discovered in May of 1997 that samples documenting the "world's richest gold find," in Busang, Indonesia, were salted) has produced tighter regulations at the Ontario Securities Commission and the Toronto Stock Exchange, but the brokers who touted the stock and then sold out before it collapsed have not been sanctioned or held accountable.

Corporate fraud is increasingly global. In most countries it is under-punished and under-reported. "British utility regulation has fallen victim to the dynamics of stock-market capitalism" (Wilks 1998:141); its only master now is the financial markets. The Bank of Credit and Commerce International (BCCI) was an organization structured to escape regulatory scrutiny by being offshore everywhere (Punch 1996). Blame for spectacular collapses such as the bankruptcy of Barings Bank and the manipulation of copper prices by Sumitomo in Japan is deflected onto individuals, the so-called "rogue traders" in world capital markets (Nick Leeson and Yasuo Hamanaka in the preceding examples). The economic system that creates, supports, legitimates and richly rewards such speculation escapes scrutiny (Levi 1993, 1995; Passas and Nelken 1993). News stories, when they discuss such frauds at all, never mention deregulation, commodity ownership and free-for-all financial capitalism in the litany of causality. Structures of world capitalism are not part of the "vocabulary of motives" employed to explain these crimes (Melossi 1993). Charges of "gross negligence" can be laid against car drivers who unintentionally cause thousand-dollar accidents, but not against corporations that cause billion-dollar losses. Citizens, we are told, clamour for government crackdowns on squeegee kids and welfare moms, not jail time for CEOs and investment companies. What we see here is the highly ideological construction of social blame. Corporate spokespeople and the business press tell defrauded investors they have only themselves to blame—they were careless or greedy or did insufficient research. Or losses are attributed to the vagaries of market forces. *Caveat emptor* reigns. Citizens who have cars stolen, however, are not encouraged to blame themselves because the vehicle was unlocked. And state law certainly does not excuse a burglar because the house contained visible and valuable goods. Blame is directed onto the perpetrator where the offence and offender are individual and low level and the financial loss is small, but onto the victim where the perpetrator is corporate and powerful.

## Social Crimes
### Occupational Health and Safety
The ideological and political losses suffered by progressive forces over the past two decades are glaringly obvious in occupational health and safety issues. The layers of regulation and assorted safeguards which established minimum standards in the workplace and put in place the rights and protective legislation workers could expect—the product of decades of struggle and debate (Snider 1993)—have been systematically attacked. Crimes against occupational health and safety, defined as illegal acts which threaten the health and safety of employees and consumers, once covered a wide range of profitable but dangerous policies and practices. Regulations governed ventilation, light levels, and temperature in mines, factories and offshore drilling rigs. They specified minimum wage levels and maximum work weeks and mandated coffee breaks, overtime pay, safety equipment, guards on machines, and air quality monitors. They were backed up by government inspectors with broad regulatory powers, at least on paper. Loopholes and lenience were legendary, and there was tremendous variation in the level and efficacy of enforcement, which varied by sector, region and nation-state (Snider 1991). However, all in all these laws were part of a network of

welfare state legislation that transformed the conditions of work in the twentieth century.

These laws, which had their beginnings in the nineteenth century, have been strenuously resisted by business (Carson 1980). The reasons are threefold: (1) occupational health and safety laws challenge ownership rights, the rights of employers to do what they like with "their" employees in "their" workplace; (2) they challenge contract rights, imposing what employers consider an artificial barrier between owners and employees; (3) they add direct costs to production while providing no corresponding benefit to capital (Ursel 1992).

Thus it is not surprising that one of the first acts of the neo-liberal Republicans in 1979 was to downsize, disembowel and disempower the Occupational Safety and Health Administration (OSHA), the federal agency responsible for occupational health and safety in the United States. Regulations requiring specific labelling of hazardous chemicals were repealed, "walk around" pay (allowing workers to accompany inspectors on tours of workplaces without having their pay docked) was ended and exposure standards for cotton dust (a cause of "brown lung" disease) were raised (Calavita 1983). By 1992, OSHA was reduced to 2,150 inspectors to cover 5.9 million employers, meaning it could at best inspect three percent of workplaces. Of the 526 "known carcinogens" to which 25 million workers are regularly exposed, exposure limits had been designated for less than one-quarter (Noble 1995). OSHA was attacked with particular fervour because it was one of the few regulatory agencies to adopt strict enforcement policies toward offenders, an exception in a world where conciliatory, "educational" approaches were the norm (Green 1994). Throughout the 1980s OSHA's most virulent critics were appointed to head key OSHA departments, and public burnings of pamphlets informing workers of their right to refuse unsafe work or to demand information about dangerous substances in the workplace were instituted (Clarke 1990: 207).

However, the traditional kinder and gentler regulatory agencies fared little better in the America of the early 1980s. Elsewhere, although the rhetoric was softer, the results were much the same. Self-regulation, in particular "the Robins system," quickly replaced state regulation, albeit with significant nation-state differences. Self-regulation allows teams of employees with different ranks, specializations and expertise to negotiate the working conditions they will accept, determine the speed and pace of work, and set their own production targets within management-determined limits. The employer rewards highly productive teams with bonuses and prestige, and penalizes groups falling below target. The discourse of individualism and the celebration of choice make self-regulation highly appealing, by promising lower costs to industry and lower taxes to all. In theory, state regulation is downsized rather than eliminated; it provides the framework for team negotiations; and state law sets the outer limits of exploitation and worker "consent." In practice, by the early 1990s, state regulation had virtually disappeared in many workplaces and nations (Hutter and Lloyd-Bostock 1992; Tombs 1996).

This is not to say there has been no resistance or that all resistance has been futile. As noted above, significant nation-state differences remain. In locales such as the American South, where neo-liberal rhetoric is strong and union ideology dangerous to espouse, what little regulation there was quickly disappeared. Britain, on the other hand, a country with a powerful union movement throughout the twentieth century, is a particularly interesting case. There Margaret Thatcher, using models copied from America, tried to destroy overnight what she called "the nanny state" (Hogwood 1996; Wilks 1998). However, she was unlucky, because dismantling the state's protective legislation led to a string of highly public disasters. The Piper Alpha oil rig exploded in the North Sea in 1988, killing 167 employees. Then 188 passengers drowned when the aptly named *Herald of Free Enterprise* sank at Zeebrugge. In addition, many newly privatized industries, touted as superior to public sector endeavours in every way, delivered overpriced and unreliable water, electricity and gas, while rewarding their executives with excessive salaries and generous bonuses. For many, the mad cow disease (bovine spongiform encephalopathy, or BSE) disaster was the last straw and limited re-regulation occurred (Hogwood 1998; Pearce and Tombs 1998; Tombs 1996). As Wilks (1998) has pointed out, in some spheres the privatization of utilities and services forced government to create entirely new regulatory structures.

However, public belief in state regulation suffered a mortal blow throughout the 1980s and 1990s, in the face of heavily promoted arguments which portrayed "government" as synonymous with inefficiency, featherbedding and corruption (Doern and Wilks 1996; Snider 1996). Monetarist economic theories that viewed the corporation as a "nexus of transacting relationships" questioned the state's moral right to regulate. Globalization and the need to remain "competitive," plus the reduction in tax levels for corporations and the richest individuals, undermined the state's fiscal ability to regulate. In the U.S. the Republican-controlled Congress has created new rights for capital, allowing companies to seek compensation for the "negative impacts of regulation" on profit levels. Moreover, the costs of regulation are to be deducted from the (already miniscule) budgets of regulatory agencies themselves (Doern and Wilks 1996: 9).

Meanwhile, in the reworked, "loosely coupled" transnational corporation of the 1990s, self-regulation delivered something very different from the more efficient but equally effective health and safety it promised. Instead of improving workplace conditions and eliminating red tape, it has changed the definition of safety, altering "the limits of acceptable discourse regarding safety regulation" and redefining the word "hazard" (Tombs 1996: 325). Now, with workplace teams setting production quotas, more "reasonable" (employer-friendly) definitions of risk have come into play (Walters et al. 1995), and conditions which would be expensive to fix are unlikely to be identified as hazards. Management's traditional responsibility for ensuring worker safety has vanished, because workers who have "freely" agreed to certain conditions and collaborated in setting safety standards are poorly positioned to complain. Indeed, there is less likely to be anybody to complain to.[8] With state watchdogs an endangered species and "flexible" workplace standards the norm, determining the meaning of worker "consent" becomes as difficult as holding management accountable for worker injury, sickness or death.

## Crimes Against the Environment

Forces seeking enhanced environmental protection by curbing the misdeeds of corporate North America have suffered heavy losses. Laws protecting the environment and targeting profitable behaviours which endanger the health, habitat and survival of all forms of life represent one of the newer forms of corporate criminalization. In the past, particularly in North America, the environment was treated as a "free good." A key competitive advantage industries in the New World had over their Old World competitors was the availability of "free" water, game, fish and other natural resources, whereas in Europe land-based aristocracies and population pressures forced new industries into expensive battles against rival claimants (Snider 1987). (The rights of First Nations people were, of course, denied and ignored.) As with legislation regulating occupational health and safety, environmental laws were fiercely resisted by industry because they added to the costs of production and threatened the rights of private property holders. But there are key differences between the two social crimes.

In occupational health and safety, workers and managers may disagree on all else, but they agree on the necessity of large-scale, resource-extracting industrial production. However, some streams of environmentalism do not hold this view and thus threaten the basic assumptions of all industrial societies. The philosophical premises of deep or radical ecology challenge the beliefs that every river, tree, idea and genome exists only to be marketed for private profit; that buying and using up commodities is always desirable; and that there are no naturally imposed limits to production and growth that modern science cannot overcome. A second difference revolves around the power of the groups supporting government regulation. In occupational health and safety it is workers (especially those in primary and secondary industry) and their unions who are most committed to state regulation and have the most to lose when it disappears. The power base of these groups, the industrial sectors they represent and the number of people they employ are all in decline, threatened by downsizing, the growth of tertiary industry and the ascendance of the knowledge economy, the new engine of growth. However, the primary proponents of environmental regulation are media-savvy middle-class groups with sizable financial and organizational resources. While this has not prevented downsizing and deregulation of environmental crimes, it has affected their pace and produced widely publicized struggles over their wisdom and feasibility.

Most environmental legislation originated in the protest movements of the 1970s. Pollution Probe was formed in Toronto in 1969, followed by the Canadian Environmental Law Association in 1970. Greenpeace was founded in 1971.

(Governments back then saw regulation as a solution to problems!) In Canada, nine new federal environmental statutes were enacted between 1968 and 1972, several provincial governments established regulatory agencies and the omnibus *Environmental Protection Act* was passed in 1988. In the United States, a new federal agency, the Environmental Protection Agency (EPA), was formed in 1970. Environmental regulation was first targeted for elimination by the Reagan Republicans, and EPA budgets were cut by 19 percent between 1980 and 1985. However, a series of environmental disasters and strong public support allowed budgets to recover to pre-Reagan levels by the early 1990s. Then the Republican victories in Congress in 1994 produced reductions of 7.5 percent in 1995 and 1996 (Hoberg 1998). (Given that many Republicans wanted much larger cuts, these 7.5 percent reductions have been hailed by some as victories.) In Canada, public support for environmental issues has always been strong, despite Canada's greater reliance on primary and secondary industry for its economic prosperity. The federal government made no real attempts to cut back on environmental protection until the early 1990s, when the infamous and misnamed "Regulatory Reform" Bill was passed (Snider 1996).

This does not mean that environmental law in Canada was stringently or effectively enforced until 1992. A mandatory review of the 1988 *Environmental Protection Act*, undertaken in 1995 by a gung-ho, environmentally friendly committee of parliamentarians, revealed that twenty-eight investigators and thirty-one inspectors were responsible for enforcing federal environmental law throughout the entire country. Environment Canada was found to be ignoring its own policy directives on enforcement, which called for "strict compliance," in favour of a permissive philosophy of "compliance promotion" (Environment Canada 1995). From 1988 to 1995, a total of sixty-six prosecutions produced fifty-one convictions, a less-than-impressive average of 7.2 actions per year. The most common "sanctions" assessed under the *Act* were warnings—in 1993–94, for example, 120 warnings and 3 prosecutions resulted from 1,548 inspections. The *Environmental Assessment Act*, passed in 1992 but not proclaimed into law until 1994, lacks standards, penalties and basic rules specifying when public reviews must be held. If a public environmental review is held (and few have been), its recommendations are not binding, Cabinet can overrule them if it wishes. Since no definition of "expert" is provided by the *Act*, companies can shop for industry-friendly "scientists" who will support their claims. There are reports of experts selling their services to the highest bidder, or redoing reports to make them "more benign" in the eyes of industry; as one policy expert concludes, the *Act* is a disaster (Nikiforuk 1997: 17). Meanwhile Canada, like most industrial countries, has more than sixty thousand industrial chemicals in use, with a thousand new ones introduced annually. Yet Environment Canada's "Domestic Substances List" designated only 44 of 28,000 substances as regulatory priorities and assessed only 5 in ten years, a rate which translates into "38 bureaucrat years per chemical" (Leiss 1996: 132).

Dominant anti-regulatory philosophies at Environment Canada, relentless and unceasing lobbying by industry (particularly the Business Council on National Issues and the chemical, forestry, and pulp and paper lobbies) and massive and continuous government downsizing are responsible for this impasse (Doern 1995b; Doern and Conway 1994; Leiss, VanNijnatten, Darier and Mitchell 1996). The *coup de grâce* was delivered by the *Regulatory Efficiency Act,* which in 1992–93 eliminated 30 percent of the budget of Environment Canada. In 1994–95 the budget was cut again, from $705 million to $507 million. Personnel have been reduced from ten thousand in 1992–93 to less than four thousand in 1994–95. As well, the department of environment lost its designation as a senior ministry, giving it less clout inside cabinet, less voice in government decisions, and even fewer resources (*Globe and Mail*, May 27, 1998: A3; July 30, 1997: A3; August 19, 1997: A1).

In Ontario the provincial government has been targeting regulation in general, and social regulation in particular, since the election of the right-wing populist Conservatives under Mike Harris in 1995. Because the Harris Conservatives came after the left-leaning New Democratic Party, in power under Bob Rae from 1991 to 1995, the contrast was particularly stark. From 1987–88 to 1993–94, Ontario's Ministry of the Environment was one of the most effective agencies in the country. It pressed two hundred to three hundred prosecutions per year and maintained high conviction rates (Gallon 1996). In 1995–96, right after the Conservatives took power, 725 enforcement and investigation officials were let go. Annual charges dropped from 1,640 in 1994 to 724 in 1996. Prosecutions in some regions dropped 74 percent, and fines declined 57 percent between 1995 and 1996. The average pollution fine dropped from a high of $3 million in 1992 to $1 million in 1997. In 1997 several hundred officials monitoring and researching air and water quality were dismissed, and the number of pollution inspectors fell by 28 percent from 1995 to 1998 (*Globe and Mail*, June 22, 1998: A1). The annual operating budget fell from $390 million in 1993–94 to $150 million in 1995–96, and then was cut by another third in 1997. And that is just the operating budget—the capital budget has fallen 81 percent and staff levels are down 32 percent. Overall, charges dropped by 50 percent from 1992 to 1997, from 2,163 to 954. Access to information was also a casualty; the "real" figures may actually be lower than those just mentioned. For example, the Canadian Institute for Environmental Law and Policy claims that pollution fine levels actually totalled a mere $955,000 (instead of $1.2 million).

Industry self-regulation has replaced the Ministry of Natural Resources in environmentally high-risk areas such as forestry, gravel pits, and petroleum. Electricity has been deregulated with no provision for the major increases in air pollution likely to result from deregulation. Ontario, once a leader in environmental protection, now lobbies *against* national initiatives to implement the Kyoto Accord, decrease levels of acid rain, reduce smog or regulate the sulphur content of gasoline. It recently removed much of the environmental science from elementary and high school curricula, and it has ended almost all of its acid rain monitoring and research. Such initiatives were quite transparently driven by ideology rather than economics—even though presented and rationalized in economic terms—because it is not in the long-term best interests of any government to allow industry to destroy the natural base on which production ultimately depends. This is especially true in a province such as Ontario, where the exploitation of fish, wood, water and other natural resources is still a mainstay of the economy, and where eco-tourism is expected to become ever more important.

All of this demonstrates that allowing industry (now "the client," or "stakeholder") to set the environmental agenda has not produced more efficient and effective environmental protection. Canada has admitted that its industries have failed to meet targets promised at the Earth Summit in Rio de Janiero in 1992; Canada's output of greenhouse gases has increased by 10 percent from 1990 to 2000. Federal decentralization and off-loading of environmental responsibility are ongoing. And the federal commitments to environmental protection made in Kyoto in December 1997, modest through they were, appear increasingly out of reach (Emmett 1998; *Globe and Mail*, August 15, 1997: A14; October 4, 1997: D1; Nikiforuk 1997; *Toronto Star*, April 11, 1998: E5).[9]

## Conclusion

This chapter has documented a significant ideological shift in ways of thinking about corporate power, corporate accountability and corporate crime. The nation-state has systematically given up its legal right and moral obligation to control the predatory, anti-social acts of its most powerful players. While strengthening state power to criminalize those at the bottom of the increasingly unequal class hierarchy, it has downsized and destroyed its capacity to criminalize those at the top. As long as the average CEO resists the urge to buy a gun and rob a bank, confining corporate theft to the stock market or consumer, such theft will escape public censure and prosecution. As long as the corporation poisons people by releasing toxins into the air, water and workplace, and not by putting cyanide into bottles of vitamins (or into the cereal bowl of a spouse or employee), it will be celebrated as model citizen. A legal and regulatory structure that took centuries of struggle to put in place has been weakened and, in many sectors, destroyed. Crime and punishment have become a cultural obsession of modernity. But this obsession is onesided. The harm that primarily powerless individuals do to themselves, their relatives and acquaintances, and occasionally to strangers is demonized, decried and exaggerated, while the harm that corporations do to their employees, communities, competitors and the environment is minimized, rationalized and denied. The cultural and ideological victory which allowed this transformation to occur must surely rank as the greatest abuse of corporate power thus far.

## Notes

1. The influence of the United States, at present the world's dominant economy, has been alternately cursed and lauded in Canada since Confed-

eration. With globalization, nations from Japan to the United Kingdom are experiencing the full pressures of American-style capitalism for the first time. Whether they will fare better than Canada at fending off U.S. cultural products and ideological demands, transmitted as they are through a country's own business and knowledge elites, remains to be seen. Given the near-total takeover and collapse of the Canadian nation-state, particularly since the Free Trade Agreement was signed, it is hard to see how they could fare any worse.

2.    The highly publicized prosecution of Bill Gates and Microsoft Corporation launched in the spring of 1998 was actively sought by Microsoft's competitors, particularly Netscape. Historical precedent—such as that set by the prosecution of big oil in the 1970s—cautions against consumer optimism. At best, the prosecution may produce benefits for a few large competitors by stopping Microsoft from tying its internet search engine to Windows (Edstrom and Eller 1998).

3.    The point here is not to praise competition laws. Economists are divided on whether government intervention to create a "true" competitive environment is good for the economy (always the criterion economists use). Certainly the idealized *laissez-faire* capitalism of the eighteenth century is long gone. My concern here is whether the so-called competitive economy is good for the majority—for employees, consumers and citizens. The evidence is mixed. In the post-war period some oligopolies did deliver job security and decent wages to a generation of employees (Simpson 1987). However, companies had to be forced by unions to do this, and the shareholders' revolution and merger mania of the 1980s ended such practices. The 1990s saw increased global concentration but few benefits for employees in "leaner, meaner" corporations intent on downsizing, outsourcing and cost-cutting. High corporate debt loads and the intensification of short-term management, linked to the globalization of stock markets and the need to show profits every quarter, may have negative consequences for all players and interests (Zey 1993).

4.    Capital as a class does not have intentions—people have motives, structures do not. The actions of capital are taken by thousands of corporate executives, stock traders and the like. But these individual actions do have a particular shape. Their intention is to maximize share prices, profit levels and productivity. This means persuading other players to put up risk capital, an enterprise which is collectively imperilled if trust in the stock exchange system disappears.

5.    Calavita et al. (1997) refer to this process of purposefully bankrupting a heretofore legitimate company as "collective embezzlement."

6.    The best estimates are that about 14 percent of all suspected offenders were prosecuted, with considerable variation between states. In Texas, of 1,515 individuals referred for prosecution from 1985–93, 13 percent were indicted by May of 1993; in California the figure was 6 percent of 1,339. In general,

employees were more likely to be indicted than officers of the company. Still, of 1,000 charged from 1988 to 1992, 580 were sentenced and 78 percent received prison terms (the median term was twenty-two months). Compared to burglars, who steal one-hundredth as much, such sentences are ridiculously light; but compared to punishments received by the the average corporate criminal, these sanctions are very harsh (Calavita et al. 1997; Snider, 1993).

7.   The discrepancy between the $4.5 billion fine total in the *Globe and Mail* and the $5.2 billion total here is caused by the fact that the former figure refers to civil fines only, while the latter includes civil and criminal fines assessed.

8.   This does not mean workers bear no responsibility for accidents and injuries. Workers, like other human beings, may smoke tobacco, abuse legal and illegal drugs, or be careless or stupid. Machismo subcultures—real men take risks, wimps wear safety helmets and whine about coal dust—prevent safety consciousness (Glasbeek and Tucker 1992). National cultures are important too—in the U.S., violent acts (such as shootings) cause 21 percent of work-related deaths (versus two percent in Canada, and negligible percentages elsewhere).

9.   Some would argue that the American influence on Canada, always strong, is in this area entirely positive because the United States has a better record of environmental protection, achieved by a serendipitous combination of litigiousness, punitiveness and faith in market forces. A federal environmental crimes unit was set up in 1982 (a peak deregulatory year everywhere else) and criminal prosecutions from the EPA increased from 59 in 1988 to 278 in 1997 (*Globe and Mail*, March 23, 1999: A7). While not impressive for a country of 220 million people, federal acts are supplemented by state and some city ordinances. New civil laws allow private parties to sue for non-compliance with federal statutes without having to prove injury. And market mechanisms such as pollution licences, tax differentials, tradeable emission permits, and insurance-based strategies have had some success when supplementing and not replacing state regulation (Grabosky and Braithwaite 1993; Gunningham 1993).

Chapter 8

# Westray and After:
Power, Truth and News Reporting of the Westray
Mine Disaster

*John McMullan*

Genesta Halloran, a family member of a dead miner, recalls being
approached by one woman who was crying. She asked, "What family
are you related to?" and the woman replied, "I am not a family member,
I am just concerned." And I said, "Well who are you?" And she said, "I
am so-and-so from the Montréal Gazette." And I literally chased her
down the field. To put on false tears! (in Richards 1999: 156)

The CBC finally discovered the name of one of the men trapped below.
They knew he was from Antigonish, a town about half an hour's drive
from the mine. They called every person in the phone book with the
surname who lived in Antigonish. According to Bob Allison, one of the
journalists, one of the people called was so angry he drove to the
community centre where the media was stationed.... He stormed over
to the CBC contingent and said that if anyone called his family again, he
would be back with a gun. (in Richards 1999: 157)

Two Westray stories. Each exposes instances of insensitivity and intrusion in the
aftermath of the mine tragedy. With the help of hindsight and reflection they are
disturbing, even contemptible, transgressing professional guidelines and the
rights of the bereaved, and eroding public trust in the media. In the heat of the
moment, decisions by reporters to enter the homes of the bereaved without their
consent and presence, and to constantly scan, record and eavesdrop on private
events and conversations, were unenviable steps taken out of desperation to
produce that unique human interest story. Not surprisingly, journalists and
reporters covering the explosion were cursed by angry relatives of the dead,
threatened by friends of the missing, stoned by grief-stricken supporters of the
bereaved and warned to "get out of town" by local community leaders (Richards
1999: 155–58).

The relentless search for emotional detail, so common in media coverage of
tragedies, resulted not only in bad feelings but also in errors, some of which
aroused shock and caused hurt. Bodies were misidentified. Family names and
local sites were misreported. Corporate and state speculations were recounted as

stubborn facts. More generally, news narratives were dramatically decontextualized. The disaster was frequently reported as a "natural" tragedy, something simply surprising rather than socially predictable (Comish 1993; McCormick 1995; McMullan and Hinze 1999). Indeed the "truth" of Westray remains a highly contested matter. Despite a criminal trial, parliamentary debates, private civil actions, countless media investigations and a public inquiry, the bereaved and their supporters remain convinced that answers to the questions "what happened" and "who is responsible" have so far been ignored, distorted, concealed or reconstructed (Dodd 1999).

This chapter examines news coverage of the Westray mine disaster and its immediate aftermath in the context of a theoretical discussion of Foucault's (1980, 1991) concept of the "politics of truth." It is one part of a larger project that considers how formal political, legal, criminal justice, and media processes and their outcomes were constituted and manipulated to degrade the truth and deny justice to the bereaved. I am especially concerned here to study how "regimes of truth" were registered by the media to protect and sustain the interests of the mine owners and the local state, and used to downplay a relationship between the tragic and the criminal in the immediate aftermath of the explosion. I will concentrate on the three months immediately following the disaster.[1]

## Truth, Power and the Press

Before discussing the news coverage of Westray, it is important to consider the process of the production of truth and the exercise of power by news providers. Truth, Hannah Arendt (1971, 1972) reminds us, is a difficult concept. Its definition, identification and verification are rarely uncomplicated and almost always implicated in complex political and communicative processes involving perception, representation and interpretation. Yet criminal investigations, civil proceedings, public courts, special state tribunals, coroners' inquests, judicial reviews, government inquiries and truth commissions all claim, in theory at least, to offer mechanisms, rules and procedures by which "truth" can be aggregated, evaluated, confirmed and denied. These agencies seek to elicit truth in people's stories, even if the narratives produced are usually restricted to formal recollections and then further refined by adversarial adjudication to narrower and narrower memories.

The evidence-bound character of these truth-seeking agencies, however, is not separate from the political context of the production of truth. The weighing of personal rights and freedoms, the balancing of political necessities and priorities, the entanglements of laws and the forgetfulness of sometimes disingenuous "official memories," together expose the myth of any simple or single truth and confirm that establishing "the facts" is not uncontroversial. Misspeaking the truth has always been regarded as a necessary weapon in the arsenal of the powerful (Arendt 1971). But more recently these groups are organizing untruthfulness as a bulwark against the discovery of unsettling facts. This active, aggressive capacity to manufacture incorrect and misleading information is no longer about protecting state secrets, confusing hostile enemies or even deceiving others without deceiving oneself. Rather it is about manipulating information about things that are not secrets at all and are known to practically everybody (Arendt 1972: 5). This is not only evident in the numerous rewritings of history denying genocide to survivors; it is equally apparent in government programs, pronouncements and publications in which, time and time again, known and established facts are ignored, decried, suppressed or rearranged if they hurt a corporate interest or subvert the credibility of a state agency (McMullan 1997).

Contemporary organized manipulations of the truth, then, do not so much tear a hole in the fabric of factuality as reconfigure the entire factual texture of society. Criminal justice institutions, for example, are just as capable of demonizing their victims, denying their truth and corrupting social justice as they are capable of acknowledging and resolving unsettling stories and troubling acts. Scraton, Jemphrey and Coleman (1995), in their study of the aftermath of the Hillsborough soccer stadium disaster in which ninety-six men, women and children died, remind us that the reconstitution and registration of truth often operated to protect police interests and accounts of events while simultaneously denying justice to the victims through deceit and the neutralization and dismissal of their voices.

Like the state, the press also functions as an important site for the production and dissemination of "truth." Codes of ethics proclaim that news should be accurate, factual and gathered with delicacy and circumspection. Journalists, we are told, must be mindful of privacy issues and show empathy in reporting cases involving grief, shock or sudden death. Of course, research on media coverage of disasters reveals that the press can behave quite differently. They can exploit grief shamelessly, stigmatize people wrongfully, report awful rumour as fact and neglect unwelcome information (Barak 1994; Ericson et al. 1989; McMullan and Hinze 1999; Potter and Kappeler 1998; Scraton et al. 1995; Surette 1998).

The transition from lived experience to news narrative, of course, does not occur in isolation. What constitutes news for the general public is usually transmitted via routine electronic or print-based media systems. This process of information acquisition and dissemination is not neutral, indifferent or unbiased. News-as-fact is highly selective, often interpretative and profoundly invented. The mediation of news depends on a number of distinct but interrelated factors: newsworthiness, market needs, advertising policy, budgets, access to and control of information sources, story "spin" and dominant discourses which enable, guide and sustain news coverage (Barak 1994; Ericson et al. 1991; Fishman 1980; Hall et al. 1978; Rock 1973; Sumner 1982; Sumner and Sandberg 1990; Surette 1998; Potter and Kappeler 1998).

While the media are often presented and viewed as independent, objective and determined in the pursuit of a "story," regardless of vested interests, the actual restrictions on critical investigative journalism are many and effective: interest group lobbying, editorial politics, information screening, pre-selected narrative plot lines and quick story deadlines are all designed to keep reporters and their text within narrow, established ideological limits (Ericson et al. 1987, 1989, 1991; Fishman 1980; Hartley 1982; Herman and Chomsky 1988; Potter and Kappeler 1998). For example, reporters and journalists typically overestimate the criminality of those most vulnerable to authoritative labelling and sanctioning (Chibnall 1977; Ericson et al. 1991; Murdock 1982) and underestimate the harms and crimes caused by the powerful (Croall 1992; Friedrichs 1996; Lofquist 1998; Lynch et al. 2000; McCormick 1995; McMullan 1992; Smith 1992; Snider 1993; Wright et al. 1995). As Evans and Lundman (1983: 539) put it, "newspapers protect corporate reputations by failing to provide frequent, prominent and criminally oriented coverage of common corporate crimes." Journalists and corporate sources often form a hermeneutic circle for "rationalizing business practices and articulating business interests" (Ericson et al. 1989: 260).

Notwithstanding the diversity of media forms and presentational styles, the press remains largely conventional in content and representation (Gamson et al. 1992; Lofquist 1998; Lynch et al. 2000; Tunnell 1998). Indeed, reporting is not only guided by internal power mechanisms, it is also constrained by market forces and exterior political realities. On the one side are investments, markets, conglomerates, oligopolies and monopolies; on the other are lobby groups, state control of knowledge and the power to censure (Adorno 1991; Herman and Chomsky 1988). At bottom, the underlying structure of communicative relationships is about power, "that deep sense of propriety and legitimacy which has assigned both authority and responsibility to certain public sources of news and interpretation" (Williams 1989: 117).

Like the state and the firm, the media proclaims and confers legitimacy on truth. And truth, as Foucault (1980: 131) notes, is produced by "virtue of multiple forms of constraint." Truth is not outside power or lacking in it. Rather, it circulates and "induces regular effects of power." Of course, there is resistance to established practices of truth-making and truth-telling. There are brave examples of investigative reporters unmasking the corruption of the powerful and bearing witness to very unwelcome facts. But as I have observed elsewhere, journalists and reporters cannot easily take a stand that subverts corporate or political interests (McMullan and Hinze 1999). The press is radically embedded in the production of *official* discourses which, as Foucault (1980: 137) suggests, form part of a society's "general politics of truth": the appropriate political technologies of truth discovery, the enunciations which a society deems acceptable or not, the mechanisms it uses to judge true and false statements, the sanctioning of statements, and the valorization of claim-makers as truth-sayers.

For Foucault, the authority of the press is not narrowly institutional, reducible to organizational structure; rather, it extends to the representation, registration and ordering of knowledge, linked in elective affinity with "systems of power which produce and sustain it, and to effects of power which it induces and which extend it" (1980: 133). What the press typically produces is a "regime of truth"—a discursive practice of immense intensity, credibility, diffusion, consumption and contestation (Foucault 1980: 132). "Regimes of truth," moreover, can be dominant or subordinated depending on relations of power and authority. Hierarchies of credibility certainly exist. Put simply, holders of state institutional power and corporate power not only manage the labels of "deviant" and "criminal" and have them applied to certain acts and not to others, they also construct and arrange the "truth" so that their versions of veracity gain credence over those of others. This occurs most visibly in their relations with the media. Corporations and governments invest in the "symbolic politics of news and advertising because sophistication in defending bad news and trafficking in good news is seen as an essential part of achieving capital gains" (Ericson et al. 1991: 14). They exercise power, then, through the production of truth which they interpolate, and the media in turn are constrained to a large degree to produce the truth of their power.

In discussing media coverage of disasters, it is important to recognize that the relationship between power and truth is organized in a highly specific fashion. "Truth" is often registered through professional discourses that strategically "take charge" of social issues: science, engineering, business, policing, medicine and law, to name a few. In turn, these disciplines are "accredited" as sources of information that allow the media to speak or write convincingly about public health, gambling, sex, crime, social disasters and the like. Not surprisingly, those in power are persistent in their efforts to construct and reconstitute their hegemony through technical investigations, scientific studies, medical reports, judicial reviews, coroner's inquests, criminal trials, public inquiries, press stories and the like (Foucault 1980, 1991).

It is where institutional and professional discourses intersect that "views from above" become strategically united and rationalized, while "views from below" become disputed or disqualified. There are, to be sure, ongoing battles around the rules and status of truth and the economic and political roles it plays. Truth-making and truth-telling are dynamic, involving processes of emergence, consolidation, contestation and displacement (Arendt 1972; Foucault 1990: 93–98, and 1991). Dominant power players may not have a monopoly on defining "truth," but in their official discourses, including news narratives, they are especially adroit at avoiding blame, shifting responsibility, condemning others and decontextualizing people and events from the structural, material world of cause and consequence (Lofquist 1998; Lynch et al. 1989; McCormick 1999; Morash and Hale 1987; Scraton et al. 1995; Smith 1992; Wright et al. 1995).

How, then, was power exercised in the immediate aftermath of the Westray explosion? What were the press procedures for the production, distribution and circulation of statements about Westray? How were they linked with corporate power to induce and extend a "regime of truth"?

## The Westray Explosion

At 5:20 a.m. on May 9, 1992, an explosion ripped through an underground mine in Plymouth, Pictou County, Nova Scotia, killing twenty-six miners, eleven of whom remain there to this day. According to the *Report of the Westray Mine Public*

*Inquiry* (Nova Scotia 1997), sparks from the cutting head of a continuous miner machine ignited methane gas, creating a large rolling flame that travelled through the mine, consuming all the oxygen in its path and leaving behind deadly carbon monoxide. The fire intensified into a methane explosion, and the shock wave stirred up coal particles, creating a coal-dust explosion.

The explosion was so strong that it blew the top off the mine entrance, more than a mile above the blast centre. In nearby villages, houses shook and windows broke. Residents were awakened from their beds, and within minutes phones began to ring and people were put on alert to cope with what one woman described as "this incredible thud ... a noise that filled the atmosphere.... Oh, my God! The vastness of this" (in Richards 1999: 144).

The explosion crushed the miners on the spot or poisoned them where they stood. In either event, death was almost certainly instantaneous. Pictures from the mine site show a scene of utter destruction. Steel roof supports were shattered. Steel doors were blown apart. Equipment lay burned and twisted into piles on the ground. The mine walls were split and cracked wide open in places. The mine floor was littered with tons of fallen debris and rock. The air was deadly poisonous; draegermen,[2] and later police investigators, had to use special breathing equipment to search for survivors and evidence. When the bodies were brought to the surface they were seen to be badly burned. Clothing had been scorched off their skin. Some bodies had turned bright red, the result of carbon monoxide poisoning. All were marked by signs of intense heat. Hair was singed and hands were closed into tight fists (personal communication, Sgt. Ullock, RCMP; Nova Scotia 1997).

In the early hours after the explosion, numerous groups positioned themselves to respond to the disaster. The families of the trapped miners gathered to provide support and await information. The media, local and international, converged on Plymouth to report the story. Curragh Resources, the owners of the Westray Mine, took control of the site, managed the incident and produced and dispersed information that became news. Draegermen arrived on the scene and quickly went into action. They spent the next week picking their way through the debris, looking for survivors (Comish 1993). On day two, they discovered eleven bodies. On day five, they retrieved four more. But on May 14, Curragh Resources announced that there were no survivors and that the search was too dangerous to pursue any further. The remaining bodies would have to stay in the mine, an unpopular decision with those committed to recovering their dead for proper burial (Dodd 1999).

The police, normally a pre-eminent group in post-disaster tragedies, were slow to develop an investigative role. The RCMP were certainly on the scene within minutes of the explosion; they organized the processing of the dead and the living, set up the identification process as bodies came to the surface and regulated traffic near the mine site. But it was not until May 21, twelve days after the explosion, that the RCMP launched a criminal investigation, and it was September 17 before they secured the mine site and seized company records and equipment. They eventually laid charges of manslaughter and criminal negligence causing death against two mine officials and Curragh. But after much legal wrangling, an abrupt trial in 1995 and a period of judicial review and reflection, the charges were stayed in 1998, not to be revived again (Jobb 1994, 1999; McCormick 1999).

The Nova Scotia government was more timely in responding to the disaster. A public inquiry was promised the day after the explosion, and on May 15, after rescue efforts were abandoned, the premier of the province, Donald Cameron, appointed a judge of the Nova Scotia Supreme Court to investigate the disaster under the *Public Inquiries Act* and the *Coal Mines Regulation Act.* "Nothing and no person with any light to shed on this tragedy," Cameron said, "will escape the scrutiny of this inquiry" (Nova Scotia, May 15, 1992: 9291). After many delays, the public inquiry finally got underway in November 1995, but many of the key players refused to participate and could not be compelled to do so. The final report, released in December 1997, concluded that the disaster was both foreseeable and preventable: "management failed, the inspectorate failed, and the mine blew up," wrote Justice Richard. The Westray tragedy, he opined, was a "complex mosaic of actions, omissions, mistakes, incompetence, apathy, cynicism, stupidity and neglect" (Nova Scotia 1997: ix).

The Nova Scotia Department of Labour had been responsible for regulating the mine site from its inception in 1988. Armed with the *Coal Mines Regulation Act* and the statute governing workplace safety under the *Occupational Health and Safety Act*, their inspectorate had visited the site more than fifty times. Violations had been cited and numerous warnings had been issued. Indeed, written orders, the last on April 29, 1992, had been forwarded to the Westray mine manager, threatening prosecution unless action was taken within fifteen days to clean up coal dust and put down limestone to prevent an explosion. Unhappily, the overdue remedy was never implemented, and no follow-up inspection to ensure compliance was conducted by the Department of Labour before the explosion. Nevertheless, six months *after* the explosion, fifty-two charges were filed against Curragh Resources and four mine officials, alleging numerous violations of the *Occupational Health and Safety Act*. These charges, however, were never acted on and in March of 1993 were dropped in favour of criminal action (Jobb 1994, 1999; Nova Scotia 1997).

Within days of the explosion, the personal and social impact of the tragedy had extended beyond those directly involved, affecting entire communities and concerned outsiders. Three separate investigations were in process and a company-paid panel of experts had been hired to conduct an internal review of the disaster. Inevitably, perhaps, personal loss had become public property.

## The Press and the Production of the Westray "Truth"

The media reflected the volatility and chaos that characterized the explosion. The demands imposed upon them were well in excess of typical emergencies or daily tragedies. Existing routines, day-to-day policies and procedures, and accepted professional practices were disrupted. The psychological and social needs of the bereaved, of witnesses and of rescuers were subordinated to the priorities of investigative agencies, including the press. The entire community was invaded. Reporters parked on people's doorsteps, commandeered local telephone lines and hounded the families of the missing and presumed dead. In the first six days of reporting, more than one hundred stories were published by the Halifax *Chronicle-Herald* alone, and, at its peak, about two hundred journalists were reporting to local, national and international audiences (McCormick 1995: 212). As Dean Jobb (1994: 52) recounts:

> The Westray explosion was the lead item on radio newscasts across the country. CBC Newsworld and local television stations were installing satellite dishes ... so they could go live with updates ... reporters for newspapers with Sunday editions were already tapping stories into portable computers ... CNN in Atlanta was beaming the story to the world.

However, the media's need to know could not always be squared with the victims' or bereaveds' rights to privacy and dignity. One reporter from the Halifax *Daily News* recalls that the community resented the media recording their grief and their funerals. "They did not want you there and hated your guts" (in Richards 1999: 155). Nor could the media's need to know be squared with the corporation's and the state's control of information. Even as the magnitude of the disaster was unfolding, Curragh hired a public relations firm to manufacture images and manage impressions surrounding the explosion. Reid Management immediately faxed instructions to Curragh's operations director telling him to advise the media of the following:

> This is a terrible human tragedy that could not be foreseen. The company has done everything physically and humanly possible to guard against dangerous conditions.... There have been no dangerous or suspicious conditions or methane gas readings; dust kept under strict control. There were no warnings of any kind. Safety always the first consideration. Dangers acknowledged daily.... Mines designed for safety and emergencies.... Procedures carefully monitored.... The families, rescue teams and other employees have demonstrated extraordinary courage.... The company will encourage a comprehensive examination of the causes of the accident to ensure against similar tragedies in the future. (in Cameron and Mitorvica 1994: 56)

Within hours of the explosion, the company initiated an operation to control the lines of communication and flow of information to the public. Their actions suggest that they were primarily concerned with crisis management rather than emergency response. The dominant post-disaster contexts affecting Curragh's decisions were criminal and civil liability, and a looming public inquiry. As Richards (1999: 150) aptly puts it, the company's top priorities were "shareholders and lenders and ultimately a judge and jury." To that end, they immediately limited and monitored the territorial site for the production of the news. The media were placed in the local community centre, and the families of the missing miners were installed across the street in the firehall. Journalists were denied entry to the company offices and the mine site, and employees and their families were instructed to stay away from the press, because "the media lied" (Jobb 1994: 59). Curragh officials, in turn, informed the press that worried families did not want to talk. The police, for their part, were cast in a secondary role in the immediate post-disaster period. They essentially patrolled the road that separated the two buildings and prevented the media from speaking to family members (Cameron and Mitorvica 1994: 58). It was a classic systems approach to a complex human event, and one in which corporate power, not police power, was preeminent.

At the outset, the press was positioned in a reactive role. They were denied access to sources except at the company's initiative. Corporate spokespersons quickly tied reporters into their perspective by stage-managing the release of relevant information: providing diagrams, maps and photographs; arranging press hearings at company convenience so stories had to be filed quickly and without reaction from others; and channelling news into technical stories that empowered themselves and their advisers as authoritative claim-makers. They converted the reporters' lack of time, informants and routines into a source tactic and created a "best news" story in the context of "bad news."[3]

These strategies allowed Curragh to circulate their "truth" about the explosion through public relations ritual and rhetoric. They wrote the central scripts, provided the stage and counselled their actors for a pop-culture drama, while reporters were left to write about the performance. One reporter observed, "We were feeding off each other ... waiting for their briefings.... There was no real news, they just felt that they had to come, and we felt that we had to write or broadcast something" (in Richards 1999: 152). The press was encouraged to frame Westray as a human interest story and not to question the role of private capital in the disaster or develop a crime angle on the causes of the explosion. In Jobb's words, the media emphasized "the trivial," "the fluff and feelies," "the peoples angles" and "the human interest" (in Richards 1999: 156). When raised, questions about safety were ignored or deflected by Curragh officials. News in the immediate aftermath of the explosion was primarily a communication between journalists and corporate sources, with much of the "public left in the position of spectator" (Ericson et al. 1989: 260).

The relationship between the exercise of power and the production and circulation of "truth" is revealed in a content analysis of random news coverage taken from the Halifax *Daily News* and *Chronicle-Herald* in the three-month period following the explosion. In this period, there were 548 articles published, of which I analyzed 137 for content.[4] Seventy-five of 137 items emphasized human interest, twenty-four raised political concerns, twenty-two reported on safety, ten focused on the public inquiry and six were miscellaneous. Most stories concerning Westray appeared in section A of both newspapers, although human interest stories were far more prevalent on the front page (52 percent of the time) than were political or safety stories (11 percent and 7 percent of the time).

The most frequent cluster of connotations was around the theme of tragedy. Human loss and hope were reported on so as to evince a powerful set of emotions: grief, sacrifice, pain, courage, fortitude, and dignity in coping with sudden death. The news items dwelled on the loss caused by the explosion, but they downplayed the *context* that had produced that harm and the critical feelings surrounding it. The causes and agents of the actual explosion were ignored in the coverage. Rather than focusing on responsibility, media attention emphasized the consequences of the explosion, an approach that reinforced an *accident discourse*. Dying underground was a brave but necessary risk—part of the culture of mining, which miners knew and accepted. The Westray story was repeatedly presented as one "of great human courage pitted against great natural hazards." It was about "brave men toiling in the face of unseen dangers in the dark" (*Chronicle-Herald*, May 11, 1992: C1). Such sentimental depictions said little about the ownership, administration and operation of the mine, the politics surrounding its construction, the regulatory regime or the practices of law enforcement. Instead, the press advanced the view that the Westray management had been a victim of events beyond its control, much like the media portrayals of Union Carbide, Imperial Food Products, Exxon and Akzo Nobel Salt in the aftermath of their corporate disasters in India and the United States (Lofquist 1998: 241–61; Lynch et al. 1989: 7–35; Smith 1992; Wright et al. 1995: 20–36).

Questions about safety were raised, but many of the news narratives stressed the dangerous *physical* properties of coal mining. Inanimate chemical reactions, hazardous by-products, coal dust and a dangerous natural environment were presented as responsible for the harm caused, not human judgements or social and political priorities. While there were hints of corporate impropriety, the overall effect of the reporting was to focus little attention on why methane gas was present but undetected and why coal dust was allowed to accumulate on the mine floor in the first place.

There had been warnings about the dangers of mining coal in Pictou County, and there had been complaints from miners about cave-ins, unsafe equipment and poor ventilation at the Westray mine. But, for the most part, these voices were unheard, ignored or disbelieved and the accident discourse was advanced to create a hegemonic understanding of the explosion that was consistent with the dominant narratives of business and state. The explosion was presented as the product of "Mother Nature," which, as Colin Brenner (a company spokesperson) noted, "cannot always be predicted or controlled" (in Richards 1999: 149, 261).

Reporters did not dwell much on the political dimensions of the explosion either. The first direct coverage of political involvement found in my sample appeared on May 23. It reviewed Premier Cameron's long association with the

Westray project and concluded that "Westray remained the government's favourite son after Cameron reached the Premier's Office in early 1991" (*Mail-Star*, May 23, 1992: C1). Westray, as a "creature of politics," appeared on line ninety-two of the article, was featured in the third section of the newspaper. While there are references in this article to much earlier political stories, there were, in fact, very few political reports printed in the immediate time frame (McCormick 1995: 208; McMullan and Hinze 1999: 191–92; Richards 1999: 144). Furthermore, these few stories tended to be buried in the newspapers and contextualized in benign terms. If he could have predicted what would happen, Premier Cameron is quoted as saying, "I am sure we would have made different judgements" (*Mail-Star*, May 23, 1992: C1). The media portrayal was that the explosion was unanticipated and that senior politicians were not implicated in the making of the disaster. Again, the vocabulary of accident, suggesting that events were beyond anyone's control, was crucial in locating political responsibility as a minor issue for news coverage during this period.

When reporters did probe the role of the state, they tended to focus on *individual* incompetence within the Department of Labour's inspectorate. These officials, and the minister responsible, were held indirectly accountable for the explosion because they had failed to enforce the rule of law at the mine site. Characteristically, these news narratives emphasized "surprise and shock" at what was frequently called a "bungling state of affairs" within this government department. While the coverage tried to establish a cause and effect relationship that was easy to name, blame and shame, it did not explore the wider conditions surrounding bureaucratic inaction. The reporting inserted, in only a minor way, the "social" alongside the "natural" causes of the event. But the focus was almost exclusively on personal impropriety and "bad apples in a good barrel" type of storytelling. No sense of cumulative collective action and responsibility—linking owners and managers, corporate officials and political elites with a production plan and schedule that may have contributed to the disaster—was ever stated.

Even the establishment of the public inquiry received minor attention in the early news coverage. Much of the news writing lacked inquisitiveness and simply recounted the terms of reference, scope and powers of the commission. Yet there was a promise of another news angle, one that might develop a critical counter-narrative based on the voices of the Westray miners.

> At least 70 Westray employees want to testify at the inquiry into the mine disaster and have asked the province to cover their costs, a miner said Wednesday. "As far as I can tell, from anybody I have talked to, there's not one person who does not want to tell their side of the story," said miner Gordon Walsh, Co-Chairman of an employee's committee formed in the wake of the May 9 explosion.... As employees, we feel we have a lot to offer the inquiry.... I really think the only fair way is to take every man who worked there and have him testify under oath. (*Mail-Star*, May 21, 1992: A1)

Unfortunately, the public inquiry was the first casualty of the legal imbroglio surrounding the Westray disaster. The inquiry did not commence until late in 1995, and while reporting certainly changed in amount and content, it did not develop a "lawandorder" narrative about the explosion.[5]

In sum, the Westray explosion was quickly and strongly constructed as a tragic accident. It was never suggested that the deaths were homicides or that the corporation or individual executives might be criminals. Indeed, the dominant sources of the news were "official" communications from Curragh or relevant government agencies, and this aided enormously in establishing and circulating Curragh's claims of the "truth" about themselves and the disaster. The press preferred predictable hegemonic voices and actively constructed and conferred legitimacy on this "regime of truth."

## Deceit, Denial and Disavowal

The most interesting aspect of this news writing was that the "regime of truth" being assembled ran contrary to the most obvious fact scenario: that is, maintaining this version of the "truth" required both effort and negligence. The Westray story contained abundant earlier evidence of inappropriate mining practices, including the widely known danger of the gaseous coal seam in Pictou County, the long history of previous mining deaths in the region, Curragh's troubled mining safety record elsewhere in Canada, public reservations about both capital and labour in the area before the explosion, and multiple problems related to the methods used in the mine and both the government and Curragh's previous knowledge of the dangers. It also contained available evidence of widespread political involvement in brokering the mine into existence, including guaranteed loans, subsidies, tax incentives, infrastructure grants, and protected coal markets at inflated prices, as well as public information regarding government reluctance to take action against occupational health and safety violations at the mine (Glasbeek and Tucker 1992; Hynes and Prasad 1999; Tucker 1995).

The company and the state had to work hard to prevent these "subversive" narratives from coming forward in the immediate aftermath of the disaster.[6] They registered their "views from above" and ordered their "facts" through professional discourses that emphasized engineering, chemistry, geology, accounting and mine administration. They promoted the view that they were running a modern, technologically sophisticated mine that could overcome any and all safety problems, and they created the perception, through their "authorized experts," that all risks in the mine had been known and accepted by the miners. In Bourdieu's (1977: 169) terms, corporate and state interests reconstituted (1) an underlying "thought element" for news coverage, a system of presuppositions and principles—an elite consensus, if you will—which was largely internalized without much questioning, and (2) an "unthought element" for news reporting, a vocabulary of impossibilisms which circumscribed critical commentary and deflected, downplayed and denied corporate and government involvement and wrongdoing in causing the explosion.

The press, for their part, functioned with a kind of "propaganda model," degrading the accounts of critics and disqualifying the complaints of miners. According to Starr (1992: 11), the reporters had been predisposed to write about Westray as a success story *before* the explosion and thus were reluctant to pick up the subversive truths they had previously marginalized after the mine blew up. Curragh was not the only party good at practising what Arendt (1972) calls "manipulating the truth about publicly-known facts"; the press was also good at "putting reality together" within the bounds of acceptable corporate premises and established political doctrines. Press coverage in May, June and July of 1992 did investigate some of the irregularities surrounding the explosion and empha-sized some of the connections between capital accumulation, political govern-ance, law enforcement, the criminal justice system and the mine explosion (Cameron and Mitorvica 1994; Jobb 1994). But this was a minority construction of news events. Reporting merged more than it diverged and, for the most part, the narrative iconography of press accounts signified remarkably conventional images and interpretations: the ideological formulation of "accident," the personalization of responsibility, the disavowal of the social, and the memorialization of human grief as truth (McCormick 1995; McMullan and Hinze 1999).

In this sense, the press was part of the story and part of the disaster, because how they covered the news before the explosion contributed to the ideological context that enabled it to happen, and how they covered the news after the explosion "silenced" any cries of corporate violence. In effect, this news reporting amounted to a subjugation of the knowledge and truth of "views from below," depicting them as partisan, fanciful or ill-conceived. News providers created an atmosphere within which criminal justice institutions, judicial reviews and ultimately the public inquiry "searched for truth," and within which the families of the bereaved were forced to establish the "innocence" of their loved ones and demand social justice for their families.

The intensity, bias and careless reporting of this early period was mirrored by the equally insensitive and continuous degradation of truth and neutralization of justice surrounding the RCMP investigation, the criminal prosecution, the trial and review, regulatory charges under the *Occupational Health and Safety Act* and the *Coal Mines Regulation Act*, and the public inquiry. While the latter laid blame for the explosion in the corridors of power, no one has ever been convicted of a crime or a breach of safety laws. Clifford Frame, the CEO of Curragh, insists to this day that the explosion was a "simple accident" (*Globe and Mail*, February 17, 1997). Former premier Donald Cameron claims that Westray's truth has nothing to do with him or his government's actions. His "truth telling" before the public inquiry openly condemned and vilified the miners as the agents of their own destruction:

> The families ... will never find any peace if they don't get to the truth. And that's why I am so upset that people wouldn't own up to what they were doing. And instead of briefly speaking about it and shoving it

under the table. The bottom line is that the mine blew up on that morning because of what was going on in there at that time. That's the bottom line. (Nova Scotia, 1997, vol. 67: 14859)

Much of the sociology of the media starts from the premise that news is invented and that the media transmits "knowledge" as truth through the creation of ideas (Gamson et al. 1992; Potter and Kappeler 1998). To some extent this is so, but a more complete analysis is that in the "construction" selection and narrative formation of news, the media transmits knowledge as truth through appealing to established conventions, ideas and ideologies. It reflects powerful beliefs and, at the same time, circulates and reinforces them (Adorno 1991; Barak 1994; Kellner 1990; Scraton et al. 1995; Sumner 1990; Surette 1998). In the Westray case, "truth" was constructed as a reflection of an established hierarchy of credibility. The "mechanisms," "technique," and "procedures" defined by Foucault (1980: 1991) as fundamental to a society's "regime of truth" lay barely disguised beneath the surface of Westray's "official discourse" and the state's legal maneuverings. They informed how the explosion was to be reported as a disaster without a cause, and they informed the degradation of the bereaved throughout the process, from the early administration of bodies[7] to the final torment of injustices: lax police practices, flawed criminal justice procedures, inappropriate regulatory responses, miniscule compensation payments and the failure to discipline those responsible.

Press reporting was and remains one crucial element in the reconstitution and registration of truth surrounding the Westray disaster. But, as Foucault (1990, 1991) suggests, it did not easily record the "truth" of the "views from below" because what it witnessed, acknowledged and memorialized was the "truth" of those with the power to define the parameters and even the substance of the reports that became news.[8] What Westray demonstrates is that this was an easily manipulated process in which the definitions were so powerful that they undermined justice and damaged lives. The brother of a dead miner stated forcefully:

> Those bastards did this and they are walking away from this.... You cannot touch Frame.... He's the ultimate. That's where the blame lies.... And yet we cannot even get at the goddamn managers that were there. So I'm trying to see where this friggin' justice system fits. It doesn't fit nowhere. Unless you happen to be a nobody, then they'll nail your ass right to the wall. It's odd, I just can't let it go that these people were able to kill twenty-six people and just walk away. (in Dodd 1999: 238–39)

There is a chilling complacency behind the state's failure to address the harm and homicide of Westray. And there is a deep resentment in the voices of the bereaved. In this context, validating the victims' experience, registering the awful "criminal truth," obtaining appropriate public recognition and apology, and dramatizing the "views from below," however difficult, are essential to a truth-telling that challenges corporate and state-sanctioned "regimes of truth."

Unhappily, the press was unable or unwilling to contribute to this process. Not only did they not have a competent plan to establish limits on permissible investigation, they were intrusive without depth. The media-hyped rush to judgement on Westray in the form of "fluff and feely" journalism undermined the search for truth in all its complexity. The deeper and more challenging questions were passed over, and a search for truth which would have exposed official discourse and wisely taught us about this shocking event was undermined by news narratives that reduced explanation and understanding to the emotion of the moment. Immediate events were stripped of context and, therefore, of meaning. In the final analysis, the press has to be called to account not only for what they wrote, but also for what they neglected to write.

## Notes

1. For a discussion of news coverage of Westray over a three-*year* period, see McMullan and Hinze (1999).
2. Miners trained in rescue operations.
3. Richards (1999) argues that Curragh was ill prepared for the disaster. They had no crisis communication plan and their relations with both the media and the families of the victims were unfriendly. But public relations was not their chief concern. Legal strategy dominated their thinking, and constructing a particular "regime of truth" was fundamental to this strategy. Thus they employed a discourse of deceit, denial and neutralization to protect their interests, even if the press was manipulated and the families were ignored.
4. An exhaustive sampling of everything written in that three-month period would be even more compelling. But I want to emphasize that I familiarized myself with the total press coverage available from the Halifax *Chronicle-Herald* and *Mail-Star* before I drew the sample, so I am convinced that my analysis identifies the basic themes of media reporting about Westray at that time.
5. The public inquiry was struck down as *ultra vires* (beyond the power) of the province of Nova Scotia on November 13, 1992, and then reinstated by a court of appeal decision on January 19, 1993. However, the inquiry was ordered to delay its hearings until all trials arising from the disaster were ended. The public inquiry finally began, after a further appeal to the Supreme Court of Canada, in November 1995. Later reporting did emphasize legal news coverage but failed to develop a critical crime focus. See McMullan and Hinze (1999).
6. Some of these "subversive" stories did receive press coverage later and especially in reporting on the public inquiry. So, media coverage was dynamic and it did change in amount and content. However, this case study suggests that reporters were unlikely to define corporate violence as criminal or to promote thinking that would "criminalize" corporate personnel for

their harm and homicide. For similar conclusions, see Evans and Lundman (1983), Lynch et al. (1989), Lynch et al. (2000), Morash and Hale (1987), Scraton et al. (1995) and Wright et al. (1995). For a more positive appraisal of the news reporter's role in the social movement against corporate crime, see Cullen et al. (1987) and Swigert and Farrell (1980).

7.   For examples of callous disregard for the trauma of sudden bereavement, see Dodd's (1999) discussion of how families were made to wait twelve to fourteen hours throughout the night and without information before being allowed to view their loved ones.

8.   I am not, however, claiming that there was no critical journalism. Dean Jobb, Ralph Surrette and Stevie Cameron were three reporters who exposed misinformation, disputed company and state accounts of events, uncovered background information and pressured the police and the courts to discover the truth and remember the dead. But this type of coverage was a minority representation of the news.

Chapter 9

# Consumers to the Rescue?
## Campaigning against Corporate Abuse of Labour

*Judy Fudge*

## Nike: Just Doing It

Picture in your mind's eye the Nike symbol. This should not be difficult to do since the "swoosh" is everywhere—on running shoes, T-shirts, baseball caps, billboards, magazines, television, even the sides of buses. What do you think of when you see the Nike symbol? Running shoes? Working out? Just doing it? High-priced athletes? Power, success and competition? A successful corporate citizen? A rapacious global corporation? Mindless consumerism? I asked my ten-year-old nephew—who is lovingly but sarcastically called "Nike Boy" by the members of his immediate family because he is draped from baseball cap to the soles of his sneakers in Nike wear—what the symbol called to his mind. He informed me that when he saw the swoosh he thought about baseball and hockey, his favourite activities. But it also means something more to my young nephew, something akin to being a successful big boy. When he wears Nike, he feels cool. His parents spend a great deal of money buying him apparel and running shoes with the Nike logo. Moreover, Nike spends millions and millions of dollars each year to ensure that affluent consumers all over the world, but especially in the rich countries of the North, spend billions of dollars on the swoosh.

Many people either are not informed or do not care about the working conditions of the people who make sportswear shoes or apparel. For those who are, finding a brand that does not exploit its workers is a difficult task, involving a lot of research and critical judgement. While many large companies have Internet sites extolling the virtues of their labour codes of conduct, in some circumstances this is a marketing ploy. Less-known companies provide no information. Moreover, the competition within this sector puts pressure on all the corporations to reduce labour costs as much as possible, further jeopardizing working conditions and wages.

What I want to focus on is what the Nike symbol signifies in the context of both the ongoing campaign to expose Nike's exploitation of women workers in Asia and the increasing popularity of consumer campaigns as a strategy for reining in transnational corporations that abuse their workers. The action against Nike is perhaps the most prominent in a campaign by students, church groups, human rights organizations and trade unions to disclose to consumers the terrible working conditions of the people who labour behind the labels of several apparel and footwear corporations and giant retailers. The goal is to mobilize consumer power to force global corporations to end labour abuse. The Nike example shows not only how such campaigns are mobilized and organized, but also how these corporations defend themselves. This case study also explores the possibilities and limitations of using consumer power to improve the working conditions of some of the most exploited employees in the world.

From its modest beginning in 1964, Nike has become the market leader in athletic footwear, controlling 37 percent of the market. It produces ninety million pairs of sports shoes every year (Clean Clothes 1999: 1). It has also diversified into the apparel (or garment) industry. In 1999, Nike had revenues of just over $9 billion (all figures in U.S. dollars). Its amazing growth and dominance in the sportswear field is largely attributable to two things: (1) its strategy—called "outsourcing"—of having a network of corporations all over the world that make Nike products and (2) its state-of-the-art marketing campaigns. The first element of its success is private or hidden, whereas the second is Nike's public face. The goal of the campaign against Nike is to expose the first aspect of its business practices and to reveal a different image from the one on which the transnational corporation spends millions of dollars.

Nike is a prime example of a modular corporation that has used outsourcing to create a competitive advantage. Modular companies focus their efforts, resources and capital on their core functions and competencies and selectively subcontract other operations to companies that specialize in those areas. Nike concentrates on design, marketing and sales and contracts out 100 percent of its shoe production, manufacturing only key technical components of its specialized "Nike Air" system. Thus, it shifts many of the risks associated with manufacturing, demand fluctuation, and labour relations onto the contractor, who also bears the burden of producing cheaply to keep the contract. Nike maintains control over the manufacturing process by establishing procedures that permit direct involvement in limited stages of the contractor's activities. It also controls the final product through trademarks and licensing agreements. In order to further limit its risks, Nike uses a number of suppliers in several countries (Quinn and Hilmer 1994; Szablowski 1995).

Manufacturing footwear, like manufacturing garments, is a labour-intensive activity. Around the world, 530,000 people make shoes and garments that bear the Nike logo, but only 16,000 are employed directly by the corporation (Clean Clothes 1999: 2; Nike 1999). The majority of direct employees are designers and marketers. Blueprints for new shoes are relayed by satellite from Nike's headquarters in Oregon to its contractors' computer-aided design and manufacturing systems (Clifford 1992). In order to keep costs low and profits high, 99 percent of Nike shoes are produced in Asian countries with large labour forces. Indonesia is Nike's biggest production centre, with seventeen footwear factories that employ ninety thousand workers, most of them young women (Clean Clothes 1999: 3; Olive 1996). China, Vietnam, Bangladesh and Malaysia also make Nike products. After the drop of the Mexican peso in 1994, Mexico too became a Nike production source because its labour was cheap (Yanz et al. 1999: 12–13). Labour costs account for only about four percent of the retail price of a pair of Nike running shoes (Nike 1999). This side of Nike's success is popular only in the business press.

The public side of Nike's success is its marketing strategy. The company has cultivated a highly popular, aggressive and performance-oriented identity through its multi-million-dollar advertising campaigns. In 1997, Nike's estimated marketing budget was $978 million. By using high-profile athlete celebrities such as Michael Jordan, Tiger Woods, Andre Agassi and Silken Lauman to endorse its products, Nike has managed to associate the swoosh with success, audacity and freedom without compromise. In 1992, Nike paid Michael Jordan the equivalent of $55,000 a day, or $20 million a year, to endorse a line of basketball shoes named after him (Air Jordans), in order to be associated with his popularity and success (Olive 1996).

What Nike does not want to be associated with is the people who actually make its shoes. Although its corporate policy is to exploit cheap labour globally, Nike does *not* want its ubiquitous swoosh to evoke a picture of someone like Sadisah, one of the tens of thousands of Asian women who toil long hours in harsh conditions piecing together Nike shoes. In 1992, Sadisah worked in a factory in Indonesia where she earned the equivalent of fourteen cents an hour or $1.03 a day. On a line with 115 workers, she produced about sixteen hundred pairs of Nike running shoes a day. After a month of working six days a week and ten and a half hours a day, Sadisah earned the equivalent of $37.46—about half the retail price of a pair of sneakers she made. This was not enough money to provide a diet considered adequate by Indonesian government standards. It would have taken Sadisah 44,492 years to earn what Nike paid Michael Jordan in one year. In 1992 the basketball superstar received from Nike more than the combined yearly income of the thirty thousand young women who made Nike running shoes for contractors in Indonesia. When Sadisah organized the other workers to protest bad working conditions, she was fired. Not only did contracting shops like the one in which Sadisah was employed fail to comply with Indonesian labour laws, several used corporal punishment to discipline the workers (Ballinger 1992; Cavanagh and Broad 1996). As David Olive, a business editor at the *Globe and Mail*, summed up:

> The success formula of Nike might best be described as ethical arbitrage. This is the tactic of buying labour cheaply in jurisdictions with substandard working conditions and selling the fruits of that labour in societies whose advanced working conditions make it possible for people to aspire to own a paid of Air Jordans. (1996)

The goal of the campaign against Nike is to change the symbolism of the swoosh—from the success and glamour of Michael Jordan to the abuse and exploitation of Sadisah—so consumers will pressure Nike to ensure that its contractors provide decent wages and working conditions for their workers. The campaign is a public relations battle for the hearts and minds of affluent consumers, between media-savvy and innovative anti-corporate campaigners whose major weapons are the Internet and creative publicity stunts, and Nike, one of the kingpins of advertising smarts and hype.

The media have been inundated with stories about people who make shoes bearing the Nike swoosh. Since 1992 there have been hundreds of articles in newspapers and magazines, dozens of television exposés, and even a series of *Doonesbury* cartoons about Nike and its exploitation of Third World workers. Groups have leafleted and picketed stores that sell Nike products. October 18, 1997, was the first of a series of international days of action against Nike. On April 12, 1998, the second international day of action, activists staged demonstrations against the labour practices of Nike contractors in thirteen cities across Canada. The Internet has been used to publicize the campaign and a number of web sites are devoted to disclosing and changing the labour practices of Nike's contractors. Moreover, the campaign is making headway in the school system. In religion and civics classes across Canada, teachers are informing high school students about the working conditions of the people who make the brand-name clothing and runners they wear. In their Catholic high school in southern Ontario, my fourteen- and sixteen-year-old nieces, the sisters of "Nike Boy," told me that they had heard about Nike's labour practices from an Indonesian woman who visited their religion class. In response, they drew protest posters and wrote to Phil Knight, CEO and one of the co-founders of Nike, to ask him to ensure that working conditions in the Asian contracting shops improved. According to one journalist, "to some the Nike swoosh is now as scary as the hammer and sickle" (Friedman 1999).

## Consumer Campaigns against Corporate Abuse of Labour

"Corporate campaigns" are increasingly the strategy of choice for activists who want to place limits on transnational corporations' power to exploit working people. The success of the trade boycott of the South African apartheid regime, the refusal of nation-states to agree to or implement international labour standards with enforcement mechanisms equivalent to those provided in trade agreements; and corporate advertising techniques and new communications technologies, especially the Internet, have combined to increase the popularity of this strategy. Throughout the 1990s the number of campaigns to expose the terrible terms and conditions under which workers, especially in the South, labour in the apparel and footwear industries surged. The targets were the super-labels and the giant retailers who sit on top of the huge apparel and footwear industry and reap the biggest profits. The Gap, Guess, Disney, Liz Claiborne, Kathy Lee Gifford, Levi Strauss and Reebok are just a few of the big-name labels that have been targeted. Transnational retailers such as Wal-Mart and Sears also have had campaigns against them (Ross 1997a). And while Canadian groups are involved in the campaigns against the international giants as well, they have also selected some homegrown targets such as the Bay and Northern Reflections (Maquila Solidarity Network 1999).

These campaigns have been organized by coalitions, composed of trade unions, student organizations, church groups and non-governmental organizations (NGOs) promoting human rights and international solidarity, to expose how big names in the apparel and sportswear industry use international subcontracting chains to keep the cost of labour down. Some of the most active anti-corporate campaigners are the National Labor Committee in the United States (Krupat 1997), the Clean Clothes Campaign based in the Netherlands (Shaw 1997) and Canada's own Labour behind the Labour Coalition (Jeffcott 1998). One of the most active new groups is United Students Against Sweatshops, which organizes university and college students across North America to put pressure on university administrators to require corporations with which they have licensing agreements to ensure that their contractors meet a stringent code of labour conduct (Students Against Sweatshops 1999). While their tactics differ, all of these organizations use consumer pressure to improve the working conditions of people making consumer products.

While the terminology of these campaigns is contemporary, the protest strategy goes back to nineteenth-century struggles against subcontracting and "sweated labour" in the garment industry. "Sweated labour" was a term first used in the 1840s in England to describe what happened when, because of new methods of garment production, many male tailors were replaced by women workers in subcontracting chains. Just before the turn of the twentieth century, a young and reform-minded William Lyon McKenzie King, who would later become Canada's longest-serving prime minister, began a campaign against sweated labour in contracting shops in Toronto. In a series of newspaper articles, he exposed the terrible working conditions of women and child workers who toiled for long hours in unhealthy conditions for poor wages. Together with the labour movement and social reform groups, he helped to mobilize a public outcry against sweatshop conditions. The federal government responded by passing a fair wages resolution that required government contractors to adhere to certain minimum labour standards (Frager 1992; McIntosh 1993; Steedman 1997).

Consumer campaigns against labour abuse have a long pedigree in Canada. Trade unions have organized consumer boycotts of goods made by non-union labour in order to force corporations to recognize unions and the rights of workers to bargain collectively. Buy union label campaigns have also been common in the garment industry (Steedman 1997). The "no sweat" slogan used by contemporary campaigners against labour abuse deliberately echoes the history of struggles against sweated labour in the garment industry (Howard 1997).

Today, however, the target of protest campaigns is multinational corporations rather than government, and women and children are being exploited in the international labour market, not domestically. Unlike a century ago, consumers are not being asked to boycott products but to pressure the super-labels and giant retailers to make their contractors adhere to fair labour practices.

These changes in the targets and demands of consumer campaigns to stop labour abuse reflect profound changes within the garment industry in particular and the political economy in general. Mobile capital, new technology, trade liberalization policies and the resurgence of a neo-liberal politics whereby the free market is elevated to an ethical imperative have driven these changes.

A recent report for Status of Women Canada characterized the globalized apparel and footwear industries as continents wide and layers deep. Trade liberalization policies and new technologies have created profound changes not only in the international division of labour, but also "in how, by whom, and under what conditions our clothes are made in Canada and other countries" (Yanz et al. 1999: 110). Many corporations have adopted the Nike model, in which the corporation, typically headquartered in the North, sits on top of a production pyramid and controls the label, design and marketing while subcontracting the manufacturing of goods to countries that provide not only a cheap labour force, but one strictly controlled through repression of union organizing or prohibition of independent unions. When Korean workers won union rights, thanks to a series of sit-down strikes timed to coincide with the 1988 Olympics in Seoul, Nike moved its production from Korea, where wages were increasing, to Indonesia, a country notorious for persecuting independent unions. Indonesia, Vietnam and especially China are now the favoured countries for mega-labels and retailers seeking cheap and docile sources of labour (Cavanagh 1997).

Governments in countries where global sweatshops are located claim that if they legislate improved labour standards or even enforce existing ones, the transnational corporations will simply move their contracts to countries with even lower labour standards. In a world where capital is free to move at will, national governments say their hands are tied because any improvements they make in labour standards will price their workers out of the global market. They argue that bad jobs are better than no jobs for their people. They also complain that efforts by governments of the rich northern countries to link trade agreements to labour standards are simply a form of disguised protectionism designed to eliminate the only competitive advantage they have to offer on the global market—their cheap and abundant labour (Bernstein 1999; *Economist* 1995).

Moreover, many governments of the northern consumer countries prefer voluntary codes of conduct directed at the private sector to legislation by the public sector. Voluntary codes are seen as "compatible with the neo-liberal model of trade liberalization, privatization, deregulation, cost-cutting, flexibility, and global competitiveness" (Yanz et al. 1999: 47). Voluntary codes are attractive to governments of the North because they reduce some of the costs associated with the traditional command and control model of government regulation such as enforcement, application across national boundaries, inflexibility and ineffi-ciency (Purchase 1996). As Kevin Thomas (n.d.: 1–2) notes:

In the earlier part of the [twentieth] century people looked to government to regulate the activities of corporations. Ever since "free market" ideology became the prevailing rationale for our economic system, however, government has been systematically reducing its ability to regulate the corporate sector. The more government tries to extricate itself from regulating corporate behaviour, the more those responsibilities fall to citizens.

Contemporary corporate campaigns target the super-labels and industry leaders such as Nike because they use global subcontracting chains built upon sweated labour. But instead of asking consumers to boycott a particular retailer or label, the campaigners ask consumers to put pressure on leading corporations to ensure that their contractors meet specific labour standards. Boycotts simply punish a particular label without being linked to an improvement in workers' rights or conditions, because there is no way to ensure that there is a "no sweat" alternative. By focusing on an industry leader, today's campaigners hope to improve working conditions and workers' rights throughout the industry while simultaneously preserving jobs and avoiding charges of protectionism.

While capital roams the globe looking for cheap sources of labour, consumer markets with enough disposable income to buy high-priced running shoes and sportswear are limited to the well-off countries of the North. The challenge for corporate campaigns is to link the 10 percent of the world's population who exercise real consumer power with the estimated 1.3 billion people who work for less than one U.S. dollar a day. Opinion polls in the United States show that most consumers would rather not shop in stores that sell sweatshop goods. And some polls indicate that U.S. shoppers would pay a dollar more on a $20 item for a guarantee that the product came from a worker-friendly supplier (Press 1997: 221; Tabb 1999: 8). Even if the number of shoppers who would act on their convictions is smaller, apparel and athletic footwear labels, and retailers, know that public concern is growing. Corporate campaigns against labour abuse have been very successful at raising consumer consciousness about the labour behind the label. In response, key corporations have not only begun to adopt codes of labour practice and implement external monitoring, they have joined together with governments to develop industry-wide codes of practice and techniques to let consumers know which labels do not use sweated labour (Ross 1997a; Yanz et al. 1999).

## The Debate over Voluntary Codes of Conduct

Two prominent activists in the Canadian corporate campaign movement have summed up the sea change in how voluntary corporate codes of conduct regarding labour practices are viewed:

Five years ago, many of us would have dismissed codes of conduct as nothing more than company attempts to protect their brand image and/

or avoid government regulation. In a remarkably short period of time the debate about codes of conduct has moved from a focus on corporate social responsibility and self-regulation toward negotiation of the terms of corporate accountability, involving not only companies and their associations, but also (usually Northern) labour, religious and non-governmental organizations. In a few years, we have moved from company codes of conduct with no provision for monitoring or verification, toward multi-company, industry-wide and multi-sectoral codes, with elaborate systems of internal monitoring and external verification, factory and company certification, and mechanisms for NGO and labour participation in monitoring and third party complaints procedures. From company codes containing vague principles about corporate responsibility, we have moved to negotiated codes with precise and fairly consistent language based on ILO [International Labour Organization] conventions and UN declarations. (Yanz and Jeffcott 1999: 1)

While there is ongoing debate between corporate campaigners, on the one side, and the corporations and retailers, on the other, about the content of codes, the meaning of external monitoring and the extent of public disclosure, codes are here to stay. The question is how they will be used and whose agenda they will serve. As Yanz and Jeffcott (1999: 1) remark, "Codes can be used to deflect public criticism or to hold corporations accountable, to avoid unionization and justify investment in countries with repressive regimes or to increase democratic space for worker organizing." Moreover, the relationship between voluntary codes and government regulation is not straightforward: "Codes can be a privatized alternative to government regulation or a catalyst for government action" (Yanz and Jeffcott 1999: 1). In the U.S. in 1996 the Clinton administration convened a task force to examine conditions in the apparel industry, and eventually helped to set up the Fair Labor Association, which involves corporate campaigners and leading labels and retailers in establishing industry-wide codes of conduct, effective external monitoring systems and the "No Sweat" label of accreditation. The Canadian federal government, albeit reluctantly, established a similar task force in 1999.[1]

Whether codes are effective in improving labour standards and the rights of workers is one question. Another concerns the broader significance of consumer campaigns and voluntary codes of conduct in the context of the global market and neo-liberal ideology. The campaigns are not directed to citizens, but rather to consumers. Disposable income, not democracy, is the measure of power, and national governments are treated as pale shadows in comparison with powerful corporations. The logic of these campaigns is that we can rely on consumers to regulate corporations and create a moral economy. But the problem is, that is precisely what free-marketers would have us believe (Thomas n.d.: 7).

## The Nike Campaign: Attack, Defence and Counterattack

It is useful to turn once again to the Nike campaign to answer two questions: (1) the pragmatic question of whether voluntary codes of conduct are simply public relations techniques employed by cynical corporations or also effective methods of ameliorating labour abuse, and (2) the philosophical question of whether corporate campaigns reinforce or challenge the logic of rampant consumerism and rapacious capitalism. The typical response by a corporation to a campaign against it can be broken into a number of stages (Bernard 1997). The first is denial: "We meet all the local standards and we are good employers." The corporation denies any knowledge of labour abuse or that any abuse is occurring. The second is to blame others: "It's not our problem. We are marketers and designers, and the companies that make the shoes that bear our trademark are independent." The third stage is damage control, which includes actions involved in the other stages, but is distinctive because the corporation goes on the offensive. Critics are dismissed as special interests with axes to grind and in the extreme case the corporation resorts to what is known as "strategic litigation against public participation" (SLAPP) to silence critics. The fourth stage is to reassert control over the damaged corporate image, typically by implementing a code of conduct regarding labour practices. The fifth stage is to seek a prestigious cover, a high-profile individual, management firm or NGO to assert that the corporation is making all reasonable efforts to ensure that its labour practices code is followed by contractors. Nike's response to the campaign against the labour practices of its contractors is a variation on what has become a classic pattern.[2]

In response to a question posed by a reporter in 1991 regarding allegations that supervisors were beating workers and other labour abuses, Nike's general manager in Indonesia replied: "It's not within our scope to investigate" (Cavanagh 1997: 39). The following year saw many stories recounting labour abuse by Nike contractors. Nike responded by denying responsibility for the actions of its contractors, whom they claimed were adhering to labour laws; discounted any examples of abuse as exceptions; and established a corporate code of conduct that banned the use of forced, prison or child labour and required Nike contractors to comply with local laws governing wages, benefits, overtime, child labour and environmental protection. But, as critics were quick to point out, the code was little more than a public relations gesture as it did not provide for any enforcement mechanism.

Stories about the abusive labour practices of Nike's contractors continued to appear in the press,[3] but the international campaign against Nike did not get off the ground until 1996 when abuse of workers in Nike's contract factories in Vietnam was documented. Former employees and union activists at factories making Nike running shoes in Indonesia began to tour countries of the North, bearing witness to the hard work, low pay and bad working conditions tolerated by Nike. The disclosure of slave labour conditions among U.S. garment contractors similar to those in the developing world prompted the Clinton administration to establish a Sweatshop Task Force composed of leaders in the apparel and footwear industries, garment unions and NGOs. Along with other leading labels, Nike pledged to ensure that its products "are manufactured under decent and humane working conditions." But at the White House ceremony, Phil Knight remained unrepentant about Nike's strategy, proclaiming: "We are not here to rewrite economic history"(Olive 1996).

However, Nike was very active in 1996 in rewriting its labour image in response to the international campaign. In addition to taking the pledge, it created a Labor Practices Division, which provided internal inspectors in the key production countries of Indonesia, China and Vietnam, and appointed Dusty Kidd as head of Nike's global labour practices. Although it already had contracts with Ernst & Young and Price Waterhouse, two huge accounting firms, to audit some of its contractors' factories, Nike responded to demands for independent monitoring. It hired Andrew Young, the former U.S. Ambassador to the United Nations under President Carter, to examine working conditions in Nike's Asian contractors' plants.

In 1997, Young's firm, GoodWorks International, reported that "Nike is doing a good job in the application of its Code of Conduct. But Nike can and should do better." However, critics pointed out that, among other shortcomings, the report did not address the issue of wages and living standards except to say that "while it is tempting to criticize a few highly visible and successful companies for paying 'low wage,' meaningful reform can only be achieved through national law or international standards that enforce a 'level playing field' for all companies, not just a few" (GoodWorks 1997; Glass 1997; Clean Clothes 1999: 14–16). Moreover, Ernst & Young's audits were strictly confidential, available to the public only if Nike chose to release them or they were leaked. One audit, which was leaked to the press, found that the Nike subcontractor was in violation of a number of Vietnamese labour and environmental laws but nonetheless concluded that the factory was in compliance with the Nike Code of Conduct (Clean Clothes 1999: 13–14). Thus, the debate shifted from whether Nike should have a code and external monitoring to the content of the code and the independence of the monitors.

In April 1997, Clinton unveiled a new apparel industry code of conduct known as the Apparel Industry Partnership. It incorporated core ILO standards regarding child and free labour, freedom of association and health and safety, and required corporations to ensure that workers received the legal minimum wage and a maximum sixty-hour week with one day off. Most significantly, it established the Fair Labor Association (FLA), whose members were committed to establishing standards for independent external monitoring and a system for accrediting companies which fulfilled the obligations of the code. Companies that met the standards could attach the "No Sweat" label to their products. In 1997, Nike updated its own code to include the provisions of the FLA. So far, only four companies, including Nike and its major rival, Reebok, have joined the FLA; the other members of the presidential task force bowed out because they found the obligations too onerous (Bernstein 1999).

At a headline-making news conference on May 12, 1998, Phil Knight admitted that the brand had become "synonymous with slave wages and arbitrary abuse." He promised to do something about it, including increasing the salaries of its Indonesian minimum-wage workers by 15 percent, involving NGOs in independent monitoring of factory conditions and making summaries of findings public (Schmit 1999).[4] According to Kidd, "people now know that if they don't accept that responsibility [for the labour practices of their contractors], they may not have consumers in the next century" (Schmit 1999). In fact, Nike and Reebok are now in a race to the top to see which of the two athletic wear giants can persuade consumers that it treats its workers better (Maquila Network Update 1999).

But all this does not mean that the corporate campaign against Nike has ended; rather it has shifted from making Nike accept responsibility for the labour practices of its contractors to making Nike live up to its promises. Web sites are full of claims and counterclaims regarding labour abuse by Nike's contractors. The public relations battle has simply increased in intensity. Moreover, there are now duelling codes of conduct and a range of different external monitoring systems (Bernstein 1999; Yanz et al 1999). If anything, consumers are confronted by a surfeit of choice in the ethical marketplace.

## The Morality of the Market

For people concerned to see the end of corporate abuse of working people, many aspects of consumer campaigns are appealing. First, such campaigns expose how corporate giants such as Nike are involved in an international chain of exploitation and hold them responsible for the labour practices of their contractors. The campaigns make the links between production (cheap labour strategies), consumption (expensive brand names) and profit transparent. Second, these campaigns also illustrate the relationship between national and international labour markets: how good jobs in the North are not only leaving for the South but also becoming bad jobs. Third, these campaigns can be used to promote international solidarity rather than national protectionism by connecting coalitions in the North that are exposing labour abuses with the NGOs and unions in the South that represent workers. Fourth, they can foster union recognition or at least some form of independent advocacy for workers in countries where trade unions are repressed by the state or employers. Fifth, these campaigns exemplify the strength of coalition politics in which trade unions, church groups, women's organizations, international solidarity groups and human rights advocates are all involved. And finally, they can be linked with a broader series of demands, including enforceable international labour standards and international investment treaties that do not sacrifice democratic politics to multinational profit (Yanz et al. 1999).

However, campaigns that mobilize consumers to use their purchasing power to stop transnational corporations from making profits on the back of abused workers also have some limitations. In order for consumers to police the marketplace, they need knowledge and power. Today's consumers are faced with a dizzying array of codes, monitoring systems, claims and counterclaims. In the marketplace of ideas, sadly, those with the biggest advertising budgets often win. Nike has vastly greater resources to get its message across than do the campaigners. How many people have heard of Nike's contractors' labour practices in comparison with the number of people who have seen Nike ads?[5] How many people have participated in a Nike Day of Action compared with the millions of people who own or have purchased an item bearing the Nike swoosh? What is the relationship between knowing about the poor working conditions of the women who make Nike products and wearing those products? I asked my sixteen-year-old niece who was wearing Nike runners, but who had also signed a protest letter against Nike's labour practices, what she thought the effect of the campaign was. She said: "You feel bad about the workers so you sign a protest letter. Later you see a pair of Nikes, you think 'cool,' and you want to buy them."

Is it possible for independent monitors and third parties to force transnational corporations to live up to codes of conduct when national governments claim that they don't have the capacity to enforce labour standards? Or will the codes simply become another marketing device, a twenty-first-century, good house-keeping seal of approval? Consumers' power is still no substitute for state regulation. According to Thomas,

> A 1994 KPMG study of the factors which are considered important in motivating Canadian corporations to take action on environmental issues found that compliance with regulations motivated 92% of companies; voluntary programs motivated only 16%. Public pressure came somewhere in between, at 40%. Perhaps the "free market" ideologue's preference for public pressure over government regulation is because public pressure is over 50% easier to ignore. (n.d.: 7)

Consumers alone cannot police the global market. Consumer campaigns against corporate abuse of labour are best regarded as one tactic in an integrated and multi-dimensional strategy to improve labour standards and rights worldwide (Thomas n.d.; Yanz et al. 1999). Moreover, the goal of any strategy cannot be limited either to ensuring that corporations simply adhere to legal standards or to putting an end to sweatshops, which increasingly are seen to be in a moral class of their own (Ross 1997b: 296). Such a narrow focus simply tends to legitimize what have been deteriorating conditions, standards and rights for working people over the globe. A concerted strategy against labour abuse must challenge the power of transnational corporations to dictate people's living standards and the hegemony of the market. When faced with complaints about the extremely low wages paid to workers by contractors in Vietnam, Nike maintains that its wages are driven by the market and are better than those paid by Vietnamese-owned shoe factories. According to Chris Helzer, Nike's manager of corporate responsibility in Vietnam, "We have to pay Michael Jordan ... what the market dictates because he sells shoes for us. We pay workers this amount because that's the market"

(Schmit 1999). In other words, the market makes Nike do it. The challenge is to make corporate campaigns part of a broader political vision that challenges the moral legitimacy of the market, consumerism as the route to human fulfillment and the subordination of democracy to profits.

It is time to tell Nike: Just don't do it.

## Notes

1.  In 1998 the Maquila Solidarity Network launched a campaign to force the federal government to set up a sweatshop task force similar to the one established by Clinton in 1996. After receiving tens of thousands of petitions and enduring a series of public demonstrations, in March 1999 the federal government launched the Canadian Partnership for Ethical Trading and appointed John English, a former liberal MP, as its facilitator. In May 1999, English convened a meeting which brought together the Canadian Labour Congress and affiliated unions, religious groups, the Maquila Solidarity Network, retailers, the Apparel Manufacturers' Association, the Shoe Manufacturers Association, the Retail Council and the Alliance of Manu-facturers and Exporters. The result of that meeting was the formation of a joint industry–civil society working group to establish a code for apparel, footwear and related consumer products and industries, and a compliance and complaint mechanism. The civil society proposal for a canadian base code of labour practice was submitted on November 17, 1999; however, as of the date of writing, the corporations were still stalling. The Maquila Solidarity network organized a number of demonstrations against key corporate members during the 1999 Christmas shopping season to keep up the pressure. See the Ethical Trading Action Group Web site at http://www.web.net/~msn/3code.htm.

2.  The history of the Nike campaign and Nike's response to it is based on the following sources: Community Aid Abroad at http://www.caa.orgac/campaigns/nike/news.htm; Clean Clothes at http://www.cleanclothes.org/companies/nikecase.htm; Maquila Solidarity Network at http://www.web.net/~msn/3nike.htm; Just do it! Boycott Nike! at http://www.geocities.com/Athens/Acropolis/5232/ and Nike at http://www.info.nike.com/labor/toc_prac.shtml.

3.  Meanwhile, labour rights activists moved to pressure Nike on another front. In 1992 they filed a petition before the U.S. trade office charging that Indonesia permitted the systematic violation of workers' rights and should be denied special trade privileges under a 1984 agreement that makes such privileges contingent on countries' respect for those rights. In 1994 the Indonesian government responded by announcing a 29 percent increase in the minimum wage, thereby forcing Nike contractors to raise wages (Cavanagh 1997: 39–49).

4.  Now Nike has a multi-tier monitoring system comprising: in-house moni-toring of contractors, an arrangement with Price Waterhouse Coopers

whereby the firm monitors each of Nike's contractors on a yearly basis; and the involvement of NGOs, in particular the Global Alliance for Workers and Communities, made up of private, public and nonprofit institutions dedicated to improving the work and life opportunities of young adult factory workers. Since 1996, Nike has severed relationships with ten suppliers who failed to meet its labour code. See Nike at http://www.info.nike.com/labor/pr_monit.shtm/.

5.    According to the Canadian Nike campaign Web site, a December 1997 Vector poll indicated that 46 percent of Canadians surveyed were aware that "Nike has third world sweatshops," while only 10 percent believed that Nike was a "good third world employer" (Clean Clothes 1999).

Part Four
# Professions

Chapter 10

# Psychological Illusions:
## Professionalism and the Abuse of Power

*Tana Dineen*

Power has long been a focus of attention for psychologists. In contrast to Freud's preoccupation with sexuality, power formed the dominant theme in Adler's approach to psychoanalysis. Subsequently, power has been studied in relation to interpersonal aggression, social dominance and family dynamics.

In recent times, as Freud's theories have once again come into vogue, a bizarre but titillating fusion of the concepts of power and sexuality has taken place within our society. As a consequence, the term "abuse of power" has lost its connotative breadth. The danger is that each publicized case of individualized power abuse involving sex and sexuality is like a tree that serves to obscure the view of the forest. In staying focused on these often sensationalized stories, we fail to notice and to address a much larger problem. In expressing outrage about individual cases of alleged power abuse, we lose sight of a pervasive and rampant abuse of power by the mental health professions themselves. It is this abuse of power committed on a grand scale in the name of professionalism that devalues, exploits, trivializes and victimizes people throughout society.

When we hear of the abuse of power by individuals, we need to look behind these reports to examine the role of psychology and to consider how it may be misusing its position and influence. We need to consider the possibility that the profession itself is victimizing people by suggesting they reinterpret events in a way that makes them experience debilitating consequences. We need to recognize the noxious influence of psychology in our society, and its role in manufacturing an entire generation of victims to further its own interests, power and profit.

In the fall of 1969, while monitoring the diagnostic decisions made by psychiatrists in an Ontario general hospital, I began to have serious reservations about the opinions and practices of mental health experts. These doubts led me, for several years, into a research area that questioned the very foundation of mental health services (Dineen 1975). During my many years of clinical work, I never lost touch with these fundamental concerns. When I closed my practice in 1993 it was because these nagging doubts were sounding an alarm. Mental health professionals have become too influential, too arrogant and too powerful. I have seen too many bogus ideas adversely affect the lives of too many people.

While remaining a licensed psychologist in two Canadian provinces, I have forced myself to step back and take a cold hard look at my profession. What I now see being done under the name of psychology is so seriously contaminated by errors in logic, popular notions, personal beliefs and political agendas, and it is doing so much harm to people, that I can no longer bite my tongue. Thus I find myself in the strange role of working to curb the influence of my own profession.

Long ago I lost any expectation that effective corrective actions would come from within the profession; so I find myself most often now addressing my concerns to people outside my profession, hoping to find among them skeptics who are willing to think critically about Canada's (and the Western world's) love affair with psychology.

The former British prime minister Benjamin Disraeli wrote that "all power is a trust—that we are accountable for its exercise—that, from the people, and for the people, all springs, and all must exist" (Disraeli 1826). Unfortunately, it seems that my profession has lost sight of this trust and, by autocratically exercising power in its own interest, has broken its covenant with those who place their trust in psychologists.

## The Psychology Industry

Before briefly examining several ways by which psychology has gained and then proven itself unworthy of this trust, two terms I will use require clarification.

First, the term "psychologist" refers not only to licensed psychologists but to psychiatrists, social workers, family and marriage counsellors and the whole array of certified or self-proclaimed "experts" who sell opinions, assessments, theories, therapies, counselling and advice.

Second, the "psychology industry" refers to the business of producing and promoting psychological products. When people think of industries, they tend to think of automobiles, computers, cosmetics or entertainment, of easily identifiable products with price tags, warranties and trademarks. Such industries are defined by their products. The psychology industry, being much broader and less definable, is harder to pin down. At its core are psychology, psychiatry, psychoanalysis, clinical social work and psychotherapy (Henry et al. 1971). No longer can clear distinctions be made between them. So, the term "psychology industry" comprises the services of all five of these mental health professions, and it also encompasses the ever-expanding array of therapists, counsellors and advisors of all persuasions, whether licensed, credentialed, proclaimed or self-proclaimed. In addition, this term acknowledges that around the edges of the industry are others whose work, whether it involves writing, consulting, lecturing or even movie making, relies on the psychology industry, which, in turn, benefits from their promotion of all things psychological.

## Manufacturing Victims

It became fashionable in the late 1980s and early 1990s to be a victim. In describing the United States as "a nation of victims," Charles Sykes (1992: 11) writes that a "don't-blame-me permissiveness is applied only to the self, not to others; it is compatible with an ideological puritanism that is notable for its shrill demands of psychological, political and linguistic correctness." Peter Novick (1999) coined the term "the Victimization Olympics" in referring to the competition between various groups and individuals who seek recognition as victims.

While I readily acknowledge that there are many authentic victims who have suffered degradation, brutality and violence, I also know that many of the people now referred to as "victims" are not authentic. Some are "counterfeit victims" who manipulate the system, intentionally lying with motives of revenge, greed or excuse-finding. Others are "synthetic victims"—people who have been taught to think of themselves as victims and to make accusations and claims based on the psychological reinterpretation of events in their lives.

By turning all of life into psychological events, then pathologizing normal feelings and behaviours, and generalizing psychological concepts so that "trauma" can refer as easily to having a fling with the boss as to being brutally raped, people are being persuaded to see themselves as victims. Rather than assuming respon-sibility for their own actions, they come to believe that they must be protected, nurtured and guided by those who are described as more powerful. Each and every week, newspapers carry articles describing victims of one type or another, and many of these articles conclude that counselling should be provided, laws put in place, funds set aside for a healing process, or programs established to increase self-esteem, teach parenting skills or combat violence.

*Cui bono?* Who gains by this revisioning of human experiences? Ironically it is those people who identify and decry the abuse of power, whose job it becomes to assist the victims as they deal with the emotional wounds said to have been inflicted. The profession of psychology is responsible for the creation of numerous concepts employed in accusations involving the abuse of power. It is psychologists who coined many of these terms and took the initiative to legitimize them. And it is psychologists who benefit most from the contamination of society by the uncontested acceptance of these ideas, which people believe reflect genuine "psychological expertise."

How many times has one heard that the "victim" was referred for counsel-ling, that the accused was ordered into treatment or that sensitivity training was made a condition of disciplinary action? All of these "therapeutic" orders are based on the unquestioned assumption that psychologists have specialized knowledge and powerful skills that make them uniquely qualified to facilitate healing and influence change. But do they?

*Manufacturing Victims: What the Psychology Industry Is Doing to People* (Dineen 1998b) shows in explicit detail that psychology has a vested interest in identifying instances of abuse of power. The book identifies a paradigm through which victims are manufactured and then converted into patients/clients for whom psychological services must be purchased. To put it in a visual form:

person => victim => patient => profit/power

It is through such processes that psychologists gain social status and maneuver themselves into positions from which they can influence governments, media and the courts.

## The Mystique of Science

Since the age of Enlightenment, science has come to be respected as providing the power to understand and control nature. In the West, the focus for hundreds of years remained on the conquest of the physical/material world; then, at the dawn of the twentieth century the psychological world came to be viewed as a new frontier. It seemed that human nature too might be tamed. Psychology was heralded as a science which held great promise.

Thirty-five years ago I was drawn to the discipline of psychology by the intriguing questions it asked. I respected its efforts to apply the scientific method to understanding human nature and to bring the disturbing and destructive aspects of human behaviour under control. For almost three decades I worked as a clinician and a consultant, striving to apply that knowledge. But now the profession gives too many answers and asks too few questions; the humble curiosity it once had has given way to arrogant certainty and crass marketing. The quest for knowledge has been replaced by the search for products to package and strategies to boost sales.

Most of psychology can no longer legitimately claim recognition as a science. Clinical experience and untested theories are exalted, allowing opinions and personal beliefs to be presented as if they constitute scientifically based knowledge.

As far back as 1949, a report by the American Psychological Association (APA) Committee on Training in Clinical Psychology expressed concern in writing about this trend:

> There is an over-emphasis upon training in clinical techniques at the expense of education in psychological theory and research methodology. It would seem that this emphasis is due, on the one hand, to pressure from students and field agencies, and on the other, to the residue of our own history of fifteen to thirty years of clinical psychology which developed as a practice almost entirely limited to the use of tests. Perhaps this is not unexpected. As a profession we are still somewhat gropingly exploring and finding our way. Perhaps because there is still considerable and reasonable doubt concerning the validity of much of our knowledge and theory in the field of personality and clinical problems, we are inclined to devote much attention to tangibles such as techniques which can be acquired rather easily and give immediate evidence of specialized knowledge.... Major effort must be exerted at this stage of our development to analyze and test many of our basic assumptions in clinical theory, practice and teaching. (APA 1949: 339–40)

Not much has changed in the intervening fifty years. As psychologist and APA Fellow Robyn Dawes notes:

> What the APA has failed to do—and in my mind failed miserably—is to assure that the professional practice of psychology is based on available scientific knowledge. Instead, something termed clinical judgement predominates as a rationale for practice; it is based on experiences—despite all the well-documented and researched flaws of making experience-based inference in the absence of a sound theoretical base. (Dawes 1989: 14)

In many ways, "science" has become merely a marketing term, used to imply to consumers, insurers and legislatures that the statements psychologists make are valid and the treatments they offer are effective. The mystique of science is used to sell a wide variety of products. Evidently "Science" is the Nike swoosh of the psychology industry, an empty word used to enhance the image and bolster the social power of psychologists.

## The Ascendance of Subjective Experience: A Practice Makes Perfect

Professional opinion and experience have gained such prestige that objective data are no longer required, allowing facts to be readily ignored and easily distorted. While some psychologists may align with Robyn Dawes and express regret that the profession has moved away from its scientific foundation, others believe that there is a greater advantage in highlighting practitioners' own values, beliefs and experience which formerly may have been obscured by bodies of theoretical knowledge and techniques (Chapman 1993: 57–62). For many psychologists, the importance of the subjective—as evidenced in their claims to many years of clinical experience or to clinical judgement, rather than to any objective proof of the effectiveness of their skills or the veracity of their opinions—is an accepted principle. Some go so far as to exalt their own personal experiences as victims over that of any professional training as qualifying them to provide treatment. Marilyn Murray, described as a specialist in the field of victim treatment, approvingly reports that, at this point, many people who choose to work with adult survivors of childhood trauma are coming to it from their own victimization (in Beigel and Earle 1990: 83). Anne Wilson Schaef (1992) supports such a view in stating, "My relationship addiction recovery process has been key in its interaction with my professional work and how I came to view my work"; as does John Bradshaw (1990), whose approach, as described on the jacket cover of his book, has its origins in his own experience: "John Bradshaw has lived everything he writes about."

But does experience, either personal or professional, enhance the effectiveness of treatment as much as it does the image of psychology? Psychologist and mental health services researcher Leonard Bickman identifies the belief that professional experience leads to greater knowledge and better skills as one of six myths "that are routinely used to bolster [psychologists'] confidence about their effectiveness." In his systematic review of the literature, he finds no evidence "that clinicians get better at producing client outcomes with more experience" (Bickman 1999: 13).

In spite of this lack of support, psychologists persist with this myth in their campaign to persuade individuals and society of their professional knowledge and expertise. The term "campaign" is intentionally chosen because persuasion takes the form of an organized political enterprise as well as an activity of individual psychologists. Consider, for example, the APA's multi-million-dollar public education campaign, Talk to Someone Who Can Help, the goals of which are "to help people understand ... how a psychologist can help with everyday life problems." The purpose is to market the image of psychologists as helpful and powerful. And the success of the campaign rests on psychologists presenting themselves as an authoritative professional group possessing specialized and powerful skills—all wrapped in an aura of science.

## The Symbols of Professionalism

Since professional boards have the power to grant and revoke the licences of practitioners, licensing and certification programs foster the public image of professional accountability and credibility. However, while these boards assert that their primary function is the protection of the public, they were actually established, and continue to function, as vehicles for protecting their members.

The prominent psychologist Rollo May, shortly before his death, recounted the events leading up to the licensing of psychologists in the United States (1992). He described the mid-1950s as "the dangerous years," when a conservative wing of the American Medical Association wanted to have psychotherapy declared a restricted medical procedure. These physicians and psychiatrists threatened to outlaw all non-medical psychotherapists and, for several years, these psycho- therapists lived in fear that physicians would put them out of business by taking ownership and control of psychotherapy. Finally, a conference was organized on psychotherapy training, practice and safeguards, out of which rose an impetus for the licensing of psychologists. From then on, as various state and provincial legislatures enacted licensing laws, it became accepted that psychologists had the skills and the right to do psychotherapy. Psychologists had succeeded in extending the therapeutic monopoly to include themselves. Ironically, they came to adore the power which they had abhorred earlier when it had been held beyond their reach, in the hands of medicine.

Rollo May went on to describe a conversation he had at that time with Carl Rogers:

> Expecting his [Rogers'] enthusiastic help, I was taken aback by his stating that he was not sure whether it would be good or not to have psychologists licensed.... During the following years, I kept thinking of

Carl Rogers' doubts about our campaign for licensing. I think he foresaw that we psychologists could be as rigid as any other group, and this certainly has been demonstrated. (1992: xx–xxvii)

While accusations of unaccountability and cover-up are difficult to prove since most of the activities of these licensing boards are conducted in camera, several provincial and state boards across North America have gained unwanted attention in recent years for their failure to act on complaints. Instead of protecting the public, they have been shown to operate as "organized gangs," "closed shops" and "old boys (and girls) clubs" (Wittmeier 1999: 42). Also, there have been repeated demonstrations that licences are no guarantee of clinical skills. "The role of licensing in affecting client outcome and therapy effectiveness is to date mythical," according to Bickman (1999: 972). Unfortunately, as mythical and meaningless as they may be, the average mental health consumer views these licences and certificates as totems of real professional power—as proof of the ability to understand, help and heal.

With a growing awareness of the potential harm of unproven assessments, therapies and theories, some individuals have taken action to address the problems as a consumer protection issue. During the 1990s a significant number of U.S. psychologists were successfully sued in civil courts and forced to pay large sums of money in damages (Eisner 2000). A letter signed by an esteemed group of concerned psychologists was sent to the U.S. Congress in 1995 warning that "these widespread, harmful practices waste millions of taxpayers' hard-earned dollars, violate the civil rights of patients and families and defile the American judicial process" and requesting open hearings into these important scientific, legal, consumer protection, and public policy issues.

Shortly after that letter was sent, legislation based on *The Truth and Responsibility in Mental Health Practices Act* began to be introduced in several states, including Indiana, which in 1996 became the first state to pass the informed consent part of the legislation.

## Controlling What the Public Is Told

While Francis Bacon promoted his empirical philosophy with the statement that "knowledge is power," it was not until four centuries later that the Canadian communications guru and University of Toronto professor Marshall McLuhan showed us that "information is power," demonstrating that those who have the information have the power! And the corollary is that those who have "the power" can decide what information is to be shared and what information is to be concealed. What they choose to tell the public becomes what we know, and their message is what we believe to be the truth.

The psychology industry, like any business enterprise, decides what it does and doesn't want the public to know. It wants people to hear about new treatments and successes, and it wants the public to believe that psychologists are trustworthy and powerful. But it doesn't tell us when therapies are shown to be ineffective or even to cause serious harm, such as the notorious repressed/ recovered memory therapy, once described by APA past-president Ronald Fox as "the black eye of psychology" (Martin 1995: 44). It never issues warnings when untested theories are heralded as scientific discoveries, nor does it alert the justice system when expert opinions expressed in courtrooms are known to be in error.

A case in point involves a consumer survey conducted by *Consumer Reports* (CR), the organization that reports on how well people like their toasters and their VCRs. In its 1994 annual survey, CR asked its subscribers for their opinions about psychotherapy. The response rate was an abysmal 1.6 percent but, nonetheless, CR (1995) and the APA (Seligman 1995) both claimed that this "groundbreaking" survey shows that psychotherapy usually works—"that nine out of ten" people got better with therapy—and that more was better—"longer psychotherapy was associated with better outcomes." Despite shockingly obvious flaws in the survey which should have made any conclusion dubious, *American Psychologist*, the flagship journal of the APA, described the result as "a message of hope for other people dealing with emotional problems." And the APA continues to make use of it in their public education program, designed to persuade the public that psychotherapy works (Farberman 1996: 5).

In contrast, the Fort Bragg Project, an $80 million project funded by the U.S. government, is not included in the APA's public education program (Bickman 1996; Bickman et al. 1995). The results of this well designed and conducted study, described by the APA as "state of the art," startled researchers and shocked psychologists. In examining the costs and clinical outcomes of psychotherapy, it found that the assumption that clinical services are in any way effective might very well be erroneous, and that longer-term treatment results in higher costs but no demonstrable improvement in clinical outcomes—more is NOT better. Leonard Bickman, the project's senior researcher, utterly surprised by the outcome, states that "clinical services ... very effectively delivered ... in a higher quality system of care were nonetheless ineffective. A very impressive structure was built on a very weak foundation." "These results," he concludes, "should raise serious doubts about some current clinical beliefs" regarding the effectiveness of psychological services. Independently replicated in Stark County, Ohio, with similar results, this study led Bickman to state that "there is scant evidence of (psychotherapy's) effectiveness in real-life community settings" (see Dineen 1998b: 54–63).

A recent controversy provides a further example of psychology's efforts to be a gatekeeper of information. In July 1998, *Psychological Bulletin*, one of the APA's premier journals, contained an article entitled "A Meta-Analytic Examination of Assumed Properties of Child Sexual Abuse Using College Samples" (Rind et al. 1998). The authors had done a critical review of the research literature on pedophilia and voiced the cautionary conclusion that, contrary to public opinion, the effects on children of "adult-child sex" (the authors' term) are not always severe. Egged on by a furious Dr. Laura Schlessinger, the talk-show host, the U.S.

House of Representatives voted unanimously on July 12, 1998, to denounce the study. The APA responded with the assurance that future articles will be more carefully considered for their "public policy implications" before publication.

The purpose in mentioning the issue here is not to voice an opinion one way or the other about the conclusions of the study, but rather to point out that the largest association of psychologists in the world, the APA, intends to vet future articles according to their political acceptability rather than their scientific merit. Despite the fact that the paper in question provided evidence to back statements regarding the resilience of children to survive life's cruelties, in "a stunning display of scientific weakness and moral posturing," the profession moved not to encourage scholarly discussion of the topic but rather to patch the puncture in its power and repair its relationship with government, "the Christian Coalition, Republican congressmen, panicked citizens, radio talk-show hosts and a consortium of clinicians" (Tavris 1999).

These examples offer a mere sampling of the many instances where the public is not told the whole story, where an advertising campaign is presented as if it were serving an educational function, and where censorship is applied in such a way that information is shaped to fit not the criteria of science but rather of political propaganda.

## Relying on "Fear Appeal" to Promote Its Services

In declaring that "The only thing we have to fear is fear itself," U.S. President Roosevelt acknowledged the power that fear can have in influencing behaviour. Not only a deterrent, fear can also motivate people into alternative ways of thinking and behaving.

"Fear appeal" is defined in marketing terms as "advertising purporting to develop anxiety within the consumer based on fear that can be overcome by purchasing a particular item or service" (Rosenberg 1995: 2–3). For example, the risk of house fires and the threat of burglaries are used in the promotion of home insurance.

The psychology industry relies on a similar emotional approach when it ominously describes the effects of traumatic events. Whether it's a tragic loss, violence, stress, abuse or a hate crime, harmful effects are predicted, graphically or through more subtle suggestion and imagery.

For example, one Canadian national newspaper on a typical day carried two articles advising readers of potential psychological danger. One, entitled "Job uncertainty unleashes health threats" (*National Post* 1999a: C2), cites psychologists warning that "despair, anger, fear, anxiety, fatigue, depression" are common responses to stress and can "exact a heavy physical and emotional toll, causing increased heart rate and blood pressure, tense muscles, rapid breathing, increased cholesterol and a weakened immune system." A few pages earlier, an article on the anniversary of the Swissair Flight 111 crash speaks of the hundreds of people involved in the recovery mission who continue, one year later, to receive treatment to overcome the trauma and deal with "unfinished business" (*National*

*Post* 1999b: A4). Both articles are graphic and emotional in their descriptions of the fearful effects of untreated problems.

Elsewhere, in the August 1999 issue of *Canadian Psychology,* it is reported that: "psychological services are underutilized by depressed individuals," and a newspaper article informs Canadians that the most recent estimate shows that on average only 13 percent of Canadians who can be clinically diagnosed as depressed avail themselves of any sort of counselling (Goodden 1999: A11). When coupled with the concurrent statement by the Canadian Mental Health Association that 15 percent of people with untreated depression, or 13.5 percent of all depressed individuals, commit suicide, the result is another instance of fear appeal used to promote psychological services.

Regarding "abuse," a popular fear-generating topic, a July 1997 Canadian newspaper headline read: "Abuse rate worse than thought, survey finds." The media reported that "31.2% of males and 21.8% of females reported physical abuse during their lifetime." And it concluded that "childhood maltreatment among Ontario residents is common" (MacMillan et al. 1997: 131–35).

But wait! If this conclusion were to be generally applied, it would mean that almost one in every three Canadians has been a victim of physical abuse during childhood, making Canada an exceedingly violent society. This study was large and publicly funded but, as in most instances of dramatic statistical reporting, no data are available for scrutiny. Although repeatedly requested, no answers to basic questions were forthcoming from the researchers. For instance, one question-naire item which was assumed to indicate previous physical abuse asked respondents if they could remember during their years of growing up being "sometimes pushed, grabbed or shoved." While being pushed down a flight of stairs would warrant the term "abuse," it is doubtful whether every instance of pushing or grabbing a child can be considered abusive. And without such differentiation and details, it becomes impossible to know what the results, as reported in the media, actually mean. The social effect, however, is to spread fear and interpersonal tension throughout society, to expand funding in the areas of violence research and education, and to increase professional staffing—all to the eventual benefit of psychologists "in the business."

One can only conclude that such fear-promoting, pseudo-scientific surveys are designed with political and self-serving, rather than scientific, intentions. The psychology industry is very effective in massaging definitions and misusing numbers for the purpose of engendering fears that are useful in promoting its services. Survey results are not necessarily trustworthy just because they appear in journals, cite statistics, receive government support or generate media headlines.

The data essential for evaluating the accuracy of the conclusions of surveys and studies are too often left unexamined. The information is rarely sought and, when requested, is often not provided. In this child abuse study, the researcher would not answer questions, claiming only that she was planning to use the data for further publications. When the Consumer's Union was asked for the data backing their *Consumer Reports* survey conclusions about the effectiveness of psychotherapy, the request was denied on the grounds that the data were proprietary. On other occasions when data are available, clear evidence of the abuse of numbers is far too frequently uncovered.

Such questioning of the accuracy of conclusions tends, however, not to have much impact, and the conclusions of these surveys and studies continue to kindle fears which encourage consumers to purchase the research, educational, preventive and therapeutic services that are offered for sale. Suicide, abuse, violence—these words are powerful for, as Dawes (1999) notes, "words can be and have been used to rouse intuitions and influence policies in ways that have absolutely nothing to do with reality." Their power derives in part from a human tendency, identified by Spinoza, to believe that whatever one hears expressed verbally is true and only later, if ever, to question exactly what it means. Without this questioning, these verbal images, especially when accentuated by numbers, create fears which translate into profit and power for the psychology industry.

## Concluding Comments

In a keynote speech at the 1997 annual conference of the National Association of Provincial Court Judges (Dineen 1997), I stressed two points for their consideration: (1) psychology is an industry masquerading as a scientifically based profession, and (2) no matter how strongly psychological beliefs and theories are expressed as facts, there is little to no certainty in the field. More recently, Peter Suedfeld, president of the Canadian Psychological Association (CPA), took it upon himself to voice the following question to the membership: "When is the taking of a position on non-guild issues a legitimate function for psychological organizations?" He answered that "it is rarely so. For CPA to get involved in this kind of advocacy, it should be necessary that as psychologists we have special knowledge—based on solid scientific data—of what the best policy would be." He encouraged members to consider "what effects [a policy statement] might have aside from allowing [psychologists] to feel virtuous, and perhaps, above all, whether [they] have particular expertise that makes [their] input significant." Perhaps mindful of Hippocrates' words—"There are in fact two things, science and opinion; the former begets knowledge, the latter ignorance"—Suedfeld concluded with the suggestion to his colleagues that "our contributions might be more valuable if we offered our knowledge and showed restraint in advocating our opinions" (Suedfield 1999: 2, 4).

Regrettably, in this world of entrepreneurial psychology in which niche-making takes priority over professional restraint, it is unlikely that his admonition will be heeded. Thus, it is important that anything said by psychologists be scrutinized carefully by judges, lawyers, the media and the public; that both the opinions and the power of this profession be challenged.

While, undeniably, some individuals within the profession of psychology will face disciplinary action and public disgrace by virtue of having seduced or been seduced by a patient or student, it must be remembered that such instances of unethical behaviour are only "the trees." It is my hope that public attention will not be forever diverted by fingers pointing at these individuals, because this finger pointing only obscures our view of the bigger issue. If one remains focused on the trees, the power of the psychology industry will never be effectively challenged. "The forest," in this instance, is the pervasive and socially sanctioned abuse of power, in the form of the profession's influence on the media, the courts, the government and those with their hands on the purse strings of private and public funds.

Some time ago, the renowned MIT professor of linguistics and philosophy, Noam Chomsky, wrote: "One waits in vain for psychologists to state the limits of their knowledge." He commented recently that: "I'm sure we'll continue to 'wait in vain.' Too many careers at stake" (personal communication 1998). And sadly that may be true.

I have been waiting a very long time for people outside my profession to set limits on the psychology industry. Society must take a look at the larger picture and ask itself whether it can any longer afford to remain blinded by the trees— forever distracted by limitations placed on our understanding of the term "abuse of power."

## Notes

1.  Now called "The Barden Letter," this document sent on January 5, 1995, was addressed to the chairman of the Judiciary Committee, U.S. House of Representatives, Washington, D.C.
2.  Franklin Delano Roosevelt, first inaugural address, March 4, 1933.
3.  Information provided by CMHA/Peel Branch, August 1999.

# Chapter 11

# Drugged, Exploited, Labelled and Blamed:
## How Psychiatry Oppresses Women

*P. Susan Penfold*

As workers in the mental health profession, my psychiatric colleagues and I like to believe that, like other medical specialties, psychiatry is a scientific discipline. We like to think that diagnostic categories represent particular sets of symptoms that can be addressed with specific treatments; that psychotropic medication is vital for most psychiatric disorders; that some people must be drugged, incarcerated or even electroshocked for their own and society's protection; and that psychiatry, more and more, has come to be based on a reliable and valid set of scientific propositions about the biological basis of human nature and the regular unfolding of the various phases of human development. Evidence that these beliefs are invalid, or perhaps only partially true, is often ignored. For we like to think of ourselves as sensitive, perceptive, compassionate, unbiased and hard-working helpers committed to healing sick people. Any different analysis, any alternative light, might do us out of a job! At the very least, our practices would have to change to reflect awareness of the effects, often extreme, of social conditions on people's lives.

An examination of psychiatric theory and practice over the last century yields many examples of how psychiatry, while purporting to be benign, compassionate and helpful, is actually a force of social control, oppression or even abuse. It may even be life-threatening. In the past, patients have been subjected to psychosurgery, made comatose with large doses of insulin (Valenstein 1986), or used as guinea pigs, as at the Allan Memorial Institute in Montreal during Ewan Cameron's collaboration with the CIA (Collins 1988). While psychiatry can be perilous for men and children as well, and many of the issues discussed apply to people in general, this chapter will focus on how women, in particular, are oppressed by psychiatry.

Women's complaints about psychiatry centre around being drugged, exploited, labelled and blamed. They are voiced in books such as *Women and Madness* (Chesler 1973), *Women Look at Psychiatry* (Smith and David 1975), *Still Sane* (Blackridge and Gilhooly 1985), *Shrink Resistant* (Burstow and Weitz 1988) and *Looney Bin Trip* (Millett 1990). Complaints emanate from women's centres, transition houses, women's groups, women's publications such as *Kinesis* and *Healthsharing*, agencies and societies that struggle with violence towards women.

## Drugged

Studies have consistently shown that women receive most of the prescriptions for anti-anxiety and anti-depressant medications. An outcry against the over-prescription of Valium in the 1970s led to a diminution of its use. Its place has been taken by other benzodiazepines such as Ativan and Xanax, and by the newer anti-depressant drugs such as Prozac, Paxil and Zoloft. Prozac, which is presently being prescribed to more than 31 million people and is the world's most profitable prescribed brand medicine (Graham 1998), has an ever-expanding range of indications—which is curious given its supposedly specific pharmacological action. In addition to depression, it is prescribed for obsessive compulsive disorder, panic disorders, eating disorders, drug and alcohol addictions, social phobia, migraine, premenstrual syndrome, autism, arthritis, attention deficit disorder, borderline personality disorder, and behavioural and emotional problems in children. It has even been touted as a "designer drug" to tailor one's personality or remake the self (Kramer 1993).

Women describe being prescribed these medications to "help" them cope with a difficult husband, overactive children or various losses and life changes. They complain that the doctor talks to them for only a few minutes, focusing only on symptoms, and does not listen to other problems or concerns. If the medication does not help, they are told that they need a different pill or an increased dose. The physician or psychiatrist does not consider another approach or question the original diagnosis. Sometimes women have taken these medications for as long as twenty years. Transition house staff, working with battered women, say that many of their clients are so heavily medicated that they are unable to grapple with the decisions they need to make about being in an abusive relationship. Psychotropic medications "dull sensitivity and reactivity, induce women to continue assuming narrow unfulfilling roles, and render patients docile and compliant"(Women and Mental Health Committee, CMHA 1987). The side effects of Ativan can include drowsiness, dizziness, weakness, fatigue, lethargy, disorientation, unsteady gait, memory problems, nausea, change in appetite or weight, depression, blurred and double vision, restlessness, sleep disturbance, vomiting, sexual problems, headaches, skin rashes, gastrointestinal symptoms, and musculoskeletal, ear, nose, throat and respiratory problems. Withdrawal of the medication usually leads to rebound anxiety and physical symptoms, and adds to the likelihood of addiction to this class of medications. Commonly observed adverse effects of Prozac include headache, nervousness, insomnia, drowsiness, fatigue, anxiety, tremor, dizziness or lightheadedness, nausea, diarrhea, dry mouth, anorexia, excessive sweating, skin rash, decreased libido and sexual difficulties. Less common and more serious adverse effects have been reported, such as addiction, abuse, suicide and becoming violent or even murderous (Breggin 1995). But the most noxious effects on a woman of being put on a psychotropic medication are the assumptions created about her illness. She, and others in her environment, may be convinced that her neurotransmitters are in total control and she is powerless and completely dependent on psychiatric treatment. She may feel sick, damaged and unable to function. Other possible factors such as an abusive partner, a stressful and demeaning job, difficult teenage children, or poverty are papered over.

The so-called biological revolution in psychiatry over the last two decades has led to the conviction that neurotransmitter abnormalities account for most psychiatric disorders. Reflecting, reinforcing and reaping gargantuan profits from this belief are the pharmaceutical companies, which are often large multinational corporations. The "brave new world of pharmocapitalism" (Critser 1996: 38–48) has embraced, enfolded and threatens to erase psychiatry as anything more than a biomedical specialty. Because of cutbacks in government research funding, pharmaceutical companies fund most of the research in departments of psychiatry across North America. To secure research grants, researchers may agree to delete negative information about a company's product or to delay publication of findings (Blumenthal et al. 1997: 1224–28). In the U.S., pharmaceutical companies own some health maintenance organizations, and doctors working in these organizations are required to prescribe medications manufactured by that pharmaceutical company.

Few new drugs offer a clear advantage over existing therapies. Most are so-called "me too" drugs, very similar to brand name medications already on the market. Thus pharmaceutical companies organize intense campaigns to change prescribers' habits and to distinguish their products from those of competitors (Kessler et al. 1994: 1350–53). To influence prescribing habits, pharmaceutical companies in the United States spend $5,000 to $8,000 annually on each physician. Doctors are showered with promotional literature, advertising in medical journals—which is often misleading or has little educational value (Wilkes et al. 1992: 912–19), and free samples of new medications. Physicians who are heavy prescribers receive perks such as free meals, free trips, free medications for their families and handsome rewards for participating in research on their own patients. This "research" amounts to little more than prescribing new or experimental drugs to a captive population, who could unknowingly be endangered (Walker 1999: 31–32).

So why has psychiatry "caved in to a conservative Social Darwinism ... embracing the long-discredited knowledge of an earlier era: to an insistent emphasis on behavioral disorders of all kinds as manifestations of a disease of the brain, the metabolism, or the chromosomes" (Shore 1988: 13–15)? This, it is argued, started in the 1970s in the U.S., when third party payers began to query whether psychiatry was a medical specialty and should qualify for payment. Many psychiatrists deserted psychoanalysis, psychodynamic therapy, community psychiatry, group therapy and family therapy and flocked back to a narrow biomedical model, determined to prove that they were real doctors. Biological psychiatrists gained ascendancy, and leadership in departments of psychiatry and resident and medical student training often veered strongly towards psychotropic medication for most disorders.

The availability and promotion of psychoactive medications have allowed general practitioners to move into the field of psychiatry. About 80 percent of anti-anxiety and anti-depressant medications are prescribed by general practitioners. Thus, when women go to psychiatrists or family doctors with complaints of depression, anxiety, stress, burnout, frustration or anger, medication is likely to result. Educated or influenced to see these symptoms as a manifestation of neurotransmitter malfunction, mindful of government edicts about cost-effectiveness and brief intervention, few practitioners will understand that a woman's distress may originate in being the sole caretaker of small children, sexually harassed or a target of male violence. The frustrations of boring, low-paid, dead-end jobs with no benefits or pensions, and the grinding poverty of many older women, are obscured. Medication, with accompanying sedation, drowsiness, apathy or other side effects, may be the last thing such a woman needs.

## Exploited

U.S. studies in the 1970s and 1980s indicated that six to ten percent of psychiatrists had been sexually involved with patients (Gartrell et al. 1986: 1126–31; Kardener 1974: 1134–36). Most abusers were male and most victims female. The profession ignored these statistics until outcries from consumers, books, newspaper articles and female professionals led to change. In the early 1990s, several Canadian provincial medical licensing bodies mounted task forces or committees to study sexual misconduct by physicians. Although some changes resulted, and more education of medical students and residents is occurring, much resistance and even backlash can be discerned. It is estimated that 95 percent of abuses go unreported, and victims who do make a complaint to police or licensing bodies, or who mount a civil case, face massive obstacles. These include the victims' own shame and self-blame, community attitudes towards them, and defensive medical bureaucracies (Penfold 1998: 162–79). Lawyers defending psychiatrists or other physicians who have been charged with sexually abusing patients have many techniques for discrediting witnesses, including strategies for blaming the victim.

Claims that sexual abuse of patients has diminished are hard to assess. The demise of most long-term psychodynamically oriented therapies where psychiatrist and patient spent several hours per week in an intense and often emotionally charged relationship might have reduced the opportunity and the incidence. Or has it merely gone underground? In any event, other types of exploitation and boundary violation are also damaging to women patients. Frequently heard is the account of the male psychiatrist who flirts, conducting erotically charged sessions with his woman patient, or the psychiatrist who indulges in role reversal, confiding about his troubles with his wife, job, family or finances.

Women's programming to be compliant and deferential, to minister to men's needs and do all the emotional work in the male-female relationship, makes them more vulnerable to abuse by male professionals. Childhood abuse may make a woman less able to avoid another victimization (Kluft 1990: 263–87). When a woman who is emotionally distressed goes to a psychiatrist, her job as a patient is to disclose her innermost feelings and fears. She is expected, and expects, to put her trust in an authority figure who has a fiduciary duty to her and is there to act in her best interests. The psychiatrist-patient relationship has some parallels with that between a parent and a child. The patient is in a trusting, vulnerable and childlike position and the psychiatrist is a parent-surrogate. Powerful transference feelings are engendered. The patient displaces onto the psychiatrist feelings that she had, as a child, about parents or other significant adults. Managed appropriately by the psychiatrist, an understanding of these emotions and related beliefs and attitudes can pave the way to change. But an unethical, disturbed or poorly trained psychiatrist can misinterpret and misuse the patient's trust, soul-baring, and childlike emotions and use her for his own needs.

Once entangled in a sexually abusive relationship with a psychiatrist, it may take a woman months or even years to escape (Penfold 1998: 64–87). At first the sense of being special may be exciting and enlivening. Feeling bound to secrecy, committed to a focus on the abusing psychiatrist's needs, and blocked from taking any action by fears of abandonment by the powerful parent surrogate, the woman often withdraws from or loses other relationships. Realization of the enormity of her betrayal and exploitation, that she has been duped and used, comes very slowly. Shame and self-blame are often paralyzing, as she is likely to share society's tendency to blame victims.

After-effects of such abuse can include loss of employment, husband or partner, children and home. Some women are hospitalized and about one percent commit suicide. Common reactions are guilt, decreased ability to trust, ongoing ambivalence about the abuser, feelings of emptiness and isolation, emotional instability, suppressed anger, sexual confusion, increased suicidal risk, role reversal and boundary disturbance, and cognitive dysfunction (Pope 1994: 117–56).

The profession's attitude to, and treatment of, these victims is shoddy indeed. Other psychiatrists, perhaps fearing embarrassing confrontations or court involvement, shy away from these victims. Understandably, victims may not be willing to see another psychiatrist. While taking some responsibility for educating their members about the dangers of sexual involvement with patients, medical and psychiatric bureaucracies do little or nothing for victims. Victims are usually left to their own devices, to try to transcend the damage they have suffered and rebuild their shattered lives.

## Labelled

Women complain about being treated impersonally and unsympathetically and given a diagnosis that has little to do with the problems and difficulties of their everyday lives. Once assigned, the diagnosis takes on a life of its own and a woman's behaviour may be reinterpreted or reframed to fit with this impression. Sometimes a diagnosis brings pejorative connotations. An example of this is borderline personality disorder, thought to be much more frequent in women than in men. The diagnosis is ostensibly applied to people who have a pattern of unstable relationships and emotional reactions, are confused about their identity and very impulsive. Contrary to popular impression, research has shown that these symptoms are actually more common in men than in women (Henry et al. 1983: 1527–29). The overuse of this diagnosis for women suggests that it is sometimes a "wastebasket diagnosis" used in a sloppy and imprecise fashion (Reiser et al. 1984: 1528–32), and "if the clinician is uncertain of the pathology or experiences negative emotions while interacting with her" (Simmons 1992: 219–23). In addition, women, and rarely men, are sometimes given informal labels by mental health professionals. For women, these include "martyr," "overprotective," "seductive," "symbiotic," "hysterical," "promiscuous" or "typical alcoholic's wife." The critical designations applied to mothers and wives appear to reflect Schur's (1984) description of the "maternity controls" imposed on women. He suggests that women's behaviour in the family is subjected to considerable normative regulation. Minor deviance may be harshly judged. Underlying folk beliefs about the nature of women also influence judgement and lead to women being seen as either good or bad, madonna or whore, earth mother or destructive temptress.

That mental health professionals' judgement of normality in woman is influenced by traditional beliefs about the nature of women was demonstrated by the classic study of Broverman et al. (1970: 1–7). This study showed that clinicians believe healthy mature women differ from healthy mature men (and healthy mature adults) by being more submissive, less independent, less adventurous, more easily influenced, less aggressive, less competitive, more excitable in minor crises, more easily hurt, more emotional, more conceited about their appearance, less objective and less interested in mathematics and science. Keller (1992: 15–36) notes that such beliefs remain entrenched and unchallenged, as masculine standards of normality continue to dominate modern culture.

Examination of the labelling process in psychiatry requires an understanding of how the system of psychiatric diagnosis developed and how the medical-psychiatric system insists that a diagnosis be made. Over the years, committees of the American Psychiatric Association have developed and refined a system of diagnosis for psychiatric disorders. The fourth edition of the *Diagnostic and Statistical Manual (DSM)* of the American Psychiatric Association succeeded the revised third edition in 1994. Unlike earlier DSMs, the third edition, published in 1980, and the fourth edition are supposedly descriptive and atheoretical. Sets of criteria have been developed for each disorder, with the assumption that clinicians and researchers using these criteria will arrive at similar conclusions and will be studying similar disorders. Research questionnaires and diagnostic tests administered by computer have been formulated based on these sets of criteria. Thus a woman can be judged as suffering from a specified disorder if she has the requisite symptoms. Unfortunately this has led to a "quick and dirty" approach to diagnosis, which allows the clinician to decide on a label and related treatment without getting detailed information about the vicissitudes of a person's life. It is a "complex and sophisticated nomenclature for quick and superficial observations" (Dumont 1987: 11). Although some psychiatrists continue to espouse a biopsychosocial approach and obtain information about all areas of a person's functioning, the busy general practitioner or emergency physician is more readily seduced by the "quick and dirty" method.

The psychiatrist working in a hospital, mental health centre or private practice needs to place a label on—needs to give a diagnosis to—every patient. Hospitals and mental health centres demand statistics, including diagnostic categories, to maintain their government funding. Psychiatrists in private practice who derive their income from government plans or insurance companies have to provide a diagnosis for each patient in order to get paid. A diagnosis such as "adjustment disorder," which describes a person's emotional or behavioural reactions to environmental circumstances will suffice, but the pattern is set. Each patient, however normal she might be, requires a diagnosis. Dumont (1987: 11) complains, "Who can calculate the wasted hours of foolish, futile discussion about how to compartmentalize patients who never seem to fit the numbered cubicles in which we are forced by insurers to place them?"

Psychiatrists deal with this labelling imperative in a variety of ways. To paint two extremes, let us suppose that a woman is living with an unemployed abusive man and they have two preschool children. She works all day as a legal secretary and gets home late after a long bus ride. He has been home with the children all day but has done no housework or cooking. When she gets home, he expects her to cook dinner, take over care of the children and do the housework. Gradually she becomes tired, lacks energy, gets easily annoyed, has crying spells, feels guilty about not meeting her children's needs, withdraws from her friends and usual activities, and feels sad and miserable. Worried about her mental state, she goes to her family doctor who arranges a psychiatric referral.

The first psychiatrist, who believes that psychiatric disorders are genetically determined and that neurotransmitters gone awry account for emotional, behavioural and personality disorders, would ask this woman questions based on the criteria for a major depressive disorder in the DSM. He would conclude that she has a depressive illness and needs anti-depressant medication. She would be given a prescription for Prozac, or similar anti-depressant medication, and told to come back in several weeks to determine if the medication was working. If she were still depressed at that time, the dose would be increased. If her depression persisted at later visits, she would probably be changed to another medication. Of course there is a possibility that the medication would help her regain energy and focus, and she herself might be able to get out of the abusive situation. But all too often this scenario ends with the woman seeing herself as the problem—as sick and disordered—and the abuse she is suffering is totally obscured.

To go to the other extreme, a second psychiatrist, who has a holistic approach, is well aware of the pervasive nature of violence towards women and knows about community resources. While the woman might still be labelled depressed, recommendations discussed with her would include addressing the problem of her abusive partner. A referral to a group for battered women might be suggested. A discussion of the impact on her children of witnessing their mother's abuse would ensue, and be related to any emotional or behavioural problems they were having. The importance of a support system and getting back in touch with her friends would be emphasized, along with the need to modify her work stresses if possible.

## Blamed

Blaming women is as old as history itself. Eve, wicked witches, evil stepmothers and vindictive goddesses have all been held responsible for the trials and tribulations of people's lives. Here, as with the other three areas of women's complaints about psychiatry, we find cultural beliefs about women's place and role appearing in psychiatric theory and practice. Blaming women was more prevalent from the 1940s to 1960s. During this time, childhood emotional or behavioural problems, and most adult disorders, were traced to pathology in the mother, according to a legion of experts. Theories and texts based on Freud's work presented behaviour and personality development as entirely dependent on the mother-child relationship during the first few years of life. The very influential work of Bowlby (1951) and Spitz (1945: 53–74) reinforced beliefs that infants required the undivided attention of their mothers for the first two or three years of life. Drawing on his work with war orphans and children who had been hospitalized for long periods, Bowlby postulated that "maternal deprivation" caused delinquency, mental retardation, dwarfism and affectionless psychopathy. Furthermore, Bowlby charged that a state of "partial deprivation" and consequent destructive effects on the child could occur when a child lacked constant attention from his mother. Needless to say, these theories were very helpful in getting women out of the workforce after World War II!

In his widely read book "The First Year of Life," Spitz (1965) depicted the mother-child relationship as a closed dyad. A variety of "psychotoxic" maternal attitudes were related to conditions such as infantile eczema, colic, rocking, and faecal play. In his concluding chapter, Spitz contended that the rapid disintegration of the traditional forms of family in Western society was due to a decrease in patriarchal authority and the mother's absence from the home. Fathers were accorded only one paragraph in this book, stressing their duty to support mothers in their role. These writings of Spitz and Bowlby had profound effects on mothers, families, professionals and child-rearing practices. Legislators used the findings to argue against readily available daycare, particularly for children under three, and all types of group residential care, and to stress the need for stay-at-home mothers.

The mother's primary responsibility for the child's adjustment appeared repeatedly in theories about families and children. Mothers of asthmatic children were accused of unconscious hostility and accompanying rejection or overprotection (Miller 1959: 40–49). Asthmatic attacks were depicted as the child's cry for help. Mothers were characterized as both seductive and prohibitive, binding their children to them and at the same time rejecting any signs of sexual interest.

Many theories about schizophrenia assigned culpability to the mother. The "schizophrenogenic mother" was portrayed as cold, aloof, dominating, nagging, hostile, destructive, engulfing, morally sadistic, critical and demanding (Arieti 1955). She was depicted as putting her child in a "double bind" by demanding affection and simultaneously rejecting it (Bateson et al. 1958). The child's only escape from this impossible situation was felt to be into the fantasy world of mental illness. Similarly, parents of autistic children, particularly mothers, were thought to have caused their child's terrible affliction. Mothers of autistic children were described as self-centred, cold, annihilating and totally uncaring (Bettelheim 1967).

While acknowledging the outrageous nature of these mother-blaming theories, most psychiatrists think that such ideas were left behind in the 1960s and have been supplanted by the supposedly value-free biomedical model. Unfortunately this is not so.

Attachment theory, which relies strongly on Bowlby's writings, appears to have recycled the old concepts of maternal deprivation and partial deprivation. Although a few authors embrace the possibility of fathers or other caregivers having a primary role in the attachment process, most focus on mothers alone. Despite many concerns about cultural and temperamental differences, the role of concurrent separation experiences such as daycare attendance, and the artificial nature of the "strange situation" (Rutter 1981), procedures for measuring attachment are often used to judge the nature of the mother-infant relationship and treatment needs. A "secure attachment" is thought to forecast later emotional health. Some infant psychiatrists, believing wholeheartedly in this construct, have sessions with mother and baby alone while downplaying or ignoring the influence of other family factors and environmental issues.

Attachment theory (Parkes et al. 1991), like earlier theories about the supreme importance of the mother-infant relationship, embraces beliefs about the sacred nature of the mother-infant bond. It flies in the face of longitudinal studies that show little relationship between early maternal behaviour and later adjustment (Clarke and Clarke 1976). It also serves—conveniently in these hard-pressed times when governments wish to terminate social programs and put all the responsibilities back on mothers and families—to obscure numerous studies which show that being rich or poor is the single most important factor in child development.

The "anorexigenic mother" appears to have replaced her schizophrenogenic counterpart. Many authors ascribe anorexia and bulimia to early defects in the mother-child relationship. Bruch (1973) thinks that the mother superimposes her own distorted perceptions on the child. As a result, the child is unable to develop a sense of who she is, how she feels and what it means to be satiated. The infant who does not have a relationship with a mother who is soothing and predictable fails to develop a cohesive sense of self and does not develop self-regulatory functions (Goodsitt 1983: 51–60). The predominance of eating disorders in girls is linked to a girl's more difficult separation and individuation from a pre-Oedipal mother and their subsequent hostile-dependent tie (Beattie 1988: 453–60).

Family therapy approaches to eating-disordered patients depict the families—and this usually means the mother—as enmeshing, overprotective and rigid (Palazzoli 1978).

These developmental and family theories of eating disorders are not substantiated by research (O'Kearney 1996: 115–27). They obscure the culture-bound nature of these syndromes (Swartz 1985: 725–30) and their relationship to Western society's extreme preoccupation with youth, slimness and beauty—an obsession that is very convenient for the multi-billion-dollar diet, fitness, fashion and cosmetic industries.

Extremes of mother blaming exist in the medical-legal arena of child custody disputes where allegations of sexual abuse have been made (Penfold 1995: 337–41). Child psychiatrist Gardner (1987), who is deeply involved in child custody litigation, claims that the vast majority of children who say that their fathers have sexually abused them are fabricators. He believes that children are brainwashed and programmed by vindictive mothers, and he recommends transfer of the children to the custody of the father. In a similar vein, Green (1986: 449–56) contends that, for four out of eleven children, false allegations were made during child custody disputes.

These two pieces of literature have been repeatedly used by skilled defence lawyers in court to buttress the allegation that the mother is lying, coaching the child, vindictive or mentally unbalanced. Media, fathers' rights groups and some mental health and legal professionals still believe that there is an epidemic of vindictive mothers who falsely allege that fathers have abused their children. Because of the strength of these beliefs, lawyers sometimes advise mothers not to mention any concerns about sexual abuse during a custody dispute (Law Society of B.C. 1992: 49).

If reports of community surveys, and articles where interview processes have been carefully documented, are perused a totally different picture emerges. In one large-scale study involving nine thousand families in custody/visitation disputes, slightly less than two percent involved sexual abuse allegations (Thoennes and Tjaden 1990: 151–63). Another study, using an objective protocol that re-examined cases investigated by a Boulder County child sexual abuse team, showed striking results. The cases considered to be "founded" jumped from 5.6 percent to 44 percent. This is slightly lower than 50 percent founded, which is the usual statistic for the general population of child sexual abuse cases. The authors conclude that the workers had prejudged allegations as false because they were made in the context of a child custody dispute (McGraw and Smith 1992: 49–62).

Mother blaming appears to stem from Western industrial society's most cherished beliefs about parenting in an isolated nuclear family. The family is viewed as a private setting where individual emotional needs are met. Despite some changes over the last few decades, the mother, even in a dual-career family, has primary responsibility for ensuring that emotional and physical needs are met. Traditionally she is the expressive member of the couple, and the emotional mediator and organizer in the family. She is expected to be caring, warm, nurturing and self-sacrificing, always putting others' needs before her own. Within the family, her "job" encompasses how the children "turn out." As already described, women's conduct is subject to considerable normative regulation (Schur 1984). A woman who does not fit with society's prescriptions for mothers in terms of dress, appearance, job, living situation, married state or behaviour may be judged as inadequate, unfit or bad.

Like biomedical theories, blaming mothers may present a seductive and simplistic solution to mental health professionals. It is facilitated by the likelihood that the mother, rather than the father, brings the child to the psychiatrist's office and is more available for sessions. She is more articulate, more expressive and more likely to participate eagerly in recommendations. Because she too has internalized our culture's tenets about mothers, she is ready to attribute blame to herself.

The psychiatrist's needs may be met by assigning responsibility to the mother. For instance, with attachment theory, the focus on the early mother–infant relationship is very appealing. It provides an emphasis on early beginnings rather than dismal outcomes, and a view that children can be inoculated against an increasingly toxic world. The approach is warm, human and compassionate, and the psychiatrist can be actively engaged in a process, rather than seeming to be merely a sales outlet for the pharmaceutical industry.

In addition, mother blaming may be very useful to less visible parties. Mother blaming, functioning as it does to locate within the family unit many of the stresses and strains emanating from society, fits well with current economic and political needs. Blaming mothers allows politicians, and society as a whole, to ignore or minimize the effects on children and families of poverty, violence, unemployment, lack of suitable accommodation, pornography, racism and other forms of discrimination.

## Conclusions

Crucial goals for the psychiatrist who wants to avoid drugging, exploiting, labelling and blaming women patients include: listening to the individual woman's story; empowering her, catalyzing her strengths; avoiding victim blaming; demystifying the treatment process; recognizing the power differential between professional and patient; and becoming educated about common problems women bring to therapy. But to achieve these goals the psychiatrist must understand the paradox—that psychiatry is part of the ideological and coercive mechanisms of industrial society and, at the same time, committed to the resolution of the very stresses and strains that society and its institutions produce. This unacknowledged interrelationship with the social system makes it possible for psychiatry to take part in the oppression of some of the same people it purports and intends to help (Penfold and Walker 1983).

Chapter 12

# The "Fuck-Your-Buddy System" And Its Adversaries

*Edgar Z. Friedenberg*

The most astonishing thing about homophobia is that it should exist at all. Why bother? Heterosexuality is well-established; homosexuality, though ubiquitous, is everywhere regarded as deviant, usually with scorn and hostility, always as an aberration to be explained.

Even the most inauspicious couplings between men and women require no such explanation; they are "natural." "I can't imagine what she sees in *him*," a puzzled observer may say of an apparently mismatched pair. But surely, the right guy will come; a consummation devoutly to be wished.

But why? In every society, and among various mammals, some members of the same sex are known to have developed intimate relationships. And that is probably the only general statement we can confidently make about the matter. All other factors wobble deceptively. Quasi-nomadic hunting and gathering societies, which our own is fast becoming, may have great difficulty sustaining intimate relationships of any kind as families and other groups are torn apart by economic stresses arising from climatic change or technological development. Tender, though temporary, relationships may be accepted as normal, even in a largely homophobic society, among warriors, cowboys, rock bands and computer technicians subject to transfer and downsizing. Where more stable social conditions prevail, homosexual relationships are likely to evoke more hostility, but such relationships are not inherently unstable. Gays are currently divided in a worldwide quest for the rights, risks and responsibilities conferred by formal marriage, an institution heterosexual couples in Western societies have been abandoning.

Societies or social enclaves that are violently outraged by certain homosexual roles and practices find others quite acceptable. Cultures with a virulent macho strain notoriously deride the male who submits to penetration while acknowledging the virility of his partner—a stressful distinction unlikely to be consistently maintained throughout a long relationship. Other homophobic cultures simply assume homosexuality to be an offence subject to mitigation and declare *intent* to be the criterion of malfeasance: "The boys were too drunk to know what they were doing; they were lusty young men long at sea and really had no choice." This approach leads to the familiar controversy over whether homosexual tendencies are innate and hereditary, and therefore not the faggot's fault; or whether we simply do it to annoy because we know it teases. Whatever. It's a gift to come down and out where you ought to be.

Straight society defines both gay and lesbian relationships as abnormal, but lesbianism is much less problematic, and there are difficulties in considering them as comparable. Gay and lesbian organizations have seriously divergent views. Politically we form tactically effective alliances, but at the cost of concealing unconscionable conflicts of interest. Censorship of pornography, which lesbians favour far more than gay men do, is a familiar example. At many meetings I have attended, lesbians have directed a litany of abuse against males—not just as oppressive, exploitive, and brutal, which many of us have been; but also as incapable of tenderness or fidelity; as dumb and insensitive, repellent and even ugly. But that's my Bill, who's not their type at all; they'd pass him in the street and never look at him.

The conventional view of males in straight society is not very favourable either; but despite their inherent blemishes, males are regarded by straight society as lovable; the love of women, however tragic and costly, is *real*. If sinful, it must be punished, perhaps; but O, the pity of it. Aida loved Rhadames, Madame Butterfly loved the caddish Benjamin Franklin Pinkerton; Othello loved Desdemona, not wisely but too well. Alberich, by forswearing love as a condition for acquiring the magic Ring, ultimately brings on *Götterdämmerung*. Love is invaluable. But when Dr. Aschenbach gasps at the oblivious Tadzio, *Ich liebe Dich*, he validates his own death warrant: there must be *death* in Venice.

The place of love in gay relationships is disputable. Our most homophobic adversaries deny that it exists and, unfortunately, some gay men accept this lethal verdict, viewing our ilk as Don Giovannis eager to reckon up their conquests by the thousands: so many boys, so little time. AIDS has dimmed this stereotype, not merely by eliminating many who may have lived it, but by leaving the survivors so manifestly crippled by grief. As Edmund White movingly argues in *A Farewell Symphony*, a one-night stand need not be loveless and without concern for the partner, even if he is a hustler—perhaps especially then, since the boy may not even know that he might be lovable. Conversely, even rent-boys sometimes find to their dismay that what they thought was a trick, their client regards as a lease whose terms provide a great deal of unsought affection: once again, the oldest profession threatened by enthusiastic amateurs.

But the point of *Don Giovanni* isn't the Don's promiscuity but his despera-tion. He hasn't had 1,003 lovers in Spain; he hasn't loved anyone anywhere; and he risks nothing by accepting the Commendatore's summons to be his guest in hell. How different could it be? People who speculate about such things suggest that Don Juan was really a repressed homosexual who sought fruitlessly to control his anxieties by chasing after women. This question is not as interesting as the assumption underlying it: that homosexuality, whether pathological or not, is a deeply rooted aspect of personality, equally essential to those who display or seek to conceal it.

Personally, I'm sure this is true. Most homophobic cultures, though, have punished homosexual *acts* but do not classify the men who perform them as a distinct, accursed race. Are we not, as other men, tendentiously claiming special rights? Have we not hands, organs, dimensions, senses, affections, passions? If you prick us, do we not bleed?

Well, yes, but I still cannot watch television without being reminded for seventeen minutes of every hour that the advertisements are designed to appeal to people quite different from myself, and to frighten me into denying it. I also recall how I felt about a warm, gentle young house painter who came to work on our house in Shreveport, Louisiana, when I was about three years old. I don't really remember *him*, just how I felt toward him, though he didn't do anything special and certainly nothing he shouldn't have. He was just kind to me seventy-five years ago; he let me watch him and think I was helping him. A little straight boy might have decided to become a house painter when he grew up; but that didn't seem, even then, to be the heart of the matter for me.

The question is not whether being gay makes us different, but why, and under what circumstances, the difference makes a difference. What is it about us, in post-modern society, that defines us as a special interest group, as interesting to others as to ourselves? What makes us threatening or disruptive in the eyes of straight people as well as, by reflection, of our own?

To argue that straight men fear and loathe men they perceive to be gay because their own unconscious homosexual longings threaten their masculinity really explains nothing; the reasoning is completely circular, like that of the etymologist who argued that "the pig is properly so-called, because it is such a filthy animal." The fury straight men traditionally feel when supposedly gay men cruise them is paradoxical; our attraction does not impugn their masculinity, it confirms it. In response, they need offer no more than common courtesy—or as much as they feel they can afford.

There are no categories in nature. Categories are designed, or at least evolve, as instruments of social control. The fact that homosexuals did not exist until straight people identified us as queer does not deny us our distinction—it means that they recognized and attacked us for what we have in common before we did. A small part of the horror the fate of Matthew Shepard inspires in me comes from knowing that I, too, would have found his murderers attractive and wanted their love—though snobbery and cowardice would have protected me. Jesus, whose failure to take note of our existence has so challenged the ingenuity of Christian conservatives, did indeed command us to love our enemies. We, and Matthew especially, took him more literally than most people do.

Whether and how homosexual behaviour will threaten the larger society depends on many factors. In technically primitive societies that depend on children to maintain them, homosexual acts will be abhorrent as, in effect, sins of omission. Hence the insistence that these acts are just a phase boys go through, like a student loan: threatening if unresolved. Persistent avoidance of sex with women is perceived as a very serious form of tax evasion, rather than a personality characteristic, and it is perilous to fall into arrears. If marriages are arranged, the very idea of "sexual orientation" becomes trivial. You sees your duty and you does it, from time to time. There is a time and a place for everything. Serious problems with love, as with most valuables, arise less from scarcity than from inept distribution.

When love and marriage become linked in the ethos of a culture, homosexuality becomes more of a problem. Marriage is a social contract involving property rights, inheritance, maybe even primogeniture; one may not render unto Aphrodite, Apollo or especially Dionysus that which is Caesar's. But extramarital liaisons, even between persons of the same gender, were not dangerous enough to threaten the established social order. Illicit relationships cannot, by definition, be legally binding. Like celibacy, our passions were inconsequential. It wasn't just our love that dared not speak its name; as a group, we didn't have one.

This still does nothing to explain the horror and loathing so widely aroused by homosexual *acts,* even in cultures that did not or do not define homosexual identity. It is especially difficult to explain the concentration of such loathing among athletes, churches and military organizations, which strengthens the petard on which many of their own most useful members have been hoist. When will the first hockey coach reply to his tormentor snarling, "Yes, those guys are beautiful! You're proud that you can't see it?" When will the first choirmaster ask his tormentor, "Do you think I could spend years trying to teach these boys to love music if I didn't love them?" When will the first priest ask absolution of his own confessor for having led certain of his parishioners to loathe themselves for loving each other? Straight women, who have some reason to fear our competition, do not usually hate us unless we have deceived or victimized them. They may even value us as understanding, undemanding friends who listen to what they have to say. Likes repel, opposites attract.

There are, however, plausible explanations for the hostility of a society like our own to gay men. There is also reason to believe that homophobia is becoming and will continue to become less acceptable and perhaps less virulent than it has been. This may not be grounds for boundless gaiety. The trajectory of acceptance for discriminated groups in America follows to some degree a similar path, despite great differences in the bases and intensity of such discrimination.

Gays usually and justly rebut persons who oppose our rights to marry or serve openly in an unsegregated military by pointing out that the same arguments were accepted against women and African-Americans until they were declared unconstitutional; and that they are now recognized as shameful and absurd. Discrimination has not ceased—there is still a badly stained glass ceiling—but disparities in earnings have lessened, and social-class barriers increasingly displace racial ones. It no longer seems surprising that there should be African-American congresspersons, jurists and major entrepreneurs, or even that some of these are quite dreadful people.

As a stigmatized group loses its stigma, its identity becomes fainter; the figure in the carpet fades. This is happening to gays and lesbians, as political candidates labour to convince us there is room for us in their big tent and that we will be encouraged to mingle as we serve the hors d'oeuvres. We may prove harder to assimilate. I see no inherent reason why African-Americans should be threatening to our socio-economic system. But there are reasons why gays should, and vice versa. Indeed, it is difficult to imagine economic arrangements more vulnerable to the emotional commitment of gay men than that of a competitive, privatized system pervaded by a false commitment to equality of opportunity, in which making paper profits is assumed to be the ultimate goal of any enterprise.

A market economy provides benefits corresponding to its enormous costs, though these are confusing to assess, since the system also defines what counts as a benefit. It claims enhanced productivity resulting from superior motivation, technological development and rational organization of the productive process as the bases of its superiority. And it does provide "real goods, worthless but real," in the words T.S. Eliot used to mock the lesser temptation in "Murder in the Cathedral."

In order to do it, though, it must emphasize and sometimes invent new virtues and vices. It is difficult to define "nepotism" to the ruling elites of Saudi Arabia or Indonesia, who see it as an expression of family values rather than as corruption. And if private ownership of natural resources is the righteous road to development—well, it's their oil, isn't it? Males do dominate most societies, and when they love one another, the consequences may rip the social fabric and become the stuff of myth as they did for quite different reasons in the cases of Achilles and, much later, Alexander. Neither of them were stigmatized as queers by the military. But, then, neither Achaia nor Macedonia were bureaucracies that claimed to abide by impersonal criteria for preferment; it took Napoleon to suggest that every private had a baton in his knapsack stiffening to emerge.

In a modern society that purports to be open and fundamentally impersonal, love between competitors is intolerably disruptive. This has also been a major factor in impeding the progress of women in a male-dominated society; but the problem of women is more easily handled. Men are expected, even required, to respond erotically to their presence; the response may simply attest to their conventionality. If it is stronger and more persistent—well, there is still that impartial glass ceiling to shield them.

In a "free market" society where success is the ultimate value, affection between individuals threatens the very basis of organization. It leads to favouritism, immobility within the organization and the profession, and devaluation of the prizes offered by the "fuck-your-buddy system." Note this locution well; especially the euphemism with which it begins. The four-letter word "love" is too threatening to be uttered in a straight-male social context or a David Mamet play. Love, which does not alter when it alteration finds, or bend with the remover to remove, tolls the knell of economic passion. "Fuck," however, commits you to nothing and no one.

The adverse relationship between affection and competition affects most relationships in our society and is reflected in the myths from its Judaeo-Christian beginnings. Genesis, in more modern terms, might have been called "A Case-

Study of Sibling Rivalry and its Sequelae." Scripture does not teach us, however, that those sequelae were so desirable that institutions should be designed to foster and exploit them, as ours are.

Of these, none is more interesting or revealing than the school system. Compulsory education at public expense was introduced in the latter third of the nineteenth century—beginning in Germany—as corporate industrialization proceeded. The state has always been the school's client; the pupils are the raw material which the school prepares to enter society, as if they had not been there all along. The process is usually more positively described as teaching pupils the skills necessary to get and hold jobs—on the employer's terms. But attitudes have always been more important to the school than skills, though some skills are zealously cultivated: social, athletic; rarely critical. "Nothing worth knowing is ever taught in school," Oscar Wilde observed, though much that is worth knowing is learned there. Truth is not suited to the curriculum, being, as Wilde noted, seldom pure and never simple. What is demanded is an understanding of how society operates that is ideologically fitting rather than accurate. It can hardly be both.

Schooling is a process of certification. The schools are required to label students as potential winners or losers to save employers time, effort and money. Though the labels provide remarkably unambiguous indications of the pupil's social origin, in an egalitarian society they must refer to putative skills and character traits rather than to social class or ethnicity. They must therefore be awarded on the basis of successful, impersonal, individual competition. Team-work on the athletic field is admirable; American history has its origins in combat between the shirts and the (usually coloured) skins. But in the classroom and examinations, collaboration is *cheating*, and grounds for severe disciplinary action. This is the foundation of the "fuck-your-buddy system," which bears a curious relationship to homophobia. Hostility toward gays, while more salient, is probably not increasing, though teachers and administrators still refuse to intervene to protect gay victims. Except in a number of schools that proudly call themselves Christian, homophobia is not officially condoned. But the prevailing value climate still incubates homophobia when it does not actively promote it, for the schools' routines and regulations encourage ruthless competition.

In athletic events, competitive animus, diverted toward the opponent, is routinely expressed in homophobic obscenities that have lost their meaning, though not their power to wound, through misuse. It isn't their sexuality as such that leads schoolboys to despise any boy who would love them; but their fear of being marked as a loser. A vicious circle is established. Precisely because homosexual desire is so stigmatized, any boy who displays it identifies himself as dangerously indomitable; not just a rebel but a serious troublemaker; a guy who wears his heart in his pants and already knows that freedom's just another word for nothing left to lose. This, indeed, is the sort of thing which authority cannot afford to put up with.

Schools may do harm just by invoking a formal policy toward gay adolescents.

When they do, they reify homosexuals and homosexuality as categories—a dubious undertaking, as we have seen. The boys in the category must then be regarded as a problem class. Homophobes respond by citing moral strictures from the Old Testament. This is harmful to everyone because it reinforces our cruel cultural practice of defining morality in terms of prohibited acts, rather than their predictable effects on oneself and other creatures and on the relationships among us. There is, indeed, much evil abroad—and even more that is domestic—and it cannot be identified by referring to a list of vile deeds.

Both the harm the school might do by reifying homosexuality as a quasi-clinical condition, and the assistance it might offer by dealing honestly with gay and lesbian students and protecting them from harassment or assault, are greatly limited by the school's avoidance of controversy. Controversy, one might assume, would be an essential skill for citizenship, but schools try desperately to avoid it. Many school districts forbid teaching anything about homosexuality except by discussing it as a deplorable abnormality; books that depict gay characters favourably are excluded from the library. Ironically, schools may still find themselves required by the courts to permit gay students to organize in social clubs and discussion groups, which is probably more useful to them than formal instruction. Except as it is thought to affect future employability, neither parents nor students have much interest in the actual curriculum. They quarrel over grades and the hours devoted to teaching, coaching or supervising students and over safety and hygiene, but when parents discuss ideas taught in school, it often means big trouble.

The schools, despite community pressure, therefore play a largely indirect though ultimately influential role in forming attitudes toward homosexuality. They provide an arena in which the "fuck-your-buddy system" develops its ideology and refines its social skills; but they do not do this by propagating homophobia as a moral obligation. The function of schooling is to socialize the young, though not by teaching them what to believe, because only the most naive student believes that what the school teaches is either true or false. What the schools teach is *right answers to questions that identify your place in society*. Galileo's offence, essentially, lay not in asserting that the sun rather than the earth lay at the centre of the solar system, but in showing that received wisdom could be challenged by observation; though science, in its turn, has been nearly as intolerant of subjectivity. Faggots are despicable for the same reason that Columbus discovered America, that all men are created equal, that a rising stock market betokens prosperity, that an electric current is composed of negatively charged particles. Essentially these statements are meaningless conventions. But schoolchildren learn, and adults recall, what it costs to contradict them. If you don't contradict them, though, you stand a better chance of reaching a position from which you can call them naive.

This is not hypocrisy; nobody is teaching something they disbelieve. The affirmation required is not "I believe!" but "I belong!" Hypocrisy has been virtually eliminated in developed democracies with the requisite commitment to a market economy, though it is still endemic in certain parts of Canada. Language is not used to convey information but to elicit action. Former president Clinton was, I am sure, genuinely hurt and bewildered by being accused of making false statements. He wasn't distorting the truth, he was sending signals; and the meaning of a signal depends on its context, not its content.

The role of the school in promoting or impeding homophobia is more instrumental than instructional. It is true that schools reflect the complex and contradictory values of their culture, which include a large measure of homophobia. But students pick it up whether the schools teach it or combat it; because the schools *do* teach, and teach relentlessly, the "fuck-your-buddy system" of insuring one's own success. Indeed, it has come to seem quite natural, though sad, that many boys who are members of fag-baiting groups behave quite civilly toward an erstwhile victim when they happen to meet him alone. Attributing such affability to freedom from peer pressure merely reasserts conventional explanations for the homophobia of the group. Fear of appearing less masculine to friends, fear of revealing one's own possibly erotic response—these elicit homophobic behaviour in groups.

But I think a much deeper factor is exhibited with magnificent irony by the Roy Cohn character in Tony Kushner's *Angels in America*. Cohn responds furiously to the physician who tells him that he is dying of AIDS. Cohn insists that he cannot possibly be suffering from AIDS; his illness is "liver cancer." AIDS is the gay plague, and Cohn cannot possibly be queer, because queers are victims; they have no power, while Cohn, though by now disbarred and dying, is still a major malign force in American politics. Cohn does not deny either that he is dying or that he takes delight in fucking and degrading boys. But he does deny that he is, or ever could be, a homosexual, because in his mind homosexuals are losers.

Schools exist to teach boys to succeed on the community's terms. This is why curriculum changes intended to motivate lower-status, ethnically insulted students, who are already convinced that they are destined to fail, seldom succeed in "reaching them." Schools and the communities that support them insist on competition as a way of training and identifying the kind of people who will do what is necessary to succeed in and advance the interests of "the private sector."

But being a loser is, literally, a fate worse than death. Suicide is now the leading cause of death for adolescent males in America, surpassing even automobile accidents, many of which are, in fact, also suicides though not counted as such. Any unconventional emotion or passion threatens productivity; in the event of disaster, "grief-counsellors" are rushed to the scene to teach students appropriate grievance techniques. Heterosexual passions are conventional, so established procedures from condescension toward "puppy love" to increasingly reliable means of birth control exist for channelling them. Frenzied worship of athletic teams and deification of jock heroes dispel and generalize homoerotic expression, but affection between individual males generates tension and disrupts teamwork. Homophobia's continued usefulness to a "free market economy" insures its position in the social scene.

That economy, along with the values it instills, is losing its grip as the depredations of downsizing, outsourcing and civil unrest leave their mark throughout the world; and as the role of the World Bank and the International Monetary Fund in the ruin of millions who live in poor nations becomes recognized. The response has so far been chaotic, but it is bringing about a substantial loss of faith in the "fuck-your-buddy system," which I believe is leading to an observable decrease in homophobia. The underlying social changes are, however, debilitating to friends and lovers of every variety, leaving us more than ever strangers lonely and afraid in a world we never made.

My understanding of these baleful processes is largely based on the elegant, clear and profound analysis provided by the sociologist and novelist Richard Sennett (1998) in his book *The Corrosion of Character*. The central theme of the work is the collapse of continuity in human and economic relationships. The primacy of the Protestant ethic, in however crude or authoritarian form, defined a set of reciprocal obligations between employer and employee which guaranteed job security and a place in the community in return for loyal service and acceptance of exploitation. The classical and until recently world-famous model was that of the Japanese employee who, so long as he did his often boring and repetitive job, could count on lifelong security and even a modicum of cautiously graded amenities. The modern corporate employer can no longer afford to provide such security; even highly skilled technicians in large corporations are imperilled. Those kept by their present employer are subject to transfer to branches where they and their new neighbours never get to know one another; instant civility replaces—actually, fails to replace—friendship. Fidelity and infidelity are obsolescent. You may see examples of them along with typewriters and rotary telephones used to establish the atmosphere of an earlier period in remakes of classical movies, but the experience they denote is seldom to be had. The very notion of a *career*, which formed the focus of the "fuck-your-buddy system," is lost; the skills which professionals developed through years of experience are no longer relevant. The skills that are now useful are real enough, but they are temporary, consisting of complex electronic procedures invoked by people who do not understand how the machines they operate actually work and cannot fix them when they go wrong. Even the specialists are lost when their narrow specialty becomes outdated; computer repairmen are irritated when I ask them for service on the eminently serviceable five-year-old clone I'm using right now. I'm supposed to have thrown it out and replaced it after, at most, three years.

Sennett does not discuss homosexuality in *The Corrosion of Conscience*, though he has on other occasions; but fidelity, though not always recommended, is a central issue in gay life. The "fuck-your-buddy system" operates in sheer contradiction to the needs, and sharpens the perceptions, of Queer Nation. We don't actually need homophobia, or at least not so much of it, but it has surely helped make us perceptive critics and penetrating ironists. The bright straight boy viewing the emperor's new clothes exclaims in astonishment, "But he has nothing on!" His gay but dour companion replies, "He has Majesty; Calvin Klein would be wasted on him. Let's go to my place; I can show you better!"

In the absence of hostile neighbours, Queer Nation would cease to exist, and our privileges of citizenship, such as they are, would be lost. Within my lifetime, "Negroes," as they were politely called, were also consigned to the role of court jester when they were heard at all. From this position, egregiously imposed, their spokespersons told us not only who they were but who we white folks were. Today, there is still Spike Lee. But Colin Powell, Michael Jordan, Vernon Jordan, Clarence Thomas, etc.—what do they have in common? Prudence, acumen, the admiration and envy of their fellow citizens. They have defeated the enemy, and now it is they.

Very similar processes are affecting what some still call "the gay community," though, lacking legal protection against discrimination in most jurisdictions, we are still reluctant to celebrate the achievements of gay individuals as such. But the signs of acceptance and assimilation are evident. The "gay community" is as riven by the narcissism of small differences as socialism was in Manhattan in the 1930s. Simultaneously, various "gay studies" programs are established in most prestigious universities, and tenure and promotion therein are achieved through research and publication comparable in quality and readability to academic writing anywhere. Gay-bashing is as horrible as, and perhaps more frequent than, ever, as fundamentalist hysteria mounts; but it now seems almost quaint as well as macabre. It takes a village to raise a scandal, and few of us live in villages any more. Ultimately, straight society will miss us and the clarity and passion we could sometimes provide. But then there won't be any more straight or gay society, just one nation, invisible, with equal malice toward all.

## Recommendations for Further Reading

As will surely have been evident, this essay is not and was not meant to be a report of a scientific investigation. Accordingly, I have selected these references because they deal directly and at some depth with the abuse of authority with reference to gays; with developments, especially among traditionally homophobic athletic subcultures, of some more favourable patterns of response; with relevant analyses of the development of the view of homosexuality as a problem and a threat to the socio-economic (dis)order; and especially with the creations of artists as diverse as Edmund White, Tony Kushner, Paul Cadmus, Thom Gunn and others, who so thoroughly integrate love, taste and passion in their work.

Eliasoph, Philip. 1981. *Paul Cadmus*. Oxford, Ohio: Miami University Art Museum.

> Despite its unabashed gender bias—nearly all the young women depicted in Cadmus' work are rather baleful figures identified as "floozies"—his work is unforgettably tender in its depiction of lustful festivals and affectionate depiction of young males. Dating from the 1930s to 1980s, Cadmus is shocking only in his bold insistence that there is nothing shocking in the scenes he so skillfully portrays.

Greenberg, David F. 1988. *The Construction of Homosexuality*. Chicago: University of Chicago Press.

> Still, after 10 years of active scholarship, perhaps the most scholarly and comprehensive treatment of the evolution of this bizarre artifact. At 635 scholarly pages, this book may well tell you more than you want to know.

Hippler, Mike. 1989. *Matlovich: The Good Soldier*. Boston: Alyson.

> The tragic story of Leonard Matlovich's battle to remain in the United States Air Force, which, partly because of his political conservatism, made his case especially newsworthy while limiting the support he received from some effective gay organizations. Matlovich finally settled his suit against the Air Force for an award of $160,000 in 1979; he died of AIDS in 1984. The book includes a summary of the struggles (to that time) of gay servicepersons against being discharged; the worst was clearly still to come.

Klein, Alan M. 1993. *Little Big Men: Bodybuilding Subculture and Gender Construction*. Albany, N.Y.: State University of New York Press.

> A thoughtful study of a rather morose, homophobic subculture of athletes, many of whom support themselves by turning tricks with outsiders they despise. An apparent exception to the rule that men who compete in individual sports like swimming or ice skating are less likely to be homophobic than team-sports players anxious to preserve their macho identity.

Kramer, Larry. 1993. *The Destiny of Me*. New York: Plume (Penguin).

> This bitterly witty and moving play by the brilliant author of *Faggots* and founder of Act Up, dramatizes the conflict between conventional and holistic views of AIDS which reflect more basic conflicts in social attitudes toward homosexuality itself.

Kushner, Tony. 1993. *Angels in America*. New York: Theatre Communications Group.

> If I had to select a single work to explain the politics of homosexuality as revealed through the development of the AIDS crisis and its effect on human relationships, the two plays that together make up *Angels in America* would be it. There is nothing to compare with it in scope and perception.

Merlin, Patrick, ed. 1996. *Boys Like Us: Gay Writers Tell Their Coming Out Stories*. New York: Avon.

> Though the coming-out experience has become a cliché genre, these short essays dealing with experiences dating from 1949 to 1995 profit from the professional skills of their narrators, while the half-century scope of the selections provides an informative background of changes in social attitudes.

Murphy, Lawrence R. 1988. *Perverts by Official Order: The Campaign Against Homosexuals by the United States Navy*. New York: Haworth.

Read in conjunction with *Matlovich* and current experience with "Don't ask, don't tell," this scholarly account of a vicious campaign against homosexuals in the navy during the period following the World War I is dispiriting evidence that, indeed, *plus ça change, plus c'est la même chose.* Or, as Yogi Berra might have told George Santayana, those who ignore the lessons of history are compelled to repeat them. Not a pleasant book.

Pollack, William. 1998. *Real Boys: Rescuing Our Sons from the Myths of Boyhood.* New York: Random House.

A detailed account, based on much case material, of the emotional distortion imposed on boys by cultural pressure to be competitive, insensitive and belligerent, suppressing tenderness and denying weakness. These are not new theses, and the book suffers from a rather pedantic, social-service style, but is notable for the depth of its analysis and its unsentimental respect for the boys whose difficulties it discusses.

Pronger, Brian. 1990. *The Arena of Masculinity.* New York: St. Martin's Press.

In contrast to *Little Big Men*, to which Pronger's book is superior in scope and empathy, *The Arena of Masculinity* presents a more diverse and cheerful history of the role of homoerotic feeling among college and professional sports teams, especially as gay men are increasingly recognized as a lucrative and well-behaved source of public support. A cheerful book and enough of a turn on to leave the reader feeling refreshed.

Rayside, David. 1998. *On the Fringe: Gays and Lesbians in Politics.* Ithaca, N.Y., Cornell University Press.

A very clear, detailed analysis and comparison of the problems and developments in achieving gains against discrimination in Britain, Canada and the United States, by a distinguished professor of political science at the University of Toronto. The historical account is illuminated by perceptive case comparisons of the careers of Chris Smith, Svend Robinson and Barney Frank as elected politicians who have operated most effectively within and against the parliamentary structures of their respective countries. In its scholarship, *On the Fringe* is undoubtedly the finest work included in this bibliography.

Sagarin, Edward (Donald Webster Cory, pseudonym). 1951. *The Homosexual in America.* New York: Julian.

A historical landmark, hailed as liberating when it was published and now regarded as pernicious. As Donald Cory, Sagarin pseudonymously identified and defended homosexuals as an unfortunate minority, more to be pitied than censured. He firmly believed, as did official medical opinion, that we were sick people whose best hope lay in marriage and the determination to adopt a conventional "lifestyle." As we became more confident and gay, Sagarin resumed his real identity and became one of Queer Nation's bitterest critics. The book is still worth reading as a landmark from which to measure how far we have come, yet how familiar the arguments against us, now couched in fundamentalist rather than psychiatric terms, remain.

Sennett, Richard. 1998. *The Corrosion of Character.* New York: Norton.
Discussed above.

Timmons, Stuart. 1990. *The Trouble with Harry Hay.* Boston: Alyson.

A biography of one of the most significant figures in the political evolution of modern gay rights. Harry Hay, born in 1912, the indomitable founder of the Mattachine Society in 1950, though impoverished in later years, remained an active force. His later obscurity has resulted less from neglect than from our reluctance to recall just how powerless and vulnerable we were.

Weinberg, Thomas, and G.W. Levi Kamel. 1983. *S and M: Studies in Sado-Masochism.* Buffalo, N.Y.: Prometheus.

An unpretentious academic work that, especially in the chapters devoted to gay S&M, conveys with remarkable insight and sensitivity the complex relationship among pain, pleasure and affection in sado-masochism among males. S&M, by definition, brings its practitioners closer together: bondage hopefully leads to bonding, if at some risk of later embarrassment. Risks are ritualized and controlled; in these mutually developed if sometimes bizarre scenarios, authority is not abused but abreacted and essentially mocked.

White, Edmund. 1980. *States of Desire: Travels in America.* New York: E.P. Dutton.

A friendly and probing examination of gay life in a dozen cities and regions of the United States that skillfully conveys the flavour of each. The information conveyed is, one surely hopes, dated after many tumultuous years. The book is a landmark because White approaches gay communities as a genial, mildly skeptical guide with a real feel for each culture and the people who compose it. The Old Curiosity Shop is now bankrupt. The book is dedicated to Patrick Merla.

White, Edmund. 1994. *The Burning Library: Essays* (David Bergman, ed.). New York: Knopf.

Some forty essays by White, many on other authors and artists, all perceptive and revealing, none bitchy; a feat unmatched in the gay community. He *liked* these people, though, as Oscar Wilde (whom White would surely have liked) might have observed, only a man with a heart of stone could read of the life of Truman Capote without bursting out laughing. Capote, whose heart surely qualified, never laughed at himself.

White, Edmund. 1997. *The Farewell Symphony.* New York: Knopf.

White calls this work "an autobiographical novel" in which he has combined the characteristics of certain of the people in his life to form the narrative; which, I suspect, is what all autobiographers do, however unwittingly. The title does not convey White's personal valedictory; it is taken from Haydn's *Farewell Symphony*, during the last movement of which the musicians, as a job-action, get up and leave the orchestra one by one. The book is nevertheless elegiac, as so many of its characters die of AIDS. White's *The Farewell Symphony* is gently witty; his writing is reassuring but never sentimental. His consistent genius lies in his grasp of the essential moral relationship between love and lust. No trick can be just a treat; as Holden Caulfield famously observed, "A horse is at least human, for God's sake!" though some of the famous horses White has known do turn out to be more headless than heedless.

Woods, Gregory. 1987. *Articulate Flesh: Male Homoeroticism and Modern Poetry*. New Haven, Conn.: Yale University Press.

Eight essays dealing with gay themes and variations among five poets: D.H. Lawrence, Hart Crane, W.H. Auden, Allen Ginsberg and Thom Gunn. A more recent work would undoubtedly have added others like James Merrill and John Ashbery; but these five are classic and the essays are perceptive and astute.

Woog, Dan. 1998. *Jocks: True Stories of America's Gay Athletes*. Los Angeles: Alyson.

Informative and ingeniously organized into twenty-eight chapters by roles (e.g., "The Wrestlers," "The Suicidal Jock," "The Soccer Coaches," "The Catholic School Girl's Coach"), this work includes, as expected, its quota of horror stories; but its overall implications are quite heartening, especially in the growing acceptance of gay athletes by their peers, especially in the absence of their elders. Even the coaches are slowly evolving into business class. Homophobia among athletes is still rampant, but lessening—the guys are gorgeous and, as Mrs. Lovett observed of the disposal of her friend Sweeney Todd's clients, "It seems such a waste, dear!"

**Editors' Note:** *Edgar Friedenberg died before this book went to press. It was our great privilege and unqualified delight to work with him on this, one of his final writing projects. Libertarian supreme, and adversary of deference and authority in equal measure, he will be sorely missed.*

Part Five
# Criminal (In)justice

Chapter 13

# Racism in Justice:
## The Report of the Commission on Systemic Racism in the Ontario Criminal Justice System

*Toni Williams*[1]

Criminal justice is an important domain in which to examine uses and abuses of state power. Events such as the brutal treatment of female prisoners at the Prison for Women (Arbour 1996), the "accidental" death of Robert Gentles at the hands of guards at the Kingston Penitentiary and the wrongful convictions of Donald Marshall, David Milgaard, Guy Paul Morin and others are spectacular reminders of the power that state officials wield, and of the terrible consequences that may follow when they make the wrong choices (Kaufman 1998; Nova Scotia 1989; *Reference re Milgaard* 1992). Questionable uses—and misuses—of power appear also in routine practices, such as the casual mistreatment of victims, especially female victims, by the police and in the courts, and police harassment of Aboriginal Canadians, blacks and other racialized people (Alberta 1991; Liao 1995).

These examples share a context in which law regulates the uses of power, in which law sets the terms and limits the extent to which officials may control, confine and coerce individuals. As law enables power, it also restrains. Only within the boundaries of law are uses of power official, authorized and legitimate; outside law's limits, the use of power becomes its abuse. It might be expected, therefore, that law would provide not only a base from which to examine misuses of power in the criminal justice system, but also a starting point for progressive responses—or better still, resistance—to the abuse of power by or within the criminal justice system. There are, however, good reasons to doubt the progressive potential of legal regulation. Despite the liberal ideology of equal application of the law, law enforcement processes serve to protect and maintain an unequal social order in which the power of the state is routinely deployed against marginalized people (Cashmore and McLaughlin 1991; Hagan and McCarthy 1994; Reiman 1990). Reforms intended to control abuses of power may leave untouched the broader problem of how power is lawfully used in ways that sustain inequality (Jefferson 1991).

Racial injustice is an important context for the exploration of this problem. One deeply disturbing feature of multiracial societies in advanced capitalist countries is the rate at which criminal justice authorities control and confine people of colour within those societies (Mann 1993). In this context, as in so many other areas of the criminal justice system, the most appalling statistics are found in the United States, where, for example, in the late 1990s about one in three young black men—as compared to one in fifteen young white men—was subject to some form of correctional control (Cole 1999; Mauer 1997, 1999). Studies in Britain, New Zealand and Canada (Hood 1992; LaPrairie 1990; New Zealand 1988; Manitoba 1991) also document inordinate and disproportionate incarceration of indigenous, black and other racialized populations, although not to the same extent as in the U.S. Such findings suggest an urgent need for change, but first it is important to understand why law enforcement tends to produce these results.

Rationalizations to the effect that people—or more specifically, young men—from racialized communities commit more crime or more serious crimes than others have currency in popular, official and academic discourses (Tonry 1995; Wilbanks 1987). Reasons given for this alleged difference in behaviour may range from the overtly racist, "they are criminals," to more socially situated analyses that link detected offending to factors such as poverty and neighbourhood conditions; and note, usually correctly, that in many multiracial societies, indigenous, black and other racialized people are on average poorer than those of European descent (Carey 2000; National Council of Welfare 2000b). Whatever the precise reason offered for why people commit crimes, explanations of racialized outcomes in terms of differential patterns of offending tend to cast the criminal justice system itself as a neutral process that simply responds to the social conflicts it confronts. Administrators of criminal justice are not responsible for the havoc their decisions may wreak in racialized communities. Solutions lie outside the realm of criminal justice, perhaps in the alleviation of poverty or the strengthening of social institutions such as the family, the "community" and the school.

An alternative explanation maintains that the criminal justice system is at least to some extent responsible for the racialized consequences of how it exercises power (Baker 1994; Cook and Hudson 1993; Hagan and Peterson 1995; Mann 1993; Nelson 1995). This approach focuses less on the objects of criminal justice power (suspects, accused and convicted persons) than its subjects (police, lawyers, judges, prison officials) and the procedures, policies, courts and prisons that comprise its institutions. It draws on a variety of studies to make the point that far from being a neutral tool to maintain social peace, the criminal justice process systematically selects particular classes of people to enjoy its protection and targets others to experience its might. Self-report studies of illegal behaviour, for example, indicate that criminal activity is rife among young males of all social classes, but the vast majority of persons suspected, accused and convicted of crimes are poor young men with tenuous connections to the formal labour market (Elliott 1994; Gabor 1994; Hagan and McCarthy 1994; National Council of Welfare 2000b). It is true that most of the crimes committed by middle-class and employed young men in the self-report studies are fairly trivial offences; but exactly the same can be said of most offences that result in convictions for working-class and unemployed young men (Hagan and McCarthy 1994; Schissel 1993). Research into corporate crimes that are committed in pursuit of profit provides additional evidence of selection biases. Corporate/white-collar crime kills, maims and robs at rates that far exceed the injuries inflicted by individual or "street" crime (Snider 1993).

Despite the harm it causes, corporate crime is much less likely than street or individual crime to be policed, prosecuted and punished by the criminal justice system. Both self-report and white-collar/corporate crime studies suggest that the exercise of law enforcement power produces outcomes that differ with the class of offenders and that this effect occurs within the boundaries of lawful action. Are similar or parallel processes responsible for racial injustice in the outcomes of criminal justice processes?

Investigation of this question was a central task of the Commission on Systemic Racism in the Ontario Criminal Justice System, a public inquiry established by the government of Ontario in October 1992 with a mandate to conduct research into "systemic racism" at all stages of the administration of criminal justice. The commission published an interim report on Ontario's prisons in February 1994 and its final report on the entire criminal justice process in Ontario at the end of 1995 (Ontario 1994, 1995). This chapter uses the commission's work to illustrate some of the complexities of relying on legal understandings of uses and abuses of power as an organizing framework for change in the criminal justice system. I shall first explore the creation of the commission as a response to mobilization of black communities in Ontario, whose initial demands were organized around abuses of police power. Second, I will consider the extent to which the commission framed its work and findings in terms of ideas about the abuse of power, and the implications of this framework for the struggle against systemic racism.

## Background and Context of the Commission[2]
Although the creation of the commission was formally an initiative of Ontario's first social democratic government, its genesis lay in the mobilization of members of Toronto's black communities in response to police shootings over the previous fifteen years (Glasbeek 1994; Williams 1999). Between August 1978 and May 1992, Ontario police officers shot one black woman and at least thirteen black men; eight of these victims were killed. Eleven of the fourteen shootings occurred in Toronto. One striking aspect of the shootings—and a factor that likely shaped the community mobilization—is that they tended to occur in clusters. Three killings happened in a fifteen-month period between August 1978 and November 1979; another four shootings occurred between August 1988 and October 1989; and in the eight months between September 1991 and May 1992, police officers shot five black men (Ontario 1995).

Members of Toronto's black communities reacted to these tragedies by organizing for change. Activist groups formed and developed an analysis that identified "racism" in policing as a contributory factor in the shootings. They also pressed for accountability for the deaths and injuries that had occurred and for reforms to policing practices to prevent future shootings. A key theme underlying the analysis was that law and legal processes did not sufficiently restrain police officers' powers to use deadly force and that this lack of restraint was in part responsible for the shootings. In calling for "accountability," the activist groups were concerned with the responsibilities of both individuals and institutions for the deaths and injuries. Individual responsibility lay with the officers who had fired the shots. Their accountability would be promoted by independent investigation, vigorous prosecution and criminal convictions. Institutional responsibility was located in the procedures, policies and practices that formed the context within which police officers shot black people with such disturbing frequency. Enhancing this form of accountability would require fundamental reforms to police recruitment, training and operations. Largely in support of this latter goal, the activist groups generally supported—and participated in—special inquiries and task forces that were struck in the aftermath of the shootings to explore the dynamics of "race relations and policing" (Metro Toronto Task Force on Human Relations 1977; Ontario 1980; Race Relations and Policing Task Force 1989).

In the early stages of mobilization, community groups focused on the shootings and their struggle to elicit acceptable responses from officials and policy-makers. During the 1980s, however, the diagnosis of "racism" as a dimension of black Ontarians' experiences of criminal justice was extended, first, to more routine aspects of policing, such as police stops and arrests, and then to encompass non-policing elements of the criminal justice system, including courts, lawyers and judges. Black people who had experienced contact with criminal justice officials and institutions complained about unfair bail and sentencing decisions, and about the conduct of trials and other hearings (Equal Opportunity Consultants 1989). Stories circulated about mistreatment in prisons and in the criminal courts. Community groups that had organized around demands for police accountability began to protest harassment and mistreatment of black people in other parts of the criminal justice process. Police violence came to be seen as part of a larger picture of pervasive (or systemic) mistreatment of black people in the criminal justice process. As the analysis developed, so also did calls for a more systematic response to what was seen as abuse of racial power.

Although the police remained the most visible and intrusive element of the criminal justice system, and the target of most of the anger and frustration, many activists insisted that police violence was just one element of a broader problem of how power is used—or misused—to control racialized people, especially black people, in urban centres. These concerns were largely ignored by the criminal justice establishment, even as it attempted to manage the anger that erupted after each shooting. A different response was warranted, however, after the events that followed the police killing of Raymond Lawrence in May 1992. This shooting coincided with the acquittal of the American police officers whose beating of an African-American man, Rodney King, had been captured on videotape, and with the riots that ensued in Los Angeles. At a rally organized by a prominent black community group in Toronto, some participants drew parallels between the failure of the U.S. legal system to hold police officers accountable for the violent abuse of their power over African-Americans and the police shootings of black Ontarians. Since few charges had been laid after the shootings in Ontario and there had been no convictions for homicide or assault, it was not difficult for the activists to characterize the administration of criminal justice in Ontario as indifferent to abuses of police power.

Some young people who had attended the rally subsequently launched a protest along Toronto's main commercial street during which they challenged police authority and damaged commercial property. Against the backdrop of the nightly visions of Los Angeles burning that were beamed across the planet, events in Toronto provoked a swift response. Then premier Bob Rae appointed a special advisor on race relations—Stephen Lewis—to develop a comprehensive action plan for resolving whatever problems lay behind the disturbances.

Lewis consulted extensively with black and other racialized people in the province. His report re-presented their demands in ways that fit into the political discourse of the time. There were three key elements to this re-presentation. First, Lewis recognized the "reality of systemic discrimination" as a pervasive characteristic of Ontario society (Lewis 1992). This recognition marked a departure from reliance on the language of "multiculturalism" and "race relations" to name and frame the experiences and concerns of people from racialized communities in their dealings with social institutions. To many who had participated in the mobilization against racial injustice, it denoted a shift from a model of racial difference that emphasized intercultural (mis)understandings to an acknowledgement that racial inequality is a manifestation of racial power.

Second, the Lewis Report identified black people as especially vulnerable to systemic racism. On this point it states:

> [W]hat we are dealing with, at root, and fundamentally, is anti-Black racism. While it is obviously true that every visible minority community experiences the indignities and wounds of systemic discrimination throughout Southern Ontario, it is the Black community which is the focus.... Just as the soothing balm of "multiculturalism" cannot mask racism, so racism cannot mask its primary target. It is important, I believe, to acknowledge not only that racism is pervasive, but that at different times in different places, it violates certain minority communities more than others. (Lewis 1992: 3)

By identifying black people as the "primary target" of systemic racism, the Lewis Report broke with the convention of earlier reports which had treated all racialized people except those of Aboriginal or First Nations heritage as undifferentiated "racial" or "visible" minorities and implicitly assumed that all such minorities had similar experiences in their dealings with social institutions.

With this move, Lewis made it more difficult to marginalize black people's complaints about systemic racism by pitting their negative experiences against the allegedly more positive experiences, or perhaps more muted complaints, of people from other racialized communities.

The third important element of Lewis's re-presentation of his consultations was his focus on the criminal justice system in its entirety. He noted significant complaints not only about policing but also about racial discrimination in non-policing phases of the criminal justice process, commenting that he had heard "anecdotal horror stories about alleged racist episodes" (Lewis 1992: 14). As is indicated by the use of terms such as "anecdotal" and "alleged," however, Lewis was not persuaded that existing knowledge about the nature and extent of any problems outside the policing sector was sufficient to justify reforms. Indeed, in his view, a central obstacle to progress was that the exclusive focus on policing in earlier inquiries had led to "a curious distortion" of knowledge about the administration of criminal justice. Many reports had documented the case for reforms to police recruitment, training and practices, but no systematic studies had examined what Lewis here described as "race relations" in other parts of the Ontario criminal justice system. To correct this "curious distortion" Lewis proposed a comprehensive investigation of racial discrimination in "those parts of the Justice System which cry out for assessment and evaluation but always seem to escape it" (Lewis 1992: 14).

By recommending such an investigation, Lewis sought a means of creating official and authorized knowledge of the complaints of black and other racialized people about abuses and misuses of power in the criminal justice system. Many people who had participated in the mobilization of black communities may have believed that there existed within the black communities sufficient authentic knowledge drawn from experiences with the criminal justice system to justify reform (Scott and Aylen 1995). Implicit in Lewis's report, however, is an assumption that the power to reform practices and procedures lay with the legal actors responsible for criminal justice processes, who, in the absence of official and authorized knowledge, would likely resist change.

A scant four months after Lewis reported, the Ontario government established a six-person commission of inquiry with a mandate to examine the extent to which "systemic racism" affects the administration of criminal justice in Ontario. Consistent with the Lewis Report, the terms of reference directed the commission to focus on "anti-black" racism but also to pay attention to the vulnerabilities of other racial minority communities (Ontario 1995: Appendix A).

Nowhere in the Lewis Report or the commission's terms of reference is the focus of the inquiry described in terms of the misuse or abuse of power. The characterization of the central problem as "systemic racism," however, created space to address one of the main claims to emerge from community demands for such an inquiry: that the failure to treat black and other racialized people equally with white people in the routine processes of criminal justice constitutes an abuse of social and legal power. Two elements of the commission's mandate were particularly important to its ability to address this claim. First, the terms of reference define "systemic racism" as "patterns and practices [in society and its institutions] ... which, although they may not be intended to disadvantage any group, can have the effect of disadvantaging or permitting discrimination against ... racial minorities" (Ontario 1995: Appendix A). This definition points to the discriminatory potential of practices and emphasizes their effects, as opposed to the underlying intentions of those engaged in them. As such, it acknowledges the risk that legally authorized processes may result in unequal treatment and insists on scrutiny of the impact of the exercise of legal power.

Second, the terms of reference direct the commission to investigate, by means of empirical research, "the extent to which the exercise of discretion, at important decision making points in the criminal justice system, has an adverse impact on racial minorities." Discretion, or the power to make choices that have significant social and legal consequences, pervades the criminal justice system (Davis 1971; Hagan and Zatz 1985; Kadish and Kadish 1973; Walker 1993). At every stage of the process, from police contact to the expiry of a sentence, officials make judgments about how to respond to events and how to treat those who are said to be responsible for them. Often they choose among options that may have radically different consequences for everyone involved. Since discretion is fundamental to the exercise of power in the criminal justice system, investigation of its uses and abuses formed a cornerstone of the commission's work.

## The Work of the Commission

### Framing the Questions: Coming to Terms with Systemic Racism

One of the major challenges confronting the commission was the development of a model of "systemic racism" to frame its research. In the early 1990s, there was considerable public discussion of systemic racism and some significant initiatives were undertaken, such as introduction of employment equity in Ontario. There was little dispute among those who make and administer the law that racial injustice was wrong and a misuse of power (Williams 1999). Equality norms built into the Canadian Constitution and human rights codes prohibit discrimination based on race and its substitutes such as national origin, ethnicity and ancestry. To exercise power in ways that contravene these prohibitions is to act outside fundamental boundaries of law. A consensus that equality norms govern institutional practices, however, does not necessarily produce shared understandings of the nature of racial inequality, especially as it may relate to legally authorized practices. Differences centre on the general meanings of (in)equality in the context of complex administrative processes and how to demonstrate that it does—or does not—exist, and on the specific meaning of *racial* inequality in these processes.

In relation to the general meaning of (in)equality, the commission emphasizes (un)equal treatment, which, it maintains, may take two apparently contradictory forms: unjustified differences in treatment and unjustified similarities in treatment. Unjustified differential treatment is the standard interpretation of discrimination within a formal equality model of law. This model is seen most often in conflicts over access to and the distribution of social goods, such as employment, housing or credit. It holds that discrimination exists when individuals who control access to key resources or who are authorized to make decisions that affect people's lives treat similar individuals differently and the difference in treatment is directly or indirectly traceable to aspects of personal or socially constructed identity, such as race, sex, disability, age or sexual orientation.

Conversely, decisions may produce racial injustice when they erase differences by treating people the same despite their different histories, contexts and needs. This substantive equality analysis recognizes that people whose histories and contexts differ may have non-comparable needs, and that in this situation similar treatment may have unjust consequences. For example, suspects, accused persons or witnesses who are not fluent in English or French need access to free and competent interpreter services at all stages of the criminal justice process, if they are to have an understanding of the process comparable to that of persons whose first language is English or French. In the absence of such services, the same treatment of persons who do and do not need them produces inequality (Fong 1995). Individuals who do not need the services are implicitly given an advantage in that they are better able to understand what is happening and to answer the case against them. This implicit advantage and the corresponding disadvantage constitute unequal treatment in a substantive equality model.

Although the commission adopts both models of (in)equality in various parts of its work, its major empirical studies—summarized below—rely heavily on the differential treatment analysis of the formal equality model. The most effective way of demonstrating differential treatment is to focus on the outcomes of discretionary power and the practices of those who exercise it. Some aspects of differential treatment may be detectable on an individual basis, particularly where the difference is directly attributable to a decision-maker's response to race, sex or other aspects of identity—as, for example, where a landlord refuses to rent to a black person who has the same employment prospects and income, and equivalent references, as a white person who is offered the tenancy. In practice, however, it can be difficult to establish discrimination on an individualized basis where, as in most social institutions and administrative processes, decisions are complex and the decision-making process is not transparent. Complexity and lack of transparency may allow decision-makers to mask differential treatment by claiming that apparently similar persons in fact differ in salient ways that do not relate to aspects of personal or socially constructed identity. One response to this problem is to focus not on individual cases but to examine numerous decisions about the treatment of similar people who differ primarily in terms of race or other aspects of personal or socially constructed identities. Where examination of such decisions reveals patterns of differential treatment, the decisions that produce this effect are implicated in the production of inequality.

By the time the commission was created, these general models of formal and substantive equality and the method of demonstrating differential treatment had been accepted in Canadian constitutional and human rights jurisprudence (*Law Society of British Columbia v. Andrews* 1989; *Ontario Human Rights Commission v. Simpson-Sears Ltd*. 1985). There remained considerable resistance, however, to the application of the models and the method in the specific context of *racial* inequality in the administration of criminal justice (Ontario 1995: 18–34). This resistance stemmed, in part, from confusion about the meanings of "systemic racism" that largely centred on the relevance of "intentional" racial bias and the role of subconscious attitudes.

Some equated "systemic racism" with the claim that officials routinely express blatant prejudice against racial minorities. Although the commission documents examples of blatant prejudice in the prisons and courts, its reports maintain that intentional racial bias is not the primary source of the unjust treatment of racialized people that it found.

A more subtle interpretation of "systemic racism" identifies subconscious attitudes that may affect personal interactions and personal judgement as signifi-cant factors in the production of differential treatment. This interpretation seeks to explain how criminal justice decision-makers who are not motivated by racial bias, and who indeed may strive to avoid it, may yet contribute to racially unjust outcomes. It draws on analyses of how historical constructions of racial differ-ences were adopted to justify imperialist exploitation and to promote racial divisions among workers under capitalism; and on cultural studies of the processes by which social constructions of racial differences are transmitted in and through social institutions, such as religion, education, culture, politics and the organiza-tion of the economy (Bolaria and Li 1988; James 1995; Miles 1988; Pieterse 1992; Razack 1998; Satzewich 1991). These social institutions may subtly inculcate ideas about the legitimacy of a social order in which material success and positions of power are enjoyed overwhelmingly by males of Northern European ancestry. Decision-makers responsible for maintaining that social order typically form a homogeneous group of common ethnicity that shares similar values and understandings of the world. Interactions among peers implicitly confirm the rightness of their world view and the legitimacy of their position in the social order. Their more limited contact with people from racialized communities— typically in situations where the decision-maker is exercising power—is unlikely to challenge the assumptions about "who belongs where" that stem from historical constructions of race.

From this starting point, the "unconscious racism" theory fashions a model of how decision-making may produce differential treatment. Believing that the social order is just, or at worst requires minor adjustments, decision-makers account for the homogeneity of their group and justify the power that they exercise by reference to personal characteristics of people who do and do not succeed. When they exercise discretionary power over individuals at the margins of society, as in the administration of criminal justice, these decision-makers may assume, again subconsciously, that individuals whose choices are so different from their own must be coerced into conformity with the social order. The greater the differences that decision-makers perceive between themselves and the persons subjected to their decisions, the less likely they are to identify with the individuals before them, and the more likely they are to believe that a severe response is warranted. Since aspects of identity associated with race, such as colour, ancestry or ethnic origin, are among the more socially salient differences among people, they are likely to contribute to the distancing effect that is implicated in differential treatment.

While this interpretation avoids allegations of intentional and overt bias, it continues to explain systemic racism in terms of attitudes, beliefs and assumptions that decision-makers may hold, albeit subconsciously, and rely upon in their daily activity. It therefore tends to favour educational solutions and to promote consciousness-raising with respect to the risks of subconscious biases. Education and training measures may be as generally beneficial in this area as in others, and many of the commission's recommendations support them. But they may not reach some critical dimensions of how the exercise of discretionary power produces racial inequality (Haney Lopez 2000). In particular, they may not address differential treatment that occurs when apparently neutral laws, policies, standards and procedures encourage the exercise of discretion in ways that have racialized consequences.

For example, one of the commission's persistent findings is that the disproportionate imprisonment of black people before trial and at sentencing is partly due to the role of employment in bail and sentencing proceedings (Ontario 1995; Doob 1995; Roberts 1995). Law encourages decision-makers to treat employment as evidence of "community ties" in bail hearings (where ties make pre-trial detention less likely) and as a factor that may militate against a prison term at sentencing. Where, as in Ontario, black accused and convicted persons are less likely than white accused and convicted persons to be employed, the legal permission to take account of employment when exercising discretion tends to produce racialized differences in imprisonment. To the extent that part of the unequal rates of imprisonment is attributable to reliance on the apparently neutral standard of employment, education aimed at eliminating subconscious biases against black people may be beside the point.

Fundamental to the commission's work is the understanding that decision-makers with good attitudes may yet act in ways that produce racial inequality if the context and environment in which they work, together with the standards that they administer, promote practices that have such effects. Conversely, even decision-makers with biased attitudes may behave in a non-discriminatory manner if the institutions in which they work require them to treat everyone equally and enforce compliance with the working norm of equality.

### Selected Findings of the Commission
The commission engaged in an ambitious program of work, which included extensive preliminary consultations with community groups and justice officials,

to define and refine its research agenda, surveys, interviews, file studies and observations of a variety of proceedings, such as trials, bail hearings and parole board hearings. It asked people what they think and examined what criminal justice decision-makers do. The commission found unjustified differences in treatment in policing, courts and prisons and unjustified similarities in treatment that fail to address the distinct needs of some racialized people. It also documented perceptions of members of the public, lawyers and judges about racial discrimination in the criminal justice system (Ontario 1995; Wortley 1995).

Much of the qualitative and quantitative research focuses on the exercise of discretionary power. These studies examine the policies, procedures and "working practices"—Ericson's "recipe rules"—that structure discretion as well as the outcomes of discretionary choices (Ericson 1981). In this very brief summary of some of the commission's most important studies, I focus on its research into imprisonment, because exercise of the discretionary power to incarcerate has the most significant consequences for people's lives.

Provincial prisons hold persons who are detained pending further criminal proceedings, the vast majority of whom are awaiting trial, and convicted persons sentenced to prison terms of less than two years. Partly because provincial prisoners are incarcerated for relatively short terms, provincial prison systems have received less scrutiny than the federal system, and little was known about the Ontario prison population when the commission began its work. Extensive analysis of prison admissions data assembled by the commission revealed some very disturbing patterns (Ontario 1995: Chapter 4).

First, there was a massive increase in the imprisonment of black people during the late 1980s and early 1990s. Between 1986/87 and 1992/93, the admission of black people to provincial prisons increased by 204 percent as compared with a 23 percent increase in the admission of white people. Over the same period the black population of Ontario grew by about 36 percent. The net effect was that, in percentage terms, black admissions to provincial prisons doubled in six years, increasing from 7 percent to 15 percent of all admissions. Within this general trend, the most dramatic pattern is the increase in admissions of persons charged with or convicted of drug offences in the Toronto area. All admissions for drug offences increased during this period, but admissions of black men and women increased by several thousand percent. In 1986/87, black people comprised about 10 percent of admissions for drug offences in most Toronto area prisons. By 1992/93, black people made up more than 50 percent of admissions for drug offences in these institutions.

Second, analysis of prison admissions in 1992/93 (the last year for which data were available to the commission) indicates that both black and Aboriginal women and men are overrepresented in Ontario prisons, as are black male youth and Aboriginal male and female youth. All other identified racial minorities are underrepresented among total prison admissions.

Third, the commission found that black people are admitted to prison at higher rates than white people across the spectrum of offences. But the overall ratio of five to one in black to white admissions masks substantial variation among charges. Differences in admission rates are much higher for charges that are usually produced by "proactive" policing rather than victim complaint. Four categories of charges stand out, because the admission rate for black people is more than nine times greater than the admission rate for white people; these charges are obstruction of justice, weapons offences, drug possession and drug trafficking.

These findings about disproportionate imprisonment of black people reinforced the commission's decision to pay close attention to the exercise of the discretionary power to commit people to jail (Doob 1995; Ontario 1995; Roberts 1995). Its major study of bail and sentencing compares the outcomes of bail and sentencing decisions about 1,653 black and white men charged with the same offences. Although the study is limited by the commission's selection of just five types of charges (robbery, drug offences, bail violation, sexual assault and serious non-sexual assault) for the comparison, it is the largest and most detailed Canadian study of the racialized impact of discretionary power in criminal proceedings.

This study showed that black men were more likely than white men to be incarcerated, both before trial and after conviction. But there was substantial variation among the different charges. For example, most black and white men convicted of robbery were sentenced to prison and there was no evidence of racial differences in incarceration rates. This finding is not surprising, because robbery is treated as a very serious crime in Canada that is usually punished by a prison term. Analysis of other charges, by contrast, indicated that black men were significantly more likely than white men to be incarcerated, both before trial and after conviction. There were no charges for which the white men were more likely than the black to receive a prison term. The most substantial differences in outcomes appeared in the decisions about pre-trial detention of men charged with drug offences. Among the sub-sample charged with these offences, black accused (31 percent) were three times more likely than white accused (10 percent) to be refused bail and imprisoned before trial. The largest differences in prison sentences also appeared among the men charged with drug offences. About one in three white men (36 percent) as compared to two in three black men (66 percent) convicted of drug charges received a prison term, whereas across the entire sentenced sample, 57 percent of white men and 69 percent of black men were sentenced to prison.

In its analysis of the data, the commission considered whether the differential imprisonment rates could be explained in terms of characteristics of the offences and how they were processed, or the men's criminal or social histories. It found that differential incarceration rates at bail and sentencing could not be justified on the basis of the seriousness of the offence charged since the offences of the white and black men were similar. Nor are the findings explicable by reference to criminal record because the black men were less likely than the white men to have criminal records and, among those with previous convictions, the black men had shorter and generally less serious records than the white men. After extensive analysis of the recorded characteristics of the individuals and their histories, the offences, and the processing of the cases, two factors stood out at both bail and sentencing as explanations for the difference in incarceration rates. One factor is race, the other is unemployment. Black men were less likely to have jobs than white men, and unemployment was strongly associated with incarceration before trial and after conviction.

This study indicates that both "race" and employment influence discretionary judgements in the criminal justice process in ways that produce racial inequality. In this sense, both factors contribute to systemic racism. But they differ in terms of their relationship to legally authorized uses and misuses of discretionary power. The commission's "inescapable conclusion" that "some black men who were imprisoned would not have been jailed had they been white and some white men who did not go to jail would have been imprisoned had they been black" is evidence of racial bias. Other commission findings suggest that such biases are likely subtle and may operate subconsciously (Ontario 1995: Chapter 7). They probably take the form of decision-makers being willing to give a white person another chance to stay out of prison but responding harshly to a similarly placed black person. Subtle or not, racial bias in decision-making is an abuse of power that law does not directly condone. Indeed, decisions influenced by racial factors breach constitutional equality norms. But law is indirectly implicated in this form of abuse of power in so far as it fails to restrain or prevent the racialized consequences of the exercise of discretion.

The role of employment factors in producing racial inequality illustrates a different point about uses and misuses of power. Law allows decision-makers to consider employment status when deciding whether to send people to prison (*R. v. Iwaniw: Overton* 1959; Ruby 1999). That unemployment is a significant factor in differential incarceration rates of white and black men demonstrates how the exercise of discretion in ways permitted by law may contribute to racial injustice. In this case the choices of decision-makers are within the immediate boundaries of the law. Whether the legal norms that indirectly produce racial inequality in the outcomes of discretion would survive a constitutional equality challenge is open to debate. The commission's findings indicate that employment status operates as a racially neutral factor in decision-making that has a racially discriminatory impact and, as such, it too should be treated as a breach of fundamental guarantees of equality. Until this is decided, however, the role that employment status plays in the exercise of discretionary power to imprison people remains an example of how legally authorized uses of power may be actively implicated in the production of systemic racism.

## Conclusion

The commission's research confirmed many of the complaints of those involved in the events that led to its creation. It produced formal knowledge of how discretionary power may be abused in ways that produce racial inequality, and it showed how the abuse of power may become embedded in routine practices.

This aspect of the commission's work has the potential to contribute significantly to the development of policy directed towards eliminating differential treatment and promoting racial equality in the criminal justice system. But the commission's findings about the abuse of power in ways that are outside the boundaries of law tell only part of the story. The criminal justice system does treat black people badly and, in many respects, worse than others. Law is not innocent of racism (Fitzpatrick 1987; Peller 1993). This critical finding should not, however, mask the broader observations that law enforcement processes treat most people badly, and that the capacity to oppress, control and harass may be built into the system and authorized by law. To put the point bluntly, equality may be a hollow goal if it means nothing more than a criminal justice system that (mis)treats poor black people no worse than it (mis)treats poor white people.

Alongside the state project of political and economic restructuring of the last twenty years, there is an intensification of punitive power, which, paradoxically, may reflect the failure, not the success, of the state in controlling crime (Garland 1996). Unable or unwilling to deliver economic and personal security to its citizens, the state responds to cultural expressions of social anxiety with a show of punitive force. It promotes initiatives that criminalize people who live and work on the streets, and adopts measures that result in rising prison populations, even as rates of recorded crime fall. In this context, the work of the Commission on Systemic Racism in the Ontario Criminal Justice System highlights the need to address the dynamic of ever-increasing repression that lies at the heart of the law enforcement enterprise. It is the use, as much as the abuse, of state power that should be the focus of strategies to promote social change.

## Notes

1. My thanks to Iain Ramsay for comments on an earlier draft, and to Emma Rhodes for diligent research assistance. All errors and oversights are my own.
2. This section is a substantially expanded version of the summary of the commission's origins in Williams (1999).

Chapter 14

# Unredressed Wrong:
## The Extradition of Leonard Peltier from Canada

*Dianne L. Martin*[1]

Three young men died violent deaths on June 26, 1975, when a firefight erupted on the Pine Ridge Indian Reservation in South Dakota, USA. Two were Federal Bureau of Investigation (FBI) "special agents" Ronald Williams and Jack Coler, who had been shot several times and were found lying face down next to Coler's bullet-ridden vehicle. The other was Joe Stuntz, a young member of the American Indian Movement (AIM), said to have been killed by a police bullet. Hundreds of bullets were fired that day from both sides. Indeed there had been many violent deaths on Pine Ridge in the days and months leading up to June 26. But the only deaths investigated, the only deaths avenged, were those of the FBI agents.

Leonard Peltier has served more than twenty years of two consecutive life sentences for the murder of the agents, but his extradition from Canada in 1976, trial in North Dakota and continued imprisonment without parole are all widely seen as unjust. The extradition from Canada is challenged because it was based on false affidavits taken by the FBI from a purported eyewitness, one Myrtle Poor Bear, under circumstances that suggest they knew she had no true evidence to give. The trial is challenged on many grounds, including non-disclosure of evidence that supported Leonard Peltier's plea of innocence. His continued imprisonment without parole is problematic given the admission by prosecutors that they do not know who actually killed the agents and hence can claim only that Peltier should be held responsible as an aider and abettor—essentially for participating in a firefight with many others. Whether or not this admission changes the legality of the conviction, it dramatically alters the moral culpability for the agents' deaths, and thus the legitimacy of denying parole to an otherwise model prisoner.

Those who refuse to reopen the case, or who support Peltier's continued imprisonment, do so on the grounds that a properly constituted court convicted him and their decision was upheld on several appeals. Others argue that the steps taken by the FBI and prosecutors can be justified, given that they were dealing with a dangerous organization like the AIM and the murder of FBI officers. In this regard, the case represents a classic miscarriage of justice.

It is also a paradigmatic case of abuse of power. Today, we are acutely aware that the state's power to prosecute and imprison is imperfectly contained and exercised:

> In some cases the innocent can find themselves in double jeopardy:
> where the police, deluding themselves into believing that a suspect is
> guilty, corrupt themselves by taking unlawful steps to ensure his
> conviction; and where Appeal Court judges, deluding themselves into
> believing the police are incorruptible, declare convictions to be safe and
> satisfactory which clearly are not. (McKee and Franey 1988: iii)

This observation has been made recently in one form or another throughout the
common law world where the problem of wrongful convictions has been shaking
confidence in criminal justice systems (Canada, Department of Justice 1998; see
also Wegg-Prosser 1982). It has particular relevance in the matter of Leonard
Peltier's conviction. His case has not yet resulted in a dramatic exoneration, but
it has troubled observers for years.

This examination of his case proceeds from the Canadian vantage point—
the extradition—and locates it as the *sine qua non* of a miscarriage of justice. There
is no real contest that the extradition was founded on false evidence. The
controversy is related to questions about who knew the evidence was false and
when; what consequences if any flow from this taint on the extradition; and
whether the serious errors in his trial should have resulted in a new trial and
exoneration. Because it is difficult to understand this or any other miscarriage of
justice without understanding the context in which it arose and the intersection
of institutional flaws and individual failures that perpetuate it, the analysis is
grounded in a chronological account of the entire case. The historical record is
closely scrutinized to tease out the linkages between official knowledge and
(in)action. As far as possible, original sources are used to map the events leading
up to the extradition and trial, and to illuminate the options available to
individuals and institutions (courts and governments) in terms of the way they
chose to deal with the issues raised. Finally, the case is examined to see what it
reveals about who and what are served by the lack of remedies for justice gone
wrong, and what, if anything, might be done about it.

## The History of a Firefight and Its Aftermath

In the 1970s American Aboriginal peoples (once again) grew vocal about the
history of broken treaties and unkept promises that mark the history of the
European incursion into North America. Some organized themselves as the
American Indian Movement (AIM) and began to fight back. It was also a time of
FBI misconduct of exceptional scope and diversity; "dirty tricks" and "counter-
intelligence" strategies were used against U.S. citizens whenever the latter
expressed dissent or made demands for civil and legal rights (Churchill and Vander
Wall 1988). Leonard Peltier is both a product and a victim of this history, which
is key to understanding the June 26, 1975, tragedy and his extradition and
conviction.

Pine Ridge Indian Reservation of South Dakota has a long and bloody
history of resistance to the U.S. government and violent reaction from govern-

ment agents. On December 17, 1890, it was the site of a massacre of hundreds of Lakota women and children by U.S. soldiers at a reservation village, the now legendary Wounded Knee. On February 27, 1973, it witnessed another legend-making confrontation when AIM joined Lakota Sioux traditionals, opposed to the Bureau of Indian Affairs (BIA) tribal government's policies and corruption, in a peaceful "occupation" at the Wounded Knee massacre site. Within hours the camp was surrounded by the self-styled Guardians of the Oglala Nation or GOONS (FBI-armed tribal police), FBI agents and U.S. marshals in an attempt to force the demonstrators out. Within days these government forces were joined by the U.S. army, which used unprecedented and massive force against American citizens. Known around the world as the "siege" of Wounded Knee, it commanded extensive publicity, largely critical of the U.S. government, and finally ended on May 7, 1973, when AIM members and their supporters left the site (Churchill and Vander Wall 1988: 141–77; Matthiessen 1991).

In the aftermath to Wounded Knee, FBI fears and concerns about AIM were as potent as those held by many Lakota about the FBI. Investigative interest in AIM and its members continued,[2] as did the violence against Pine Ridge residents, with more than sixty murders committed on the reserve from 1973 to 1976 and almost none solved or even investigated despite the massive FBI presence in the area (Matthiessen 1991: 5).[3] The FBI blamed AIM for the violence. Even before the occupation ended, local FBI had prepared a briefing paper for the attorney general of the United States about plans to use FBI special agents in a "paramilitary law enforcement operation" in the "event of a major confrontation in Indian Country." The paper discussed AIM and the situation on Pine Ridge, and problems the FBI encountered during the siege of Wounded Knee with obtaining necessary equipment from the army, such as armoured personnel carriers, and concluded that in the future the FBI must control all such "operations."[4]

This was the FBI protocol and this was the climate of fear at Pine Ridge when two FBI special agents, Ronald Williams and Jack Coler, entered the reservation on June 26, 1975. They were reportedly there to make a straightforward arrest of AIM member Jimmy Eagle for theft and possession of a pair of stolen cowboy boots (Churchill and Vander Wall 1988: 236–40). Somehow a firefight started. There is no consensus as to who fired first or precisely when a massive police and military force was again unleashed against Pine Ridge. However, the ensuing deaths of the two agents were not permitted to go unavenged.

## Connecting Leonard Peltier to the Murders
### Circumstantial Evidence
On February 6, 1976, Royal Canadian Mounted Police (RCMP) arrested Leonard Peltier in Hinton, Alberta. Before he could be brought to trial in the United States for the reservation murders, he had to be extradited on those charges from Canada, where he had sought refuge. To obtain a warrant of extradition, the American government, represented on the extradition by a prosecutor with the Canadian Department of Justice, merely had to establish a *prima facie* case of

murder against him. In February 1976, the FBI could offer only circumstantial evidence to that end.

The firefight at Pine Ridge had begun at approximately 11:50 a.m. and continued "from many sources" until approximately 6:00 p.m. The three young men were killed at some point during that period. One early report from FBI sources described thirty to forty residents of Pine Ridge returning police fire over that four-to-six-hour period. By the time the shooting was over, the scene of the three deaths had been completely disrupted. The agents' cars had been stripped, including the tires; all of their weapons and some personal possessions were missing; and Joe Stuntz's body was found wearing a jacket belonging to one of the agents.[5]

An investigation into the deaths of the agents began, with AIM as the focus.[6] Basically, everyone who could be accused of having fired on June 26, 1975, was considered to be an AIM member and a suspect in the deaths of the agents. The FBI began with a list of forty-seven suspects that was eventually narrowed down to four people: Dino Butler, Robert Robideau, Jimmy Eagle and Leonard Peltier. All were committed AIM members; all initially escaped from Pine Ridge and all were ultimately co-indicted. Only Leonard Peltier was ever convicted.

FBI interest in Peltier as a suspect began to crystallize early, despite initial information suggesting that he had been shot and killed during the siege:

> Inasmuch as solid evidence has been uncovered placing Leonard Peltier at the scene of the crime firing at Law Enforcement, consideration is being given to obtaining a warrant for aiding and abetting murder.... Even though Peltier might be deceased, *much benefit could be obtained from national press showing type of individuals agents faced in battle.*[7]

The FBI became particularly interested in Leonard Peltier when they learned about an outstanding charge against him in Wisconsin of attempted murder of a police officer (which they described in press releases as a conviction). Although Peltier was readily acquitted by a jury on the Wisconsin charge and has no criminal record apart from the reservation murders, by July 16, 1975, the FBI had a strategy in place to begin building a case against him. The goal was to "develop information to lock Peltier ... into this case" and to "develop additional confidential informants and sources." This aspect of the strategy was separate from the task of "examining the evidence and connecting it to the suspects."[8]

Meanwhile, ballistics tests were being conducted. By July 3, 1975, hundreds of shells and cartridges from the scene had been sent for crucial forensic examination.[9] On October 2, 1975, the FBI firearms examiner, Evan Hodge, sent a teletype to the Rapid City field office in charge of the investigation: "Recovered .223 calibre Colt rifle received from S.A. Batf, contains different firing pin than that in rifle used at RESMURS [an FBI term for the reservation murders] scene."[10] By the time of the trial, this .223 calibre Colt rifle would be directly connected to Peltier, but in October 1975 the FBI's firearms examiner had apparently *excluded* him from a direct role in the agents' deaths. Indeed, Hodge concluded that what would be developed into Peltier's rifle could not be linked to any of the .223 casings found at the scene. This teletype was never disclosed to the defence at the extradition or at the trial.

The last piece of evidence used at the extradition was obtained in November 1975 when agent Coler's handgun was located in a paper bag inside a motor home Peltier had recently vacated. A fingerprint on the bag was identified as Peltier's.[11] The weight of this evidence must be viewed against the fact that by the end of the day on June 26, 1975, all of the weapons belonging to the agents had been dispersed and were located in various hands, none of whom were prosecuted for murder because of that fact.

Thus, the evidence available to prosecutors when Peltier was arrested in Canada for the purpose of making a *prima facie* case of murder was that he had been at Pine Ridge, armed and firing with many others; no ballistics evidence connected him to the deaths; and he had handled material from the scene at some point months later. It was not enough. Direct evidence was required and eventually produced in the form of affidavits from Myrtle Poor Bear.

### The Myrtle Poor Bear Extradition Affidavits

Shortly after Peltier's arrest in February 1976 in Hinton, Alberta, the FBI learned that Canadian prosecutor Paul William Halprin, their counsel on the extradition, was reluctant to proceed on the reservation murders. Before he would agree to seek extradition on the murders—the true focus of the extradition arrest—the FBI would have to tell him that they had more evidence; the implication being that it would need to be eyewitness testimony. On February 12, 1976, the FBI described the resolution to the problem: "After extensive deliberations, Halprin agreed to file additional charges based upon information furnished by FBI February 11, 1976."[12]

Paul William Halprin in fact became very active in preparing for the extradition. Between February 17 and 19, 1976, he was in Rapid City, South Dakota, and Boise, Idaho, interviewing witnesses and preparing the extradition case[13] when the affidavits, essential to the extradition, were obtained from Myrtle Poor Bear. According to his subsequent sworn deposition, Halprin was advised while in Rapid City of a "potential eyewitness."[14] It is reasonable to infer that Myrtle Poor Bear was the witness and that her affidavits were the "information furnished by F.B.I. February 11, 1976" which had induced Halprin to agree to seek extradition on the reservation murders.

On February 19, 1976, Myrtle Poor Bear swore an affidavit that she was *not* on the Pine Ridge Reservation the day the FBI agents were killed, although she claimed that Peltier described his plans for murdering the FBI agents to her and then confessed to the reservation murders. This affidavit was not presented to the Canadian extradition court, nor did the prosecution disclose its existence to the Canadian lawyers acting on the extradition.[15] On February 23, 1976, Myrtle Poor Bear swore another affidavit. It is identical to the undisclosed affidavit of February 19, 1976, except that, instead of saying, "I left Jumping Bull hall and did not return," she says that she saw Peltier shoot the agents: "I was present the day the Special Agents of the Federal Bureau of Investigation were killed. I saw Leonard Peltier shoot the FBI agents."[16] On March 31, 1976, Myrtle Poor Bear signed a third affidavit, consistent with that of February 23, 1976, after Halprin sought clarification of the February 23, 1976, affidavit, the February 19, 1976, affidavit, or both (in which case he was aware of the inconsistencies and complicit in the non-disclosure).[17] The affidavits of February 23, 1976, and March 31, 1976, along with affidavits establishing the circumstantial facts detailed earlier, represent the evidence presented at the extradition hearing. Despite inconsistencies, the affidavits make a clear case of murder—but it is a fiction.

First, today it is uncontroverted and conceded by both U.S. and Canadian prosecutors that the affidavits were utterly false. In 1977, Myrtle Poor Bear retracted all three affidavits. Every key point of that retraction was independently corroborated: she was not Peltier's girlfriend and in fact had never even met him; she had never been to the Pine Ridge Reservation, except later, when the FBI agents took her there; and she had most certainly not witnessed a murder. While her last claim, that the FBI forced her to sign the affidavits, is nowhere directly corroborated, it is clear that someone composed them for her. Apart from the fact that the undisclosed February 19 affidavit is copied verbatim into the altered February 23 affidavit, it is almost inconceivable that she would have used the language found in these documents.

Second, the affidavits were known to be false *before* Peltier's extradition was ordered on June 18, 1976, and well before he was surrendered to the United States. The more difficult and contested question concerns *when* the FBI and/or prosecutors knew that she had no truthful evidence to give. The chronology of disclosure and evidence at the trial of Dino Butler and Robert Robideau—who were co-indicted with Peltier but tried separately—establishes that legal authorities definitely knew at some time leading up to that trial in June 1976. Chief prosecutor Evan Hultman later confirmed under oath that he was aware during the Butler-Robideau trial that Poor Bear could have no truthful evidence to give based on the evidence of the other prosecution witnesses.[18]

Third, whether or not they knowingly suborned Poor Bear into this perjury, FBI agents and prosecutors were dealing with a witness that by June 1976 prosecutors were describing as so emotionally and intellectually frail that she was legally incompetent to testify. Moreover, the FBI had used her as a witness in other questionable cases (Churchill and Vander Wall 1988: 335–42)[19] and both the FBI and prosecutors knew of her frailty.[20] On Poor Bear's evidence, coercion took place. In 1977 she testified that around the time she signed the affidavits she spent a lot of time in the company of the two FBI agents in charge of the Peltier investigation. She said they kept her in protective custody for several weeks and brought her to the Pine Ridge Reservation to familiarize her with its geography—she had never been there before. She also alleged that these agents threatened her life and the lives of members of her family, which caused her to sign the false affidavits.[21]

When Poor Bear's evidence and the manner by which it was obtained were put in issue on Peltier's first appeal, U.S. prosecutors described her as being incompetent in the "utter, utter, utter, ultimate sense of incompetency."[22] Moreover, this key eyewitness, whose testimony obtained Peltier's extradition, was never presented as a government witness at either the Butler-Robideau trial or at Peltier's trial in Fargo, North Dakota, apparently because of her incompetence. Defence efforts to call her as a witness to prove government misconduct were prevented in both trials.

In the end, all of the U.S. prosecutors were aware that she had no evidence to give relevant to Peltier's guilt, and at best they could be said to have turned a blind eye to the manner in which it was obtained and used at the extradition hearing. One of the prosecutors at Peltier's trial , Lynn Crooks, commented in a television documentary on the case:

> Crooks: "What Judge Ross was saying is that we should have spotted what a fruitcake Myrtle Poor Bear was right from the start and therefore using and relying upon her testimony really in and of itself was not good judgement…. I don't know why they shipped up what they did, because I wasn't involved in it, but I can guarantee if I would have been I would have shipped up her affidavits."
>
> Q: "No matter how you cut it, you can't get away from the fact that it was her testimony that got Leonard Peltier extradited from Canada to stand trial."
>
> Crooks: "I guess I don't ultimately know and ultimately I don't really care…. If everything they say is right on that, doesn't bother my conscience one bit. The man's a murderer. He got convicted on fair evidence…. Now I don't agree that we did anything wrong with that, but I can tell you it don't bother my conscience if we did."[23]

If Poor Bear was knowingly used to produce worthless evidence solely for the purpose of obtaining Peltier's extradition, such a use would constitute fraud. Evidence that pointed to this fraud surfaced *before* Leonard Peltier was turned over to the U.S. justice system. Shortly after the hearing which committed him for extradition, Peltier's lawyers obtained a copy of the February 19, 1976, affidavit which had been sworn by Poor Bear *prior* to the two affidavits presented at the extradition hearing.[24] It had been disclosed to the defence in the Butler-Robideau trial but was never disclosed by prosecutors to the Peltier extradition defence.[25] There was, however, no remedy in the courts for this material non-disclosure, nor, indeed, for any of the other improprieties that combined to ensure a conviction.

## The Legal Proceedings

The chronology of the many court proceedings in this case, the positions of the prosecution and defence, and the court rulings are crucial to understanding why there has been no remedy for Leonard Peltier and why his supporters continue to describe his case as a miscarriage of justice. It also demonstrates why Canada has been complicit.

### The Butler-Robideau Trial and the Peltier Extradition Hearing

On June 6, 1976, when the Peltier extradition hearing was still going on, discovery hearings were being held in Cedar Rapids, Iowa, in the trial of Dino Butler and Robert Robideau, the men indicted with Leonard Peltier. As noted above, the February 19, 1976, affidavit of Myrtle Poor Bear (and the evidence of Wilfrid Draper, which made it clear that Poor Bear had never been at Pine Ridge and did not know Leonard Peltier) was disclosed to defence counsel.[26] At that trial, which formally commenced on June 8, 1976, Poor Bear was listed as a prosecution witness but not called because prosecutor Sikma determined that she was "so emotionally out of control that [he] decided that she would never be used as a witness by the government."[27]

The Butler-Robideau trial proceeded on the basis that there had been a firefight on Pine Ridge in which they had participated. The jury acquitted them on July 16, 1976,[28] because the case had not been proved, FBI tampering with witnesses and evidence was manifest and, as the foreman explained,

> The jury agreed with the defence contention that an atmosphere of fear and violence exists on the reservation, and that the defendants arguably could have been shooting in self defence. While it was shown that the defendants were firing guns in the direction of the agents, it was held that this was not excessive in the heat of passion. (in Matthiessen 1991: 318)

Meanwhile, on June 18, 1976, Justice Schultz of the British Columbia Supreme Court had ordered Peltier committed for extradition on the reservation murders. His judgement made clear that Myrtle Poor Bear was the heart of the case, but he was unaware that she had sworn inconsistent affidavits and that she had no truthful evidence to give in any event. His discussion of the evidence on the FBI murders was very brief: "Direct evidence relating to each alleged crime is contained in Ex. 18N, the deposition of Myrtle Poor Bear, sworn February 23, 1976, and Ex. 18 'O,' sworn March 31, 1976, her further deposition." In his only reference to the evidence that the Canadian government later tried to argue justified the extradition, he said, "There is, in addition, circumstantial evidence comprising other affidavits of Exhibit 18, relating to each of the two alleged murders, which it is unnecessary to relate."

After discussing a range of legal issues raised in regard to all the charges on which extradition was being sought, he concluded in regard to four of the five charges, including the reservation murder charges, that:

> With respect to *each* of the other four (4) charges ... the evidence
> produced in this hearing would, according to the law of Canada, justify
> the committal of Peltier for trial, if the crime had been committed in
> Canada. Accordingly, with respect to *each* of these four extradition
> crimes, with which Peltier is charged, I commit Leonard Peltier,
> pursuant to section 18 (1) of the *Act*, to the nearest convenient prison;
> namely Lower Mainland Regional Correction Centre, there to remain
> until surrendered to the U.S.A. [29]

One month later, on July 20, 1976, the FBI analyzed the Butler–Robideau acquittal
and devised a strategy to ensure Peltier's conviction. That strategy included a
change of judge and venue[30] to keep the evidence of FBI misconduct and of
violence on the reservation away from any jury trying Peltier. By August 10, 1976,
the strategy also included dropping charges against Jimmy Eagle "so that the full
prosecutive weight of the Federal Government could be directed against Leonard
Peltier."[31]

### Appeal of the Extradition

Although the proof that Myrtle Poor Bear's affidavits were false came too late to
be used at the extradition hearing, counsel for Peltier did try to bring this
important fact to light on appeal. The manner in which the appeal court dealt
with the Poor Bear issue has been an important part of the Canadian government's
refusal to do anything about it. They continually argue that the appeal court
"considered" the fraud and leave the impression that a Canadian court reassessed
the extradition request on the basis that the key evidence was known to be untrue.
However, the facts are quite different.

The appeal was heard on October 25, 1976, before the Federal Court of
Appeal of Canada. An application to introduce evidence concerning the Poor
Bear fraud was made to the court as a separate and preliminary matter. If the court
agreed to receive and consider the fresh evidence, the appeal would be heard on
the basis that key evidence on the extradition was untrue. If, on the other hand,
the court refused to receive the evidence, the appeal would be argued and decided
as if there were nothing wrong with the Poor Bear affidavits. The application was
dismissed, without reasons, after less than two hours of deliberation over a lunch
hour. The only official account is found in the notes of the registrar: "October
25, 1976 application made at 11:11 am by Mr. Rush, concludes at 12:37; reserved
on application at 12:46 pm. 2:30 pm Mr. Justice Gibson denies the motion for
new evidence."[32]

The next day, on October 27, 1976, the court dismissed the appeal. The
court had listened to a number of arguments, but none of them had concerned
the crucial fact that the essence of the extradition case was utterly worthless. The
court's only reasons were as follows:

For some days prior to the hearing we have had the advantage of considering the case and the extensive memoranda of points of argument provided by counsel for the Applicant and for the Respondent, respectively, and the cases and authorities referred to in such memoranda, and we have, at the hearing, allowed counsel to make their submissions at considerable length without restriction as to time or subject matter; and, on the whole, we are of the opinion that no sufficient cause or reason has been shown for this court to set aside the warrant of committal dated the 18th day of June, 1976, referred to in the Originating Notice herein. Therefore the application is dismissed.[33]

The order of a judge that extradition is warranted is not the end of the matter, however. Each case of extradition involves matters of foreign affairs in the sense that one nation is making a request of another, and thus the minister of justice always has the final word on whether someone will be surrendered to another country to stand trial. After the appeal was dismissed, the minister of justice for Canada was required to decide whether he would surrender Peltier to the United States. If he determined that the extradition was being sought for political motives, he could refuse to surrender the prisoner. Counsel made submissions on Peltier's behalf, but on December 17, 1976, the justice minister, Ron Basford, ordered his extradition as it had "not been demonstrated" to him that the offences were of a political character. Dismissing the evidence about the state of siege at Pine Ridge as essentially irrelevant to his decision, the minister of justice stated that: "it will be the courts and not the F.B.I. or the B.I.A. who will be trying Mr. Peltier."[34]

In a press release justifying the decision to surrender, the minister did not respond in any direct way to the issue of the deliberate suppression of relevant evidence raised by the defence and the presentation of false evidence to a Canadian court. Instead, he characterized the matter as one of "inconsistency" and said that it had already been dealt with in Canada: "One of the matters referred to in the submission was the alleged inconsistency in the affidavits of Myrtle Poor Bear. This is a legal matter for the courts *which have dealt with it in Canada and will undoubtedly do so in the U.S.* [35]

It is technically true but misleading at best to say that the Federal Court of Appeal "dealt with" the Poor Bear fraud when they ruled that they would not hear any evidence on the subject, and to assert that the American courts would "undoubtedly" address the Poor Bear question. Presumably he knew that American law is unconcerned about how a person is brought before the court, up to and including by means of kidnapping. Moreover, prosecutors in the Butler-Robideau trial had already decided that Poor Bear could not be used as a witness. Why the minister of justice thought the situation would change in Peltier's trial is unknown.

*Leonard Peltier's Trial and Conviction:*
When Peltier's trial for the murder of the FBI agents was moved from Cedar Rapids to Fargo, North Dakota, almost none of the evidence that had helped Butler and Robideau explain the events of June 26, 1975, was heard by the jury. The prosecution had "corrected" all of the mistakes of the first trial. On April 12, 1977, the U.S. prosecutors also decided not to call Myrtle Poor Bear, once again rejecting her testimony.[36] The defence attempted to have her evidence heard, in part to place before the jury FBI misconduct in the extradition. But on April 14, 1977, Judge Benson, the trial judge, ruled against a defence motion to have Poor Bear called as a witness to FBI wrongdoing in the conduct of the investigation:

> The offer of proof related to a collateral matter and under the Rules of Evidence is therefore inadmissible. If the witness as she testified yesterday were to be a believable witness [as to FBI wrongdoing] the court would have seriously considered allowing her testimony to go to the jury on the grounds that if believed by the jury the facts testified to were such that they would shock the conscience of the Court and in the interests of justice should be considered by the jury. However, for reasons given on the record yesterday the Court concluded the danger of confusion of the issues misleading the jury and unfair prejudice [to the prosecution] outweighed the possibility that the witness was believable.[37]

On April 18, 1977, Leonard Peltier was convicted of the murder of the two agents.

A day after the conviction, a story in the *Vancouver Sun* asserted that: "The Canadian government through its Justice Department has been complicit in the misconduct by the American State and the F.B.I." (April 19, 1977). The Department of Justice prosecutor representing the United States, Paul William Halprin, successfully sued the newspaper and defence counsel for libel. His case is significant given the subsequent position of the Canadian government that the Poor Bear evidence had not been needed on the extradition. Halprin, of course, had initially said that there was insufficient evidence for an extradition, which is when the Poor Bear affidavits surfaced. Not surprisingly, therefore, he acknowledged at the libel trial that her testimony "formed a vital part of the case against Peltier" since at the extradition she was offered as the only eyewitness.[38] On May 3, 1978, in concluding that Halprin had been libelled, Justice Anderson of the B.C. Supreme Court characterized the suppression of the affidavit by the FBI and the United States government as "unusual and reprehensible conduct."[39]

### The Post-Conviction Appeals
Since the U.S. trial court had not "dealt with" the Poor Bear issue, neither did the U.S. appeal courts. However, the U.S. position about her testimony was reinforced once again on April 12, 1978, during oral argument on Peltier's appeal to the United States Court of Appeals for the Eighth Circuit. U.S. prosecutor Evan

Hultman confirmed that Myrtle Poor Bear had no truthful evidence to give against Peltier and was otherwise "utterly" incompetent to be a witness. Following this statement, Judge Ross said concerning the FBI conduct in obtaining the Poor Bear affidavits:

> Anybody who read those affidavits would know that they contradict each other. And why the FBI and Prosecutor's office continued to extract more to put into the affidavits in the hope to get Mr. Peltier back to the United States is beyond my understanding.... Because you should have known and the FBI should have known, that you were pressurizing the woman to add to her statements.[40]

The same court said that the use of the affidavits "was, to say the least, a clear abuse of the investigative process by the FBI," and the court recognized the essence of the misconduct:

> But can't you see, Mr. Hultman, what happened happened in such a way that it gives some credence to the claim of the Indian people that the United states is willing to resort to any tactic in order to bring somebody back to the United States from Canada.... And if they are willing to do that, they must be willing to fabricate other evidence. And it's no wonder that they are unhappy and disbelieve the things that happened in our courts when things like this happen.[41]

After the appeal was dismissed on June 22, 1979, counsel brought an action under the U.S. *Freedom of Information Act*. It produced six thousand pages of evidence (from the approximately eighteen thousand page FBI "Resmurs" file), including the ballistics evidence which established that the gun linked to Peltier was *not* the murder weapon. In 1984, Peltier appealed again.

The second appeal dealt with the non-disclosure of important information discrediting the prosecution theory that Peltier had shot the agents. The United States Court of Appeals for the Eighth Circuit viewed the non-disclosure as serious, but they were not prepared to grant a remedy:

> There is a *possibility* that the jury would have acquitted Leonard Peltier had the records and data improperly withheld from the defense been available to him in order to better exploit and reinforce the inconsistencies, casting strong doubts upon the government's case. Yet, we are bound by the *Bagley* test requiring that we be convinced, from a review of the entire record, that had the data and records withheld been made available, the jury *probably* would have reached a different result. We have not been so convinced.[42]

On September 11, 1986, the appeal was dismissed. When the United States Supreme Court refused to hear a further appeal, attention returned to Canada.

On March 30, 1989, an application for leave to appeal the October 27, 1976, decision of the Federal Court of Appeal, together with an application to extend the time in which appeals may be brought and to introduce new evidence, was filed in the Supreme Court of Canada (SCC) on Peltier's behalf. That evidence was the additional proof confirming that the Poor Bear evidence was false, and that prosecutors in the United States at least knew it. The argument was simple. An order, even an extradition order, obtained by fraud is a nullity. The remedy was rather more difficult, as Peltier had already been extradited, tried and convicted.

On April 28, 1989, the U.S. Department of Justice received an airtel from the director of criminal prosecutions, Canadian Department of Justice, seeking instructions from their client (the United States), as to how or whether to respond to the ground of appeal that Peltier's extradition had been secured fraudulently on the basis of false evidence.[43] No such instructions were received. Counsel for the United States could not and did not deny that a fraud on the Canadian government had occurred, but they argued that this was a matter for the Canadian government, not the courts.

On June 21, 1989, the application for leave to appeal to the Supreme Court of Canada was dismissed without written reasons. However, during oral argument, and in light of the Crown's failure to deny that the Poor Bear evidence was false, Justice LaForest suggested that the Poor Bear episode raised questions about the *bona fides* of the extradition process. Nonetheless, he seemed to agree with the prosecution's position that any lack of *bona fides* had to be dealt with by the parties to the extradition treaty—the governments of the United States and Canada—and not by the courts.[44]

One final legal battle was fought in an effort to cut through the "Catch-22," whereby politicians and state officials referred the matter to the courts, which then declared it a matter for state officials and government. On July 7, 1993, the U.S. Court of Appeals for the Eighth Circuit dismissed a third *habeas corpus* appeal. The application had been made on two grounds: (1) that since the government conceded it could no longer prove who had actually killed the agents, it was improper to continue Peltier's imprisonment, and (2) that Peltier's conviction was tainted by a pattern of outrageous government conduct in regard to the evidence. Forty-nine members of the Parliament of Canada were permitted to make oral arguments as *amicis curiae* in regard to the extradition fraud. Ironically, but not surprisingly given the history of the case, the argument of the Canadian members of Parliament was disregarded because it was made in their capacity as members and was *not* a claim from the government of Canada.[45]

## The Political Battles

Political strategies were pursued concomitantly with legal battles. In Canada these efforts were assisted by the comments that Justice Ross of the Eighth Circuit

Court of Appeals had made about the Poor Bear affidavits and the extradition in 1978 on the first appeal. On August 11, 1978, Stuart Rush, one of Peltier's counsel in Canada, wrote to Minister of Justice Otto Lang and provided him with the transcript of Judge Ross's remarks regarding the use of the affidavits in Peltier's extradition. He also advised the minister that U.S. Department of Justice prosecutors knew that Poor Bear was untrustworthy and had no evidence to give in any event.[46] Demonstrations and a sit-in took place in Vancouver, and an application to the United Nations was prepared on Peltier's behalf.

Because of the level of public concern, political staff got involved. On October 30, 1978 Michael Phelps, a "special advisor" to the justice minister, sent a memorandum to two senior deputies, Douglas Rutherford and Fred Jordan, and copied it to Paul William Halprin, the prosecutor who had conducted the extradition and the appeal. Phelps described the matter as "one of great sensitivity, both legally and politically," and advised that a response was needed in order to prevent a recurrence of the Vancouver sit-in which had attracted considerable publicity. He reminded them as well of the need to respond effectively to the complaint before the United Nations. He set out the four issues they needed to address and thereby established the Canadian government strategy that is still being followed. First, he asked if there was "other evidence" warranting extradition. Stuart Rush had written Justice Minister Otto Lang that the extradition was based on fraud. "Can we reply to the effect that this does not change things one bit?" Second, since "clearly there is no basis for re-opening the extradition hearings," a legal memo to justify this apparently "obvious" fact is needed. Third, he asked whether the FBI in fact obtained the affidavit and whether this aspect of the investigation was "sloppy." He wondered also whether this sloppiness should be condemned (apart from the "political wisdom" of such a move)? Finally, he asked, if "we" sought to complain about the extradition, what would the vehicle to accomplish this be? The replies he received to each of the four questions have a consistent theme—we didn't do anything wrong, but even if we did, it doesn't matter.[47]

### The Significance of the Poor Bear Fraud

In his reply to Phelps on November 8, 1978, Paul Halprin included a copy of a letter that he wrote to F.J. Jordan on April 19, 1978, in response to the application to the United Nations. He pointed out that although he did not know about the first affidavit and would have presented it to the court if he had, the inconsistencies do not rob the two he did introduce of evidentiary value. He said that all three affidavits were consistent about planning and a subsequent confession. Moreover, he would have argued before Justice Schultz that, even if Poor Bear was not an eyewitness, the other (circumstantial) evidence in the impugned affidavits was "sufficient during an extradition hearing to justify the conclusion that the fugitive was probably guilty of the crimes alleged."[48] Finally, he claimed that: "This was the text of the ruling of the three judges of the Federal Court of Appeal."[49]

His position is disingenuous. The concern about the Poor Bear affidavits was not only that an inconsistent one had been suppressed but also, and more importantly, that she had not even been on Pine Ridge at the time in question and didn't know Leonard Peltier. In other words, the heart of the matter was that the extradition was based on worthless eyewitness evidence. Given his earlier position—first with the FBI before the extradition and then at his own libel action—about how crucial the affidavits were, Halprin was even less credible in claiming that the circumstantial evidence was sufficient on its own. He also had to be aware that the Federal Court of Appeals had simply refused to consider the evidence of the extradition fraud.

The reply to Stuart Rush's letter of August 8, 1978, that finally came from the new minister of justice, Marc Lalonde, took the position that fraudulently filed or not, untrue or not, the Poor Bear affidavits could be ignored. This position was framed (incorrectly) as if it were the view of the Federal Court of Appeal: "the Court held that the fresh evidence should not be introduced *in that there was other sufficient evidence to justify the committal for surrender.*" [50]

This position has survived. On June 18, 1990, Douglas Rutherford, who had acted as counsel for the United States on the Supreme Court appeal and who by then had become associate deputy minister, wrote on behalf of Kim Campbell, Minister of Justice: "The Federal Court of Appeal dismissed Mr. Peltier's appeal, apparently on the strength of the circumstantial evidence implicating him in the murders, apart from the Poor Bear evidence." [51] On October 13, 1992, W.H. Corbett, senior general counsel, Department of Justice (who took over the Peltier file after Rutherford's appointment to the bench) wrote to the minister's special advisor Peter Lugli in similar terms, this time adding that Leonard Peltier *accepted* this position. "The Federal Court, on review of the committal for extradition was made aware of the contradictory statements and found, apparently, *sufficient other evidence or corroboration to affirm the committal.... Apparently content with the Federal Court decision, Peltier appealed to Mr. Basford, Minister of Justice"* [52]

Similarly, on November 10, 1993, in a "secret" memorandum authorized by Associate Deputy Minister Eric A. Bowie, Corbett wrote: "The Federal Court of Appeal dismissed Mr. Peltier's appeal, apparently on the strength of the circumstantial evidence implicating him in the murders, *apart from the Poor Bear evidence.*" [53] More recently, on October 15, 1999, the Canadian Minister of Justice released a letter she wrote to the U.S. attorney general. In advising her client (Canada still represents the U.S. government in the matter of the extradition) that the extradition was lawful, she said:

> Furthermore, the third Poor Bear affidavit was considered by the Federal Court of Appeal and the Minister of Justice before Mr. Peltier was extradited to the United States. Subsequently, further submissions respecting the third Poor Bear affidavit were made to the Supreme Court of Canada, as well as the appellate courts in the United States. The

record demonstrates that the case was *fully considered* by the courts and by the then Minister of Justice.[54]

Of course the record does no such thing, if "fully considered" means anything substantive.

## Who Was Responsible?

The next plank in Phelps' strategy was to deflect blame, if any should be accorded, at least to the extent of calling the Poor Bear incident "investigative sloppiness." In his letter dated November 8, 1978, Halprin admitted that the affidavit should have been disclosed to the extradition judge, but he was initially unwilling to lay any blame on the FBI:

> With respect to the investigation carried out by the Federal Bureau of Investigation, I cannot characterize the same to be "sloppy." I think that the witness Myrtle Poor Bear was difficult to assess and handle and that it would not be unusual for such a person to give additional evidence in the course of such a long investigation.[55]

However, the FBI has always maintained that at least three prosecutors, including Halprin, were responsible for the suppression of the original affidavit, and the original sequence of events set out earlier certainly suggests that Halprin participated in obtaining all three affidavits. A May 2, 1979, telex is the first known statement from the FBI to this effect:

> The affidavits of February 23 and March 31, 1976, were selected to be used as evidence in support of the extradition request of Leonard Peltier … the selection of the two affidavits was based upon the recommendation of Paul William Halprin [who] represented the United States in the extradition proceedings. It was in this capacity that he travelled to Rapid City, South Dakota, to confer with Special Prosecutor Robert Sikma, and to review available evidence in this case. It was upon Halprin's recommendation, with concurrence of the Special Prosecutors, that only two of the three Affidavits were used in the extradition proceedings. In fact, the Affidavit of March 31, 1976, was obtained at the request of Halprin who indicated he desired amplification of certain issues.[56]

On May 10, 1979, Ronald W. Moore Jr., Assistant Director of the FBI, wrote in a similar vein to Robert Keuche, Deputy Assistant Attorney General, regarding the Canadian inquiry:

> Halprin was aware of the contents of all three affidavits, and, in fact, he was the reason Myrtle Poor Bear furnished the third affidavit, as he

requested certain issues previously furnished by her be amplified. It was on Halprin's recommendation, with the concurrence of special prosecutors Evan L. Hultman and Robert Sikma, that only Myrtle Poor Bear's second and third affidavits were used in the Peltier extradition.[57]

On June 12, 1979, in a response to Doug Rutherford's memorandum of June 7, 1979, concerning the FBI position that he knew about all three Poor Bear affidavits, Halprin stopped supporting the FBI. Instead he claimed that their position was false, provided copies of correspondence to support his position and concluded: "the Federal Bureau of Investigation are still 'covering up' the suppression of the first affidavit."[58] Mr. Rutherford pursued Halprin's claim until receiving a February 18, 1980, memorandum from the FBI stating that there were "no records of the discussions" about the "selection" of which Myrtle Poor Bear affidavit(s) to submit to the Canadian courts. He accepted the "explanation" that the FBI assertions of May 2 and 10, 1979, that Halprin was actively involved in this process were now only their "best recollection." On February 21, 1980, Rutherford informed Halprin that this position "adequately explains" both the FBI claim that Halprin decided not to disclose the February 19, 1976, affidavit and Halprin's position that this claim is an FBI "cover up."[59]

Although by 1986 some members of the Department of Justice of Canada recognized that "there may be reason to suspect that the FBI and the Prosecutor's office may have known that the Poor Bear affidavits were false or unreliable before those documents were transmitted to Canada for use in the extradition hearing," that recognition has never led to Canadian government action on Peltier's behalf; "no such admission has ever been made and the evidence is not sufficient to support that conclusion."[60] The issue did not even arise in the most recent position. When Justice Minister McLellan took the unusual steps of writing the U.S. attorney general and releasing her letter, she did not refer to the manner of obtaining the affidavits, nor to the fact that they were known very early in the process to be false. In effect she washed Canada's hands:

> In 1994, my predecessor, the Honourable Allan Rock, asked Department of Justice officials to conduct a review of Mr. Peltier's extradition file. That process has been completed and I am now publicly releasing the file review, which I enclose for your information. I bring this matter to your attention because the release of the review may generate renewed publicity regarding Mr. Peltier's extradition from Canada and his subsequent prosecution and conviction in the United States. Given the unique circumstances of this case and its connection to both Canada and the United States, I felt it appropriate to relay to you the conclusions I have reached regarding Mr. Peltier's extradition. In short, after reviewing this matter, I have concluded that Mr. Peltier was lawfully extradited to the United States.[61]

## Conclusion

To date there has been no legal, executive or political remedy in Canada or the United States for the wrongs done to Leonard Peltier, an Aboriginal person, to Canada and to justice. As this book was going to press, Peltier was pursuing an application for clemency with the president of the United States that was being actively supported by defence committees in both countries and a growing coalition of activists, Aboriginal people, organized labour and faith communities. The FBI has launched an aggressive media campaign to oppose it. No body independent of the parties has ever reviewed the misconduct of state agents in the events at Pine Ridge, the development of the case against Leonard Peltier or the establishment of the case for extradition. In this, as with most other cases of suspected miscarriage of justice, the absence of independent review is significant. Not only does this lack make it almost impossible to achieve individual justice, but it also demonstrates how closely tied the exercise of the criminal sanction is to political agendae and the use and abuse of political power.

## Notes

1.   Thanks to many who have worked to understand this injustice and have contributed to this research—in particular, Leonard Peltier, the Leonard Peltier Defence Committee (Canada), colleague Bruce Ryder and former Osgoode Hall law students Michele Moore, Matt Stone and Robert Christie.

2.   Orders were given to develop informants and sources and to create extensive files on all AIM members and "unaffiliated Indians arrested or involved in takeover of Wounded Knee" (Airtel, "America Indian Movement (AIM) Extremist Matters," acting director of the FBI to the Special Agent in Charge (SAC) Albany, for "all offices except Honolulu," mailed May 7, 1973; in Martin 1995).

3.   See Martin (1995) for material on the FBI's dealings with AIM and with Lakota traditionals that was made available to Leonard Peltier through a *Freedom of Information Act* application after his extradition, trial and first appeal. The 1995 submission to the United Nations relied heavily on original documents, many of which had never been disclosed to Peltier's defence at the time of the extradition and trial. Hereinafter, the reference "undisclosed" is made to identify that circumstance.

4.   Memorandum, J.E. O'Connell to R.E. Gebhardt, "The Use of Special Agents of the FBI in a Paramilitary Law Enforcement Operation in the Indian Country," April 24, 1975 (undisclosed, Martin 1995).

5.   Memorandum, Gebhardt to O'Connell, June 27, 1975, which summarizes what the FBI knew the day following the firefight (undisclosed, Martin 1995).

6.   By June 30, 1975, the FBI was expressing concern about media portrayals of the deaths and the importance of focusing on AIM. Memorandum, B.H.

Cooke to Gebhardt, subject "Resmurs," June 30, 1975 (undisclosed, Martin 1995).

7.  Teletype, SAC Richard G. Held, Pine Ridge, to director, July 6, 1975 (undisclosed, Martin 1995), emphasis added.

8.  Rapid City FBI to director, "Daily Summary Teletype," July 16, 1975 (undisclosed, Martin 1995).

9.  Memorandum, B.H. Cooke to Gebhardt, subject "Physical Evidence," July 3, 1975. Airtel, Rapid City to director, July 21, 1975 (undisclosed, Martin 1995).

10. Airtel, Rapid City to director, attn. FBI laboratory, July 21, 1975. Teletypes, director to SAC Rapid City, "Reference your teletype 9/12/75," October 2, 1975, and Rapid City to director, "Re Minneapolis letter," October 2, 1975 (undisclosed, Martin 1995).

11. Oregon State Trooper William P. Zeller testified at the extradition that he developed one latent print on the bag and identified it as Peltier's. Special Agent Evan Hodge, FBI Firearms ID Section, swore on April 6, 1976, that on December 29, 1975, he had recovered the obliterated serial number from a .357 magnum Smith and Wesson revolver (the property of Agent Coler) [affidavit of Dean Ray, extradition exhibit 18 'K', 18 'J'] (Martin 1995).

12. Teletype, Minneapolis to director, February 12, 1976 (undisclosed, Martin 1995).

13. Teletype, director FBI, February 20, 1976 (undisclosed, Martin 1995).

14. Halprin swore that he did not learn her name and did not see her (undisclosed) February 23, 1976, affidavit until March 26, 1976. *Richard Marshall v. Herman Solem*, U.S. District Court, District of S. Dakota, file CIV 82-4072, deposition of P.W. Halprin, sworn July 20, 1983, at 1512–1715 (Martin 1995).

15. Affidavit of Myrtle Poor Bear sworn before Clerk B. Berry, February 19, 1976, filed, Supreme Court of Canada (SCC) (Martin 1995).

16. Affidavit of Myrtle Poor Bear sworn before Clerk B. Berry, February 23, 1976, filed, SCC.

17. Teletype, director FBI, February 20, 1976 (undisclosed, Martin 1995). Affidavit of Myrtle Poor Bear sworn before Clerk B. Berry, March 31, 1976, filed, SCC (Martin 1995).

18. Hultman before the U.S. Court of Appeals for the Eighth Circuit on April 12, 1978 (no. 77-1487), excerpts from argument from magnetic tape at 7326-7 (Martin 1995).

19. *Richard Marshall v. Herman Solem*, U.S. District Court, District of S. Dakota, file CIV 82-4072, deposition of Evan L. Hultman, sworn August 23, 1983, at 5513, line 20–6412 (Martin 1995).

20. Excerpts from oral argument, memorandum, Michael Phelps to Doug Rutherford and Fred Jordan, October 30, 1978, part of exhibit 8, Halprin deposition.

21. For a record of her retraction and description of the coercion, see *United*

*States v. Leonard Peltier*, April 13, 1977, transcript of proceedings, pp. 4584–4679 (Martin 1995).

22. *Leonard Peltier v. United States*, U.S. Court of Appeals for the Eighth Circuit (no.77-1487), excerpts from argument from magnetic tape at pp. 7326–27.

23. U.S. prosecutor Lynn Crooks was interviewed by Steve Kroft for a 1992 documentary shown on the U.S. television news program "West 57th." The transcript was filed with the Supreme Court of Canada on the leave to appeal application, June 1989.

24. Mr. Justice Schultz committed Leonard Peltier for extradition on June 18, 1976; *United States of America v. Leonard Peltier*, reasons for judgement, B.C. Supreme Court, no. 760176, Vancouver, pp. 86–87. The Butler Robideau trial began June 7, 1976, and the third affidavit was disclosed at a disclosure hearing on June 6, 1976 (Martin 1995).

25. Affidavit, Stuart Rush, sworn April 22, 1989, application for leave to appeal, Supreme Court of Canada, filed, SCC (Martin 1995).

26. October 20, 1976, affidavit of Leonard Peltier in support of the Federal Court of Appeal application to introduce fresh evidence, exhibit "I," filed, SCC. This chronology has never been disputed (Martin 1995).

27. Memorandum, Lawrence Lippe, Acting Chief, General Litigation and Legal Advice Section, to Murray Stein, April 26, 1979, p. 4; exhibit 12, Halprin deposition.

28. FBI memorandum, B.H. Cooke to Gallagher, "Subject: Resmurs, Purpose: to advise of Jury verdict," July 16, 1976 (Martin 1995).

29. *United States of America v. Leonard Peltier*, B.C. Supreme Court, no. 760176, Vancouver, BC (Martin 1995).

30. FBI teletype, Rapid City to director, "Re Resmurs, Re Analysis of Robideau and Butler Trial, July 20, 1976. See also Messerschmidt (1983).

31. Memorandum, B.H. Cooke to Gallagher, "Purpose: To record the decision to dismiss prosecution of James Theodore Eagle and to vigorously prosecute Leonard Peltier in the murders of SAs Jack R. Coler and Ronald A. Williams," August 10, 1976 (Martin 1995).

32. *Leonard Peltier v. United States*, Federal Court of Appeal, file no. A-441-76, minutes of appeal taken by registrar (Martin 1995).

33. *Leonard Peltier v. United States*, Federal Court of Appeal, file no. A-441-76, judgement, October 27, 1976 (Martin 1995).

34. Press release, Minister of Justice, December 17, 1976, p. 4, "In the Matter of the Extradition of Leonard Peltier—Political Character Submission," filed with the Minister by Donald Rosenbloom and Stuart Rush, counsel for Leonard Peltier (Martin 1995).

35. Press release, Minister of Justice, December 17, 1976, p. 4 (Martin 1995).

36. *United States v. Leonard Peltier*, April 13, 1977, transcript of trial proceedings, pp. 4584–4679 (Martin 1995).

37. *United States v. Leonard Peltier*, April 14, 1977, transcript of trial proceedings, ruling, pp. 4707–08, Exhibit "J," SSC.

38. *Halprin v. Sun Publishing Co.*, [1978] 4 WWW 685 (BCSC) at 688.

39. *Ibid.*

40. *Leonard Peltier v. United States*, 585 F.2d 314 (8th Cir. 1978) (no. 77-1487), excerpts from argument from magnetic tape at 7326–27.

41. *Ibid.* 7327–28.

42. *United States v. Leonard Peltier*, 800 F.2d 772 (8th Cir. 1986) at 775, 779–80.

43. *Leonard Peltier v. United States*, SCC, (no. 21409), judgement, Thursday, June 22, 1989.

44. *Ibid.*

45. Application for *habeas corpus*, October 2, 1991, Bismarck, North Dakota, denied; appeal denied by the Eighth Circuit Court of Appeals; *Peltier v. Henman*, 997 F.2d 461 (8th Cir. 1993).

46. Stuart Rush to Otto Lang, August 11, 1978, part of exhibit 8, deposition of Paul William Halprin, May 27, 1983, in the U.S. District Court, District of South Dakota, *Richard Marshall v. Herman Solem, Warden and Mark Meirhenry, Attorney General for the State of South Dakota*, file no. CIV 82-4072. The matter involved another challenge to the use of Poor Bear as a witness.

47. Memorandum, Michael Phelps to Doug Rutherford and Fred Jordan, October 30, 1978, part of exhibit 8, Halprin deposition.

48. Paul William Halprin to Michael Phelps, November 8, 1978, exhibit 9, deposition of Paul William Halprin, May 27, 1983; Paul William Halprin to F.J.E. Jordan, April 19, 1978, exhibit 10, Halprin deposition.

49. But the prosecution's argument at the Federal Court of Appeal of Canada presented by Halprin relies not on the circumstantial case but on Poor Bear's evidence. The respondent's argument was augmented by written "Submissions on the Circumstantial Evidence." *Leonard Peltier v. United States*, Federal Court of Appeal, file no. A-441-76, October 27, 1976.

50. Marc Lalonde to Stuart Rush, undated, released to Jim Fulton, M.P., pursuant to *Freedom of Information Act* application; emphasis added.

51. Douglas Rutherford, Associate Deputy Minister on behalf of the Honourable Kim Campbell, Minister of Justice, to Jim Fulton and to Dianne L. Martin, June 18, 1990.

52. W.H. Corbett to Peter Lugli, "Memorandum," October 13, 1992; emphasis added.

53. William H. Corbett, Q.C., "Secret Memorandum," November 10, 1992; emphasis added.

54. Letter, A. Ann McClellan, Minister of Justice, Canada, to The Honourable Janet Reno, Attorney General of the United States, October 15, 1999; emphasis added.

55. Letter, Paul William Halprin to Michael Phelps, November 8, 1978.

56. FBI teletype, May 2, 1979, referring to a facsimile of April 25, 1979, inquiries from the Canadian Department of Justice.

57. Letter, Ronald Moore Jr. to Robert L. Keuch, May 10, 1979, exhibit 14 Halprin deposition.

58. Exhibit 14, Halprin deposition, p. 1.
59. Memorandum, Douglas J.A. Rutherford to William Halprin, February 21, 1980, referring to letter, Francis Mullen, Asst. Director FBI, to Robert Keuch, Deputy Asst. Attorney General, January 29, 1980; exhibit 13, Halprin deposition.
60. Undated, unsigned memorandum, "Leonard Peltier Case," p. 4. A memorandum concerning Leonard Peltier from D.A. Avison, Criminal Prosecution Section, to Minister of Justice, July 29, 1986, refers to a "comprehensive memorandum prepared June 1986."
61. Letter, A. Ann McClellan to Janet Reno, October 15, 1999.

Chapter 15

# Women's Imprisonment and the State:
## The Praxis of Power

*Gayle K. Horii*

> There will never be a really free and enlightened state until the state comes to recognize the individual as a higher and independent power, from which all its own power and authority are derived, and treats him [or her] accordingly. (Thoreau 1965 [c. 1854]: 271)

I had never truly understood the concepts of the powerful and the powerless until I was sentenced to life in prison. Though walls of office towers and houses, restrictions of labels and identities, constraints of illnesses and barriers of age, sexism, prejudice and judgement had all confined me to varying degrees for forty-one years, I had viewed them all as surmountable obstacles or as temporary boundaries. Looking back, it is as if everything changed in one blazing flash. I knew nothing about criminal law. Its thickly bound and codified papers of mystification seemed to purposefully mask any understanding of the legal concepts applied to me. I felt like an actor in a symbolic, ritualized display. I was an outsider in the midst of the pomp and ceremony of wigged, black-frocked barristers and a tribunal laid out in gleaming hardwoods and polished brass—the power and authority which had once divinely rested within the body of the king and the church, now vested in the body of the laws of the state. Handcuffed and shackled, my hundred-pound frame squeezed easily into the metal-screened cage of the waiting prison van and instantly personified my internalization of the systematic reaffirmation of privilege and power that is the legal process. As I watched the many commuters rushing along the freeway to their homes, I realized I would never revisit that previous state of naiveté, my self-proclaimed guilt now intensified by my absolute lack of power.

While many of my experiences of imprisonment may be uncommon, my sentence was standard. When I pled guilty to second-degree murder for killing my stepmother, the statutory minimum term of life imprisonment was imposed.[1] The prisons and the conditions under which I survived my sentence were unique and informed my criticism of imprisonment and my existential understanding of power relations. Reading the thoughts of Aristotle on *Equity* helped me to make sense of my existence. He advised, "to ask not what a [wo]man is now but what [s]he has always or usually been" (in Greenland 1987: 8). I then realized that less than five minutes of my life had dictated my punishment, but they need not wipe out the woman I had been for forty-two years prior to my particular madness nor dictate how I would live the remainder of my life. Because of the crime I had committed, it might be difficult to accept my assertions that I should be granted human rights and that I could still maintain decent values. It is a most abstract conundrum, to wrap one's mind around the fact that a killer and/or prisoner can also be a good person. These are definitively contrary pictures—the "self" and the "not-self" coexist (see Geertz 1988). The prisoner contains a complete picture of herself—an open window—in stark contrast to the powerful, duplicitous organizations of the Correctional Service of Canada (CSC) and B.C. Corrections (BCC).

For seven years I stumbled over the confusing mandates of various penitentiaries. I served my first thirty-three months from April 1986 until February 1989 under maximum-security custody, which included six months in a women's prison under B.C. provincial jurisdiction. I served twenty-seven months at the former women's penitentiary, the Prison for Women (P4W),[2] and was the lone woman incarcerated in a men's low medium-security penitentiary for two months, and for fifty months in a men's high medium-security penitentiary.[3] I also completed three years on day parole in a men's halfway house, all under Canadian federal jurisdiction. On February 29, 1996, I was granted full parole and returned to live in the community.

In the first few months of my incarceration, a forensic psychiatrist asked me whether I understood just how mammoth the system was. I did not understand then that his question was actually a suggestion that I not "fight the system," a battle he considered fruitless. Accused of being self-centered or proprietary in my actions—the first red herring hurled to dissuade me from protesting—I pulled back, drawn into the accusers' scheme of distraction. However, I grasped a stronger and better-informed sense of what is right and eventually returned to pursue the argument. I realized that though there might not be a satisfactory outcome, I needed to see things through, since the alternative of doing nothing was highly defeating and often self-deprecating. This sense of what was right was my real world dynamic and this is what I was committed to in the unreal world of prisons.

During the long ordeal of imprisonment, I earned the label "political" because my interpretations of various rules and regulations were often contradictory to those espoused by guards and administrators. For example, while in Kingston's Prison for Women (P4W) I did not agree that the policy of segregating a woman who had slashed herself was compatible with their justifications used: "for the maintenance of good order and discipline in the institution, or in the best interests of an inmate."[4] How could more punishment be the righteous response to a bleeding woman?

Had I been serving a shorter sentence, I might not have been quite as "political," but when serving life, one is assured of only one thing: no definite release date. As a lifer, when each issue of depravity raised its ugly head, I concluded that the only choices I had were to struggle now or to struggle later.

Paulo Freire captured my dilemma:

> The central problem is this: How can the oppressed, as divided, inauthentic beings, participate in developing the pedagogy of their liberation? … As long as they live in the duality in which "to be" is "to be like," and "to be like" is "to be like the oppressor," this contribution is impossible.… The solution cannot be achieved in idealistic terms. In order for the oppressed to be able to wage the struggle for their liberation, they must perceive the reality of oppression not as a closed world from which there is no exit, but as a limiting situation which they can transform (1982: 33–34).

Prisoners are automatically oppressed by the generic and absolute imbalance of power within prison systems. With no power, few uncoerced choices are available and that includes the choice to say, "No," which is the most terrifying consequence of being a prisoner. As my friend Karlene Faith (1991: 18) said, "The power to act is precisely what freedom is about, and that includes the act of refusal." Knowing the hows, whens and whys of saying "No" is an exercise in embracing the authority within oneself. One must hold tightly to rightness and embrace the inherent rights of one's position in the human family. Only with this reference as a basis can the cruelties imposed upon prisoners by prison authorities be challenged and eliminated. "In the law, rights are islands of empowerment" (Williams 1991: 233). However, in practical terms, it is only through claims under the *Canadian Charter of Rights and Freedoms* that there is any possible recourse.

Federal penitentiaries are administered under acts passed by Parliament. The *Corrections and Conditional Release Act (CCRA)* of 1992 provides the regulations; however, these are interpreted by the CSC on their terms, using their methods, with impunity. The basic tools of the authorities, which are commissioner's directives (CDs), regional instructions (RIs) and standing orders (SOs), should be mastered first by those intending to enter the fray. If Claire Culhane, founder of the Prisoners' Rights Group in Vancouver, B.C. in 1975, were still with us, it would be she who could best conduct this effort.[5] Claire understood the "language of oppression" within these tools of authority. Under law (*CCRA*, section 98.1.2), prisoners in each penitentiary are entitled access to the Canada-wide CDs, but they have no access to the more specific RIs or to the most pertinent interpretations, SOs, which are penned by their own warden for the control of the prison in which they are incarcerated. Prisoners may grieve their treatment with reference to specific CDs; however, grievances are easily discounted. The final level of grievance (no further appeals) is outlined in part III of the *CCRA*, where sections 57–198 are devoted to the description, functions and duties of the office of the correctional investigator (CI), yet the *Act* itself gives the CI's office no clout. "Neither the Commissioner nor the Chairperson of the National Parole Board is bound to act on any finding or recommendation made under this section" (part III 179.3).

Even the CI can be refused a hearing by the CSC, who will simply *deny* any wrongdoing and paralyze any criticisms with tactical language designed to permanently block any requested solution. For example, in a letter to the CI, John Edwards, the Commissioner of Corrections, pointed out:

> The significant difference between our two perspectives, a difference I am increasingly realizing, explains just how difficult it is for our two agencies to agree on what needs to be done in respect of the issues you report each year. As you finalize the report, we would want to know what changes are made to any comment that is critical of CSC or any of its employees.... I do hope that these comments will have an impact on the tone and civility of your final report. (in Stewart 1995a: 113–14)

When the "final report" was issued, the commissioner of corrections commented: "The Correctional Service cannot accept the general negativism of the Correctional Investigator's observations" (Stewart 1995a: 116).

You can see why even the appointment of a woman CI to examine complaints by women prisoners cannot stop the many levels of violations of women inside penitentiaries. The CSC's appointment of Nancy Stableforth as deputy commissioner for women (DCW) simply added another deceptive layer to the bureaucracy. Her "rank equivalent to that of a Regional Deputy Commissioner" (CSC 1997:1) carries no real power. The DCW has no line authority, and no warden in any of the regional prisons for women must be accountable to her! The wardens must only "keep her fully informed" (CSC 1997: 2). Her presence is simply a strategic screen with which the CSC may block truth-seeking inquiries (like the plexiglass partition specifically designed by the CSC to slide in front of Marlene Moore's cage in segregation so she could not throw her blood out of the cell as she slashed herself unmercifully[6]). This also underscores the unlikelihood that any panel like the 1989 Task Force on Federally Sentenced Women (TFFSW), with its report *Creating Choices* (TFFSW 1990), or commission of inquiry (like that of Arbour 1996)[7] can be expected to alter the course of cruelty inside the walls. No matter how well-meaning and astute the investigators are, or how well researched, witnessed and documented the incidents of cruelty are, a prison is a prison is a prison. The structure of authority that produces the oppressed and the oppressor alike is the key to understanding the problem (see Zimbardo 1971). Contained within this structure is the authoritative power to agendize language, which is simply another control mechanism. "To name is to know; to know is to control" (Paglia 1991: 5).

The language of the oppressor, with its reams of rhetoric and countless nice-nellyisms, effectively masks the barbarity of imprisonment. Hidden behind policies fronted by cardboard people and programs are the devices of this structure which must be strictly opposed. Overlooking the power of euphemisms to conceal becomes blind acceptance.

The CSC applies the term "treatment" without definitional challenge.

"Treatment" can include the "involuntary transfer" of women to special handling units (SHUs, super maximum security units for men) where they suffer the gamut of isolation punishments, like the kind that provoked three women to hang themselves at P4W.[8] Meanwhile, the task force members met and consulted, the CSC digested *Creating Choices* and two more women enjoyed "treatment" before they eventually "strung themselves up."[9] Though the Daubney Committee (1988) recommended "that the Solicitor General convene a Task Force on Federal Female Offenders" (recommendation 96), it took the aftermath of Marlene Moore's December 1988 suicide to finally prompt the CSC to convene the TFFSW in the spring of 1989.

There is, of course, a duality of discourse inherent in the ubiquitous structure of the CSC, "typically a disparity between the public transcript deployed in the open exercise of power and the hidden transcript expressed safely only offstage" (Scott 1992: 73). Both transcripts must be laid open to multi-layered examination. It is through language that the process of dehumanization becomes acceptable, just as "the process of humanization is not founded in the conscious production of the necessities of life (Marx) or in the use of tools (Rousseau), but rather in the use of language" (Horster 1992: 63). When the CSC uses labels like "violent," without knowing and accepting the prisoner's challenge of the contextual framework within which the so-called violence was enacted, and uses euphemisms for "programs," such as "special needs units," which are really modern torture chambers, where "treatment" (mental and physical cruelty) is applied without reproach, they ensure the consequences of a divorced understanding accompanied by ongoing confusion and tragedy. As Williams states,

> an accurate understanding of critical theory requires recognition of the way in which the concept of indeterminacy questions the authority of definitional cages; it is not "nihilism" but a challenge to contextualize, because it empowers community standards and the democratization of interpretation. (1991: 109)

Most people remember the U.S. government's use of euphemisms to sanitize the killing of unarmed men, women and children during the 1991 Gulf War, calling it "collateral damage." Euphemisms used by the CSC are less understood. It is punishment, not "treatment," that is administered within the fortified sensory-deprivation cells called "enhanced security and/or special needs units." Segregation or solitary confinement is clearly *not* a "program."

The "management" that a "correctional manager," "unit manager" or "case manager" does is primarily his or her own job management. It is not about assisting prisoners. The titles used in prisons should describe the function of the worker—warden, keeper, jailer, record keeper. "Prisoner" is the only correct term to describe a person locked into a cage or cell within a facility not of her choice and whose quality of existence depends upon the keepers. A prisoner does not "live" in her house, home or room—one always has the key to one's house and has the freedom to enter and leave at will, as well as the right to refuse entry to anyone. An "inmate" is an inpatient of a mental hospital who may or may not have voluntarily entered the "institution." A "client" is a person who has purchased the services of a chosen deliverer, is a patron of the one hired and/or is an outpatient; someone chooses to be a client. The term "resident" is also an obvious corruption. "Institution" attempts to civilize the penitentiary, since it brings to mind other familiar institutions like hospitals, the family, marriage, etc. All of these euphemisms are used to normalize and sanitize the experience of imprisonment, which is clearly not "normal" at all. Tragically, many prisoners internalize this fake normalcy and become totally "manageable" (institutionalized). After years inside, many are completely "programmed" (debilitated), unable to apply critical thinking, and have lost familiarity with the "real world" interrelationships between work, family and community. When released, many "good inmates" fail at "reintegration," returning to prison (their "normal" "homes") over and over and over again. Prison "treatment" and "programs" produce good "recidivists," not good citizens.

The continual use of the term "offender" justifies everything done to an inmate "in the name of the law." Yet "offender" describes a person who is committing an offence—a current transgression, one that is occurring at that time. Charged with an offence, the person is tried and, if convicted, becomes a prisoner. The offence has already happened. It is in the past. A prisoner in prison is not offending. She or he has already offended. She or he may have "offended" once and may never "offend" again, but using the label "offender" permits an ongoing and static reference that justifies the brutalization and degradation that is euphemistically referred to as "treatment of the offender" and enables the continuum of power distinctions. On December 31, 1987, at four in the morning I was startled awake in my cell at Mission Medium-Security Penitentiary for Men by the brilliant light of a video camera trained on me while guards surrounded my bed. I was handcuffed and shackled in my pajamas and carried to a prison van. At the Abbotsford airport, two waiting P4W guards tossed me into a Lear Jet to fly me back to Kingston, Ontario. They call this the "involuntary transfer" of an "inmate." I call this assault and violation of my prisoner's rights.

"Corrections" is plainly a misnomer, since reformatories, lock-ups, jails, prisons and penitentiaries correct nothing; rather they err. The correct description for the "business" of the CSC would be the "Penal Services Among Canada (PSAC)." Since many of the "front-line" workers (those in the front, facing the "enemy" first) are Public Service Alliance of Canada members, the general public would then be reminded of the clear link between jails and jobs. Should the "War Against Crime" (an ever-present threat) justify the "war against prisoners" (a former threat)? Given that the absolute costs of war are borne by the citizenry, a fact which parallels the costs of incarceration borne by taxpayers, perhaps penalties for betraying the trust of those footing the bills should be mandated under law.

Compliance with the law ultimately depends upon an interdependent trust—trust in the rightness of the law and in the right enforcement of that law which "reflects ideals of liberty, equality and fairness (*nullum crimen sine lege nulla poena sine lege*—there can be no crime, nor punishment, without law)" (Arbour 1996: 179). Richard Goldstone, chief prosecutor of war criminals from the former Yugoslavia, and Louise Arbour, the then Chief Justice of the U.N. Tribunal on War Crimes, recommended that the Hague should mandate an ongoing series of war crimes tribunals to ensure that abuses of power would be internationally judged. If correctional abuses were also faced with the potential of penalties for infractions exacted by a high court and not by an arm of its own body of power, it might definitively mitigate the brutality of many prison officers and erase the arbitrary imposition of punishments such as segregation.

As it now stands, prison employees whose conduct would be judged outrageous and often unlawful outside of prisons are normally protected by transfer and often promoted. Abuses of power within prison corporations are publicly minimized with carefully manipulated media management. When media manipulation fails, an occasional token resignation of a powerful figure may occur, like that of the commissioner of corrections, John Edwards, who resigned on March 29, 1996, after Arbour's "blistering judicial report said he heads a branch of the criminal justice system that violated six women prisoners' rights and generally operates without concern for the rule of law" (*Globe and Mail,* April 2, 1996: A1, A4). Following the tradition of cover-ups, Edwards had stated that "I can see so easily how the well-trained ERT [Emergency Response Team] from Kingston Penitentiary would professionally carry out its instructions" and "no-one at the Prison for Women was physically injured during the ERT interventions" (Solicitor General of Canada 1995: 2). As Arbour explained, "The deplorable defensive culture that manifested itself during this inquiry has old, established roots within the Correctional Service … they are, it would seem, simply entrenched in it" (1996: 174). Edward's reward was a position on the privy council. He has now retired with what I assume would be a most generous pension.

In 1991, in Saskatchewan Penitentiary, two prisoners on their knees from the effects of tear gas died from ERT bullets fired into their backs. The CSC called it "legal intervention." Claire Culhane called it killing. In her December 14, 1994, letter to R.L. Stewart, CI, addressing his annual reports for 1992 to 1994, Claire stated,

> You will recall that the Administration also failed to notify me, in my capacity as prisoners' advocate, of the request made by the hostage-takers that I be brought in to assist them in their efforts to proceed with their attempts at a peaceful negotiation process. It is quite conceivable, in our view, that these two tragic deaths might have been avoided had that effort been made.

In 1994, when the ERT—simply a gang of hooded, armed guards (often "recreational officers") trained to inflict pain and fear—stomped into the segregation unit at P4W to carry out "cell extractions" (the enforced removal of prisoners from their cells), they easily justified their terrifying assaults on unarmed and naked women. I remember similar incidents. The last one I witnessed was on December 31, 1988. About twelve women had refused to lock into their cells on "A" range before midnight, the customary lock-up time on New Year's Eve at P4W. We normally remained just outside of our cells so that we could personally wish each other a happy new year. At about 10:45 p.m., the keeper announced over the intercom that since we had been rude that day the usual 11 p.m. lock-up would be enforced. Fifteen minutes before midnight, with shields and batons raised and accompanied by two Dobermans, the ERT from the Kingston Penitentiary for Men (KP)[10] stormed onto the range. The women ran into any cell they could lock into before being battered and/or bitten. Then in the darkness, one-by-one, each woman was "cell extracted." The dull thuds of heads banging on gloved concrete, shrieks of terror and whimpers of subjection, the clanging of cell doors opening and crashing closed, and the loud, hoarse-voiced commands competed with the cries of outrage from those of us already locked. We knew well the macing, stripping and degradation protocol that would follow later in segregation. The next day, all that was left of the struggle was the odd tangle of long hair entwined in bars, the reverberations of boots, batons and shields, and the disturbing memory of excited glints in the eyes behind the helmets. "A" range was locked down for the next four days while five of us went to segregation in protest.

Although the Prison for Women is closed now, it is a grave error to think that any one commission or other such reactive formation will stop "certain events" from occurring again at other prisons. One must focus less on the "events of unrest" and instead realize the urgency for a constraint of the process. The unmitigated power granted under law to immeasurable layers of authority has no analogous penalties for violations of that trust. One needs a thorough understanding of the *practice* of power.

Consider the end-results of the process of "classification," a process used to justify CSC actions and misdeeds. The new regional facilities in Edmonton, Maple Creek (Saskatchewan), Kitchener, Joliette and Truro were initially classified as "reception centres" since all federally sentenced women (FSW) were to be transferred to these penitentiaries at sentence. The CSC reneged on its 1990 promise to close P4W, and in 1991 placed mainly Aboriginal women in a "separated unit." According to Sally Willis, then executive director of the Elizabeth Fry Society of Kingston and member of the TFFSW, this action was "in total antithesis to the Task Force Report." Her 1991 "Report to CAEFS [Canadian Association of Elizabeth Fry Societies] Social Action Committee" explicitly stated that it was "not reasonable, safe, secure and humane control," and added, "such treatment cannot lead to a positive outcome." Over the next three years of increasingly harsh conditions, the "unrest" of the women segregated on "B" range was resolved with ERT (goon squad) "interventions." Attempts by

Aboriginal women to protest with hunger strikes were answered with more lockdowns. The unanswered smashing (two weeks prior to the April 27 events) of the grandmother drum in the women's sweat lodge erupted in a chain of extreme violations, forcing the warden, Mary M. Cassidy, to acknowledge previous queries. In a confidential letter dated April 29, 1994, Cassidy wrote, "The destruction of the drum is most unfortunate. I have not determined it was done 'by guards' and in fact have no evidence of the manner or the culprit. We'll keep trying to sort it out."

Following the ERT "interventions," the women remained in segregation, handcuffed and shackled for eight to nine months. The last woman was released from segregation on January 23, 1995 (Stewart 1995b: 12). When the courts blocked the "involuntary transfers" of these women to permanent isolation in KP, the CSC continued to operate P4W as a SHU-like facility. On September 12, 1996, Ole Ingstrup, commissioner of corrections, issued a memo to all CSC directives holders which stated that, "no federally sentenced woman who is designated as a maximum-security inmate will be accommodated at any of the new regional facilities for women" (Ingstrup 1996a). This measure ensured that maximum-security women could not benefit from CSC's former agreement with the TFFSW to "allow female inmates to live closer to their families and friends" (*Vancouver Sun,* September 26, 1990: A6). It also meant that more women must be classified maximum security for transfer to P4W in order to justify the employment costs of keeping P4W open (in November 1999, half a year before its closure, there were twelve women incarcerated in P4W and about fifty staff members). This necessitated the reclassification of the regional prisons which now "are not reception centres as provided for in paragraph 4 of CD 500"; casually added to this interim CD was the provision that "placement or subsequent transfer of female inmates may be made to an institution other than a women's institution" (Ingstrup 1996a).

These "involuntary transfers" to men's SHUs illustrated the alternate strategy of the CSC. If they couldn't classify enough women as maximum security to justify the expense of keeping P4W open, the CSC could add another label to these women to warrant their move to a men's maximum-security penitentiary or an SHU. However, because women "having significant mental health issues" may not always be classified maximum security, on September 19, 1996, the commissioner issued a further Instruction: "Effective immediately and until further notice the portion of Springhill Institution[11] accommodating federally sentenced women is classified as multi-level" (Ingstrup 1996b). Multi-level is the catch-all classification for prisons that incarcerate prisoners of any security level. A multi-level prison is required to maintain the security level of the highest classified prisoner held in that location. Therefore, as Kim Pate, Executive Director of CAEFS, has forcefully argued, even if a woman is considered a minimum security risk, if she is labelled as "having a significant mental health issue," she is punished as if she were a maximum security problem!

This summarily justified process illustrates how easily even harsher controls over women have emerged after both *Creating Choices* and the Arbour Inquiry. The most heinous of punishments—sensory deprivation—is imposed upon the least powerful women who have little education and/or resources, and/or few friends and/or family members powerful or astute enough to build the legal and public support required to stop this intentional barbarity.

Joey, Diane and Sandy have suffered more than eighteen years of this CSC "treatment." Heaped upon their short, outside-prison life histories disfigured with abuse are their lengthy prison histories scarred with more violations. It is beyond comprehension how these women have survived years of isolation. Joey and Diane have already served more than double their minimum sentences of seven years before eligibility for day parole. Each has been incarcerated in P4W for over eighteen years on sentences that carried a minimum ten-year term before eligibility for full parole![12]

Sandy, according to a reporter (*Vancouver Sun*, April 6, 1993: A15), "was going to be a nun." Instead "she became an armed robber. She entered here [P4W] at age 18. Problems in prison, including a hostage taking, have left her with 14 more years to serve." It was in 1986, in P4W, that I met this amiable young woman whose focus was simply to gain access to the yard. I will never forget how her brilliant smile lit up the gym when she danced at Pow-Wows. There is ample evidence that Sandy was wrongfully charged and convicted of murder early in 1994 (prior to the additional abuses she suffered during the "events" of April 27). Though the CSC will tell you that Sandy voluntarily transferred from KP to the Prince Albert SHU for men in May of 1994, they will not tell you that they promised she would be transferred to the Healing Lodge when it opened. In 1995, when the Okimaw Ohci Healing Lodge finally did open in Maple Creek, Saskatchewan, no maximum security women were permitted transfer. Since then the Healing Lodge has undergone a severely negative transition. Rather than implementing the vision whereby Aboriginal community and task force member involvement would create a focus on meaningful choices and healing, the CSC has predictably directed the focus towards their control model of punishment-risk-security (Monture-Angus 2000: 53) The CSC has the unfailing history of pirating and then bastardizing every positive idea presented to it "in order to expand [its] own power" (see Kendall 2000: 92). Sandy is now forty years old, a product of severe, state-authorized abuse—incarcerated under maximum-security and segregated conditions for over twenty-two years. She remains powerless. The CSC labels her one of the "worst mental health problems in the system,"[13] yet when I spoke to Sandy several months later she sounded perfectly rational. As Edelman wrote in 1977 (in Kendall 1994: 2), "it appears that people can deliberately hurt others only by persuading themselves and as wide a public as possible that it serves a therapeutic purpose."

These three women have endured the majority of their years under various forms of isolation. The CSC continues their blatant abuse with constant reference to its newest slippery slope "profiling": "high needs = high risk." And yet, with merely the stroke of a pen in May 2000, the CSC reclassified many of the remaining women in P4W (previously held there because of their "high risk profiles") to medium-security and transferred them to regional facilities![14] This CSC "profiling" enabled P4W to remain operative for ten years past the promised 1990 closure—a postponement estimated to have cost taxpayers over $25 million[15] (excluding costs of $750,000 expended for new segregation cells, the Arbour Inquiry, the civil actions arising from the violations of six women and any and all other miscellaneous "corporate" and "executive" expenditures).

There are also women serving life in the Burnaby Correctional Centre for Women (BCCW). Before BCCW was built, I applied to BCC seven times for return from P4W but was denied. However, when BCCW opened in 1991, because the federal funds contributed to its operating budget are based on the number of beds occupied by FSW, I became a sought-after commodity. My lawyer, John Conroy, Q.C., successfully obtained an injunction[16] to stop my "involuntary transfer" to this modernized jail because the medium-security conditions I lived under at Matsqui Penitentiary were vastly superior to what I would have faced at BCCW. There they boast 114 surveillance cameras to observe 114 maximum-security prisoners separated into tiny units, each commanded by a plexiglass-surrounded guard station. Constant "in-your-face" aggravation, no communal dining, very restricted movement through countless electronically locked doors and very few activities ensure the ultimate in deprivation for FSW, and the ultimate in control and job security for staff. Nearly 70 percent of the women held in this "ultra-max" prison are serving provincial sentences of less than two years—many just a few months. The distress suffered is directly related to the amount of time one is forced to exist within this harsh environment. Juvenile boys,[17] prisoners on remand or serving weekends, environmental protesters and "illegal Chinese immigrants" all compete for their meagre share of space and "resources."

Even though the planned fortress, the BCCW, was still only a conceptual drawing when the TFFSW was established, FSW in B.C. were excluded from the TFFSW. The B.C. Federal Exchange of Services Agreement (BCESA), which eliminates federal standards of treatment for FSW, was not signed until March 29, 1990. *Creating Choices* was published a few days later. In 1988, while incarcerated in P4W, I was told that B.C. is simply too far away from Ottawa for the CSC to be "concerned about"—out of sight, out of mind. Nothing has changed. FSW in B.C. still have no power and absolutely no choices. BCCW, however, was granted the federal power to "involuntarily transfer" FSW to P4W and/or to a men's federal penitentiary as they did in July 1999.[18] This is called "power-sharing."

Certainly *Creating Choices* stands as a classic document (as do the Arbour recommendations), but like the office of the correctional investigator, its power is limited to that of any group without the authority under law to enforce their recommendations. Open to the discretion of the CSC, the perversion of the recommendations was slickly accomplished. Perhaps if the TFFSW had referred to the authority of the Daubney committee's suggestions in *Taking Responsibility* (1988), the task force might have enlisted the potency of a parliamentary committee. Instead, the CSC used *Creating Choices* to conveniently and effectively usurp the authority of the Daubney committee's recommendations, in particular the focus on community placements for FSW. The CSC noted:

> The 1988 report of the Standing Committee on Justice and Solicitor General ... takes a rare view of the situation facing federally-sentenced women ... [and] 17 of its 97 recommendations to improvements [related to them. One recommendation was that]...no further prison construction take place without establishing halfway houses for women at the same time [and another was for the] closure of the Prison for Women in the next five years.... [The CSC added that] it is not clear at this point whether the government will formally respond to the Daubney report. (Solicitor General 1989: 8–9)

At the time of writing there were no halfway-house beds designated specifically for FSW west of Ontario, a fact that is explained by the lack of funding for this type of arrangement. There is funding for inside contracts, which many professionals continue to spar for. To those of us inside who are designated "subjects for research," many find that "the scholar appears as an authoritative (and often well-paid) voyeur bound in hierarchical relations to her relatively impoverished subject" (in Duggan 1992: 27).

The priority prison axiom, "for the good order of the institution," belies the real mission and private discourse of the "correctional" authorities—growth of their "industry," job security and safety, and concealment. Those employed by and under contract for the CSC must promise that "nondisclosure of wrongs," termed "confidentiality," is an acceptable condition for employment. This effectively silences any dissent from disgruntled employees and also ensures the ongoing commission of terrible crimes, all in the name of the state. With regard "to the mindset of the entire organization," as Arbour (1996: 162) observed, "it would seem that the admission of error is perceived as an admission of defeat by the Correctional Service." When accused of "mismanagement," the CSC, like other policing agencies, simply "closes ranks" (Arbour 1996: 174).

Never underestimate the gluttony of "correctional" enterprises. The CSC has ready access to funding and is audited only every five years. They need not wait for approval from anyone before acting. Rather, they act and then justify their multi-billion-dollar expenditures with the moralistic platitude that they are "keeping the *public* safer." Witness the rapid, April 1995 completion in P4W of "a new, higher security segregation unit ... of 10 cells with steel doors ... at a cost of $750,000" (*Kingston Whig Standard,* April 20, 1995: 16) *before* the Arbour Inquiry was announced. Along with the twenty-two segregation cells and the twenty-five "separated" cells on "B" range, there were fifty-seven segregation cells, more than 42 percent of the 135 single-bed capacity of P4W! Are women ten times more "dangerous" than the men incarcerated in the maximum-security Archambault Penitentiary, which has sixteen segregation cells (less than four percent) out of its 425 single-bed capacity? Or could it be that the examples of unarmed women with obviously indefatigable courage—enough to protest their violations in the face of the overwhelming odds of impending physical assault—must be obliterated?

The military-control model (adjusted and amended to computerized requirements) was designed by and for the patriarchal, male-dominated culture and is as appropriate for attending to the "needs" of women in prison as circumcision is. We must attack the processes to illustrate that band-aids do not stop the jugular flow. We need to declare that language and behavioural euphemisms meant to disarm advocates for justice will be obliterated. And we must fully grasp that "there is little hope that the Rule of Law will implant itself within the correctional culture without assistance and control from Parliament and the courts" (Arbour 1996: 182).

Let us understand that the "correctional" bastions will only use inquiries, commissions, task forces and the like as smoke screens to increase their numbers and their budgets, not to redress their abuses of power. We should stop the construction of more maximum-security units, the addition of more security devices, more barriers in the bureaucratic maze, and more levels of "authority" that only result in greater numbers of potential abusers being funded for a greater number of years. We have to understand that reform of any corrupt enterprise will only result in reformed corruption.

> Every reform raises the question of whether, in Gramsci's terms, it is a revolutionary reform, one that has liberatory potential to challenge the status quo, or a reform which may ease the problem temporarily or superficially but reinforces the status quo by validating the system through the process of improving it. We do liberal reform work because real women in real crises occupy the prisons, and they can't be ignored. Revolutionary reform work is educative: it raises questions of human rights (and thereby validates prisoners as human beings) and demonstrates that the state apparatus which is mandated to uphold human rights is one of the worst abusers. (Faith 2000: 12)

We should enlist the weapons of critical education, dissent and protest to decriminalize and decarcerate wherever possible. Community resources, education, legal and policy initiatives and public awareness can bring an end to the incarceration of the majority now imprisoned and perhaps an end to incarceration as a business specializing in protected abuses of power. We can learn much from the proceedings of International Conferences on Penal Abolition (ICOPA).[19] As Karlene Faith writes:

> When appraising whether or not a project is reformist reform or has revolutionary reform potential, the question to ask is "Cui Bono?", that is, "Who Benefits?" If it benefits women in the long run, strengthens communities, and reduces the numbers of prisoners, it is revolutionary;

> if it eases conditions for a few women temporarily but at the same time reinforces a correctional ideology which benefits the state and a philosophy of retribution, it's reform. (Faith 2000: 12)

The office of the correctional investigator must be mandated to report *only* to Parliament. It is there that recommendations can be enforced. Members of Parliament, independent tribunals and community boards must be given powers of entry into any place where people are imprisoned in Canada without notice to correctional authorities. Only with unrestrained, constant vigilance can it be assured that the abuses of power entrusted to civil servants may possibly be mitigated. This battle needs a logistical plan or nothing will change except "now they are modern, now they wear polyester" (Horii 1989: 23). "Modern institutions" are not the panacea for crime, just as "modern weapons" are not the panacea for war.

> Along with feminism, postmodernism opposes modernism by reference to the choice—hairesis, heresy—made possible by the existence of competing possibles and to the explicit critique of the sum total of the alternatives not chosen that the established [modernist] order implies. (Bourdieu 1977: 169)

This era of postmodernism has graced us with key thinkers and actors in the human rights struggle. They compassionately demand accountability for abuses of power and insist that prisoner voices be included and accepted as authentic. We are forever grateful to those who have forged this path.

On behalf of those who have been, are or will be abused in prisons, I implore you to put your faith and trust in experts within global circles of humanitarians, academics, creatively strong feminists, socio-political activists, penal abolitionists and constitutional scholars. We need to open doors to the solutions available within postmodernist and feminist intellectual analyses, true spiritual endeavours and constitutional challenges. These analyses can best ensure humane treatment within the walls while a practical, cross-disciplinary strategy is formulated to end the use of imprisonment as the first reaction to "criminal behaviour." A few experts come quickly to mind, because I know them and their work well, such as the indomitable Claire Culhane, MP Svend Robinson,[20] Des Turner,[21] Wayne Northey,[22] Karlene Faith,[23] Liz Elliott,[24] Kim Pate,[25] Patricia Monture-Angus,[26] June Callwood,[27] John Conroy[28] and Sasha Pawliuk.[29] They continue to serve as role models for me as I continue to serve my life sentence reporting to a CSC parole officer.

> But man, proud man,
> Drest in a little brief authority
> Most ignorant of which he is most assured,
> His glassy essence, like an angry ape,

Plays such fantastic tricks before high heaven
As make the angels weep.
—Shakespeare, *Measure for Measure*

## Notes

1. *Criminal Code of Canada,* section 235—with ten years served before eligibility for full parole.
2. On May 9, 2000, Theresa Ann G. was the last woman transferred out of P4W. CSC held an official closing ceremony on July 6, 2000, attended by nearly two hundred people (including only a handful of advocates, since CSC would not pay for travel). No mention was made of the many women who had died in P4W over its sixty-six-year history.
3. With the exception of Mary B. and Mary A., who were fasting in protest of their incarceration in the spring of 1990 in Matsqui Penitentiary for Men, Abbotsford, B.C.
4. Commissioner's Directives [CD] 40.1.(a)(b) 1987-05-01. *Administrative Consolidation Penitentiary Service Regulations (PSR).* In 1992 the PSR was replaced by the *Corrections and Conditional Release Act (CCRA),* 31.(3)(a-c), which added "and the institutional head is satisfied that there is no reasonable alternative to administrative segregation."
5. Claire lived from September 2, 1918, to April 28, 1996. Her work was honoured by the following: Commemorative Medal for the 125th Anniversary of Confederation, 1992, "for Canadians who have made a significant contribution to their fellow citizens, to their community or to Canada; Marlene Moore Award, "for leadership in the field of community based programs in Canada, or for furthering the goals of deinstitutionalization, or for outstanding service within a community based program which has had significant impact on the lives of the individuals who have been helped" (Ontario Board of Parole); "Canada Volunteer Award Medal and Certificate of Honour"; "Member of the Order of Canada" (1995). See also her several books (Culhane 1972, 1979, 1985, 1991) and Lowe's (1992) account of her life. Claire suffered a heart attack on January 2, 1995. Though under strict orders to cease her activities, she continued her work and while working on a crucial project—to close down all segregation units—she suffered a stroke and died on Sunday, April 28, 1996. We miss her so.
6. Witnessed by myself on November 24, 1988, in segregation at P4W. Nine days later, on December 3, 1988, Marlene choked herself to death in the prison hospital. See Kershaw and Lasovitch (1991).
7. Honourable Madam Justice Louise Arbour of the Ontario Court of Appeal (in 1999 appointed Justice of the Supreme Court of Canada) headed the Commission of Inquiry into Certain Events at the Prison for Women in Kingston (April 1994). The commission conducted hearings in November 1995 and submitted its report to the solicitor general in March 1996.
8. Pat Bear, March 1989; Sandy Sayer, October 1989; and Marie Ledoux,

February 1990.

9. Careen Daignault, September 1990; and Johnie Neudorf, November 1990.

10. The Kingston Penitentiary for Men was located across the street from P4W, which enabled quick access to the ERT by guards eager for stimulation from their usual boredom.

11. A men's maximum security penitentiary in Nova Scotia. FSW are also isolated in the men's Regional Psychiatric Centre in Saskatoon, Saskatchewan Penitentiary in Prince Albert, and the Ste. Anne-des-Plaines Penitentiary in Québec.

12. Joey is now in a medium-security regional facility. Diane is now incarcerated in a women's unit in the men's SHU in Ste. Anne-des-Plaines. Further information may be obtained by your request in writing, accompanied by a letter of introduction upon which I will ask the women for their consent to be contacted.

13. As expressed to me by a CSC employee during a break from proceedings at the National Stakeholder's Meeting, January 1998, Montreal.

14. Known exceptions include Diane in the men's SHU at Ste. Anne-des-Plaines.

15. Calculated according to the 1993 stated costs of about $100,000 per year per woman x 25 women x 10 years. This is a low estimate since over 100 women were held in P4W in the years prior to the opening of regional facilities beginning in 1995.

16. As of June 26, 2000, my *Charter* writ claiming discriminatory treatment by the CSC is still active. We were served "Notice of Pre-Trial Conference" set for August 16, 2000. Decisions on two outstanding Canadian human rights complaints (filed in 1988 at P4W and 1992 at Matsqui Penitentiary) are "stood down" subject to the outcome of my trial.

17. The boys were transferred out of BCCW in 1998. It doesn't mean that they won't be returned at some point in the future.

18. As the injunction to stop this "involuntary transfer" to Saskatchewan Penitentiary for men was being prepared, the woman signed a waiver on July 22, 1999, in exchange for a guarantee from the warden that she would be returned to BCCW in three months. That guarantee is now disclaimed.

19. ICOPA I was held in Toronto in 1983. Toronto was the venue once again for ICOPA IX in 2000. For more information contact Rittenhouse: ritten@interlog.com.

20. As NDP justice critic for many years, he saved many lives (mine included), in particular by entering segregation units from 1982 (Archambault) through to the early 1990s (P4W).

21. A social and environmental activist par excellence who continues to rally support from Archbishop Michael Peers, Primate of the Anglican Church of Canada, and does countless charitable acts for women in BCCW and prisoners elsewhere.

22. M2W2 Association (an organization of Christian volunteers). Wayne was editor until 1998 of *The Accord*, a Mennonite Central Committee newsletter.

A social activist and penal abolitionist, Wayne is internationally known for his in-depth and challenging contextual analyses of the meaning of Christianity.

23. Professor of Criminology at Simon Fraser University (SFU), Karlene has worked in prison rights activism and many social justice arenas since the 1950s. She facilitated the founding of our advocacy group, the Strength In Sisterhood (SIS) Society. Among her many writings see Faith (1991, 1993, 1995, 1999 and 2000).

24. Coordinator of the field practice program in criminology at SFU, Liz has worked with the John Howard and Elizabeth Fry societies, and is editor of the *Prisoners' Journal on Prisons* and board member of the West Coast Prison Justice Society, Abbotsford, B.C.

25. Lawyer and teacher by training, Kim has worked on a wide range of social justice issues for more than a decade, was with the John Howard Society and in 1992 became executive director of the Canadian Association of Elizabeth Fry Societies (CAEFS). Kim has received international recognition for her prison advocacy work and participated in the 10th U.N. Congress on Crime Prevention in Vienna.

26. I met this distinguished member of the Mohawk Nation through Native Sisterhood in P4W (1986). She enabled the inclusion of voices of Aboriginal women in prison while a member of the TSFFSW. She is now a tenured associate professor at the University of Saskatchewan. Trish challenged the constitutionality of the requirement to swear allegiance to the Queen as a requisite for being called to the Bar. She continues to provide venues for Aboriginal voices (see Monture-Angus 1995, 1999).

27. Humanitarian, former *Globe and Mail* columnist, VISION TV host of "Callwood's National Treasures," author of forty books, friend of Marlene Moore, and founder of Casey House, the first hospice in Canada for AIDS patients.

28. Chair of the Canadian Bar Association and chief partner in Conroy and Co. Barristers and Solicitors, Abbotsford, B.C. Among many landmark cases in prison law, see most recently *Landry v. Regina* and *Winters v. Regina*, and series of submissions by the Committee on Imprisonment and Release of the National Criminal Justice Section of the Canadian Bar Association.

29. A lawyer and former advocate with Prisoners' Legal Services, Abbotsford, B.C., Sasha is board member of the West Coast Prison Justice Society. See her most recent *Charter* challenge: *Alcorn et al v. The Commissioner of Corrections et al.* (March 10, 1999).

# References

Abella, Irving M., and Harold Troper. 1982. *None Is Too Many: Canada and the Jews of Europe, 1933–1948*. Toronto: Lester and Orpen Dennys.

Adachi, Ken. 1991. *The Enemy That Never Was: A History of the Japanese Canadians*. Toronto: McClelland and Stewart.

Adams, Walter, and James W. Brock. 1986. *The Bigness Complex: Industry Labour and Government in the American Economy*. New York: Pantheon.

Adorno, Theodor W. 1991. *The Culture Industry: Selected Essays on Mass Culture*. London: Routledge.

Ahmed, Leila. 1992. *Women and Gender in Islam: Historical Roots of a Modern Debate*. New Haven: Yale University Press.

Alberta. 1991. *Report of the Task Force on the Criminal Justice System and its Impact on the Indian and Metis People of Alberta* (Chair, R.W. Cawsey). Edmonton.

American Psychological Association (APA). 1949. Committee on Training in Clinical Psychology. "Doctoral Training Programs in Clinical Psychology: 1949." *American Psychologist* 4.

_____. 1999. *Talk to Someone Who Can Help*. Washington: APA Office of Public Affairs.

Amos, Valerie, and Pratibha Parmar. 1984. "Challenging Imperial Feminism." *Feminist Review* 17 (July).

Anderson, Barrie, with Dawn Anderson. 1998. *Manufacturing Guilt: Wrongful Convictions in Canada*. Halifax: Fernwood.

Anderson, Frank W. 1973. *Hanging in Canada: A Concise History of a Controversial Topic*. Calgary: Frontier.

Anonymous. 1972. "U.S. electronic espionage: A memoir." *Ramparts* (August).

_____. 1983. "Secret listening agency expands its operations." *Globe and Mail*, November 12.

_____. 1987. "Government eavesdroppers need stricter controls, says Liberal MP." *Ottawa Citizen*, March 31.

Arat-Koc, Sedef. 1992. "Immigration Policies, Migrant Domestic Workers and the Definition of Citizenship in Canada." In Vic Satzewich, (ed.), *Deconstructing a Nation: Immigration, Multiculturalism and Racism in '90s Canada*. Halifax: Fernwood.

Arbour, The Honourable Justice Louise, Commissioner. 1996. *Report of the Commission of Inquiry into Certain Events at the Prison for Women in Kingston*. Ottawa: Public Works and Government Services Canada.

Arendt, Hannah. 1971. *Between Past and Future*. New York: Viking Press.

_____. 1972. *Crises of the Republic: Lying in Politics, Civil Disobedience on Violence, Thoughts on Politics, and Revolution*. New York: Harcourt Brace Jovanovich.

Arieti, Silvano. 1955. *Interpretation of Schizophrenia*. New York: Brunner.

Backer, Larry Catá. 1993. "Of Handouts and Worthless Promises: Understanding the Conceptual Limitations of American Systems of Poor Relief." *Boston College Law Review* 34.

_____. 1995. "Welfare Reform at the Limit: The Futility of 'Ending Welfare as We Know It'." *Harvard Civil Rights/Civil Liberties Law Review* 30.

Backhouse, Constance. 1991. *Petticoats and Prejudice: Women and Law in Nineteenth Century Canada*. Toronto: Women's Press.

Bakan, Abigail B. 1987. "The International Market for Female Labour and Individual Deskilling: West Indian Women Workers in Toronto." *Canadian Journal of Latin American and Caribbean Studies* 12, 24.

Baker, David, ed. 1994. *Reading Racism and the Criminal Justice System*. Toronto: Canadian Scholars' Press.

Balibar, Etienne. 1991. "Racism and Nationalism." In Etienne Balibar and Immanuel Wallerstein, (eds.), *Race, Nation, Class: Ambiguous Identities*. London: Verso.

Ballinger, Jeffrey. 1992. "The New Free-Trade Heel: Nike Profits Jump on the Back of Asian Workers." *Harper's* (August).

Barak, Gregg, ed. 1991. *Crimes by the Capitalist State: An Introduction to State Criminality*. New York: State University of New York Press.

_____. 1994. *Media, Process, and the Social Construction of Crime: Studies in Newsmaking Criminology*. New York: Garland Publishing.

Barbee, Evelyn, and Marilyn Little. 2000. "Health, Social Class and African-American Women." In Estelle Disch, (ed.), *Reconstructing Gender: A Multicultural Anthology*. Second edition. Mountain View, Calif.: Mayfield.

Barker, Martin. 1981. *The New Racism: Conservatives and the Ideology of the Tribe*. London: Junction.

Barlow, Maude. 1990. *Parcel of Rogues: How Free Trade is Failing Canada*. Toronto: Key Porter.

Barrett, Michèle. 1991. *The Politics of Truth: From Marx to Foucault*. Palo Alto, Calif.: Stanford University Press.

Barroso, Carmen, and Cristina Bruschini. 1991. "Building Politics from Personal Lives: Discussions on Sexuality among Poor Women in Brazil." In Chandra Mohanty, Ann Russo and Lourdes Torres, (eds.), *Third World Women and the Politics of Feminism*. Bloomington: Indiana University Press.

Bateson, Gregory, Don D. Jackson, Jay Haley and John Weakland. 1958. "Towards a Theory of Schizophrenia." *Behavioral Science* 1.

Battle, Ken. 1998. "Transformation: Canadian Social Policy since 1985." *Social Policy and Administration* 32.

Bauman, Zygmunt. 1993. *Postmodern Ethics*. Oxford: Blackwell.

Beattie, Hilary J. 1988. "Eating Disorders and the Mother-Daughter Relationship." *International Journal of Eating Disorders* 7.

Beigel, Joan Kaye, and Ralph H. Earle. 1990. *Successful Private Practice in the 1990s: A New Guide for the Mental Health Professional*. New York: Brunner/Mazel.

Benzie, Robert. 1995. "Operative says Ottawa Spied on Canadians," *Edmonton Sun*, November 14.

Bernard, Elaine. 1997. "Ensuring Monitoring is not Co-opted." Presentation to Independent Monitoring: A Forum, sponsored by the National Labor Committee, Queen's College, New York, April 4.

Bernstein, Aaron. 1999. "Sweatshop Reform: How to Solve the Standoff." *Business Week*, May 31.

Bettelheim, Bruno. 1967. *Infantile Autism and the Birth of the Self.* New York: Free Press.

Bickman, Leonard. 1996. "A Continuum of Care: More is Not Always Better." *American Psychologist* 51, 7.

_____. 1999. "Practice Makes Perfect and Other Myths about Mental Health Services." *American Psychologist* 54, 11.

Bickman, Leonard, Pamela R. Guthrie, E. Michael Foster, E. Warren Lambert, William T. Summerfelt, Carolyn S. Breda and Craig A. Heflinger. 1995. *Evaluating Managed Mental Health Services: The Fort Bragg Experiment.* New York: Plenum.

Biggs, Lesley, and Mark Stobbe, eds. 1991. *Devine Rule in Saskatchewan: A Decade of Hope and Hardship.* Saskatoon: Fifth House.

Bishop, Matthew. 2000. "The Mystery of the Vanishing Taxpayer: A Survey of Globalisation and Tax." *The Economist*, January 29.

Blackridge, Persimmon, and Sheila Gilhooly. 1985. *Still Sane.* Vancouver: Press Gang.

Blakely, Edward, and Mary Gail Snyder. 1997. *Fortress America: Gated Communities in the United States.* Washington, D.C.: Brookings Institution.

Blank, Rebecca M. 1997. *It Takes a Nation: A New Agenda for Fighting Poverty.* Princeton, N.J.: Princeton University Press.

Bloomberg Business News. 1995. "Bond Buyers Bullish on Welfare State's Demise." *Globe and Mail*, November 15.

Blumenthal, David, Eric G. Campbell, Melissa S. Anderson, Nancyanne Causino and Karen Seashore Louis. 1997. "Withholding Research Results in Academic Life Science: Evidence from a National Survey of Faculty." *Journal of the American Medical Association* 277.

Boddy, Trevor. 1992. "Underground and Overhead: Building the Analogous City." In Michael Sorkin, (ed.), *Variations on a Theme Park: The New American City and the End of Public Space.* New York: Hill and Wang.

Bolaria, B. Singh. 1992. "From Immigrant Settlers to Migrant Transients: Foreign Professionals in Canada." In Vic Satzewich, (ed.), *Deconstructing a Nation: Immigration, Multiculturalism and Racism in '90s Canada.* Halifax: Fernwood.

Bolaria, B. Singh, and Peter S. Li. 1985. *Racial Oppression in Canada.* Toronto: Garamond.

_____. 1988. *Racial Oppression in Canada.* Second edition. Toronto: Garamond.

Bonnycastle, Kevin D., and George S. Rigakos. 1998. *Unsettling Truths: Battered Women, Policy, Politics, and Contemporary Research in Canada.* Vancouver: Collective Press.

Boomer, Rachel. 1999. "Former Premier Regan to Face New Sex Charges." *Vancouver Sun*, December 3.

Bothwell, Robert, Ian Drummond and John English. 1981. *Canada Since 1945: Power, Politics and Provincialism*. Toronto: University of Toronto Press.

Bourdieu, Pierre. 1977. "Structures, Habitus, Power: Basis for a Theory of Symbolic Power." In Pierre Bourdieu, *Outline of a Theory of Practice*. New York: Cambridge University Press.

_____. 1980. "The Production of Belief." *Media, Culture and Society* 2, 3.

Bowlby, John. 1951. *Maternal Care and Mental Health*. Geneva: World Health Organisation.

Box, Steven. 1983. *Power, Crime and Mystification*. London: Tavistock.

Boyd, Susan B., ed. 1997. *Challenging the Public/Private Divide: Feminism, Law and Public Policy*. Toronto: University of Toronto Press.

Boyer, Robert, and Daniel Drache, eds. 1996. *States Against Markets: The Limits of Globalization*. London: Routledge.

Brackey, Harriet Johnson. 2000. "Now May Be Time to Make a Change." *London Free Press*, January 19.

Bradshaw, John. 1990. *Home Coming: Reclaiming and Championing Your Inner Child*. New York: Bantam.

Bradsher, Keith. 1996. "Need to Cut Costs? Order Out." *New York Times*, April 11.

Braithwaite, John. 1989. *Crime, Shame, and Reintegration*. New York: Cambridge University Press.

Breggin, Peter R. 1995. *Talking Back to Prozac*. New York: St Martin's Press.

Breggin, Peter R., and David Cohen. 1999. *Your Drug May Be Your Problem: How and Why to Stop Taking Psychiatric Drugs*. Reading, Mass.: Perseus.

British Columbia, Ministry of Advanced Education, Training and Technology. 1999. *Federal Spending on Post-Secondary Education Transfers to Provinces: Trends and Consequences*. Victoria.

Brodie, Janine. 1995. *Politics on the Margins: Restructuring and the Canadian Women's Movement*. Halifax: Fernwood.

Broverman, Inge K., Donald M. Broverman, Frank E. Clarkson, Paul S. Rosenkrantz and Susan R. Vogel. 1970. "Sex Role Stereotypes and Clinical Judgements of Mental Health." *Journal of Consulting and Clinical Psychology* 34.

Brown, Lorne, and Caroline Brown. 1973. *An Unauthorized History of the R.C.M.P.* Toronto: James and Samuel.

Brown, Mark, and John Pratt, eds. 2000. *Dangerous Offenders: Punishment and Social Order*. London: Routledge.

Bruch, Hilde. 1973. *Eating Disorders: Obesity, Anorexia Nervosa, and the Personality Within*. New York: Basic Books.

Buchignani, Norman, and Doreen M. Indra, with Ram Srivastava. 1985. *Continuous Journey: A Social History of South Asians in Canada*. Toronto: McClelland and Stewart.

Bumiller, Elisabeth. 1999. "In Wake of Attack, Giuliani Cracks Down on Homeless." *New York Times*, November 20.

Burstow, Bonnie, and Don Weitz. 1988. *Shrink Resistant*. Vancouver: Press Gang.

Business Council on National Issues (BCNI). 2000. *Global Champion or Falling Star? The Choice Canada Must Make*, statement at the CEO Summit 2000, April 5. Ottawa.

Calavita, Kitty. 1983. "The Demise of the Occupational Safety and Health Administration: A Case Study in Symbolic Action." *Social Problems* 30, 4.

Calavita, Kitty, Henry N. Pontell and Robert H. Tillman. 1997. *Big Money Crime: Fraud and Politics in the Savings and Loan Crisis*. Berkeley: University of California Press.

Cameron, Stevie. 1994. *On the Take: Crime, Corruption and Greed in the Mulroney Years*. Toronto: Macfarlane, Walter and Ross.

Cameron, Stevie, and Andrew Mitorvica. 1994. "Burying Westray." *Saturday Night* 109, 4 (May).

Canada. "External Review Mechanism for Communications Security Establishment Announced." News release no. NR-96.061, June 19, 1996.

Canada, Bureau of Competition Policy. 1989. *Competition Policy in Canada: The First Hundred Years*. Ottawa: Consumer and Corporate Affairs.

Canada, Commissioner of the Communications Security Establishment. 1998. *Annual Report, 1997–1998*. Ottawa: Minister of Public Works and Government Services Canada.

Canada, Communications Security Establishment (CSE), Commissioner. 1998–99. *Annual Report*. Ottawa.

Canada, Department of Justice. 1998. "Remedies for Wrongful Convictions: Review of s.690." Ottawa.

Canada, Environment Canada. 1995. *It's About Our Health: Towards Pollution Prevention*. Report of the House of Commons Standing Committee on the Environmental and Sustainable Development. Ottawa: House of Commons, no 81 (a.k.a. CEPA Review).

Canada, House of Commons. 1975. Standing Committee on Miscellaneous Estimates. *Minutes of Proceedings and Evidence* 18 (March 24).

_____. 1990a. Special Committee on the Review of the CSIS Act and Security Offences Act, *Minutes of Proceedings and Evidence* 9 (January 16).

_____. 1990b. Special Committee on the Review of the CSIS Act and Security Offences Act. *Minutes of Proceedings and Evidence* (February 20).

_____. 1990c. Special Committee on the Review of the CSIS Act and Security Offences Act. *Minutes of Proceedings and Evidence* 19 (March 8).

_____. 1990d. Special Committee on the Review of the CSIS Act and Security Offences Act. *Minutes of Proceedings and Evidence* 27 (April 24).

_____. 1990e. Special Committee on the Review of the CSIS Act and Security Offences Act. *Minutes of Proceedings and Evidence* 28 (April 25).

_____. 1993. Standing Committee on Justice and the Solicitor General, Sub-Committee on National Security. *Minutes of Proceedings and Evidence* 11 (June

15).

_____. 1995. Standing Committee on National Defence and Veterans Affairs. *Minutes of Proceedings and Evidence* 22 (May 2).

Canada, Independent Advisory Team on the Canadian Security Intelligence Service (IAT). 1987. *People and Process in Transition*. Ottawa: Solicitor General of Canada.

Canada, Industry Canada. 1997. *Annual Report of the Director of Investigation and Research, Competition Act* (for the year ending March 31, 1996). Ottawa.

_____. 1998. *Annual Report of the Director of Investigation and Research, Competition Act* (for the year ending March 31, 1997). Ottawa.

Canada, Office of the Auditor General [OAG]. 1996. *Annual Report 1996—* Chapter 27. *The Canadian Intelligence Community—Control and Accountability.* Ottawa: Office of the Auditor General.

_____. 1998. *Follow-up Report on the Canadian Intelligence Community—Control and Accountability—1996.* Chapter 27 (December). Ottawa.

Canada, Privacy Commissioner. 1996. *Annual Report 1995–96.* Ottawa: Ministry of Supply and Service of Canada.

Canada, Royal Commission. 1946. *Royal Commission to Investigate the Facts Relating to and the Circumstances Surrounding the Communication, by Public Officials and Other Persons in Position of Trust of Secret and Confidential Information to Agents of a Foreign Power.*

Canada, Senate. 1983a. *Proceedings of the Special Committee on the Canadian Security Intelligence Service* Issue No.9 (September 15).

_____. 1983b. *Proceedings of the Special Committee on the Canadian Security Intelligence Service* 11 (September 22).

Canada, Standing Committee on Public Accounts. 1991. *Minutes of Proceedings* 10 (October).

Canadian Centre for Justice Statistics. 1999. *The Juristat Reader: A Statistical Overview of the Canadian Justice System.* Toronto: Thompson.

Canadian Press. 1983. "Called Grave Threat: Secret Listening Agency Expands its Operations." *Globe and Mail,* November 12.

Cardinal, Harold. 1969. *The Unjust Society: The Tragedy of Canada's Indians.* Edmonton: Hurtig.

Carey, Elaine. 2000. "Race, Income Splits Toronto, Study Warns: 'Huge' Inequality Shown in Survey of Census Figures." *Toronto Star,* July 7.

Carruthers, Jeff. 1974. "Few in Ottawa Know of the Secret NRC Group." *Globe and Mail,* January 11.

Carson, W.G. 1980. "The Institutionalization of Ambiguity: Early British Factory Acts." In Gilbert Geis and Ezra Stotland, (eds.), *White Collar Crime: Theory and Research.* Beverly Hills: Sage.

Cashmore, Ellis, and Eugene McLaughlin, eds. 1991. *Out of Order: Policing Black People.* London: Routledge.

Cavanagh, John, 1997. "The Global Resistance to Sweatshops." In Andrew Ross, (ed.), *No Sweat: Fashion Free Trade and the Rights of Garment Workers.*

London: Verso.

Cavanagh, John and Robin Broad. 1996. "Global Reach: Workers Fight the Multinationals." *The Nation*, March 18.

Cayley, David. 1997. *The Expanding Prison: The Crisis in Crime and Punishment and the Search for Alternatives*. Toronto: House of Anansi.

Cernetig, Miro. 1998. "Crackdown on the Outstretched Palm." *Globe and Mail*, May 18.

Chambliss, William J., and Robert B. Seidman. 1982. *Law, Order and Power*. Second edition. Reading, Mass.: Addison-Wesley.

Chapman, Jane. 1993. "Politics and Power in Therapy: A Discussion on the Implications of Postmodern Ideas for Therapeutic Practices." *Australian & New Zealand Journal of Family Therapy* 14, 2.

Chesler, Phyllis. 1973. *Women and Madness*. New York: Avon.

Chevigny, Paul. 1995. *Edge of the Knife: Police Violence in the Americas*. New York: New Press.

Chibnall, Steve. 1977. *Law and Order News: An Analysis of Crime Reporting in the British Press*. London: Tavistock.

Chomsky, Noam. 1998. Private communication. April 2.

Christie, Nils. 1993. *Crime Control as Industry*. New York: Routledge.

Chunn, Dorothy E., and Dany Lacombe, eds. 2000. *Law as a Gendering Practice*. Toronto: Oxford University Press.

Chunn, Dorothy E., and Robert Menzies. 1995. "Canadian Criminology and the Woman Question." In Nicole Rafter and Frances Heidensohn, (eds.), *International Feminist Perspectives in Criminology*. Milton Keynes, U.K.: Open University Press.

Churchill, Ward, and Jim Vander Wall. 1988. *Agents of Repression: The FBI's Secret Wars Against the Black Panther Party and the American Indian Movement*. Boston: South End Press.

Citizenship and Immigration Canada (CIC). 1994a. *Facts and Figures: Overview of Immigration*. Ottawa: Minister of Supply and Services.

_____. 1994b. *Canada and Immigration: Facts and Issues*. Ottawa: CIC.

_____. 1994c. *The Report of Working Group #8: "How Do We Realize the Benefits of Immigration to Canada in Areas such as Regional Impact, Workforce Skills, Job Creation and International Competitiveness?"* Ottawa: CIC.

_____. 1994d. *Canada 2005: A Strategy for Citizenship and Immigration*. Background Document. Ottawa: CIC.

_____. 1994e. *Canada 2005: A Strategy for Citizenship and Immigration*. Conference Proceedings. Ottawa: CIC.

_____. 1994f. *Immigration Consultations Report*. Ottawa: Minister of Supply and Services.

_____. 1994g. *A Broader Vision: Immigration and Citizenship Plan 1995–2000*. Annual report to Parliament. Ottawa: Minister of Supply and Services.

_____. 1994h. *Employee Consultation Report*. Ottawa: CIC.

_____. 1995. *Strengthening Family Sponsorship*. Ottawa: Minister of Supply and

Services.

Clarke, Ann M., and A.D.B. Clarke. 1976. *Early Experience: Myth and Evidence*. London: Open Books.

Clarke, Michael. 1990. *Business Crime*. Cambridge: Polity.

Clean Clothes Campaign. 1999. "Nike Case." http://www.cleanclothes.org/companies/nikecase.htm.

Clifford, Mark. 1992. "The China Connection." *Far Eastern Economic Review*, November 6.

Clinard, Marshall B., and Peter C. Yeager. 1980. *Corporate Crime*. New York: Free Press.

Cohen, Stanley. 1988. *Against Criminology*. New Brunswick, N.J.: Transaction.

Cole, David. 1999. *No Equal Justice: Race and Class in the American Criminal Justice System*. New York: The New Press.

Coleman, James W. 1994. *The Criminal Elite: The Sociology of White Collar Crime*. Third edition. New York: St. Martin's Press.

Collins, Anne. 1988. *In the Sleep Room: The Story of the CIA Brainwashing Experiments in Canada*. Toronto: Lester and Orpen Dennys.

Comack, Elizabeth. 1993. *Feminist Engagement with the Law: The Legal Recognition of the Battered Woman Syndrome*. Ottawa: Canadian Research Institute for the Advancement of Women.

_____, ed. 1999. *Locating Law: Race/Class/Gender Connections*. Halifax: Fernwood.

Comack, Elizabeth, and Stephen Brickey, eds. 1991. *The Social Basis of Law: Critical Readings in the Sociology of Law*. Halifax: Garamond.

Comish, Shaun. 1993. *The Westray Tragedy: A Miner's Story*. Halifax: Fernwood.

Condon, Mary. 1992. "Following Up on Interests: The Private Agreement Exemption in Ontario Securities Law." *Journal of Human Justice* 3, 2.

*Consumer Reports*. 1995. "Mental Health: Does Therapy Help?" November.

Conway, John F. 1993. "The Saskatchewan Electoral Boundaries Case, 1990–91." *Proceedings of the CPSA Annual Meetings*. Microfiche. Ottawa: Canadian Political Science Association.

_____. 1994. *The West: The History of a Region in Confederation*. Toronto: James Lorimer.

Cook, Dee, and Barbara Hudson, eds. 1993. *Racism and Criminology*. London: Sage.

Corea, Gena. 1979. *The Mother Machine*. London: Harper & Row.

Correa, Sonia. 1994. *Population and Reproductive Rights: Feminist Perspectives from the South*. London: Zed.

Correctional Service of Canada (CSC). 1997. *CSC Action Plan*. November 26 (protected). Ottawa: Correctional Service of Canada.

Cory, Donald Webster, *pseud*. Edward Sagarin. 1981. *Paul Cadmus*. Oxford, Ohio: Miami University Art Museum.

Courtney, John C., Peter MacKinnon and David E. Smith, eds. 1992. *Drawing Boundaries: Legislatures, Courts, and Electoral Values*. Saskatoon: Fifth House.

Coyne, Andrew. 1997. "Statistics Show the Poverty Rate Is an Elusive Creature." *Toronto Star*, July 17.

Cranston, Ross. 1982. "Regulation and Deregulation: General Issues." *University of New South Wales Law Journal* 5.

Critser, Greg. 1996. "Oh, How Happy We Will Be: Pills, Paradise and the Profits of Drug Companies." *Harper's* (June).

Croall, Hazel. 1992. *White Collar Crime: Criminal Justice and Criminology*. Buckingham: Open University Press.

CTV National News. 1995. "Communications Security Establishment," November 12, 13, 14.

Culhane, Claire. 1972. *Why is Canada in Vietnam?* Toronto: NC Press.

_____. 1979. *Barred from Prison: A Personal Account*. Vancouver: Arsenal Pulp Press.

_____. 1985. *Still Barred from Prison*. Montreal: Black Rose.

_____. 1991. *No Longer Barred from Prison*. Montreal: Black Rose.

Culhane, Dara. 1997. *The Pleasure of the Crown: Anthropology, Law and First Nations*. Burnaby, B.C.: Talonbooks.

Cullen, Francis T., William J. Maakestad and Gray Cavender. 1987. *Corporate Crime Under Attack: The Ford Pinto Case and Beyond*. Cincinnati: Anderson.

Cunningham, Rob. 1996. *Smoke and Mirrors: The Canadian Tobacco War*. Ottawa: Canadian Development Research Centre.

Dale, Stephen. 1999. *Lost in the Suburbs: A Political Travelogue*. Toronto: Stoddart.

Daubney, David. M.P., Chairman. 1988. *Taking Responsibility. The Report of the Standing Committee on Justice and Solicitor General on its Review of Sentencing, Conditional Release and Related Aspects of Corrections*. Ottawa: Queen's Printer.

Davis, Angela. 2000. "Women, Punishment and Globalization." Lecture to Vancouver Status of Women, Vancouver, 12 February.

Davis, Kenneth Culp. 1971. *Discretionary Justice: A Preliminary Inquiry*. Urbana: University of Illinois Press.

Dawes, Robyn. 1989. "Letter to Members of the APA Council of Representatives." Reprinted in *APS Observer* (January).

_____. 1999. "Irrationality: Theory and Practice." Unpublished manuscript.

Dean, Mitchell. 1999. *Governmentality: Power and Rule in Modern Society*. London: Sage.

Desbarats, Peter. 1997. *Somalia Coverup: A Commissioner's Journal*. Toronto: McClelland and Stewart.

DeVoretz, Don J. 1995. "New Issues, New Evidence, and New Immigration Policies for the Twenty-First Century." In Don J. DeVoretz, (ed.), *Diminishing Returns: The Economics of Canada's Recent Immigration Policy*. Ottawa: C.D. Howe Institute.

Dicken, Peter. 1998. Global Shift: Transforming the World Economy. Third edition. New York: Guilford Press.

Dineen, Tana. 1975. "Diagnostic Decision Making in Psychiatry." Doctoral thesis, University of Saskatchewan, Saskatoon.

_____. 1997. "Judicial Skepticism: Judging Psychology and Psychologists."

Annual Conference of the Canadian Association of Provincial Court Judges, Halifax, N.S., September 25.

_____. 1998a. "Psychotherapy: The Snake Oil of the 90's?" SKEPTIC 8, 3.

_____. 1998b. Manufacturing Victims: What the Psychology Industry Is Doing to People. Second edition. Montreal: Robert Davies Multimedia.

Dion, Robert. 1982. Crimes of the Secret Police. Montréal: Black Rose.

Disraeli, Benjamin. 1826. Vivian Grey. Book VI Chapter 7. London: Longmans, Green.

DiTomaso, Nancy. In press. "The Loose Coupling of Jobs: The Subcontracting of Everyone?" In Ivar Berg and Arne L. Kalleberg, (eds.), Sourcebook on Labor Markets: Evolving Structures and Processes. New York: Plenum.

Dobbin, Murray. 1998. The Myth of the Good Corporate Citizen: Democracy Under the Rule of Big Business. Toronto: Stoddart.

Dodd, Susan. 1999. "Unsettled Accounts after Westray." In Christopher McCormick, (ed.), The Westray Chronicles: A Case Study of Corporate Crime. Halifax: Fernwood.

Doern, G. Bruce. 1995a. "Sectoral Green Politics: Environmental Regulation and the Canadian Pulp and Paper Industry." Environmental Politics 4.

_____. 1995b. Fairer Play: Canadian Competition Policy Institutions in a Global Market. Toronto: C.D. Howe Institute, policy study no. 25.

Doern, G. Bruce, and Thomas Conway. 1994. The Greening of Canada: Federal Institutions and Decisions. Toronto: University of Toronto Press.

Doern, G. Bruce, and Steven Wilks, eds. 1996a. Comparative Competition Policy: National Institutions in a Global Market. Oxford: Clarendon.

Doob, Anthony N. 1995. Race, Bail and Imprisonment. Research report of the Commission on Systemic Racism in the Ontario Criminal Justice System. Toronto: Queen's Printer.

Duggan, Lisa. 1992. Presentation to conference on "Queer Theory," Rutgers University, November 1991. Voice Literary Supplement.

Dumont, Matthew P. 1987. "A Diagnostic Parable (First Edition—Unrevised)." Readings: A Journal of Reviews and Commentary in Mental Health 2, 4.

Dyck, Noel. 1991. What is the Indian "Problem"?: Tutelage and Resistance in Canadian Indian Administration. St. John's: Institute of Social and Economic Research.

Economic Council of Canada. 1969. Interim Report on Competition Policy. Ottawa: Information Canada.

_____. 1990. Good Jobs, Bad Jobs: Employment in the Service Economy. Ottawa: Supply and Services Canada.

Economist. 1995. "Ethical Shopping," June 3.

Edelhertz, Herbert. 1970. The Nature, Impact and Prosecution of White-Collar Crime. Washington, D.C.: National Institute for Law Enforcement and Criminal Justice, Department of Justice.

Edstrom, Jennifer, and Marlin Eller. 1998. Barbarians Led By Bill Gates. New York: Holt and Co.

Ehrenreich, Barbara. 1999. "Nickel-and-Dimed: On (not) Getting By in America." *Harper's* (January).

Eisner, Donald. 2000. *The Death of Psychotherapy: From Freud to Alien Abductions.* Westport, Conn.: Praeger.

Eliasoph, Philip. 1981. *Paul Cadmus.* Oxford, Ohio: Miami University Art Museum.

Elliott, Delbert S. 1994. "Serious Violent Offenders: Onset, Developmental Course and Termination—The American Society of Criminology 1993 Presidential Address." *Criminology* 32.

Ellis, Desmond. 1987. *The Wrong Stuff: An Introduction to the Sociological Study of Deviance.* Don Mills, Ont.: Collier Macmillan.

Emmett, Brian. 1998. *Annual Report to the House of Commons.* Ottawa, May 25.

Employment and Immigration Canada (EIC). 1983. *Canada's Immigration Law: An Overview.* Ottawa: Supply and Services Canada.

Equal Opportunity Consultants. 1989. *Perceptions of Racial Minorities Related to the Services of the Ministry of the Attorney General.* Toronto: Ontario Ministry of the Attorney General.

Ericson, Richard V. 1981. "Rules for Police Deviance." In Clifford D. Shearing, (ed.), *Organizational Police Deviance: Its Structure and Control.* Toronto: Butterworths.

Ericson, Richard V., and Patricia M. Baranek. 1982. *The Ordering of Justice.* Toronto: University of Toronto Press.

Ericson, Richard V., Patricia M. Baranek and Janet B.L. Chan. 1987. *Visualizing Deviance: A Study of News Organization.* Toronto: University of Toronto Press.

_____. 1989. *Negotiating Control: A Study of News Sources.* Toronto: University of Toronto Press.

_____. 1991. *Representing Order: Crime, Law, and Justice in the News Media.* Toronto: University of Toronto Press.

Ericson, Richard V., and Kevin D. Haggerty. 1997. *Policing the Risk Society.* Toronto: University of Toronto Press.

Ermann, M. David, and Richard J. Lundman. 1987. *Corporate and Governmental Deviance: Problems of Organizational Behavior in Contemporary Society.* Third edition. New York: Oxford University Press.

Esping-Andersen, Gøsta. 1997. "Towards a Post-industrial Welfare State." *Internationale Politik und Gesellschaft* 3.

Evans, Robert G. 1997a. "Health Care Reform: Who's Selling the Market, and Why?" *Journal of Public Health Medicine* 19.

_____. 1997b. "Going for the Gold: The Redistributive Agenda behind Market-Based Health Care Reform." *Journal of Health Politics, Policy and Law* 22.

Evans, Robert G. and Morris L. Barer. 1998. "Financing and Delivering Health Care in Canada: Lots of Sound and Fury, but Little 'Reform'." *Korean Review of Public Administration* 3.

Evans, Sandra S., and Richard J. Lundman. 1983. "Newspaper Coverage of

Corporate Price Fixing." *Criminology* 21, 4.

Faith, Karlene. 1991. "Gender, Power, and Foucault." *Institute for the Humanities* 4, 2 (Spring). Simon Fraser University.

_____. 1993. *Unruly Women: The Politics of Confinement and Resistance.* Vancouver, B.C.: Press Gang.

_____. 1995. "Up Against Foucault: Explorations of Some Tensions between Foucault and Feminism." *Crime, Law and Social Change* 23, 3.

_____. 1999. "In Praise of Political Education." *Social Justice* 26, 2 (Summer).

_____. 2000. "Reflections on Inside/Out Organizing." Critical Resistance Publications Committee, Berkeley. In submission.

Farberman, Rhea K. 1996. "Public Campaign Nears Roll-out: Public Communications Report." *The APA Monitor* (January).

Ferrell, Jeff, and Neil Websdale, eds. 1999. *Making Trouble: Cultural Constructions of Crime, Deviance and Control.* New York: Aldine de Gruyter.

Fishman, Mark. 1980. *Manufacturing the News.* Austin: University of Texas Press.

_____. 1998. "Crime Waves as Ideology." In Gary W. Potter and Victor E. Kappeler, (eds.), *Constructing Crime: Perspectives on Making News and Social Problems.* Prospect Heights, Ill.: Waveland.

Fishman, Ted C. 1997. "The Joys of Global Investment." *Harper's* (February).

_____. 1998. "Up in Smoke." *Harper's* (December).

Fitzpatrick, Peter. 1987. "Racism and the Innocence of Law." *Journal of Law and Society* 14.

Fleming, Thomas O'Reilly, ed. 1985. *The New Criminologies in Canada: Crime, State, and Control.* Toronto: Oxford University Press.

Fong, Siu. 1995. *Interpretation Services in the Criminal Justice System.* Research report of the Commission on Systemic Racism in the Ontario Criminal Justice System. Toronto: Queen's Printer.

Foss, Krista. 1999a. "Hospital Crisis Long in the Making, Administrators Say." *Globe and Mail,* December 8.

_____. 1999b. "Hospital Chaos Sign of a System Splitting at the Seams." *Globe and Mail,* December 15.

Foucault, Michel. 1980. "Truth and Power." In Colin Gordon, (ed.), *Power/Knowledge: Selected Interviews and Other Writings, 1972–1977.* New York: Pantheon.

_____. 1990. *The History of Sexuality: An Introduction.* Vol 1. New York: Vintage.

_____. 1991. "Politics and the Study of Discourse." In Graham Burchill, Colin Gordon and Peter Miller, (eds.), *The Foucault Effect Studies in Governmentality.* Chicago: University of Chicago Press.

Fox Piven, Frances. 1993. "Reforming the Welfare State." In Gregory Albo, David Langille and Leo Panitch, (eds.), *A Different Kind of State? Popular Power and Democratic Administration.* Toronto: Oxford University Press.

Frager, Ruth. 1992. *Sweatshop Strife: Class, Ethnicity and Gender in the Jewish Labour Movement in Toronto, 1900–1939.* Toronto: University of Toronto Press.

Fraser, Nancy. 1989. *Unruly Practices: Power, Discourse and Gender in Contemporary Social Theory*. Minneapolis: University of Minnesota Press.

Freeman, Christopher, and Carlota Perez. 1988. "Structural Crises of Adjustment, Business Cycles and Investment Behaviour." In Giovanni Dosi et al., (eds.), *Technical Change and Economic Theory*. London: Frances Pinter.

Freire, Paulo. 1982. *Pedagogy of the Oppressed*. N.Y.: Continuum.

Frideres, James S. 1990. "Policies on Indian People in Canada." In Peter S. Li, (ed.), *Race and Ethnic Relations in Canada*. Ontario: Oxford University Press.

Friedenberg, Edgar Z. 1980. *Deference to Authority: The Case of Canada*. White Plains, N.Y.: M.E. Sharpe.

Friedland, Martin L. 1979. *National Security: The Legal Dimensions*. Study prepared for the Commission of Inquiry Concerning Certain Activities of the Royal Canadian Mounted Police. Ottawa: Supply and Services Canada.

Friedman, Thomas. 1999. "New Human Rights World Order." [*Mexico*] *News*, August 12.

Friedrichs, David O. 1996. *White Collar Crime: Trusted Criminals in Contemporary Society*. Belmont: Wadsworth.

Frost, Mike, and Michel Gratton. 1994. *Spyworld: Inside the Canadian and American Intelligence Establishments*. Toronto: Doubleday.

Gabor, Thomas. 1994. *Everybody Does it! Crime by the Public*. Toronto: University of Toronto Press.

Gallon, Gary. 1996. "Ontario Government Backsliding on Environment." *Canadian Environmental Business Letter: The Gallon Report*, 11, 46, November 20.

Galt, Virginia. 1999. "I Can't Afford It Any More. I'm 20 Grand In Debt." *Globe and Mail*, December 13.

Gamson, William A., David Croteau, William Hoynes and Theodore Sasson. 1992. "Media Images and the Social Construction of Reality." *Annual Review of Sociology* 18.

Gardner, R.A. 1987. *The Parental Alienation Syndrome and the Differentiation Between Fabricated and Genuine Child Sexual Abuse*. Cresskill, N.J.: Creative Therapeutics.

Garland, David. 1996. "The Limits of the Sovereign State: Strategies of Crime Control in Contemporary Society." *British Journal of Criminology* 37.

Gartrell, Nanette J., Judith Herman, Silvia Olarte, Michael Feldstein and Russell Localio. 1986. "Psychiatrist-Patient Sexual Contact: Results of a National Survey, I: Prevalence." *American Journal of Psychiatry* 143.

Gauthier, James, and Richard Roy. 1997. *Diverging Trends in Self-Employment in Canada*, Research paper no. R-97-13E. Ottawa: Human Resources Development Canada.

Geertz, Clifford. 1988. "Us/Not Us." In Clifford Geertz, (ed.), *Works and Lives: The Anthropologist as Author*. Palo Alto, Calif.: Stanford University Press.

Gilroy, Paul. 1991. *"There Ain't no Black in the Union Jack": The Cultural Politics of Race and Nation*. Chicago: The University of Chicago Press.

Glasbeek, Harry J. 1994. *Police Shootings of Black People in Ontario*. Research report of the Commission on Systemic Racism in the Ontario Criminal Justice System. Toronto: Queen's Printer.

Glasbeek, Harry J., and Eric Tucker. 1992. "Death by Consensus: The Westray Story." Unpublished paper, York University, November.

Glass, Stephen. 1997. "The Young and the Feckless: Andrew Young, Nike and the Reputation Racket." *New Republic* (September).

*Globe and Mail.* 1996. "Corrections System Head Resigns." April 2.

Goff, Colin H., and Charles E. Reasons. 1978. *Corporate Crime in Canada: A Critical Analysis of Anti-Combines Legislation.* Scarborough, Ont.: Prentice-Hall.

Goodden, Herman. 1999. "Therapy's Many Barriers." *London Free Press*, August 11.

Goodsitt, Alan. 1983. "Self-Regulatory Disturbances in Eating Disorders." *International Journal of Eating Disorders* 2.

GoodWorks International. 1997. "The Nike Code of Conduct." http://www.digital release.com.cgi–...htdocs/../companies/@goodworks/ib

Goold, Douglas, and Andrew Willis. 1997. *The Bre-X Fraud.* Toronto: McClelland and Stewart.

Grabosky, Peter N., and John Braithwaite, eds. 1993. *Business Regulation and Australia's Future.* Canberra: Australian Institute of Criminology.

Graham, Jill. 1998. "Prozac is 10, So What's Next for Lilly?" *Pharmaceutical Marketing* (August).

Granatstein, J.L. 1981. *A Man of Influence: Norman A. Robertson and Canadian Statecraft, 1929–68.* Toronto: Deneau.

Gray, Dave. 1999. "The Crisis Facing Our Hospitals." *Globe and Mail*, December 15.

Green, Arthur H. 1986. "True and False Allegations of Sexual Abuse in Child Custody Disputes." *Journal of the American Academy of Child Psychiatry* 5.

Green, Gary S. 1994. *Occupational Crime.* Chicago: Nelson-Hall.

Green, Joyce A. 1995. "Towards A Détente With History: Confronting Canada's Colonial Legacy." *International Journal of Canadian Studies* 12 (Fall).

Green, Mark J., with Beverly C. Moore Jr. and Bruce Wasserstein. 1972. *The Closed Enterprise System: Ralph Nader's Study Group Report on Antitrust Enforcement.* New York: Grossman.

Greenaway, Norma. 1999. "Ramsey Should Resign, Friends, Foes Advise. The Reform MP Was Found Guilty of Attempted Rape and Faces up to 10 Years in Jail." *Vancouver Sun*, November 26.

Greenberg, David F. 1988. *The Construction of Homosexuality.* Chicago: University of Chicago Press.

Greenland, Cyril. 1987. "Twenty Years of Research in the Field of Dangerousness." *Liaison* (May).

Gringeri, Christina. 1994. "Assembling 'Genuine GM Parts': Rural Homeworkers and Economic Development." *Economic Development Quarterly* 8.

Gunningham, Neil. 1993. "Occupational Health and Safety, Future Markets and Environmental Law." In Peter N. Grabosky and John Braithwaite, (eds.), *Business Regulation and Australia's Future*. Canberra: Australian Institute of Criminology.

Guy, Kathleen A. 1997. *Our Promise to Children*. Ottawa: Canadian Institute of Child Health.

Hackler, James C. 2000. *Canadian Criminology: Strategies and Perspectives*. Second edition. Scarborough, Ont.: Prentice-Hall, Allyn and Bacon Canada.

Hagan, John, and Bill McCarthy. 1994. "Double Jeopardy: The Abuse of Punishment of Homeless Youth." In George S. Bridges and Martha A. Myers, (eds.), *Inequality, Crime and Social Control*. Boulder, Colo: Westview Press.

Hagan, John, and Ruth D. Peterson. 1995. "Criminal Inequality in America: Patterns and Consequences." In John Hagan and Ruth D. Peterson, (eds.), *Crime and Inequality*. Palo Alto, Calif.: Stanford University Press.

Hagan, John, and Marjorie S. Zatz. 1985. "The Social Organization of Criminal Justice Processing: An Event History Analysis." *Social Science Research* 14.

Hall, Stuart, Chas Critcher, Tony Jefferson, John Clarke and Bruce Roberts. 1978. *Policing the Crisis: Mugging, the State, and Law and Order*. London: Macmillan.

Hammonds, Keith. 1994. "The New World of Work." *Business Week*, October 17.

Haney Lopez, Ian F. 2000. "Institutional Racism: Judicial Conduct and a New Theory of Racial Discrimination." *Yale Law Journal* 109.

Hannah-Moffat, Kelly, and Margaret Shaw, eds. 2000. *An Ideal Prison? Critical Essays on Women's Imprisonment in Canada*. Halifax: Fernwood.

Hardin, Herschel. 1991. *The New Bureaucracy: Waste and Folly in the Private Sector*. Toronto: McClelland & Stewart.

Harris, Jerry. 1998. "Globalisation and the Technological Transformation of Capitalism." *Race and Class* 40, 2/3.

Harris, Michael. 1986. *When Justice Fails: The Law Versus Donald Marshall*. Toronto: Macmillan.

Hartley, John. 1982. *Understanding News*. London: Methuen.

Hartmann, Betsy. 1995. *Reproductive Rights and Wrongs: The Global Politics of Population Control*. Boston: South End Press.

Hatfield, Michael. 1997. *Concentrations of Poverty and Distressed Neighbourhoods in Canada*, Working paper no. W-97-1E. Ottawa: Applied Research Branch, Human Resources Development Canada.

Hawkins, Freda. 1972. *Canada and Immigration: Public Policy and Public Concern*. Montreal: McGill-Queen's University Press.

_____. 1989. *Critical Years in Immigration: Canada and Australia Compared*. Montreal: McGill-Queen's University Press.

Heeney, Arnold. 1946. "Cabinet Government in Canada: Some Recent Developments in the Machinery of the Central Executive." *Canadian Journal of*

*Economics and Political Science* 10, 2 (August).

Helleiner, Eric. 1994. "Freeing Money: Why Have States Been More Willing to Liberalize Capital Controls than Trade Barriers?" *Policy Sciences* 27.

Henry, Katherine A., and Carl I. Cohen. 1983. "The Role of Labeling Processes in Diagnosing Borderline Personality Disorder." *American Journal of Psychiatry* 140.

Henry, William E., John H. Sims and S. Lee Spray. 1971. *The Fifth Profession: Becoming a Psychotherapist.* San Francisco: Jossey Bass.

Herman, Didi. 1994. *Rights of Passage: Struggles for Lesbian and Gay Legal Equality.* Toronto: University of Toronto Press.

Herman, Edward S., and Noam Chomsky. 1988. *Manufacturing Consent: The Political Economy of the Mass Media.* New York: Pantheon.

Herszenhorn, David M. 1999. "Citywide Sweep Leads to 23 Arrests of the Homeless." *New York Times*, November 22.

Hessing, Melody, and Michael Howlett. 1998. *Canadian Natural Resource and Environmental Policy: Political Economy and Public Policy.* Vancouver: University of British Columbia Press.

Hill, Diane. 1997. *Metro Toronto: A Community At Risk—Demographic, Economic, Social, and Funding Trends in Metropolitan Toronto.* Toronto: United Way of Greater Toronto.

Hinch, Ronald, ed. 1994. *Readings in Critical Criminology.* Scarborough, Ont.: Prentice-Hall.

Hippler, Mike. 1989. *Matlovich: The Good Soldier.* Boston: Alyson.

Hoberg, George. 1998. "North American Environmental Regulation." In G. Bruce Doern and Steven Wilks, (eds.), *Changing Regulatory Institutions in Britain and North America.* Toronto: University of Toronto Press.

Hoberg, George; Keith Banting and Richard Simeon. 1999. "North American Integration and the Scope for Domestic Choice: Canada and Policy Sovereignty in a Globalized World." Mimeo. Meeting of the Association of Canadian Studies of the United States, November 17–20. Vancouver.

Hogg, Peter W. 1992. *Constitutional Law of Canada.* Third edition. Scarborough, Ont.: Carswell.

Hogwood, Brian W. 1996. "Regulatory Institutions in the United Kingdom: Increasing Regulation in the 'Shrinking State.'" In G. Bruce Doern and Steven Wilks, (eds.), *Comparative Competition Policy: National Institutions in a Global Market.* Oxford: Clarendon.

Hood, Roger. 1992. *Race and Sentencing: A Study in the Crown Court—A Report for the Commission for Racial Equality.* Oxford, Clarendon Press.

Horii, Gayle. 1989. "Progress." *Tightwire* (Kingston Prison for Women newsletter) 23, 1 (Spring).

Horster, Detlef. 1992. *Habermas: An Introduction.* Philadelphia: Pennbridge.

House, J. Douglas (Cle Newhook, ed.). 1987. *But Who Cares Now? The Tragedy of the Ocean Ranger.* St. John's: Breakwater.

Howard, Alan. 1997. "Labor, History and Sweatshops in the New Global

Economy." In Andrew Ross, (ed.), *No Sweat: Fashion Free Trade and the Rights of Garment Workers.* London: Verso.

Howard, Ross. 1991. *Poisoned Skies: Who'll Stop Acid Rain?* Toronto: Stoddart.

Human Resources Development Canada (HRDC). 1998. *An Analysis of Employment Insurance Benefit Coverage.* Working paper no. W-98-35E. Ottawa.

Hutter, Bridget M., and Sally M. Lloyd-Bostock. 1992. "Field-Level Perceptions of Risk in Regulatory Agencies." In James F. Short and Lee Clarke, (eds.), *Organizations, Uncertainties and Risk.* Boulder, Colo.: Westview.

Hyde, Christopher. 1991. *Abuse of Trust: The Career of Dr. James Tyhurst.* Vancouver: Douglas and McIntyre.

Hynes, Timothy, and Pushkala Prasad. 1999. "The Normal Violation of Safety Rules." In Christopher McCormick, (ed.), *The Westray Chronicles: A Case Study in Corporate Crime.* Halifax: Fernwood.

Ignatieff, Michael. 1987. "The Myth of Citizenship." *Queen's Quarterly* 99.

Inciardi, James A., ed. 1980. *Radical Criminology: The Coming Crises.* Beverly Hills, Calif.: Sage.

Ingstrup, Ole, Commissioner, Correctional Service of Canada (CSC). 1996a. "Interim Instruction: Regional Women's Facilities Are Not Reception Centres." CD 500. Memo. September 12.

_____. 1996b. "Interim Instruction: Security Classification of the Portion of Springhill Institution Accommodating Federally Sentenced Women." Annex "A," CD 006. September 19.

Isaac, Jeffrey C. 1987. *Power and Marxist Theory: A Realist View.* Ithaca, N.Y.: Cornell University Press.

Jakubowski, Lisa Marie. 1997. *Immigration and the Legalization of Racism.* Halifax: Fernwood.

James, Carl E. 1995. *Seeing Ourselves: Exploring Race, Ethnicity and Culture.* Toronto: Thompson.

Jeffcott, Bob. 1998. "Brief History of the Labour Behind the Label Coalition." Unpublished paper.

Jefferson, Tony. 1991. "Discrimination, Disadvantage and Police-work." In Ellis Cashmore and Eugene McLaughlin, (eds.), *Out of Order: Policing Black People.* London: Routledge.

Jenkins, Richard. 1992. *Pierre Bourdieu.* London: Routledge.

Jobb, Dean. 1994. *Calculated Risk: Greed, Politics and the Westray Tragedy.* Halifax: Nimbus.

_____. 1999. "Legal Disaster: Westray and the Justice System." In Christopher McCormick, (ed.), *The Westray Chronicles: A Case Study of Corporate Crime.* Halifax: Fernwood.

Johnson, Hugh J.M. 1989. *The Voyage of the* Komagata Maru: *The Sikh Challenge to Canada's Colour Bar.* Second edition. Vancouver: University of British Columbia Press.

Jones, Gerry. 2000. *SaskScandal: The Death of Political Idealism in Saskatchewan.* Saskatoon: Fifth House.

Kadish, Mortimer R., and Sanford H. Kadish. 1973. *Discretion to Disobey: A Study of Lawful Departures from Legal Rules*. Palo Alto, Calif.: Stanford University Press.

Kaminer, Wendy. 1995. *It's All the Rage: Crime and Culture*. Reading, Mass.: Addison-Wesley.

Kappeler, Victor E., Mark Blumberg and Gary W. Potter. 2000. *The Mythology of Crime and Criminal Justice*. Third edition. Prospect Heights, Ill.: Waveland.

Kardener, Sheldon H. 1974. "Sex and the Physician-Patient Relationship." *American Journal of Psychiatry* 131.

Karp, Carl, and Cecil Rosner. 1991. *When Justice Fails: The David Milgaard Story*. Toronto: McClelland and Stewart.

Kashmeri, Zuhair. 1991. *The Gulf Within: Canadian Arabs, Racism, and the Gulf War*. Toronto: Lorimer.

Kaufman, Fred (Chair). 1998. *Report of the Ontario Commission on Proceedings Involving Guy Paul Morin*. Toronto: Queen's Printer.

Kealey, Linda, and Joan Sangster, eds. 1989. *Beyond the Vote: Canadian Women and Politics*. Toronto: University of Toronto Press.

Keller, Evelyn Fox. 1992. *Secrets of Life, Secrets of Death: Essays on Language, Gender and Science*. New York: Routledge.

Kellner, Douglas. 1990. *Television and the Crisis of Democracy*. Boulder, Colo.: Westview.

Kendall, Kathleen. 1994. "Therapy Behind Prison Walls: A Contradiction in Terms?" *Prison Service Journal* 96.

_____. 2000. "Psy-ence Fiction." In Kelly Hannah-Moffat and Margaret Shaw, (eds.), *An Ideal Prison? Critical Essays on Women's Imprisonment in Canada*. Halifax: Fernwood.

Kersell, John E. 1960. *Parliamentary Supervision of Delegated Legislation*. London: Steven and Sons.

Kershaw, Anne, and Mary Lasovitch.1991. *Rock-A-Bye Baby: A Death Behind Bars*. Toronto: McClelland and Stewart.

Kessler, David A., Janet L. Rose, Robert J. Temple, Renie Schapiro and Joseph P. Griffin. 1994. "Therapeutic Class Wars—Drug Promotion in a Competitive Marketplace." *New England Journal of Medicine* 331.

Khosla, Punam. 1993. *Review of the Situation of Women in Canada, 1993*. Toronto: National Action Committee on the Status of Women.

Kilborn, Peter T. 1995. "A City Built on $4.25 an Hour." *New York Times*, February 12.

*Kingston Whig Standard*. 1995. "P4W Upgrades Security in Wake of Prison Riot." April 20.

Kinsman, Gary W. 1996. *The Regulation of Desire: Homo and Hetero Sexualities*. Second edition. Montréal: Black Rose.

Klein, Alan M. 1993. *Little Big Men: Bodybuilding Subculture and Gender Construction*. Albany, N.Y.: State University of New York Press.

Klein, Naomi. 1999. *No Logo: Taking Aim at the Brand Bullies*. Toronto: A.A.

Knopf Canada.

Kluft, Richard P. 1990. "Incest and Subsequent Revictimisation: The Case of Therapist-Patient Sexual Exploitation with a Description of the Sitting Duck Syndrome." In Richard P. Kluft, (ed.), *Incest Related Syndromes of Adult Psychopathology*. Washington, D.C.: American Psychiatric Press.

Kozol, Jonathan. 1991. *Savage Inequalities: Children in America's Schools*. New York: Crown.

Kramer, Larry. 1993. *The Destiny of Me*. New York: Plume (Penguin).

Kramer, Peter D. 1993. *Listening to Prozac*. New York: Viking.

Krupat, Kelly. 1997. "From War Zone to Free Trade Zone: A History of the National Labor Committee." In Andrew Ross, (ed.), *No Sweat: Fashion Free Trade and the Rights of Garment Workers*. London: Verso.

Kushner, Tony. 1993. *Angels in America*. New York: Theatre Communications Group.

LaPrairie, Carol. 1990. "The Role of Sentencing in the Over-representation of Aboriginal People in Correctional Institutions." *Canadian Journal of Criminology* 32.

Larin, Kathryn, and Elizabeth McNichol. 1997. *Pulling Apart: A State-by-State Analysis of Income Trends*. Washington, D.C.: Center on Budget and Policy Priorities, 1997.

Lash, Scott. 1990. *Sociology of Postmodernism*. London: Routledge.

Law Society of British Columbia, Gender Bias Committee. 1992. *Gender Equality in the Justice System 2*.

*Law Society of British Columbia v. Andrews*, [1989] 1 S.C.R. 143 (S.C.C.).

Leiss, William. 1996. "Governance and the Environment." Working paper no. 96-1. Kingston: Environmental Policy Unit, School of Policy Studies, Queen's University.

Leiss, William, Debora L. VanNijnatten, Éric Darier and Holly Mitchell. 1996. *Lessons Learned from ARET: A Qualitative Survey of Perceptions of Stakeholders*. Working paper no. 96-4. Kingston: Environmental Policy Unit, School of Policy Studies, Queen's University.

Leslie, Graham. 1991. *Breach of Promise: Socred Ethics under Vander Zalm*. Madeira Park, B.C.: Harbour.

Levi, Michael. 1993. *The Investigation, Prosecution, and Trial of Serious Fraud*. Research study no. 14. London: Royal Commission on Criminal Justice.

_____. 1995. "Serious Fraud in Britain: Criminal Justice versus Regulation." In Frank Pearce and Laureen Snider, (eds.), *Corporate Crime: Contemporary Debates*. Toronto: University of Toronto Press.

Lewis, Stephen. 1992. *Report to the Premier of Ontario*. Toronto: Ontario.

Lexchin, Joel. 1984. *The Real Pushers: A Critical Analysis of the Canadian Drug Industry*. Vancouver: New Star.

Leyton, Elliott. 1997. *Dying Hard: The Ravages of Industrial Carnage*. Toronto: Oxford University Press.

Liao, Katherine. 1995. *Report on Youth and Street Harassment*. Research report of the Commission on Systemic Racism in the Ontario Criminal Justice System. Toronto: Queen's Printer.

Lindblom, Charles. 1977. *Politics and Markets*. New York: Basic.

Littleton, James. 1986. *Target Nation: Canada and the Western Intelligence Network*. Toronto: Lester and Orpen Dennys.

Lofquist, William F. 1998. "Constructing 'Crime': Media Coverage of Individual and Organizational Wrongdoing." In Gary W. Potter and Victor E. Kappeler, (eds.), *Constructing Crime: Perspectives on Making News and Social Problems*. Prospect Heights: Waveland.

Loomis, Dan G. 1997. *Somalia Affair: Reflections on Peacemaking and Peacekeeping*. Ottawa: DGL.

Lowe, Mick. 1992. *One Woman Army*. Toronto: Macmillan.

Lowman, John, and Brian D. MacLean, eds. 1992. *Realist Criminology: Crime Control and Policing in the 1990s*. Toronto: University of Toronto Press.

Lukes, Steven. 1974. *Power: A Radical View*. London: Macmillan.

Lynch, Michael J., Mahesh K. Nalla and Keith W. Miller. 1989. "Cross Cultural Perceptions of Deviance: The Case of Bhopal." *Journal of Research in Crime and Delinquency* 26, 1.

Lynch, Michael J., Paul Stretsky and Paul Hammond. 2000. "Media Coverage of Chemical Crimes, Hillsborough County, Florida, 1987–97." *British Journal of Criminology* 40.

Lynch, Peter. 1996. "In Defense of the Invisible Hand." *Worth* 5, 6 (September).

MacDonald, Gayle. 2000. "Going Broke on $300K." *Globe and Mail*, February 26.

Macdonald, Neil. 1985. "Ottawa Paves the Way to Snoop on Friend or Foe." *Montreal Gazette* (September 10).

Mackie, Richard. 1999. "Ontario Tories Turn Into a Fund-raising Juggernaut." *Globe and Mail*, September 16.

MacKinnon, Mark. 1998. "Debt Pressure Mounts for Canadians." *Globe and Mail*, November 9.

MacLean, Brian D., ed. 1986. *The Political Economy of Crime*. Scarborough, Ont.: Prentice-Hall.

MacLean, Brian D., and Dragan Milovanovic, eds. 1991. *New Directions in Critical Criminology*. Vancouver: Collective Press.

MacMillan, Harriet L., Jan E. Fleming, Nico Trocmé, Michael H. Boyle, Maria Wong, Yvonne A. Racine, William R. Beardslee and Richard Offord. 1997. "Prevalence of Child Physical and Sexual Abuse in the Community." *Journal of the American Medical Association*, July 9.

Makin, Kirk. 1992. *Redrum the Innocent: The Murder of Christine Jessup*. Toronto: Viking.

Mallory, James R. 1982. "Curtailing 'Divine Right': The Control of Delegated Legislation." In Onkar P. Dwivedi, (ed.), *The Administrative State in Canada: Essays in Honour of J.E. Hodgetts*. Toronto: University of Toronto Press.

Manitoba, Public Inquiry into the Administration of Justice and Aboriginal

People. 1991. *Report of the Aboriginal Justice Inquiry of Manitoba.* Winnipeg.

Mann, Coramae Richey. 1993. *Unequal Justice: A Question of Color.* Bloomington: Indiana University Press.

Mann, Edward, and John Alan Lee. 1979. *The RCMP vs The People.* Don Mills. Ont.: General.

*Maquila Network Update.* 1999. "Are Nike and Reebok in a Race to the Top?" 4, 2.

Maracle, Lee. 1993. "Racism, Sexism and Patriarchy." In Himani Bannerji, (ed.), *Returning the Gaze: Essays on Racism, Feminism and Politics.* Toronto: Sister Vision.

Marchak, M. Patricia. 1995. *Logging the Globe.* Montréal-Kingston: McGill-Queen's University Press.

Marshall, G. Duncan. 1998. *A Dictionary of Sociology.* Second edition. Oxford: Oxford University Press.

Martin, Dianne. 1995. "The Extradition of Leonard Peltier from Canada." Submission to the United Nations Working Group on Indigenous Peoples. Available at Osgoode Hall Law School Library, York University.

Martin, Sara. 1995. "Fox Identifies Top Threats to Professional Psychology." *The APA Monitor* (March).

Marx, Karl. 1967 [1867]. *Capital: A Critique of Political Economy,* Vol. 1 (Friedrich Engels, ed.). New York. International Publishers.

Marx, Karl, and Friedrich Engels. 1998 [1848]. *The Communist Manifesto.* London: Verso.

Matthiessen, Peter. 1991 [c. 1984]. *The Spirit of Crazy Horse.* Second edition. New York: Viking.

Mauer, Marc. 1997. *Intended and Unintended Consequences of State Racial Disparities in Imprisonment.* Washington D.C.: The Sentencing Project.

_____. 1999. *The Crisis of the Young African American Male and the Criminal Justice System Report Prepared for U.S. Commission on Civil Rights.* Washington, D.C.: The Sentencing Project.

May, Rollo. 1992. "Foreword." In Donald K. Feedheim, (ed.), *History of Psychotherapy: A Century of Change.* Washington, D.C.: American Psychological Association.

McCormick, Christopher, ed. 1995. *Constructing Danger: The Mis/Representation of Crime in the News.* Halifax: Fernwood.

_____. 1999. *The Westray Chronicles: A Case Study in Corporate Crime.* Halifax: Fernwood.

McDonald, Donna. 1996. *Lord Strathcona: A Biography of Donald Alexander Smith.* Toronto: Dundurn.

McGraw, J. Melbourne, and Holly A. Smith. 1992. "Child Sexual Abuse Allegations Amidst Divorce and Custody Proceedings: Refining the Validation Process." *Journal of Child Sexual Abuse* 1.

McIntosh, Robert. 1993. "Sweated Labour: Female Needleworkers in Industrializing Canada." *Labour/Le Travail* 32.

McKee, Grant, and Ross Franey. 1988. *Time Bomb: Irish Bombers, English Justice, and the Guildford Four.* London: Bloomsbury.

McKenzie, Evan. 1994. *Privatopia: Homeowner Associations and the Rise of Residential Private Government.* New Haven: Yale University Press.

McMullan, John L. 1992. *Beyond the Limits of the Law: Corporate Crime and Law and Order.* Halifax: Fernwood.

_____. 1997. "State/Corporate Crime and Social Justice: Reflections on Politics, Power and Truth." In Atlantic Human Rights Centre, (ed.), *Social Justice, Social Inequality and Crime.* Fredericton: St. Thomas University.

McMullan, John L., and Sherman Hinze. 1999. "Westray: The Press, Ideology and Corporate Crime." In Christopher McCormick, (ed.), *The Westray Chronicles: A Case Study of Corporate Crime.* Halifax: Fernwood.

McQuaig, Linda. 1991. *Shooting the Hippo: Death by Deficit and Other Canadian Myths.* Toronto: Penguin.

_____. 1998. *The Cult of Impotence: Selling the Myth of Powerlessness in the Global Economy.* Toronto: Viking.

Melossi, Dario. 1993. "Gazettee of Morality and Social Whip." *Social and Legal Studies* 2, 2.

Merlin, Patrick, ed. 1996. *Boys Like Us: Gay Writers Tell Their Coming Out Stories.* New York: Avon.

Messerschmidt, James. 1983. *The Trial of Leonard Peltier.* Boston: South End Press.

Metro Toronto Task Force on Human Relations (Chair Walter Pitman). 1977. *Now Is Not Too Late.* Toronto: Council of Metropolitan Toronto.

Mies, Maria. 1986. *Patriarchy and Accumulation on a World Scale.* London: Zed.

Miles, Robert. 1988. *Racism.* London: Routledge.

Miller, J.R. 1996. *Shingwauk's Vision: A History of Native Residential Schools.* Toronto: University of Toronto Press.

Miller, Milton L. 1959. "Allergy and Emotions: A Review." *International Archives of Allergy and Applied Immunology* 1.

Miller, Ronnie. 1994. *Following the Americans to the Gulf: Canada, Australia, and the Development of the New World Order.* Rutherford, N.J.: Fairleigh Dickinson University Press.

Millett, Kate. 1990. *Looney Bin Trip.* New York: Simon and Schuster.

Mills, C. Wright. 1956. *The Power Elite.* New York: Oxford University Press.

Milner, Brian. 1998. "Competition Cops Flex Muscle." *Globe and Mail, Report on Business*, March 30.

Mintzes, Barbara, Anita Hardon and Jannemieke Hanhart, eds. 1993. *Norplant: Under Her Skin.* Delft, Netherlands: Eburon.

Mishel, Lawrence, Jared Bernstein and John Schmitt. 1999. *The State of Working America, 1998–99.* Ithaca, N.Y.: ILR Press, an imprint of Cornell University Press.

Monture-Angus, Patricia. 1995. *Thunder in My Soul: A Mohawk Woman Speaks.* Halifax: Fernwood.

_____. 1999. *Journeying Forward: Dreaming First Nations' Independence.* Halifax:

Fernwood.

_____. 2000. "Aboriginal Women and Correctional Practice." In Kelly Hannah–Moffat and Margaret Shaw, (eds.), *An Ideal Prison? Critical Essays on Women's Imprisonment in Canada.* Halifax: Fernwood.

Moon, Peter. 1987a. "Top-Secret Spy Agency Backs Ailing Ottawa Firm." *Globe and Mail,* March 30.

_____. 1987b. "Parliamentary Review Urged for Secretive Spy Agency." *Globe and Mail,* March 31.

_____. 1991a. "Secrecy Shrouds Spy Agency." *Globe and Mail,* May 27.

_____. 1991b. "Agency Tackles Foreign Missions." *Globe and Mail,* May 29.

_____. 1991c. "Spy Agency Left Minister in the Dark." *Globe and Mail,* June 3.

Morash, Merry, and Donna C. Hale. 1987. "Unusual Crime or Crime as Unusual? Images of Corruption in the Interstate Commerce Commission." In Timothy S. Bynum, (ed.), *Organized Crime in America: Concepts and Controversies.* Monsey, N.Y.: Criminal Justice.

Morrison, Ian. 1998. "Ontario Works: A Preliminary Assessment." *Journal of Law and Social Policy* 13.

Morriss, Peter. 1987. *Power: A Philosophical Analysis.* Manchester: Manchester University Press.

Moscovitch, Allan. 1997. "The Canada Health and Social Transfer." In Raymond B. Blake, Penny E. Bryden and J. Frank Straith, (eds.), *The Welfare State in Canada: Past, Present and Future.* Concord, Ont.: Irwin.

Moses, Barbara. 1999a. "Do You Have to Reinvent Yourself Every Few Years?" *Globe and Mail,* April 26.

_____. 1999b. "Career Intelligence: The 12 New Rules for Success." *The Futurist,* August–September.

_____. 1999c. "Older Workers Can Protect Their Future." *Globe and Mail,* September 28.

Mowat, Farley. 1984. *Sea of Slaughter.* Toronto: McClelland and Stewart.

Murdock, Graham. 1982. "Disorderly Images." In Colin S. Sumner, (ed.), *Crime, Justice and the Mass Media.* Cambridge: Institute of Criminology.

Murphy, Lawrence R. 1988. *Perverts by Official Order: The Campaign Against Homosexuals by the United States Navy.* New York: Haworth Press.

Murray, Charles. 1984. *Losing Ground: American Social Policy, 1950–1980.* New York: Basic.

Nader, Ralph, and Mark J. Green, eds. 1973. *Corporate Power in America.* New York: Viking.

Nasar, Sylvia. 1995. "Only a Paper Boom: Consumers Aren't Spending Their Profits from Surging Stocks," *New York Times,* June 9.

National Council of Welfare. 1999. *Poverty Profile, 1997.* Ottawa.

_____. 2000a. *Welfare Incomes 1997 and 1998.* Ottawa.

_____. 2000b. *Justice and the Poor.* Ottawa: Public Works and Services Canada.

*National Post.* 1999a. "Job Uncertainty Unleashes Health Threats." August 28.

_____. 1999b. "The Unfinished Business." August 28.

Nelson, James F. 1995. *Disparities in Processing Felony Arrests in New York State, 1990–1992*. Albany, N.Y.: Division of Criminal Justice Services.

New Zealand, Department of Justice. 1988. *The Maori and the Criminal Justice System, A New Perspective: He Whaipaanga Hou*. Wellington.

Newman, Katharine. 1988. *Falling from Grace: The Experience of Downward Mobility in the American Middle Class*. New York: Free Press.

Niezen, Ronald. 1998. *Defending the Land: Sovereignty and Forest Life in James Bay Cree Society*. Boston: Allyn and Bacon.

Nike. 1999. Annual Report.

Nikiforuk, Andrew. 1997. *The Nasty Game: The Failure of Environmental Assessment in Canada*. Toronto: Walter and Duncan Gordon Foundation.

Noble, Charles. 1995. "Regulating Work in a Capitalist Society." In Frank Pearce and Laureen Snider, (eds.), *Corporate Crime: Contemporary Debates*. Toronto: University of Toronto Press.

Nottingham, Stephen. 1998. *Eat Your Genes: How Genetically Modified Food is Entering Our Diet*. London: Zed.

Nova Scotia. 1989. *Report of the Royal Commission on the Donald Marshall, Jr. Prosecution*. Halifax.

_____. 1992. *Debates of the House of Assembly*, May 15.

_____. 1997. *The Westray Story: A Predictable Path to Disaster*. Report of the Westray Mine Public Inquiry. 3 vols. Halifax: Queen's Printer.

Novick, Peter. 1999. *The Holocaust in American Life*. New York: Houghton-Mifflin.

O'Kearney, Richard. 1996. "Attachment Disruption in Anorexia Nervosa and Bulimia Nervosa: A Review of Theory and Empirical Research." *International Journal of Eating Disorders* 20.

O'Malley, Pat, ed. 1998. *Crime and the Risk Society*. Aldershot, U.K.: Dartmouth.

Olive, David. 1996. "The Vast Pay Gap in Nike's World." *Globe and Mail*, August 27.

Onstad, Katrina. 1996. "No Job? No Problem!" *Canadian Business* (August).

Ontario. 1980. *Report of the Task Force on the Racial and Ethnic Implications of Police Hiring, Training, Promotion and Career Development* (Chair, Reva Gerstein). Toronto: Solicitor General.

Ontario, Ministry of Finance. 1999. *1999 Ontario Budget Papers: Foundations for Prosperity. Paper C: Details of Revenue Measures*. Toronto.

Ontario, Commission on Systemic Racism in the Ontario Criminal Justice System. 1994. *Racism Behind Bars: Interim Report of the Commission on Systemic Racism in the Ontario Criminal Justice System* (Co-chairs Margaret Gittens and Judge David P. Cole). Toronto: Queen's Printer.

_____. 1995. *Report of the Commission on Systemic Racism in the Ontario Criminal Justice System* (Co-chairs Margaret Gittens and Judge David P. Cole). Toronto: Queen's Printer.

*Ontario Human Rights Commission v. Simpson-Sears Ltd.*, [1985] 2 S.C.R. 536 (S.C.C.).

Orovan, William. 1998. "The Real Health-Care Problem is the Canada Health Act." *Globe and Mail*, November 16.

Osberg, Lars, and Andrew Sharpe. 1999. "An Index of Economic Well-Being for Canada." Paper R-99-3E. Ottawa: Applied Research Branch, Strategic Policy, Human Resources Development Canada.

Pacific Institute of Resource Management (PIRM). 1999. "The Secret Government." http://www.converge.org.nz/pirm/frames/elite!f.htm.

Paglia, Camille. 1991. *Sexual Personae*. N.Y.: Vintage.

Palazzoli, Mara Selvini. 1978. *Self-Starvation: From Individual to Family Therapy in the Treatment of Anorexia Nervosa*. New York: Aranson.

Palmer, Bryan. 1994. *Capitalism Comes to the Backcountry: The Goodyear Invasion of Napanee*. Toronto: Between the Lines.

Parkes, Colin Murray, Joan Stevenson-Hinde and Peter Morris, eds. 1991. *Attachment Across the Life Cycle*. London: Routledge.

Passas, Nikos, and David Nelken. 1993. "The Thin Line between Legitimate and Criminal Enterprise: Subsidy Frauds in the European Community." *Crime, Law and Social Change* 19.

Passell, Peter. 1998. "Benefits Dwindle Along with Wages for the Unskilled." *New York Times*, June 14.

Pearce, Frank. 1976. *Crimes of the Powerful: Marxism, Crime and Deviance*. London: Pluto.

Pearce, Frank and Laureen Snider, eds. 1995. *Corporate Crime: Contemporary Debates*. Toronto: University of Toronto Press.

Pearce, Frank and Steve Tombs. 1998. *Toxic Capitalism: Corporate Crime and the Chemical Industry*. Aldershot: Ashgate/Dartmouth.

Pearce, Frank and Michael Woodiwiss, eds. 1993. *Global Crime Connections: Dynamics and Control*. Toronto: University of Toronto Press.

Peller, Gary. 1993. "Criminal Law, Race and the Ideology of Bias: Transcending the Critical Tools of the Sixties." *Tulane Law Review* 67.

Penfold, P. Susan. 1995. "Mendacious Moms or Devious Dads? Some Perplexing Issues in Child Custody/Sexual Abuse Allegation Disputes." *Canadian Journal of Psychiatry* 40.

_____. 1998. *Sexual Abuse by Health Professionals: A Personal Search for Meaning and Healing*. Toronto: University of Toronto Press.

Penfold, P. Susan, and Gillian A. Walker. 1983. *Women and the Psychiatric Paradox*. Montréal: Eden.

Pepinsky, Harold E., and Paul Jesilow. 1984. *Myths That Cause Crime*. Cabin John, Md: Seven Locks.

Pepinsky, Harold E., and Richard Quinney, eds. 1993. *Criminology as Peacemaking*. Bloomington: University of Indiana Press.

Peppin, Patricia. 1993. "Emergency Legislation and Rights in Canada: The War Measures Act and Civil Liberties." *Queen's Law Journal* 18 (Spring).

Peritz, Ingrid, and André Picard. 2000. "Backlog So Bad, Hospital Asked for 48 hour Patient Bypass." *Globe and Mail*, January 5.

Peterson, Erik R. 1995. "Surrendering to Markets." *Washington Quarterly* 18, 4.

Pieterse, Jan Nederveen. 1992. *White on Black: Images of Africa and Blacks in Western Popular Culture*. New Haven: Yale University Press.

Pitsula, James, and Ken Rasmussen. 1990. *Privatizing a Province: The New Right in Saskatchewan*. Vancouver: New Star.

Piven, Frances Fox. 1992. "Reforming the Welfare State." *Socialist Review* 22, 3.

Pollack, William. 1998. *Real Boys: Rescuing Our Sons from the Myths of Boyhood*. New York: Random House.

Pope, Kenneth S. 1994. *Sexual Involvement with Therapists: Patient Assessment, Subsequent Therapy, Forensics*. Washington, D.C.: American Psychological Association.

Potter, Gary W., and Victor E. Kappeler, eds. 1998. *Constructing Crime Perspectives on Making News and Social Problems*. Prospect Heights: Waveland.

Press, Eyal. 1997. "Sweatshopping." In Andrew Ross, (ed.), *No Sweat: Fashion Free Trade and the Rights of Garment Workers*. London: Verso.

Prince, Michael J. 1999. "From Health and Welfare to Stealth and Farewell: Federal Social Policy, 1980–2000." In Leslie Pal, (ed.), *How Ottawa Spends, 1999–2000— Shape Shifting: Canadian Governance Toward the 21st Century*. Toronto: Oxford University Press.

Pronger, Brian. 1990. *The Arena of Masculinity*. New York: St. Martin's.

Pue, W. Wesley. 2000. *Pepper in Our Eyes: The APEC Affair*. Vancouver: University of British Columbia Press.

Purchase, Bryne. 1996. "Political Economy of Voluntary Codes: Executive Summary." http://strategis.ic.gc.ca/ssg/ca00796e.html (September).

Punch, Maurice. 1996. *Dirty Business: Exploring Corporate Misconduct*. London: Sage.

Quinn, James B., and Frederick G. Hilmer. 1994. "Strategic Outsourcing." *Sloan Management Review* (Summer).

Quinney, Richard. 1974. *Critique of Legal Order*. Boston: Little, Brown.

*R. v. Iwaniw: Overton,* (1959) 127 C.C.C. 40 (Man. C.A.).

Race Relations and Policing Task Force (Chair, Clare Lewis). 1989. *Report of the Race Relations and Policing Task Force*. Toronto.

Ralph, Diana. 1996. "How to Beat the Corporate Agenda: Strategies for Social Justice." In Jane Pulkingham and Gordon Ternowetsky, (eds.), *Remaking Canadian Social Policy*. Halifax: Fernwood.

Rattner, Steven. 1993. "If Productivity's Rising, Why Are Jobs Paying Less?" *New York Times Magazine*, September 19.

Rayside, David. 1998. *On the Fringe: Gays and Lesbians in Politics*. Ithaca, N.Y.: Cornell University Press.

Razack, Sherene H. 1998. *Looking White People in the Eye: Gender, Race, and Culture in Courtrooms and Classrooms*. Toronto: University of Toronto Press.

Reasons, Charles E., Lois L. Ross and Craig Paterson. 1981. *Assault on the Worker: Occupational Health and Safety in Canada*. Toronto: Butterworths.

Rebick, Judy. 2000a. *Imagine Democracy*. North York: Stoddart.

_____. 2000b. "A Budget For the Rich." *CBC Newsworld Viewpoint*. http://www.cbc.ca/news/viewpoint/columns/rebick/rebick000229.html.

Rebick, Judy, and Kiké Roach. 1996. *Politically Speaking*. Vancouver, B.C.: Douglas & McIntyre.

*Reference re Milgaard*, [1992] 1 S.C.R. 866. (S.C.C.).

Reich, Robert. 1991. "Secession of the Successful." *New York Times Magazine*, January 20.

_____. 1992. *The Work of Nations: Preparing Ourselves for 21st-Century Capitalism*. New York: Vintage.

Reiman, Jeffrey. 1990. *The Rich Get Richer and the Poor Get Prison*. Third edition. New York: Macmillan.

Reiser, David E., and Hanna Levenson. 1984. "Abuses of the Borderline Diagnosis: A Clinical Problem with Teaching Opportunities." *American Journal of Psychiatry* 141.

Revenue Canada. 1998. *Income Statistics: 1996 Tax Year*. Ottawa.

Richards, Trudy. 1999. "Public Relations and the Westray Mine Explosion." In Christopher McCormick, (ed.), *The Westray Chronicles: A Case Study of Corporate Crime*. Halifax: Fernwood.

Rind, Bruce, Phillip Tromovitch and Robert Bauserman. 1998. "A Meta-Analytic Examination of Assumed Properties of Child Sexual Abuse Using College Samples." *The Psychological Bulletin* 124, 1 (July).

Roberts, Barbara. 1988. *Whence They Came: Deportation from Canada, 1900–1935*. Ottawa: University of Ottawa Press.

Roberts, Julian V. 1995. *The Influence of Race on Sentencing Patterns in Toronto: Report for the Commission on Systemic Racism in the Ontario Criminal Justice System*. Toronto: Queen's Printer.

Robinson, Bill. 1991. "The Fall and Rise of Cryptanalysis in Canada." *Cryptanalysis* 16, 1 (January).

Rock, Paul. 1973. "News as Eternal Recurrence." In Stanley Cohen and Jock Young, (eds.), *The Manufacture of News*. London: Constable.

Rodrik, Dani. 1997. *Has Globalization Gone Too Far?* Washington, D.C.: Institute for International Economics.

Rosen, Philip. 1981. "The Official Secrets Act." *Current Issue Review* 79-15E (October 13).

Rosenberg, Jerry M. 1995. *The Dictionary of Marketing and Advertising*. New York: John Wiley and Sons.

Rosoff, Stephen M., Henry N. Pontell and Robert Tillman. 1998. *Profit Without Honor: White-Collar Crime and the Looting of America*. Upper Saddle River, N.J.: Prentice-Hall.

Ross, Andrew, ed. 1997a. *No Sweat: Fashion Free Trade and the Rights of Garment Workers*. London: Verso.

_____. 1997b. "After the Year of the Sweatshop." In Andrew Ross, (ed.), *No Sweat: Fashion Free Trade and the Rights of Garment Workers*. London: Verso.

Ross, Becki L. 1995. *The House That Jill Built: A Lesbian Nation in Formation*.

Toronto: University of Toronto Press.

Ross, Gary. 1987. *Stung: The Incredible Obsession of Brian Moloney*. Toronto: Stoddart.

Ross, Jen. 1999. "Garment Work Turns Homes Into Sweatshops." *Globe and Mail*, June 21.

Rousseau, Jean Jacques. 1762. *The Social Contract*, Chapter XV. Translated by George D.H. Cole. Jon Roland, Constitution Society, http://www.constitution.org/jjr/socon.txt.

Ruby, Clayton C. 1999. *Sentencing*. Fifth edition. Toronto: Butterworths.

Rutter, Michael. 1981. *Maternal Deprivation Reassessed*. Second edition. Middlesex, England: Penguin.

Sachs, Jeffrey D. 1996. "The Social Welfare State and Competitiveness." In *The Global Competitiveness Report, 1996*. Geneva: World Economic Forum.

Sagarin, Edward (Donald Webster Cory, pseudonym). 1951. *The Homosexual in America*. New York: Julian Press.

Said, Edward W. 1978. *Orientalism*. New York: Pantheon.

Sallot, Jeff. 1984a. "Top-Secret Eavesdropping Agency Doesn't Tap Phones, Kaplan Says." *Globe and Mail*, April 7.

_____. 1984b. "Kaplan Refuses Legislation for Top-Secret Agency." *Globe and Mail*, April 11.

_____. 1985. "Majority Would Accept Rights Suspension in Crisis, Defence Department Poll Shows." *Globe and Mail*, December 17.

Sassen, Saskia. 1996. *Losing Control? Sovereignty in an Age of Globalization*. New York: Columbia University Press.

Satzewich, Vic. 1991. *Racism and the Incorporation of Foreign Labour: Farm Labour Migration to Canada Since 1945*. London: Routledge.

Sawatsky, John. 1991. *Mulroney: The Politics of Ambition*. Toronto: Macfarlane, Walter and Ross.

Schaef, Anne Wilson. 1992. *Beyond Therapy, Beyond Science*. San Francisco: Harper San Francisco.

Schafer, Art. 1998. *Down and Out in Winnipeg and Toronto: The Ethics of Legislating Against Panhandling*. Ottawa: Caledon Institute of Social Policy.

Schellenberg, Grant. 1997. *The Changing Nature of Part-time Work*. Social research paper no. 4.. Ottawa: Canadian Council on Social Development.

Scheper-Hughes, Nancy, and Daniel Hoffman. 1998. "Brazilian Apartheid: Street Kids and the Struggle for Urban Space." In Nancy Scheper-Hughes and Carolyn Sargent, (eds.), *Small Wars: The Cultural Politics of Childhood*. Berkeley: University of California Press.

Schissel, Bernard. 1993. *Social Dimensions of Canadian Youth Justice*. Toronto: Oxford University Press.

Schissel, Bernard, and Linda Mahood, eds. 1996. *Social Control in Canada: A Reader on the Social Construction of Deviance*. Toronto: Oxford University Press.

Schmit, Julie. 1999. "Nike's Image Problem." *U.S.A. Today*, October 4.

Schrecker, Ted. 1998. "Private Health Care for Canada: North of the Border, an Idea Whose Time Shouldn't Come?" *Journal of Law, Medicine & Ethics* 26.

_____, ed. 1997. *Surviving Globalism: The Social and Environmental Challenges*. New York: St. Martin's Press.

Schur, Edwin M. 1984. *Labeling Women Deviant: Gender, Stigma and Social Control*. Philadelphia: Temple University Press.

Scott, David, and John Aylen. 1995. *Participation by Racial Minority Community Groups in Criminal Justice Policy Development*. Research report of the Commission on Systemic Racism in the Ontario Criminal Justice System. Toronto: Queen's Printer.

Scott, James C. 1992. "Domination, Acting, and Fantasy." In Carolyn Nordstrom and JoAnn. Martin, (eds.), *The Paths to Domination: Resistance and Terror*. Berkeley: University of California Press.

Scraton, Phil, Ann Jemphrey and Sheila Coleman. 1995. *No Last Rights: The Denial of Justice and the Promotion of Myth in the Aftermath of the Hillsborough Disaster*. Liverpool: Alden Press/Liverpool City Council.

Seligman, Joel. 1982. *The Transformation of Wall Street: A History of the Securities and Exchange Commission and Modern Corporate Finance*. New York: Houghton Mifflin.

Seligman, Martin E.P. 1995. "The Effectiveness of Psychotherapy: The *Consumer Reports* Study." *American Psychologist* 50, 12.

Sennett, Richard. 1998. *The Corrosion of Character: The Personal Consequences of Work in the New Capitalism*. New York: Norton

Sharma, Nandita. 1997. "Cheap Myths and Bonded Lives: Freedom and Citizenship in Canadian Society." *Beyond Law* 6, 17.

Shaw, Linda. 1997. "The Labor Behind the Label: Clean Clothes Campaigns." In Andrew Ross, (ed.), *No Sweat: Fashion Free Trade and the Rights of Garment Workers*. London: Verso.

Shearing, Clifford D., ed. 1981. *Organizational Police Deviance*. Toronto: Butterworths.

Sher, Jonathan. 2000. "ERs Clogged with Patients." *London Free Press*, January 5.

Shkilnyk, Anastasia M. 1985. *A Poison Stronger than Love: The Destruction of An Ojibwa Community*. New Haven: Yale University Press.

Shore, Milton F. 1988. "Follow the Leader." *Readings: A Journal of Reviews and Commentary in Mental Health* 3, 2.

Silverman, Robert A., James J. Teevan and Vincent F. Sacco, eds. 2000. *Crime in Canadian Society*. Sixth edition. Toronto: Harcourt Brace.

Simmons, Debra. 1992. "Gender Issues and Borderline Personality Disorder: Why Do Females Dominate the Diagnosis?" *Archives of Psychiatric Nursing* 6, 4.

Simon, David R. 1999. *Elite Deviance*. Sixth edition. Needham Heights, Mass.: Allyn and Bacon.

Simon, David R., and Frank E. Hagan. 1999. *White-Collar Deviance*. Needham Heights, Mass.: Allyn and Bacon.

Simon, Harry. 1995. "The Criminalization of Homelessness in Santa Ana, California: A Case Study." *Clearinghouse Review* 29.

Simpson, Jeffrey. 2000. "The Tax Gap About to Widen." *Globe and Mail*, January 13.

Simpson, Sally S. 1987. "Cycles of Illegality: Antitrust Violations in Corporate America." *Social Forces* 65, 4.

Sinclair, Timothy J. 1994. "Between State and Market: Hegemony and Institutions of Collective Action Under Conditions of International Capital Mobility." *Policy Sciences* 27.

Skelton, Chad. 2000. "Statistics Show Drop in Crime, but B.C. Posts Most Murders." *Vancouver Sun*, July 19.

Smith, Conrad. 1992. *Media and Apocalypse: New Coverage of the Yellowstone Forest Fires, Exxon Valdez Oil Spill, and Loma Prieta Earthquake*. Westport: Greenwood.

Smith, Dorothy E. 1987. *The Everyday World as Problematic*. Toronto: University of Toronto Press.

_____. 1990. *The Conceptual Practices of Power*. Toronto: University of Toronto Press.

Smith, Dorothy E., and Sara J. David. 1975. *Women Look at Psychiatry*. Vancouver: Press Gang.

Smith, Juliette. 1996. "Arresting the Homeless for Sleeping in Public." *Columbia Journal of Law and Social Problems* 29.

Snider, Laureen. 1978. "Corporate Crime in Canada: A Preliminary Report." *Canadian Journal of Criminology* 20.

_____. 1987. "Towards a Political Economy of Reform, Regulation and Corporate Crime." *Law and Policy* 9, 1.

_____. 1991. "The Regulatory Dance: Understanding Reform Processes in Corporate Crime." *International Journal of Sociology of Law* 19.

_____. 1993. *Bad Business: Corporate Crime in Canada*. Scarborough: Nelson.

_____. 1996. "Options for Public Accountability." In Michael D. Mehta, (ed.), *Regulatory Efficiency and the Role of Risk Assessment*. Kingston: School of Policy Studies, Queen's University.

_____. 1998. "Understanding the Second Great Confinement." *Queen's Quarterly* (Spring).

Solicitor General Canada. 1989. "Too Few to Count: Profiling Women Offenders." *Let's Talk* (September).

_____. 1995. "Commissioner's Column, Prison for Women Video." *Let's Talk* (March).

Spitz, René A. 1945. "Hospitalism: An Inquiry into the Genesis of Psychiatric Conditions in Early Childhood." Part I. *Psychoanalytic Study of the Child* 1.

_____. 1965. *The First Year of Life: A Psychoanalytic Study of Normal and Deviant Development of Object Relations*. New York: International University Press.

St. John, Peter. 1984. "Canada's Accession to the Allied Intelligence Community, 1940–45." *Conflict Quarterly* 4, 4.

Stackhouse, John. 2000. "ER Diary: The Crisis Up Close." *Globe and Mail,* January 22.

Stanbury, William T. 1977. *Business Interests and the Reform of Canadian Competition Policy, 1971–75.* Toronto: Carswell/Methuen.

_____. 1986–87. "The New Competition Act and Competition Tribunal Act: Not with a Bang but a Whimper?" *Canadian Business Law Journal* 12.

Starr, Richard. 1992. "Where was the Warning at Westray?" *Content* (December).

Stasiulis, Daiva. 1997. "The Political Economy of Race, Ethnicity and Migration." In Wallace Clement, (ed.), *Understanding Canada: Building on the New Canadian Political Economy.* Montreal: McGill–Queen's University Press.

Stasiulis, Daiva and C. Radha Jhappan. 1995. "The Fractious Politics of a Settler Society: Canada." In Daiva Stasiulis and Nira Yuval-Davis, (eds.), *Unsettling Settler Societies: Articulations of Gender, Race, Ethnicity and Class.* London: Sage.

Statistics Canada. 1999a. *Income After Tax: Distribution by Size in Canada, 1997.* Catalogue no. 13-210-XPB. Ottawa: Supply and Services Canada.

_____. 1999b. *Labour Force Update: Supplementary Measures of Unemployment.* Catalogue no. 71-005-XPB, Summer. Ottawa: Supply and Services Canada.

Steedman, Mercedes. 1997. *Angels of the Workplace: Women and the Construction of Gender Relations in the Canadian Clothing Industry, 1890–1940.* Toronto: Oxford University Press.

Stewart, Ron L. 1995a. "Letter from John Edwards to Ron Stewart. May 18, 1995." *Annual Report of the Correctional Investigator, 1994–1995.* Ottawa: Supply and Services Canada.

_____. 1995b. *Special Report of the Correctional Investigator Pursuant to Section 193 CCRA Concerning the Treatment of Inmates and Subsequent Inquiry Following Certain Incidents at the Prison for Women in April 1994 and Thereafter.* February 14. Ottawa: Supply and Services Canada.

Students Against Sweatshops—Canada. 1999. http://www.web.net/~msn/3sas.htm).

Suedfeld, Peter. 1999. "CPA and Public Policy." *Psynopsis* (Spring).

Sumner, Colin S. 1982. *Crime, Justice and the Mass Media.* Cropwood series no. 14. Cambridge, U.K.: Cambridge Institute of Criminology.

_____. 1990. "Rethinking Deviance: Towards a Sociology of Censure." In Colin S. Sumner, (ed.), *Censure, Politics and Criminal Justice.* Milton Keynes: Open University Press.

Sumner, Colin S., and Simon Sandberg. 1990. "The Press Censure of 'Dissent Minorities': The Ideology of Parliamentary Democracy, Thatcherism and Policing the Crisis." In Colin S. Sumner, (ed.), *Censure, Politics and Criminal Justice.* Milton Keynes: Open University Press.

Surette, Ray. 1998. *Media, Crime and Criminal Justice: Images and Realities.* Belmont, Calif.: West/Wadsworth.

Surowiecki, James. 1998. "Company Man: Once Tom Peters Redefined the American Corporation. Now He Wants to Destroy It." *New Yorker,* January 19.

Swartz, L. 1985. "Anorexia Nervosa as a Culture-Bound Syndrome." *Social Science and Medicine* 7.

Swigert, Victoria L., and Ronald A. Farrell. 1980. "Corporate Homicide: Definitional Processes in the Creation of Deviance." *Law and Society Review* 15.

Sykes, Charles. 1992. *A Nation of Victims*. New York: St. Martin's Press.

Szablowski, David. 1995. "Towards an Effective International Social Charter: A Case Study of Manufacturing Workers in the Athletic Shoe Sector." Unpublished LL.B. paper, Osgoode Hall Law School.

Tabb, William. 1999. "Progressive Globalism: Challenging the Audacity of Capital." *Monthly Review* 5, 9.

Taber, Jane. 1999. "Slash Taxes to U.S. Levels: [Industry Minister John] Manley." *Ottawa Citizen*, May 1.

Task Force on Federally Sentenced Women (TFFSW). 1990. *Creating Choices*. Ottawa.

Tavris, Carol. 1999. "The Politics of Sex Abuse." *Los Angeles Times*, July 19.

Taylor, Ian. 1983. *Crime, Capitalism and Community: Three Essays in Socialist Criminology*. Toronto: Butterworths.

Taylor, Ian, Paul Walton and Jock Young. 1973. *The New Criminology: For A Social Theory of Deviance*. London: Routledge & Kegan Paul.

Thobani, Sunera. 1998. *"Nationalizing Citizens, Bordering Immigrant Women": Globalization and the Racialization of Women's Citizenship in Late 20th Century Canada*. Ph.D. dissertation, Simon Fraser University.

Thoennes, Nancy, and Patricia G. Tjaden. 1990. "The Extent, Nature and Validity of Sexual Abuse Allegations in Custody/Visitation Disputes." *Child Abuse and Neglect* 14.

Thomas, Kevin. n.d. "The Power and Limits to Consumer Action." In *From Corporate Responsibility to Social Accountability,* issue paper no. 5, Moderator's Consultation on Faith and the Economy. http://www.faith-and-the-economy.ocg/Thm4 Paper5-Thomas.htm.

Thoreau, Henry David. 1965 [c. 1854]. *Walden or, Life in the Woods and On the Duty of Civil Disobedience*. New York: Harper and Row.

Timmons, Stuart. 1990. *The Trouble with Harry Hay*. Boston: Alyson.

Tombs, Steve. 1996. "Injury, Death and the Deregulation Fetish: The Politics of Occupational Safety Regulation in United Kingdom Manufacturing Industries." *International Journal of Health Services* 26, 2.

Tonry, Michael H. 1995. *Malign Neglect: Race, Crime and Punishment in America*. New York: Oxford University Press.

Toronto Children's Services. 1999. *Toronto Report Card on Children, 1999*. Toronto: City of Toronto.

Tucker, Eric. 1990. *Administering Danger in the Workplace*. Toronto: University of Toronto Press.

_____. 1995. "The Westray Mine Disaster and its Aftermath: The Politics of Causation." *Canadian Journal of Law and Society* 10, 1 (Spring).

Tunnell, Kenneth D. 1998. "Reflections on Crime, Criminals and Control in News Magazine and Television Programs." In Frankie Y. Bailey and Donna C. Hale, (eds.), *Popular Culture, Crime and Justice*. Belmont, Calif.: West/ Wadsworth.

U.S. Department of Justice. 1999a. *Prisoners in 1998*. Washington: Bureau of Justice Statistics.

_____. 1999b. *Prison and Jail Inmates at Midyear 1998*. Washington: Bureau of Justice Statistics.

_____. 1999c. *Bulletin (Update of). Prison and Jail Inmates at Midyear 1977*. Washington: Bureau of Justice Statistics.

_____. 1999d. *Fact Sheet: Drug Data Summary*. Washington: Bureau of Justice Statistics.

Uchitelle, Louis. 1993. "'Good' Jobs in Hard Times." *New York Times*, October 3.

_____. 1995. "More Downsized Workers are Returning as Rentals." *New York Times*, December 8.

Uchitelle, Louis, N.R. Kleinfield, Rick Bragg, Sara Rimer, Kirk Johnson, Elizabeth Kolbert, Adam Clymer, David E. Sanger and Steve Lohr. 1996. *The Downsizing of America*. New York: Times Books.

Ursel, Jane. 1992. *Private Lives, Public Policy: 100 Years of State Intervention in the Family*. Toronto: Women's Press.

Useem, Michael. 1996. *Investor Capitalism: How Money Managers are Changing the Face of Corporate America*. New York: Basic.

Valenstein, Elliot S. 1986. *Great and Desperate Cures: The Rise and Decline of Psychosurgery and Other Radical Treatments for Mental Illness*. New York: Basic.

Vallières, Pierre. 1971. *White Niggers of America*. Toronto: McClelland and Stewart.

*Vancouver Sun*. 1990. "Antiquated Women's Prison to Close Doors." September 26.

_____. 1993. "A Prison Break With Old Ideas." April 6.

Vandenbroucke, Frank. 1998. *Globalisation, Inequality and Social Democracy*. London: Institute for Public Policy Research.

Walker, Robert. 1999. "The Growth of Office Research." *The Medical Post*, August 10.

Walker, Samuel. 1993. *Taming the System: The Control of Discretion in Criminal Justice, 1950–1990*. New York: Oxford University Press.

Walters, Vivienne, Wayne Lewchuk, R. Jack Richardson, Lea Ann Moran, Ted Haines and Dave Verma. 1995. "Judgements of Legitimacy regarding Occupational Health and Safety." In Frank Pearce and Laureen Snider, (eds.), *Corporate Crime: Contemporary Debates*. Toronto: University of Toronto Press.

Walton, Paul, and Jock Young, eds. 1998. *The New Criminology Revisited*. New York: St. Martin's Press.

Wark, Wesley. 1987. "Cryptographic Innocence: The Origins of Signals Intelligence in Canada in the Second World War." *Journal of Contemporary History* 22.

Washington, Frank. 1995. "The Underground Workforce: The Murky, Controversial World of Automotive 'Contract' Workers." *Ward's Auto World* (August).

Weber, Max. 1954 [1925]. *Max Weber on Law in Economy and Society*. (Max Rheinstein, ed.). Second edition. Cambridge, Mass.: Harvard University Press.

Wegg-Prosser, Charles. 1982. "The French System." In *Wrongful Imprisonment*. London: Committee on Compensation for Wrongful Imprisonment.

Weinberg, Thomas, and G.W. Levi Kamel. 1983. *S and M: Studies in Sado-Masochism*. Buffalo, N.Y.: Prometheus.

Whitaker, Reg, and Gary Marcuse. 1994. *Cold War Canada: The Making of a National Insecurity State, 1945–1957*. Toronto: University of Toronto Press.

White, Edmund. 1980. *States of Desire: Travels in America*. New York: E.P. Dutton
_____. 1994. *The Burning Library: Essays* (David Bergman, ed.). New York: Knopf.

_____. 1997. *The Farewell Symphony*. New York: Knopf.

Wilbanks, William. 1987. *The Myth of a Racist Criminal Justice System*. Monterey, Calif.: Brooks/Cole.

Wilkes, Michael S., Bruce H. Doblin and Martin F. Shapiro. 1992. "Pharmaceutical Advertisements in Leading Medical Journals: Experts' Assessments." *Annals of Internal Medicine* 116.

Wilks, Steven. 1998. "Utility Regulation, Corporate Governance, and the Amoral Corporation." In G. Bruce Doern and Steven Wilks, (eds.), *Changing Regulatory Institutions in Britain and North America*. Toronto: University of Toronto Press.

Williams, Patricia J. 1991. *The Alchemy of Race and Rights*. Cambridge: Harvard University Press.

Williams, Raymond. 1989. *What I Came to Say*. London: Hutchinson.

Williams, Toni. 1999. "Sentencing Black Offenders." In David P. Cole and Julian V. Roberts, (eds.), *Making Sense of Sentencing*. Toronto: University of Toronto Press.

Willis, Sally. 1991. *Report to CAEFS Social Action Committee*. Ottawa: Canadian Association of Elizabeth Fry Societies.

Wilson, Garrett, and Lesley Wilson. 1985. *Deny, Deny, Deny: The Rise and Fall of Colin Thatcher*. Toronto: Lorimer.

Withorn, Ann. 1996. "'Why Do They Hate Me So Much?' A History of Welfare and Its Abandonment in the United States." *American Journal of Orthopsychiatry* 66.

Wittmeier, Carmen. 1999. "An 'Organized Gang.'" *Alberta Report*, July 26.

Women and Mental Health Committee, CMHA. 1987. *Women and Mental Health in Canada: Strategies for Change*. Toronto: CMHA National Office.

Woods, Gregory. 1987. *Articulate Flesh: Male Homoeroticism and Modern Poetry*.

New Haven: Yale University Press.

Woog, Dan. 1998. *Jocks: True Stories of America's Gay Athletes*. Los Angeles: Alyson.

World Bank. 1995. *World Development Report, 1995: Workers in an Integrating World*. New York: Oxford University Press.

_____. 1999. *Entering the 21st Century: World Development Report, 1999/2000*. New York: Oxford University Press.

Wortley, Scot. 1995. *Perceptions of Bias and Racism within the Ontario Criminal Justice System: Results from a Public Opinion Survey*. Research report of the Commission on Systemic Racism in the Ontario Criminal Justice System. Toronto: Queen's Printer.

Wright, John P., Francis T. Cullen and Michael B. Blankenship. 1995. "The Social Construction of Corporate Violence: Media Coverage of the Imperial Food Products Fire." *Crime and Delinquency* 41, 1.

Wuthnow, Robert. 1994 "Religion and Economic Life." In Neil Smelser and Richard Swedberg, (eds.), *The Handbook of Economic Sociology*. Princeton, N.J.: Princeton University Press.

Wysocki, Bernard Jr. 1995. "The Outlook: Foreigners Find U.S. A Good Place to Invest." *Wall Street Journal*, August 7.

Yalnizian, Armine. 1998. *The Growing Gap: A Report on Growing Inequality Between the Rich and the Poor in Canada*. Toronto: Centre for Social Justice.

Yanz, Linda, and Bob Jeffcott. 1999. "Codes of Conduct: From Corporate Responsibility to Social Accountability." http://www.web.net/~msn/5codes1.htm.

Yanz, Linda, Bob Jeffcott, Deena Ladd and Joan Atlin. 1999. *Policy Options to Improve Standards for Women Garment Workers in Canada and Internationally*. Ottawa: Status of Women Canada.

Zacharias, Yvonne. 1999. "Hospitals Near State of Crisis: Too Many Patients, Not Enough Nurses Mean a Weekend of Chaos at Lower Mainland Hospitals." *Vancouver Sun*, December 13.

Zey, Mary. 1993. *Banking on Fraud: Drexel, Junk Bonds and Buyouts*. New York: Aldine de Gruyter.

Zimbardo, Philip G. 1971. "The Psychological Power and Pathology of Imprisonment." Statement prepared for U.S. House of Representatives Committee on the Judiciary, Subcommittee No. 3, Hearings on Prison Reform, San Francisco., October 25.